Logic in Computer Science:
Modelling and Reasoning about Systems

Logic in Computer Science:
Modelling and Reasoning about Systems

MICHAEL HUTH
Kansas State University

MARK RYAN
University of Birmingham

CAMBRIDGE
UNIVERSITY PRESS

PUBLISHED BY THE PRESS SYNDICATE OF THE UNIVERSITY OF CAMBRIDGE
The Pitt Building, Trumpington Street, Cambridge, United Kingdom

CAMBRIDGE UNIVERSITY PRESS
The Edinburgh Building, Cambridge, CB2 2RU, UK   http://www.cup.cam.ac.uk
40 West 20th Street, New York, NY 10011-4211, USA   http://www.cup.org
10 Stamford Road, Oakleigh, Melbourne 3166, Australia
Ruiz de Alarcón 13, 28014 Madrid, Spain

First published 2000

Printed in the United Kingdom at the University Press, Cambridge

Typeface Times 11/13pt   *System* LATEX2ε   [UPH]

A catalogue record for this book is available from the British Library

Library of Congress Cataloguing in Publication data
Huth, Michael, 1962–
Logic in computer science : modelling and reasoning about systems / Michael Huth, Mark Ryan.
p.   cm.
Includes bibliographical references (p.   )
ISBN 0 521 65200 6. – ISBN 0 521 65602 8 (pbk.)
1. Computer logic. I. Ryan, Mark, 1962– . II. Title.
QA76.9.L63H88   1999   99-15233   CIP

ISBN 0 521 65200 6 hardback
ISBN 0 521 65602 8 paperback

Contents

Foreword

by   Edmund M. Clarke
     FORE Systems Professor of Computer Science
     Carnegie Mellon University
     Pittsburgh, PA

Formal methods have finally come of age! Specification languages, theorem provers, and model checkers are beginning to be used routinely in industry. Mathematical logic is basic to all of these techniques. Until now textbooks on logic for computer scientists have not kept pace with the development of tools for hardware and software specification and verification. For example, in spite of the success of model checking in verifying sequential circuit designs and communication protocols, until now I did not know of a single text, suitable for undergraduate and beginning graduate students, that attempts to explain how this technique works. As a result, this material is rarely taught to computer scientists and electrical engineers who will need to use it as part of their jobs in the near future. Instead, engineers avoid using formal methods in situations where the methods would be of genuine benefit or complain that the concepts and notation used by the tools are complicated and unnatural. This is unfortunate since the underlying mathematics is generally quite simple, certainly no more difficult than the concepts from mathematical analysis that every calculus student is expected to learn.

Logic in Computer Science by Huth and Ryan is an exceptional book. I was amazed when I looked through it for the first time. In addition to propositional and predicate logic, it has a particularly thorough treatment of temporal logic and model checking. In fact, the book is quite remarkable in how much of this material it is able to cover: linear and branching time temporal logic, explicit state model checking, fairness, the basic fixpoint theorems for computation tree logic (CTL), even binary decision diagrams and symbolic model checking. Moreover, this material is presented at a level that is accessible to undergraduate and beginning graduate students. Numerous problems and examples are provided to help students master the material in the book. Since both Huth and Ryan are active researchers in logics of programs and program verification, they write with considerable authority.

In summary, the material in this book is up-to-date, practical, and elegantly presented. The book is a wonderful example of what a modern text on logic for computer science should be like. I recommend it to the reader with greatest enthusiasm and predict that the book will be an enormous success.

Preface

Our motivation for writing this book

Recent years have brought about the development of powerful tools for verifying specifications of hardware and software systems. By now, the IT industry has realised the impact and importance of such tools in their own design and implementation processes. Major companies, such as Intel, Siemens, BT, AT&T and IBM, are now actively investigating this technology and its incorporation into their planning and production departments. This necessitates the availability of a basic formal training which allows *undergraduate* students as well as working programmers and beginning graduate students to gain sufficient proficiency in using and reasoning with such frameworks.

The recent shift of information technologies towards internet-based data access and processing means that there is also an increase in demand for qualified individuals who can reason about sophisticated autonomous agent-based software which is able to interact with other agents and gather desired information on large networks.

This book addresses these needs by providing a sound basis in logic, followed by an introduction to the logical frameworks which are used in modelling and reasoning about computer systems. It provides simple and clear presentation of material. A carefully chosen core of essential terminology is introduced; further technicalities are introduced only where they are required by the applications.

We believe that our proposed course material makes a vital contribution to preparing undergraduate students for today's fast paced and changeable professional environments. This confidence stems not only from the topicality of our proposed applications, but also from the conviction that a solid background in logical structures and formalisms can very well serve as a buoy in the rough waters of future software and hardware developments.

There is an abundance of books on mathematical logic or logic in computer science on the market. However, we are not aware of any book that suits the contemporary and applications-driven courses that we teach and are beginning to be taught in most computer science curricula. Existing books tend to be written for logicians rather than computer science students and are thus too 'heavy' and overloaded with technical terminology. The ties to computer science are merely of a foundational nature, such as the Curry-Howard isomorphism, or cut-elimination in sequent calculi. There is an evident need for a book which introduces the contemporary applications of logic which are beginning to be taken up by industry; the book should be accessible to students who do not want to learn logic for its own sake.

It is important to say what the book does not provide: we completely omitted applications like the design and use of theorem-provers and the exposure to constructive type theories (such as the calculus of constructions and the logical framework) as a mathematical foundation for program synthesis; and the design, analysis and implementation of programming languages. This decision is by no means meant to represent a judgment of such topics. Indeed, we hope and anticipate that others will address these important issues in a text that is suitable for undergraduates.

Reasons for adopting this book

Our book zooms in on concepts at the heart of logic and presents them in a contemporary fashion. In that way, and by discussing the implementation of such principles, our material creates stimulating overlaps with other standard courses such as *Formal Language Theory* and an *Introduction to Data Types and Programming*.

It differs from existing books on that subject in the following ways:

- New technical concepts are introduced as they are needed, never for their own sake. The emphasis is always on applications rather than on mathematical technicalities. Yet, technicalities are always treated with the necessary rigour.
- We introduce, at an accessible level, a framework for program verification (symbolic model checking) which is currently available only in research papers. This is at present a hot topic in industry, so graduates fluent in this material are highly sought.
- Our text is supplemented by a worldwide-web site[1] which offers additional material useful for classroom presentations, such as postscript files of all

[1] www.cs.bham.ac.uk/research/lics/

the figures and text files of the program code featured in the book. There is also a multiple-choice interactive tutor.

• All sections of the book have several exercises marked with an * as in

EXERCISES 0.1
* 1. ...
  2. ...
* 3. ...
  4. ...

———

for which we have provided sample solutions in LATEX. Bona fide teachers and instructors may obtain the PDF files directly from Cambridge University Press (email to dtranah@cup.cam.ac.uk). Exercises end with a short bar, as shown, in order that the reader know where to pick up the text.

Outline of the book

One of the leitmotifs of our book is the observation that most logics used in the design, specification and verification of computer systems fundamentally deal with a *satisfaction relation*

$$\mathcal{M} \vDash \phi$$

where $\mathcal{M}$ is some sort of *situation* or *model*, like the snapshot of a system, and ϕ is a specification, a formula of that logic, expressing what should be true in situation $\mathcal{M}$. For example, $\mathcal{M}$ could model a communications protocol and ϕ the property that the protocol be fair. At the heart of this set-up is that $\vDash$ is actually computable in a compositional way. Fixing the situation $\mathcal{M}$, we determine whether $\mathcal{M} \vDash \phi$ holds by recursively determining this for all subformulas of ϕ. We expand this view for a particular logic (CTL), where this computation and the modelling of a situation may be done purely symbolically using boolean formulas. Tools which support this reasoning make the approach applicable to quite a few realistic systems and designs.

Here is a brief synopsis of what the book covers:

Chapter 1, on propositional logic, should be the common starting point and backbone for any course based on this book; it might also be used as a reference text for courses that presuppose a knowledge of propositional logic. Its sections provide

- a complete presentation of a natural deduction-style proof system for propositional logic with a discussion of the intuitionistic fragment;
- a section on propositional logic as a formal language; and
- the semantics of propositional logic, where:

  - we constructively prove soundness *and* completeness of the proof system with respect to the usual truth-table semantics;
  - we discuss the notions of equivalence, satisfiability and validity;
  - we cover the principle of mathematical induction, which is needed for soundness, often employed in our book and is one of the central reasoning tools in computer science; and
  - we feature a section on disjunctive normal forms and Horn formulas; our presentation highlights the development of algorithms computing such normal forms as well as discussing their correctness.

Chapter 2 addresses predicate logic. In this chapter we

- first motivate the need for richer logics via symbolic representations of natural language sentences;
- define and study predicate logic as a formal language with the standard notions of static scoping (free and bound variables) and substitution;
- familiarize students with its semantics,
- introduce a natural deduction style proof system for predicate logic by 'enriching' the proof system of Chapter 1 with the introduction and elimination rules for quantifiers; we use this system to prove the standard quantifier equivalences; and
- present Church's proof of the undecidability of satisfaction in predicate logic (via reduction to the Post correspondence problem).

Chapter 3 introduces students to *model checking*, a state-of-the-art technique in verifying concurrent systems. We

- focus on the syntax and semantics of CTL (computation tree logic), and derive the standard algorithm for model checking of CTL formulas;
- let students practice the synthesis and interpretation of practically relevant, and frequently occurring, specifications in CTL;
- present two case studies in great detail: a mutual exclusion protocol and an alternating bit protocol; both protocols are developed as labelled transition systems;

- introduce the symbolic model verifier SMV, provide SMV code for our case studies and discuss the relevant CTL specifications;
- explain how CTL and SMV manage to incorporate fairness constraints;
- discuss the logics LTL and CTL* and compare their expressive power with that of CTL;
- give a fixed-point characterization of those CTL operators which express invariant behaviour; and
- conclude by pointing out that practical specifications often obey common patterns and offer pointers to web sites, where such patterns are developed, surveyed and documented.

Chapter 4 covers program verification by discussing deductive reasoning about imperative programs; it presents a Floyd-Hoare-style program logic for a sequential imperative core programming language, reminiscent of a fragment of the C programming language. The emphasis will be on correctness proofs (partial and total correctness) for fairly simple programs. The main objective is to challenge students to systematically develop small programs meeting required input/output behaviour. In particular, they need to develop the ability to come up with characterizing invariants of while-loops.

Chapter 5 discusses modal logics and agents. Modal logics are motivated through a desire to have possible world semantics.

- We discuss general syntax, semantics and an extension of the propositional logic deduction calculus for basic modal logic. The theme of the first part of this chapter is that of 'logic engineering': e.g. if $\Box \phi$ means that an agent *knows* ϕ, then what axioms and inference rules for $\Box$ should we engineer? We carry out such a task for various meanings of $\Box$.
- The second part of this chapter is devoted to the study of a modal logic modelling general reasoning about knowledge in a multi-agent system ($\mathrm{KT45}^n$). It carefully explains how some epistemological puzzles can be solved using this modal logic.

Chapter 6 introduces binary decision diagrams, which are a data structure for boolean functions.

- We describe ordered binary decision diagrams (OBDDs) and their accompanying algorithms;
- We discuss extensions and variations of OBDDs as well as their limitations;
- We explain how CTL models can be coded as boolean formulas;

- We present the syntax and semantics of the relational mu-calculus within which we code CTL models and their specification in the presence of simple fairness constraints.

  That chapter should create stimulating links to courses on algorithms and data structures and to courses on circuit design, and can also be used as a foundation for implementation projects which develop tools supporting reasoning with the concepts developed in other chapters.

At the end of each chapter, we provide pointers to the literature and to sites from which free software may be downloaded, if applicable. A detailed index should allow the quick discovery of cross-connections between most of these chapters.

The inter-dependence of chapters and prerequisites. The book requires that students know the basics of elementary arithmetic and naive set theoretic concepts and notation. The core material of Chapter 1 (everything except Sections 1.4.3 to 1.5.3) is essential for all of the chapters that follow. Other than that, only Chapter 6 depends on Chapter 3 and a basic understanding of the static scoping rules covered in Chapter 2 — although one may easily cover Sections 6.1 and 6.2 without having done Chapter 3 at all. The inter-dependence graph of chapters can be seen below:

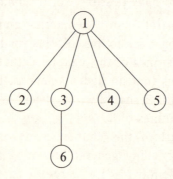

Suggested course outlines

We suggest at least three different ways of teaching with this text (based on a 12-15-week course).

- A course based on Chapters 1, 2 and 5 would be suitable for students specialising in database and information systems or artificial intelligence;

this choice of material should prepare them for more advanced topics in database programming and automated deduction.

- A course based on Chapters 1, 3 and 6 would focus on the complete development of a verification framework for concurrent systems down to the implementation level.
- A course based on Chapters 1, 3 and 4 would provide a broader presentation of the logical foundations of programming.

Suitable courses based on the book. This book can be used as the main text book in a course on the introduction to logic in computer science and the specification and verification of computer systems and programs. It may be quite useful as an additional text in courses on algorithms and data structures, the introduction to logic in artificial intelligence, sequential circuit and chip design and validation, discrete mathematics for computer scientists and formal language theory, as well as courses in networks and operating systems.

WWW page

This book is supported by a WWW page, which contains a list of errata, text files for all the program code, and all the figures. There is an interactive tutor based on multiple-choice questions. There are also details of how to obtain the solutions to exercises in this book which are marked with a *. There are also links to other relevant pages. The URL for the book's page is

`www.cs.bham.ac.uk/research/lics/`

Acknowledgments

Many people have, directly or indirectly, assisted us in writing this book. David Schmidt kindly provided serveral exercises for Chapter 4. Krysia Broda has pointed out some typographical errors and she and the other authors of [BEKV94] have allowed us to use some exercises from that book (notably Exercises 1.6(1(b)), 2.2(5) and 2.5(4, 9, 10)). We also borrowed exercises or examples from [Hod77] and [FHMV95]. Zena Matilde Ariola, Josh Hodas, Jan Komorowski, Sergey Kotov, Scott A. Smolka and Steve Vickers have corresponded with us about this text; their comments are appreciated. Matt Dwyer and John Hatcliff made useful comments on drafts of Chapter 3. Kevin Lucas provided insightful comments on the content of Chapter 6, and notified us of numerous typographical errors in several drafts of the book. Achim Jung read several chapters and gave useful feedback.

Additionally, a number of people read and provided useful comments on several chapters, including Moti Ben-Ari, Graham Clark, Christian Haack, Anthony Hook, Roberto Segala, Alan Sexton and Allen Stoughton. Numerous students at Kansas State University and the University of Birmingham have given us feedback of various kinds, which has influenced our choice and presentation of the topics. We acknowledge Paul Taylor's LaTeX package for proof boxes. About half a dozen anonymous referees made critical, but constructive, comments which helped to improve this text in various ways. In spite of these contributions, there may still be errors in the book, and we alone must take responsibility for those.

1

Propositional logic

The aim of logic in computer science is to develop languages to model the situations we encounter as computer science professionals, in such a way that we can reason about them formally. Reasoning about situations means constructing arguments about them; we want to do this formally, so that the arguments are valid and can be defended rigorously, or executed on a machine.

Consider the following argument:

Example 1.1 If the train arrives late and there are no taxis at the station, then John is late for his meeting. John is not late for his meeting. The train did arrive late. *Therefore*, there were taxis at the station.

Intuitively, the argument is valid, since if we put the *first* sentence and the *third* sentence together, they tell us that if there are no taxis, then John will be late. The second sentence tells us that he was not late, so it must be the case that there were taxis.

Much of this book will be concerned with arguments that have this structure, namely, that consist of a number of sentences followed by the word 'therefore' and then another sentence. The argument is valid if the sentence after the 'therefore' logically follows from the sentences before it. Exactly what we mean by 'follows from' is the subject of this chapter and the next one.

Consider another example:

Example 1.2 If it is raining and Jane does not have her umbrella with her, then she will get wet. Jane is not wet. It is raining. *Therefore*, Jane has her umbrella with her.

This is also a valid argument. Closer examination reveals that it actually

1

has the same structure as the argument of the previous example! All we have done is substituted some sentence fragments for others:

Example 1.1	Example 1.2
the train is late	it is raining
there are taxis at the station	Jane has her umbrella with her
John is late for his meeting	Jane gets wet.

The argument in each example could be stated without talking about trains and rain, as follows:

If *p* and not *q*, then *r*. Not *r*. *p*. *Therefore, q.*

In developing logics, we are not concerned with what the sentences really mean, but only in their logical structure. Of course, when we *apply* such reasoning, as done above, such meaning will be of great interest.

1.1 Declarative sentences

In order to make arguments rigorous, we need to develop a language in which we can express sentences in such a way that brings out their logical structure. The language we begin with is the language of propositional logic. It is based on *propositions*, or *declarative sentences* which one can, in principle, argue as being true or false. Examples of declarative sentences are:

(1). The sum of the numbers 3 and 5 equals 8.
(2). Jane reacted violently to Jack's accusations.
(3). Every even natural number is the sum of two prime numbers.
(4). All Martians like pepperoni on their pizza.
(5). Albert Camus était un écrivain français.
(6). Die Würde des Menschen ist unantastbar.

These sentences are all declarative, because they are in principle capable of being declared 'true', or 'false'. Sentence (1) can be tested by appealing to basic facts about arithmetic (and by tacitly assuming an Arabic, decimal representation of natural numbers). Sentence (2) is a bit more problematic. In order to give it a truth value, we need to know who Jane and Jack are and perhaps to have a reliable account from someone who witnessed the situation described. In principle, e.g., if we had been at the scene, we feel that we would have been able to detect Jane's *violent* reaction, provided that it indeed occurred in that way. Sentence (3), known as Goldbach's conjecture, seems straightforward on the face of it. Clearly, a fact about *all* even numbers is either true or false. But to this day nobody knows whether sentence (3) expresses a truth or not. It is even not clear whether this could be shown by some finite means, even if it were true. However, in this text we will be content with sentences as soon as they can, in principle, attain some truth value regardless of whether this truth value reflects the actual state of affairs suggested by the sentence in question. Sentence (4) seems a bit silly, although we could say that *if* Martians exist and *if* they occasionally, or frequently, eat pizza, then all of them will either like pepperoni on it or not. Again, for the purposes of this text sentence (4) will do. Et alors, qu'est-ce qu'on pense des phrases (5) et (6)? Sentences (5) and (6) are fine if you happen to read French and German a bit. Thus, declarative statements can be made in any natural, or artificial, language.

The kind of sentences we *won't* consider here are non-declarative ones, like

- Could you please pass me the salt?
- Ready, steady, go!
- May fortune come your way.

Primarily, we are interested in precise declarative sentences, or *statements* about the behaviour of computer systems, or programs. Not only do we want to specify such statements but we also want to *check* whether a given program, or system, fulfils a specification at hand. Thus, we need to develop a calculus of reasoning which allows us to draw conclusions from given assumptions, like initialised variables, which are reliable in the sense that they preserve truth: if all our assumptions are true, then our conclusion ought to be true as well. A much more difficult question is whether, given any true property of a computer program, we can find an argument in our calculus that has this property as its conclusion. The declarative sentence (3) above might illuminate the problematic aspect of such questions in the context of number theory.

The logics we intend to design are *symbolic* in nature. We translate a certain sufficiently large subset of all English declarative sentences into strings of symbols. This gives us a compressed but still complete encoding of declarative sentences and allows us to concentrate on the mere mechanics of our argumentation. This is important since specifications of systems or software are sequences of such declarative sentences. It further opens up the possibility of automatic manipulation of such specifications, a job that computers just love to do[1]. Our strategy is to consider certain declarative

---

[1] There is a certain, slightly bitter, circularity in such endeavours: in proving that a certain computer program P satisfies a given property, we might let some other computer program Q try to find a proof that P satisfies the property; but who guarantees us that Q satisfies the property of producing only correct proofs? We seem to run into an infinite regress.

sentences as being *atomic*, or *indecomposable*, like the sentence

'The number 5 is even.'.

We assign certain distinct symbols $p, q, r, \ldots$, or sometimes $p_1, p_2, p_3, \ldots$ to each of these atomic sentences and we can then code up more complex sentences in a *compositional* way. For example, given the atomic sentences

p: 'I won the lottery last week.'
q: 'I purchased a lottery ticket.'
r: 'I won last week's sweepstakes.'

we can form more complex sentences according to the rules below:

¬: The *negation* of p is denoted by $\neg p$ and expresses 'I did **not** win the lottery last week.', or equivalently 'It is **not** true that I won the lottery last week.'.

∨: Given p and r we may wish to state that *at least one of them* is true: 'I won the lottery last week, **or** I won last week's sweepstakes.'; we denote this declarative sentence by $p \lor r$ and call it the *disjunction* of p and r[1].

∧: Dually, the formula $p \land r$ denotes the rather fortunate *conjunction* of p and r: 'Last week I won the lottery **and** the sweepstakes.'.

→: Last, but definitely not least, the sentence '**If** I won the lottery last week, **then** I purchased a lottery ticket.' expresses an *implication* between p and q, suggesting that q is a logical consequence of p. We write $p \to q$ for that[2]. We call p the *premise* of $p \to q$ and q its *conclusion*.

Of course, we are entitled to use these rules of constructing propositions repeatedly. For example, we are now in a position to form the proposition

$$p \land q \to \neg r \lor q$$

which means that '**if** p **and** q **then not** r **or** q'. You might have noticed a potential ambiguity in this reading. One could have argued that this sentence

---

[1] Its meaning should not be confused with the often implicit meaning of **or** in natural language discourse as **either** ... **or**. In this text **or** always means *at least one of them* and should not be confounded with *exclusive or* which states that *exactly one* of the two statements holds.

[2] The natural language meaning of '**if** ... **then** ... ' often implicitly assumes a *causal role* of the premise somehow enabling its conclusion. The logical meaning of implication is a bit different, though, in the sense that it states the *preservation of truth* which might happen without any causal relationship. For example, 'If all birds can fly, then Bob Dole was never president of the United States of America.' is a true statement, but there is no known causal connection between the flying skills of penguins and effective campaigning.

has the structure 'p is the case **and if** q **then** ... '. A computer would require the insertion of brackets, as in

$$(p \wedge q) \rightarrow ((\neg r) \vee q)$$

to disambiguate this assertion. However, we humans get annoyed by a proliferation of such brackets which is why we adopt certain conventions about the *binding priorities* of these symbols.

Convention 1.3 $\neg$ binds more tightly than $\vee$ and $\wedge$, and the latter two bind more tightly than $\rightarrow$.

EXERCISES 1.1
Use $\neg$, $\rightarrow$, $\wedge$ and $\vee$ to express the following declarative sentences in propositional logic; in each case state what your respective propositional atoms p, q, etc. mean:

* 1. If the sun shines today, then it won't shine tomorrow.
  2. Robert was jealous of Yvonne, or he was not in a good mood.
  3. If the barometer falls, then either it will rain or it will snow.
  4. If you have read the lecture notes and if you have done the first three homework assignments, then you should be in good shape for the first exam; otherwise, you will have a problem.
* 5. If a request occurs, then either it will eventually be acknowledged, or the requesting process won't ever be able to make progress.
  6. Cancer will not be cured unless its cause is determined and a new drug for cancer is found.
* 7. If Dick met Jane yesterday, they had a cup of coffee together, or they took a walk in the park.
  8. He coughs often and loudly.
  9. My sister wants a black and white cat.
  10. The formulas of propositional logic below implicitly assume the binding priorities of the logical connectives put forward in Convention 1.3. Make sure that you fully understand those conventions by reinserting as many brackets as possible. For example, given $p \wedge q \rightarrow r$, change it to $(p \wedge q) \rightarrow r$ since $\wedge$ binds more tightly than $\rightarrow$.

    * (a) $\neg p \wedge q \rightarrow r$
      (b) $(p \rightarrow q) \wedge \neg (r \vee p \rightarrow q)$
    * (c) $(p \rightarrow q) \rightarrow (r \rightarrow s \vee t)$
      (d) $p \vee (\neg q \rightarrow p \wedge r)$
    * (e) $p \vee q \rightarrow \neg p \wedge r$

(f) $p \vee p \to \neg q$

* (g) Why is the expression $p \vee q \wedge r$ problematic?

___

1.2 Natural deduction

How do we go about constructing a calculus for reasoning about propositions, so that we can establish the validity of Examples 1.1 and 1.2? Clearly,
we would like to have a set of rules each of which allows us to draw a
conclusion given a certain arrangement of premises.

In natural deduction, we have such a collection of *proof rules*. They
allow us to *infer* formulas from other formulas. By applying these rules in
succession, we may infer a conclusion from a set of premises.

Let's see how this works. Suppose we have a set of formulas[1] ϕ_1, ϕ_2,
ϕ_3, ..., ϕ_n, which we will call *premises*, and another formula, ψ, which we
will call a *conclusion*. By applying proof rules to the premises, we hope to
get some more formulas, and by applying more proof rules to those, to
eventually obtain the conclusion. This intention we denote by

$$\phi_1, \phi_2, \ldots, \phi_n \vdash \psi.$$

This expression is called a *sequent*; it is *valid* if a proof for it can be
found. The sequent for Examples 1.1 and 1.2 is $p \wedge \neg q \to r, \neg r, p \vdash q$.
Constructing such a proof is a creative exercise, a bit like programming. It is
not necessarily obvious which rules to apply, and in what order, to obtain the
desired conclusion. Additionally, our proof rules should be carefully chosen;
otherwise, we might be able to 'prove' invalid patterns of argumentation. For
example, we expect that we won't be able to show the sequent $p, q \vdash p \wedge \neg q$.
For example, if p stands for 'Gold is a metal.' and q for 'Silver is a metal.',
then knowing these two facts should not allow us to infer that 'Gold is a
metal whereas silver isn't.'.

Let's now look at our proof rules. We present about fifteen of them in

___

[1] It is traditional in logic to use Greek letters. Lower-case letters are used to stand for formulas and
upper-case letters are used for sets of formulas. Here are some of the more commonly used Greek
letters, together with their pronunciation:

	Lower-case		Upper-case
ϕ	phi	Φ	Phi
ψ	psi	Ψ	Psi
χ	chi	Γ	Gamma
η	eta	Δ	Delta
α	alpha		
β	beta		
γ	gamma		

total; we will go through them in turn and then summarise at the end of this section.

1.2.1 Rules for natural deduction

The rules for conjunction

Our first rule is called the rule for conjunction ($\wedge$): and-introduction. It allows us to conclude $\phi \wedge \psi$, given that we have already concluded ϕ and ψ separately. We write this rule as

$$\frac{\phi \qquad \psi}{\phi \wedge \psi} \wedge i.$$

Above the line are the two premises of the rule. Below the line goes the conclusion. (It might not yet be the final conclusion of our argument; we might have to apply more rules to get there.) To the right of the line, we write the name of the rule; $\wedge i$ is read 'and-introduction'. Notice that we have introduced a $\wedge$ (in the conclusion) where there was none before (in the premises).

For each of the connectives, there is one or more rules to introduce it and one or more rules to eliminate it. The rules for and-elimination are these two:

$$\frac{\phi \wedge \psi}{\phi} \wedge e_1 \qquad\qquad \frac{\phi \wedge \psi}{\psi} \wedge e_2. \tag{1.1}$$

The rule $\wedge e_1$ says: if you have a proof of $\phi \wedge \psi$, then by applying this rule you can get a proof of ϕ. The rule $\wedge e_2$ says the same thing, but allows you to conclude ψ instead. Observe the dependences of these rules: in the first rule of (1.1), the conclusion ϕ has to match the first conjunct of the premise, whereas the exact nature of the second conjunct ψ is irrelevant. In the second rule it is just the other way around: the conclusion ψ has to match the second conjunct ψ and ϕ can be any formula. It is important to engage in this kind of *pattern matching* before the application of proof rules.

Example 1.4 Let's use these rules to prove that $p \wedge q, r \vdash q \wedge r$. We start by writing down the premises; then we leave a gap and write the conclusion:

$$p \wedge q$$
$$r$$

$$q \wedge r$$

The task of constructing the proof is to fill the gap between the premises and the conclusion by applying a suitable sequence of proof rules. In this case, we apply $\wedge e_2$ to the first premise, giving us q. Then we apply $\wedge i$ to this q and to the second premise, r, giving us $q \wedge r$. That's it! We also usually number all the lines, and write in the justification for each line, producing this:

1	$p \wedge q$	premise
2	r	premise
3	q	$\wedge e_2$ 1
4	$q \wedge r$	$\wedge i$ 3, 2

Demonstrate to yourself that you've understood this by trying this one on your own: $(p \wedge q) \wedge r, s \wedge t \vdash q \wedge s$. Notice that the ϕ and ψ can be instantiated not just to atomic sentences, like p and q in the example we just gave, but also to compound sentences. Thus, from $(p \wedge q) \wedge r$ we can deduce $p \wedge q$ by applying $\wedge e_1$, instantiating ϕ to $p \wedge q$ and ψ to r.

If we applied these proof rules literally, then the proof above would actually be a tree with root $q \wedge r$ and leaves $p \wedge q$ and r, like this:

$$\frac{\dfrac{p \wedge q}{q} \wedge e_2 \qquad r}{q \wedge r} \wedge i$$

However, we flattened this tree into a linear presentation which necessitates the use of pointers as seen in lines 3 and 4 above. These pointers allow us to recreate the actual proof tree. Throughout this text, we will use the flattened version of presenting proofs. That way you have to concentrate only on finding a proof, not on how to fit a growing tree onto a sheet of paper.

EXERCISES 1.2
1. Prove the sequent $(p \wedge q) \wedge r, s \wedge t \vdash q \wedge s$.
2. Prove the sequent $p \wedge q \vdash q \wedge p$.
* 3. Prove the sequent $(p \wedge q) \wedge r \vdash p \wedge (q \wedge r)$.

————

If a sequent is valid, there may be many different ways of proving it. So if you compare your solution to these exercises with those of others, they need not coincide. The important thing to realise, though, is that any correct proof can be *checked* for correctness by checking each individual line starting at the top.

The rules of double negation

Intuitively, there is no difference between a formula ϕ and its *double negation* $\neg\neg\phi$, which expresses no more and nothing less than ϕ itself. The sentence

'It is **not** true that it does **not** rain.'

is just a more contrived way of saying

'It rains.'.

Conversely, knowing 'It rains', we are free to state this fact in this more complicated manner if we wish. Thus, we obtain rules of elimination and introduction for double negation:

$$\frac{\neg\neg\phi}{\phi}\ \neg\neg e \qquad\qquad \frac{\phi}{\neg\neg\phi}\ \neg\neg i.$$

(There are rules for single negation on its own, too, which we will see later.)

Example 1.5 The proof of the sequent $p, \neg\neg(q \wedge r) \vdash \neg\neg p \wedge r$ below uses most of the proof rules discussed so far:

1	p	premise
2	$\neg\neg(q \wedge r)$	premise
3	$\neg\neg p$	$\neg\neg i$ 1
4	$q \wedge r$	$\neg\neg e$ 2
5	r	$\wedge e_2$ 4
6	$\neg\neg p \wedge r$	$\wedge i$ 3, 5

Example 1.6 We now prove the sequent $(p \wedge q) \wedge r, s \wedge t \vdash q \wedge s$ which you were invited to prove by yourself in the last section. Please compare the proof below with your solution:

1	$(p \wedge q) \wedge r$	premise
2	$s \wedge t$	premise
3	$p \wedge q$	$\wedge e_1$ 1
4	q	$\wedge e_2$ 3
5	s	$\wedge e_1$ 2
6	$q \wedge s$	$\wedge i$ 4, 5

The rule for eliminating implication

There is one rule to introduce → and one to eliminate it. The latter is one of the best known rules of propositional logic and is often referred to by its Latin name *modus ponens*. We will usually call it by its modern name, implies-elimination (sometimes also referred to as arrow-elimination). This rule states that, given ϕ and knowing that ϕ implies ψ, we may rightfully conclude ψ. In our calculus, we write this as

$$\frac{\phi \quad \phi \to \psi}{\psi} \;\to e.$$

Let us justify this rule by spelling out instances of some declarative sentences p and q. Suppose that

$$p : \text{It rained.}$$
$$p \to q : \text{If it rained, then the street is wet.}$$

so q is just 'The street is wet.'. Now, *if* we know that it rained and *if* we know that the street is wet in the case that it rained, then we may combine these two pieces of information to conclude that the street is indeed wet. Thus, the justification of the →e rule is a mere application of common sense. Another example from programming is:

$$p : \text{The value of the program's input is an integer.}$$
$$p \to q : \text{If the program's input is an integer, then the program outputs}$$
$$\text{a boolean.}$$

Again, we may put all this together to conclude that our program outputs a boolean value for all integer inputs. However, it is important to realise that the presence of p is absolutely essential for the inference to happen. For example, our program might well satisfy $p \to q$, but if it doesn't satisfy p, then we will not be able to derive q.

As we saw before, the ϕ and the ψ can be instantiated to any sentence, including compound ones:

1	$\neg p \wedge q$	premise
2	$\neg p \wedge q \to r \vee \neg p$	premise
3	$r \vee \neg p$	→e 2, 1

Of course, we may use any of these rules as often as we wish. For example, given p, $p \rightarrow q$ and $p \rightarrow (q \rightarrow r)$, we may infer r:

1	$p \rightarrow (q \rightarrow r)$	premise
2	$p \rightarrow q$	premise
3	p	premise
4	$q \rightarrow r$	$\rightarrow$e 1, 3
5	q	$\rightarrow$e 2, 3
6	r	$\rightarrow$e 4, 5

Before turning to implies-introduction, let's look at a hybrid rule which has the Latin name *modus tollens*. It is like the $\rightarrow$e rule in that it eliminates an implication. Suppose that $p \rightarrow q$ *and* $\neg q$ are the case. Then, *if* p holds we can use $\rightarrow$e to conclude that q holds. Thus, we then have that q *and* $\neg q$ hold, which is impossible. Therefore, we may infer that p must be false. But this can only mean that $\neg p$ is true. We summarise this reasoning into the rule *modus tollens*, or MT for short:[1]

$$\frac{\phi \rightarrow \psi \quad \neg \psi}{\neg \phi} \text{ MT.}$$

Again, let us see an example of this rule in the natural language setting:

'If Abraham Lincoln was Ethiopian, then he was African. Abraham Lincoln was not African; therefore he was not Ethiopian.'.

Example 1.7 In the following proof of

$$p \rightarrow (q \rightarrow r),\, p,\, \neg r \vdash \neg q$$

we use several of the rules introduced so far:

1	$p \rightarrow (q \rightarrow r)$	premise
2	p	premise
3	$\neg r$	premise
4	$q \rightarrow r$	$\rightarrow$e 1, 2
5	$\neg q$	MT 4, 3

Examples 1.8 Here are two example proofs which combine the rule MT with

---

[1] We will be able to *derive* this rule from other ones later on, but we introduce it here because it allows us already to do some pretty slick proofs. You may think of this rule as one on a higher level insofar as it does not mention the lower-level rules upon which it depends.

either $\neg\neg$e or $\neg\neg$i:

1	$\neg p \rightarrow q$	premise
2	$\neg q$	premise
3	$\neg\neg p$	MT 1, 2
4	p	$\neg\neg$e 3

proves that

$$\neg p \rightarrow q, \neg q \vdash p$$

and

1	$p \rightarrow \neg q$	premise
2	q	premise
3	$\neg\neg q$	$\neg\neg$i 2
4	$\neg p$	MT 1, 3

shows

$$p \rightarrow \neg q, q \vdash \neg p.$$

Note that the order of applying double negation rules and MT is different in these examples; this order is driven by the particular sequent one is trying to show.

EXERCISES 1.3

1. Use $\neg$, $\rightarrow$, $\wedge$ and $\vee$ to express the following declarative sentences in propositional logic; in each case state what your respective propositional atoms p, q, etc. mean:

   (a) If interest rates go up, share prices go down.
   (b) If Smith has installed central heating, then he has sold his car, or he has not paid his mortgage.
   * (c) Today it will rain or shine, but not both.

2. Find proofs for the following sequents:

   (a) $p \rightarrow (p \rightarrow q), p \vdash q$
   * (b) $q \rightarrow (p \rightarrow r), \neg r, q \vdash \neg p.$

The rule implies introduction

The rule MT made it possible for us to show

$$p \to q, \neg q \vdash \neg p.$$

But the sequent

$$p \to q \vdash \neg q \to \neg p$$

seems just as plausible; it is, in a certain sense, saying the same thing. Yet, so far we have no rule which *builds* implications that do not already occur as premises in our proofs. The mechanics of such a rule are more involved than what we have seen so far. So let us proceed with care. Let us suppose that $p \to q$ is the case. If we *temporarily* assume that $\neg q$ holds, we can use MT to infer $\neg p$. Thus, assuming $p \to q$ we can show that $\neg q$ **implies** $\neg p$; but the latter we express *symbolically* as $\neg q \to \neg p$. To summarise, we have found an argumentation for $p \to q \vdash \neg q \to \neg p$:

1	$p \to q$	premise
2	$\neg q$	assumption
3	$\neg p$	MT 1, 2
4	$\neg q \to \neg p$	$\to$i 2–3

The box in this proof serves to demarcate the scope of the temporary assumption $\neg q$. What we are saying is: let's make the assumption of $\neg q$. To do this, we open a box and put $\neg q$ at the top. Then we continue applying other rules as normal, for example to obtain $\neg p$. But this still depends on the assumption of $\neg q$, so it goes inside the box. Finally, we are ready to apply $\to$i. It allows us to conclude $\neg q \to \neg p$, but that conclusion no longer *depends* on the assumption $\neg q$. Compare this with saying that

'If you are French, then you are European.'.

The truth of this sentence does not depend on whether you are French or not. Therefore, we write the conclusion $\neg q \to \neg p$ outside the box. This works also as one would expect if we think of $p \to q$ as a *type* of a procedure. For example, p could say that the procedure expects an integer value x as input and q might say that the procedure returns a boolean value y as output. The validity of $p \to q$ amounts now to an assume-guarantee assertion: if the input is an integer, then the output is a boolean. This assertion can be true about a procedure while that same procedure could compute strange things in the case that the input is not an integer. Showing $p \to q$ using the rule

→i is now called *type checking*, an important topic in the construction of compilers for typed programming languages.

We thus formulate the rule →i as follows:

$$\frac{}{\phi \to \psi} \to i$$

It says: in order to prove $\phi \to \psi$, make a temporary assumption of ϕ and then prove ψ. In your proof of ψ, you can use ϕ and any of the other formulas such as premises and provisional conclusions that you have made so far. Proofs may nest boxes or open new boxes after old ones have been closed. There are rules about which formulas can be used at which points in the proof. Generally, we can only use a formula ϕ in a proof at a given point if that formula occurs *prior* to that point and if no box which encloses that occurrence of ϕ has been closed already.

The line immediately following a closed box has to match the pattern of the conclusion of the rule that uses the box. For implies-introduction, this means that we have to continue after the box with $\phi \to \psi$, where ϕ was the first and ψ the last formula of that box. We will encounter two more proof rules involving proof boxes and they will require similar pattern matching.

Example 1.9 Here is another example of a proof using →i:

1		$\neg q \to \neg p$	premise
2		p	assumption
3		$\neg\neg p$	$\neg\neg$i 2
4		$\neg\neg q$	MT 1, 3
5		$p \to \neg\neg q$	→i 2–4

which verifies the sequent

$$\neg q \to \neg p \vdash p \to \neg\neg q.$$

Notice that we could apply the rule MT to formulas occurring in or above the box: at line 4, no box has been closed that would enclose line 1 or 3.

At this point it is instructive to consider the one-line argument

| 1 | | p | premise |

which demonstrates

$$p \vdash p.$$

The rule →i (with conclusion $\phi \to \psi$) does not prohibit the possibility that ϕ and ψ coincide. They could both be instantiated to p. Therefore we may extend the proof above to

1	p	assumption
2	$p \to p$	→i 1 − 1

We write

$$\vdash p \to p$$

to express that the argumentation for $p \to p$ does not depend on any assumptions at all.

Definition 1.10 Logical formulas ϕ such that $\vdash \phi$ holds are called *theorems*.

Example 1.11 Here is an example of a theorem whose proof utilises most of the rules introduced so far:

1	$q \to r$	assumption
2	$\neg q \to \neg p$	assumption
3	p	assumption
4	$\neg\neg p$	¬¬i 3
5	$\neg\neg q$	MT 2, 4
6	q	¬¬e 5
7	r	→e 1, 6
8	$p \to r$	→i 3−7
9	$(\neg q \to \neg p) \to (p \to r)$	→i 2−8
10	$(q \to r) \to ((\neg q \to \neg p) \to (p \to r))$	→i 1−9

Therefore

$$\vdash (q \to r) \to ((\neg q \to \neg p) \to (p \to r))$$

showing that $(q \to r) \to ((\neg q \to \neg p) \to (p \to r))$ is another theorem.

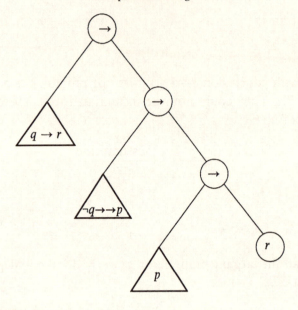

Fig. 1.1. Part of the structure of the formula $(q \rightarrow r) \rightarrow ((\neg q \rightarrow \neg p) \rightarrow (p \rightarrow r))$ to show how it determines the proof structure.

Remark 1.12 Indeed, this example indicates that we may transform any proof of

$$\phi_1, \phi_2, \ldots, \phi_n \vdash \psi$$

in such a way as to obtain a proof of the theorem

$$\vdash \phi_1 \rightarrow (\phi_2 \rightarrow (\phi_3 \rightarrow (\cdots \rightarrow (\phi_n \rightarrow \psi)\ldots)))$$

by 'augmenting' the previous proof with n lines of the rule $\rightarrow$i applied to ϕ_n, $\phi_{n-1}, \ldots, \phi_1$ in that order.

The nested boxes in the proof of Example 1.11 reveal a pattern of using elimination rules first, to deconstruct assumptions we have made, and then introduction rules to construct our final conclusion. More difficult proofs may involve several such phases.

Let us dwell on this important topic for a while. How did we come up with the proof above? Parts of it are *determined* by the structure of the formulas we have, while other parts require us to be *creative*. Consider the logical structure of $(q \rightarrow r) \rightarrow ((\neg q \rightarrow \neg p) \rightarrow (p \rightarrow r))$ schematically depicted in Figure 1.1. The formula is overall an implication since $\rightarrow$ is the root of the tree in Figure 1.1. But the only way to build an implication is by means of the rule →i. Thus, we need to state the premise as an assumption (line 1) and have to show the conclusion (line 9). If we managed to do that, then we know how to end the proof in line 10. In fact, as we already remarked, this is the only way we could have ended it. So essentially lines 1, 9 and 10 are completely determined by the structure of the given formula; further, we have reduced the problem to filling the gaps in between lines 1 and 9. But again, the formula in line 9 is an implication, so we have only one way of showing it: assuming its premise in line 2 and trying to show its conclusion in line 8; as before, line 9 is obtained by →i. The formula $p → r$ in line 8 is yet another implication. Therefore, we have to assume p in line 3 and hope to show r in line 7, then →i produces the desired result in line 8. In summary, the question now is this: how can we show r, using the three assumptions in lines 1–3? This, and only this, is the creative part of this proof. We see the implication $q → r$ in line 1 and know how to get r (using →e) if only we had q. So how could we get q? Well, lines 2 and 3 almost look like a pattern for the MT rule, which would give us $¬¬q$ in line 5; the latter is quickly changed to q in line 6 via ¬¬e. However, the pattern for MT does not match right away, since it requires $¬¬p$ instead of p. But this is easily accomplished via ¬¬i in line 4.

The moral of this discussion is that the logical structure of the formula to be shown tells you a lot about the structure of a possible proof and it is definitely worth your while to exploit that information in trying to prove sequents. Before ending this section on the rules for implication, let's look at some more examples (this time also involving the rules for conjunction).

Example 1.13 Using the rule ∧i, we can prove the sequent

$$p ∧ q → r ⊢ p → (q → r):$$

1	$p ∧ q → r$	premise
2	p	assumption
3	q	assumption
4	$p ∧ q$	∧i 2, 3
5	r	→e 1, 4
6	$q → r$	→i 3–5
7	$p → (q → r)$	→i 2–6

Example 1.14 Using the two elimination rules $\wedge e_1$ and $\wedge e_2$, we can show the 'converse' of the sequent above, i.e.

$$p \to (q \to r) \vdash p \wedge q \to r :$$

1	$p \to (q \to r)$	premise
2	$p \wedge q$	assumption
3	p	$\wedge e_1$ 2
4	q	$\wedge e_2$ 2
5	$q \to r$	$\to$e 1, 3
6	r	$\to$e 5, 4
7	$p \wedge q \to r$	$\to$i 2–6

Since we have shown $p \to (q \to r) \vdash p \wedge q \to r$ and $p \wedge q \to r \vdash p \to (q \to r)$, these two formulas are equivalent in the sense that we can prove one from the other. We denote this by

$$p \wedge q \to r \dashv\vdash p \to (q \to r).$$

Since there can be only one formula to the right of $\vdash$, we observe that $\dashv\vdash$ can only relate *two* formulas to each other.

Example 1.15 Here is an example of a proof that uses introduction *and* elimination rules for conjunction; it is a proof of the sequent $p \to q \vdash p \wedge r \to q \wedge r$:

1	$p \to q$	premise
2	$p \wedge r$	assumption
3	p	$\wedge e_1$ 2
4	r	$\wedge e_2$ 2
5	q	$\to$e 1, 3
6	$q \wedge r$	$\wedge$i 5, 4
7	$p \wedge r \to q \wedge r$	$\to$i 2–6

The rules for disjunction

The rules for disjunction are different in spirit from those for conjunction. The case for conjunction was concise and clear: proofs of $\phi \wedge \psi$ are essentially nothing but a concatenation of a proof of ϕ and a proof of ψ, plus an additional line invoking $\wedge$i. In the case of disjunctions, however, it turns out that the *introduction* of disjunctions is by far easier to grasp than their elimination. So we begin with the rules $\vee i_1$ and $\vee i_2$. From the premise ϕ we can infer that 'ϕ **or** ψ' holds, for we already know that ϕ holds. Note that this inference is valid for any choice of ψ. By the same token, we may conclude 'ϕ **or** ψ' if we already have ψ. Similarly, that inference works for any choice of ϕ. Thus, we need the proof rules

$$\frac{\phi}{\phi \vee \psi} \vee i_1 \qquad\qquad \frac{\psi}{\phi \vee \psi} \vee i_2.$$

So if p stands for

'Agassi won a gold medal in 1996.'

and q denotes the sentence

'Agassi won Wimbledon in 1996.'

then $p \vee q$ is the case because p is true, regardless of the fact that q is false. Naturally, the constructed disjunction depends upon the assumptions needed in establishing its respective disjunct p or q.

Now let's consider or-elimination. How can we use a formula of the form $\phi \vee \psi$ in a proof? Again, our guiding principle is to *disassemble* assumptions into their basic constituents so that the latter may be used in our argumentation such that they render our desired conclusion. Let us imagine that we want to show some proposition χ by assuming $\phi \vee \psi$. We then have to give *two* separate proofs which we need to combine into one argument:

1. First, we assume that ϕ holds and have to come up with a proof of χ.
2. Next, we assume ψ and need to give a proof of χ as well.
3. Given $\phi \vee \psi$ and these two proofs, we can infer χ, since our case analysis above is exhaustive.

Therefore, we write the rule $\vee e$ as follows:

$$\frac{\phi \vee \psi \quad \begin{array}{|c|} \hline \phi \\ \vdots \\ \chi \\ \hline \end{array} \quad \begin{array}{|c|} \hline \psi \\ \vdots \\ \chi \\ \hline \end{array}}{\chi} \vee e$$

It is saying that: if we have $\phi \vee \psi$ and, no matter whether we assume ϕ or we assume ψ, we can get a proof of χ, then we are entitled to deduce χ anyway.

Let's look at the example $p \vee q \vdash q \vee p$:

$$
\begin{array}{lll}
1 & p \vee q & \text{premise} \\
\end{array}
$$

$$
\begin{array}{lll}
2 & p & \text{assumption} \\
3 & q \vee p & \vee i_2\ 2 \\
\end{array}
$$

$$
\begin{array}{lll}
4 & q & \text{assumption} \\
5 & q \vee p & \vee i_1\ 4 \\
\end{array}
$$

$$
\begin{array}{lll}
6 & q \vee p & \vee e\ 1, 2{-}3, 4{-}5 \\
\end{array}
$$

Here are some points you need to remember about applying the $\vee e$ rule.

- For it to be a sound argument we have to make sure that the conclusions in each of the two cases (the χ in the rule) are actually the same formula.
- The work done by the rule $\vee e$ is the combining of the arguments of the two cases into one.
- In each case you may not use the temporary assumption of the other case, unless it is something that has already been shown before those case boxes began.

If we use $\phi \vee \psi$ in an argument where it occurs only as an assumption or a premise, then we are missing a certain amount of information: we know ϕ, or ψ, but we don't know which one of the two it is. Thus, we have to make a solid case for each of the two possibilities ϕ or ψ; this resembles the behaviour of a CASE or IF statement one would write in Pascal, or any other programming language.

Example 1.16 Here is a more complex example illustrating these points. We prove $q \to r \vdash p \vee q \to p \vee r$.

$$
\begin{array}{lll}
1 & q \to r & \text{premise} \\
\end{array}
$$

$$
\begin{array}{lll}
2 & p \vee q & \text{assumption} \\
3 & p & \text{assumption} \\
4 & p \vee r & \vee i_1\ 3 \\
5 & q & \text{assumption} \\
6 & r & \to e\ 1, 5 \\
7 & p \vee r & \vee i_2\ 6 \\
8 & p \vee r & \vee e\ 2, 3{-}4, 5{-}7 \\
\end{array}
$$

$$
\begin{array}{lll}
9 & p \vee q \to p \vee r & \to i\ 2{-}8 \\
\end{array}
$$

Note that the propositions in lines 4, 7 and 8 coincide, so the application of $\vee e$ is legitimate.

We give some more example proofs which use the rules $\lor e$, $\lor i_1$ and $\lor i_2$.

Example 1.17 The proof of the sequent

$$(p \lor q) \lor r \vdash p \lor (q \lor r)$$

below is surprisingly long and seemingly complex. But this is to be expected, since the elimination rules break $(p \lor q) \lor r$ up into its atomic constituents p, q and r, whereas the introduction rules then built up the formula $p \lor (q \lor r)$.

1	$(p \lor q) \lor r$	premise
2	$(p \lor q)$	assumption
3	p	assumption
4	$p \lor (q \lor r)$	$\lor i_1$ 3
5	q	assumption
6	$q \lor r$	$\lor i_1$ 5
7	$p \lor (q \lor r)$	$\lor i_2$ 6
8	$p \lor (q \lor r)$	$\lor e$ 2, 3−4, 5−7
9	r	assumption
10	$q \lor r$	$\lor i_2$ 9
11	$p \lor (q \lor r)$	$\lor i_2$ 10
12	$p \lor (q \lor r)$	$\lor e$ 1, 2−8, 9−11

Example 1.18 From boolean algebra, or circuit theory, you may know that disjunctions distribute over conjunctions. We are now able to prove this in natural deduction. The following proof:

1	$p \land (q \lor r)$	premise
2	p	$\land e_1$ 1
3	$(q \lor r)$	$\land e_2$ 1
4	q	assumption
5	$(p \land q)$	$\land i$ 2,4
6	$(p \land q) \lor (p \land r)$	$\lor i_1$ 5
7	r	assumption
8	$(p \land r)$	$\land i$ 2,7
9	$(p \land q) \lor (p \land r)$	$\lor i_2$ 8
10	$(p \land q) \lor (p \land r)$	$\lor e$ 3, 4−6, 7−9

verifies the sequent

$$p \wedge (q \vee r) \vdash (p \wedge q) \vee (p \wedge r)$$

and you are encouraged to show the other direction yourself: $(p \wedge q) \vee (p \wedge r) \vdash p \wedge (q \vee r)$.

A final proof rule is required in order to allow us to conclude a box with a formula which has already appeared earlier in the proof. Consider the sequent $\vdash p \rightarrow (q \rightarrow p)$, which may be proved as follows:

1	p	assumption
2	q	assumption
3	p	copy 1
4	$q \rightarrow p$	$\rightarrow$i 2–3
5	$p \rightarrow (q \rightarrow p)$	$\rightarrow$i 1–4

The rule copy allows us to repeat something that we know already. We need to do this in this example, because the rule $\rightarrow$i requires that we end the inner box with p. The copy rule entitles us to copy formulas that appeared before, unless they depend on temporary assumptions whose box has already been closed. Though a little inelegant, this additional rule is a small price to pay for the freedom of being able to use premises, or any other 'visible' formulas, more than once.

EXERCISES 1.4
1. Find proofs for the following sequents:
  * (a) $\vdash (p \wedge q) \rightarrow p$
    (b) $p \vdash q \rightarrow (p \wedge q)$
  * (c) $p \vdash (p \rightarrow q) \rightarrow q$.

2. Prove the sequents below:
  * (a) $(p \rightarrow r) \wedge (q \rightarrow r) \vdash p \wedge q \rightarrow r$
  * (b) $q \rightarrow r \vdash (p \rightarrow q) \rightarrow (p \rightarrow r)$
    (c) $p \rightarrow (q \rightarrow r), p \rightarrow q \vdash p \rightarrow r$
  * (d) $p \rightarrow q, r \rightarrow s \vdash p \vee r \rightarrow q \vee s$
    (e) $p \vee q \vdash r \rightarrow ((p \vee q) \wedge r)$
  * (f) $(p \vee (q \rightarrow p)) \wedge q \vdash p$
  * (g) $p \rightarrow q, r \rightarrow s \vdash p \wedge r \rightarrow q \wedge s$
    (h) $p \rightarrow q \vdash ((p \wedge q) \rightarrow p) \wedge (p \rightarrow (p \wedge q))$
    (i) $\vdash q \rightarrow (p \rightarrow (p \rightarrow (q \rightarrow p)))$
  * (j) $p \rightarrow q \wedge r \vdash (p \rightarrow q) \wedge (p \rightarrow r)$

   (k) $(p \rightarrow q) \wedge (p \rightarrow r) \vdash p \rightarrow q \wedge r$

   (l) $\vdash (p \rightarrow q) \rightarrow ((r \rightarrow s) \rightarrow (p \wedge r \rightarrow q \wedge s))$; here you might be able to 'recycle' and augment a proof from a previous exercise.

   (m) $p \rightarrow q \vdash \neg q \rightarrow \neg p$

 * (n) $p \vee (p \wedge q) \vdash p$

   (o) $r, p \rightarrow (r \rightarrow q) \vdash p \rightarrow (q \wedge r)$

 * (p) $p \rightarrow (q \vee r), q \rightarrow s, r \rightarrow s \vdash p \rightarrow s$

 * (q) $(p \wedge q) \vee (p \wedge r) \vdash p \wedge (q \vee r)$.

The rules for negation

We have seen the rules $\neg\neg$i and $\neg\neg$e, but we haven't seen any rules that introduce or eliminate single negations. These rules involve the notion of *contradiction*. This detour is to be expected since our reasoning is concerned about the inference, and therefore the preservation, of truth. Hence, there cannot be a direct way of inferring $\neg\phi$, given ϕ.

Definition 1.19 Contradictions are expressions of the form

$$\phi \wedge \neg\phi$$

or

$$\neg\phi \wedge \phi,$$

where ϕ is any formula.

Examples of such contradictions are $r \wedge \neg r$, $(p \rightarrow q) \wedge \neg(p \rightarrow q)$ and $\neg(r \vee s \rightarrow q) \wedge (r \vee s \rightarrow q)$.

   Contradictions are a very important notion in logic. As far as logic is concerned, they are all equivalent; that means we should be able to prove

$$\neg(r \vee s \rightarrow q) \wedge (r \vee s \rightarrow q) \dashv\vdash (p \rightarrow q) \wedge \neg(p \rightarrow q)$$

since both sides are contradictions. We'll be able to prove this later, when we have introduced the rules for negation.

   Indeed, it's not just that contradictions can be derived from contradictions; actually, *any* formula can be derived from a contradiction. This can be confusing when you first encounter it; why should we endorse the argument

$$p \wedge \neg p \vdash q,$$

where

$$p : \text{The moon is made of green cheese.}$$

$$q : \text{I like pepperoni on my pizza.}$$

since my taste in pizza doesn't have anything to do with the constitution of the moon?

Nevertheless, natural deduction does have this feature that any formula can be derived from a contradiction and therefore it does endorse this argument. The reason it takes this stance can be understood if you think about the information content of a formula. The formula $\phi \wedge \psi$ has the information content of ϕ and of ψ together, while $\phi \vee \psi$ has less-or-equal the information of ϕ and less-or-equal the information of ψ. Intuitively, ϕ having at least as much information as ψ should coincide with our ability to write $\phi \vdash \psi$.

Now, how much information is there in $\phi \wedge \neg\phi$? The answer is that $\phi \wedge \neg\phi$ is some kind of information overload. It's more information than can possibly be true. It's so much information that any *sensible* amount of information is less than it. If you think in terms of strength, $\phi \wedge \neg\phi$ is the strongest formula you can have; it's so strong, it allows you to prove any other formula. This indicates that contradictions are merely useful as a technical device in inferring other propositions.

Since all contradictions are equivalent (i.e. interderivable), we use a single symbol to represent them all: the symbol $\bot$, pronounced 'bottom'. (By the way, formulas of the form $\phi \vee \neg\phi$ are the weakest ones in logic, since they're all interderivable theorems which we will prove at the end of this section. They, too, have a special symbol reserved for them: $\top$, pronounced 'top'.)

The fact that $\bot$ can prove anything is encoded in our calculus by the rule bottom-elimination:

$$\frac{\bot}{\phi} \; \bot e.$$

The fact that $\bot$ itself represents a contradiction is encoded by the rule not-elimination:

$$\frac{\phi \quad \neg\phi}{\bot} \; \neg e.$$

Example 1.20 As an example of these rules at work, let's do $\neg p \lor q \vdash p \to q$:

1	$\neg p \lor q$				
2	$\neg p$	assumption	q	assumption	
3	p	assumption	p	assumption	
4	$\bot$	$\neg e\ 3, 2$	q	copy 2	
5	q	$\bot e\ 4$	$p \to q$	$\to i\ 3{-}4$	
6	$p \to q$	$\to i\ 3{-}5$			
7	$p \to q$			Ve 1, 2{-}6	

Notice how, in this example, the proof boxes are drawn side by side instead of on top of each other. It doesn't matter which way you do it.

What about introducing negations? Well, suppose we make an assumption which gets us into a contradictory state of affairs, i.e. gets us $\bot$. Then our assumption cannot be true; so it must be false. This intuition is the basis for the rule $\neg i$:

$$\frac{\begin{array}{|c|}\hline \phi \\ \vdots \\ \bot \\ \hline \end{array}}{\neg \phi}\ \neg i$$

Example 1.21 Here are some examples of these rules in action: the sequent

$$p \to q, p \to \neg q \vdash \neg p$$

may be proved thus:

1	$p \to q$	premise
2	$p \to \neg q$	premise
3	p	assumption
4	q	$\to e\ 1, 3$
5	$\neg q$	$\to e\ 2, 3$
6	$\bot$	$\neg e\ 4, 5$
7	$\neg p$	$\neg i\ 3{-}6$

Lines 3–6 contain all the work of the $\neg i$ rule. Here is a second example:

$p \rightarrow \neg p \vdash \neg p$ is proved by

1	$p \rightarrow \neg p$	premise
2	p	assumption
3	$\neg p$	$\rightarrow$e 1, 2
4	$\bot$	$\neg$e 2, 3
5	$\neg p$	$\neg$i 2–4

On the face of it, the statement $p \rightarrow \neg p \vdash \neg p$ seems absurd. Why would anybody even assume such nonsense as $p \rightarrow \neg p$? Well, the point of $\vdash$ is that it tells us all the things we may infer, if we assume the formulas to the left of it. This process does not care whether such premises make any sense. This has at least the advantage that we can match $\vdash$ to checks based on semantic intuitions which we formalise later by using truth tables: if all the premises compute to 'true', then the conclusion must compute 'true' as well. In particular, this is not a constraint in the case that one of the premises is false.

Example 1.22 We prove $p \rightarrow (q \rightarrow r)$, p, $\neg r \vdash \neg q$ without using the MT rule:

1	$p \rightarrow (q \rightarrow r)$	premise
2	p	premise
3	$\neg r$	premise
4	q	assumption
5	$q \rightarrow r$	$\rightarrow$e 1, 2
6	r	$\rightarrow$e 5, 4
7	$\bot$	$\neg$e 6, 3
8	$\neg q$	$\neg$i 4–7

Example 1.23 Finally, we return to the argument of Examples 1.1 and 1.2, which can be coded up by the sequent

$$p \wedge \neg q \rightarrow r, \ \neg r, \ p \vdash q.$$

Here is a proof:

1	$p \land \neg q \to r$	premise
2	$\neg r$	premise
3	p	premise
4	$\neg q$	assumption
5	$p \land \neg q$	$\land$i 3, 4
6	r	$\to$e 1, 5
7	$\bot$	$\neg$e 6, 2
8	$\neg\neg q$	$\neg$i 4–7
9	q	$\neg\neg$e 8

EXERCISES 1.5

* 1. Find proofs for the following sequents:

   (a) $\neg p \to \neg q \vdash q \to p$
   (b) $\neg p \lor \neg q \vdash \neg(p \land q)$
   (c) $\neg p, p \lor q \vdash q$
   (d) $p \lor q, \neg q \lor r \vdash p \lor r$
   (e) $p \to (q \lor r), \neg q, \neg r \vdash \neg p$ *without* using the MT rule
   (f) $\neg p \land \neg q \vdash \neg(p \lor q)$
   (g) $p \land \neg p \vdash \neg(r \to q) \land (r \to q)$
   (h) $\neg(\neg p \lor q) \vdash p$.

2. Prove the sequents below:

   (a) $\neg p \to p \vdash p$
   (b) $\neg p \vdash p \to q$
   (c) $p \lor q, \neg q \vdash p$
   * (d) $\vdash \neg p \to (p \to (p \to q))$
   (e) $\vdash (p \to q) \lor (q \to p)$
   (f) $\vdash (p \to q) \lor (q \to r)$
   (g) $\neg(p \to q) \vdash q \to p$
   (h) $p \to q \vdash \neg p \lor q$
   (i) $\vdash \neg p \lor q \to p \to q$.

1.2.2 Derived rules

When describing the rule *modus tollens* (MT), we mentioned that it is not a primitive rule of natural deduction, but can be derived from some of the other rules. Here is a proof of

$$\frac{\phi \to \psi \quad \neg\psi}{\neg\phi} \text{ MT}$$

from →e, ¬e and ¬i:

1	$\phi \to \psi$	premise
2	$\neg\psi$	premise
3	ϕ	assumption
4	ψ	→e 1, 3
5	$\bot$	¬e 4, 2
6	$\neg\phi$	¬i 3–5

We could now go back through the proofs in this chapter and replace applications of MT by this combination of →e, ¬e and ¬i. However, it is convenient to think of MT as a shorthand (or a macro).

The same holds for the rule

$$\frac{\phi}{\neg\neg\phi} \text{ ¬¬i.}$$

It can be derived from the rules ¬i and ¬e, as follows:

1	ϕ	premise
2	$\neg\phi$	assumption
3	$\bot$	¬e 1, 2
4	$\neg\neg\phi$	¬i 2–3

There are (unboundedly) many such derived rules which we could write down. However, there is no point in making our calculus fat and unwieldy; and some purists would say that we should stick to a minimum set of rules, all of which are independent of each other. We don't take such a purist view. Indeed, the two derived rules we now introduce are extremely useful. You will find that they crop up frequently when doing exercises in natural deduction, so it is worth giving them names as derived rules. In the case of the second one, its derivation from the primitive rules is not very obvious.

The first one has the Latin name *reductio ad absurdum* (RAA for short). It means 'reduction to absurdity' and we will simply call it *proof by contradiction*. The rule says: if from $\neg\phi$ we obtain a contradiction, then we are entitled to deduce ϕ:

$$\frac{}{\phi}\ \text{RAA}$$

This rule looks rather similar to $\neg$i, except that the negation is in a different place. This is the clue to how to prove it from our basic rules. Suppose we have a proof of $\bot$ from $\neg\phi$. By $\rightarrow$i, we can transform this into a proof of $\neg\phi \rightarrow \bot$ and proceed as follows:

1	$\neg\phi \rightarrow \bot$	given
2	$\neg\phi$	assumption
3	$\bot$	$\neg$e 1, 2
4	$\neg\neg\phi$	$\neg$i 2–3
5	ϕ	$\neg\neg$e 4

This shows that RAA can be derived from $\rightarrow$i, $\neg$i, $\neg$e and $\neg\neg$e.

The final derived rule we consider in this section is arguably the most useful to use in proofs, because its derivation is rather long and complicated, so its usage often saves time and effort. It also has a Latin name, *tertium non datur*; the English name is the law of the excluded middle, or LEM for short. It simply says $\phi \vee \neg\phi$. Whatever ϕ is, it must be either true or false; in the latter case, $\neg\phi$ is true. There is no third possibility (hence *excluded middle*). Its validity is implicit, for example, whenever you write an if-statement in a programming language: 'if B then C_1 else C_2' relies on the fact that $B \vee \neg B$ is always true (and that B and $\neg B$ can never be true at the same time). Here is a proof of the law of the excluded middle in our calculus:

1	$\neg(\phi \vee \neg\phi)$	assumption
2	ϕ	assumption
3	$\phi \vee \neg\phi$	$\vee i_1$ 2
4	$\bot$	$\neg e$ 3, 1
5	$\neg\phi$	$\neg i$ 2—4
6	$\phi \vee \neg\phi$	$\vee i_2$ 5
7	$\bot$	$\neg e$ 6, 1
8	$\neg\neg(\phi \vee \neg\phi)$	$\neg i$ 1—7
9	$\phi \vee \neg\phi$	$\neg\neg e$ 8

Example 1.24 We use this law to prove the sequent $p \rightarrow q \vdash \neg p \vee q$:

1	$p \rightarrow q$	premise
2	$\neg p \vee p$	LEM
3	$\neg p$	assumption
4	$\neg p \vee q$	$\vee i_1$ 3
5	p	assumption
6	q	$\rightarrow e$ 1, 5
7	$\neg p \vee q$	$\vee i_2$ 6
8	$\neg p \vee q$	$\vee e$ 2, 3—4, 5—7

1.2.3 Natural deduction in summary

The rules for natural deduction are summarised in Figure 1.2. The explanation of the rules we have given so far in this chapter is *declarative*; we have presented each rule and justified it in terms of our intuition about the logical connectives. However, when you try to use the rules yourself, you'll find yourself looking for a more *procedural* interpretation; what does a rule do and how do you use it? For example,

- $\wedge i$ says: to prove $\phi \wedge \psi$, you must first prove ϕ and ψ separately and then use the rule $\wedge i$.
- $\wedge e_1$ says: to prove ϕ, try proving $\phi \wedge \psi$ and then use the rule $\wedge e_1$. Actually, this doesn't sound like very good advice because probably proving $\phi \wedge \psi$ will be harder than proving ϕ alone. However, you might find that you

The basic rules of natural deduction:

	introduction	elimination

$\wedge$ $\qquad$ $\dfrac{\phi \quad \psi}{\phi \wedge \psi} \wedge i$ $\qquad\qquad$ $\dfrac{\phi \wedge \psi}{\phi} \wedge e_1$ $\quad$ $\dfrac{\phi \wedge \psi}{\psi} \wedge e_2$

$\vee$ $\qquad$ $\dfrac{\phi}{\phi \vee \psi} \vee i_1$ $\quad$ $\dfrac{\psi}{\phi \vee \psi} \vee i_2$

$$\cfrac{\phi \vee \psi \quad \boxed{\begin{array}{c}\phi \\ \vdots \\ \chi\end{array}} \quad \boxed{\begin{array}{c}\psi \\ \vdots \\ \chi\end{array}}}{\chi} \vee e$$

$\rightarrow$ $\qquad$ $\dfrac{\boxed{\begin{array}{c}\phi \\ \vdots \\ \psi\end{array}}}{\phi \rightarrow \psi} \rightarrow i$ $\qquad\qquad$ $\dfrac{\phi \quad \phi \rightarrow \psi}{\psi} \rightarrow e$

$\neg$ $\qquad$ $\dfrac{\boxed{\begin{array}{c}\phi \\ \vdots \\ \bot\end{array}}}{\neg \phi} \neg i$ $\qquad\qquad$ $\dfrac{\phi \quad \neg \phi}{\bot} \neg e$

$\bot$ $\quad$ (no introduction rule for $\bot$) $\qquad\qquad$ $\dfrac{\bot}{\phi} \bot e$

$\neg\neg$ $\qquad\qquad\qquad\qquad\qquad\qquad$ $\dfrac{\neg\neg\phi}{\phi} \neg\neg e$

Some useful derived rules:

$$\dfrac{\phi \rightarrow \psi \quad \neg \psi}{\neg \phi} MT \qquad\qquad \dfrac{\phi}{\neg\neg\phi} \neg\neg i$$

$$\dfrac{\boxed{\begin{array}{c}\neg\phi \\ \vdots \\ \bot\end{array}}}{\phi} RAA \qquad\qquad \dfrac{}{\phi \vee \neg\phi} LEM$$

Fig. 1.2. Natural deduction rules for propositional logic.

already have $\phi \wedge \psi$ lying around, so that's when this rule is useful. Compare this with the example sequent in Example 1.15.

- $\vee i_1$ says: to prove $\phi \vee \psi$, try proving ϕ. Again, in general it is harder to prove ϕ than it is to prove $\phi \vee \psi$, so this will usually be useful only if you've already managed to prove ϕ. For example, if you want to prove $q \vdash p \lor q$, you certainly won't be able simply to use the rule $\lor i_1$, but $\lor i_2$ will work.

- $\lor e$ has an excellent procedural interpretation. It says: if you have $\phi \lor \psi$, and you want to prove some χ, then try to prove χ from ϕ and from ψ in turn. (In those subproofs, of course you can use the other prevailing premises as well.)

- Similarly, $\rightarrow i$ says, if you want to prove $\phi \rightarrow \psi$, try proving ψ from ϕ (and the other prevailing premises).

- $\neg i$ says: to prove $\neg \phi$, prove $\bot$ from ϕ (and the other premises).

At any stage of a proof, it is permitted to introduce any formula as assumption, by opening a box. As we saw, natural deduction employs boxes to control the scope of assumptions. When an assumption is introduced, a box is opened. Discharging assumptions is achieved by closing a box according to the pattern of its particular proof rule.

It's useful to make assumptions by opening boxes, but don't forget you have to close them. Naturally, it is sensible to open a box only when you know which rule you are going to use to close it.

OK, but how do we actually go about constructing a proof?

You write the premises at the top of your page and the conclusion at the bottom. Now, you're trying to fill in the gap, which involves working simultaneously on the premises (to bring them towards the conclusion) and on the conclusion (to massage it towards the premises).

Look first at the conclusion. If it is of the form $\phi \rightarrow \psi$, then apply the rule $\rightarrow i$. This means drawing a box with ϕ at the top and ψ at the bottom. So your proof, which started out like this:

$$\vdots$$

$$\text{premises}$$

$$\vdots$$

$$\phi \rightarrow \psi$$

now looks like this:

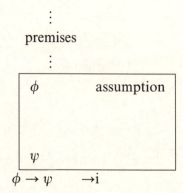

You still have to find a way of filling in the gap between the ϕ and the ψ. But you now have an extra formula to work with and you have simplified the conclusion you are trying to reach.

The rule $\neg i$ is very similar to $\rightarrow i$ and has the same beneficial effect on your proof attempt. It gives you an extra premise to work with and simplifies your conclusion.

At any stage of your proof, several rules are likely to be applicable. Before applying any of them, list the applicable ones and think about which one is likely to improve the situation you are in. You'll find that $\rightarrow i$ and $\neg i$ most often improve it, so always use them whenever you can. There is no easy recipe for when to use the other rules; often you have to make judicious choices.

1.2.4 Provable equivalence

Definition 1.25 Let ϕ and ψ be formulas of propositional logic. We say that ϕ and ψ are *provably equivalent* iff (we write 'iff' for 'if, and only if' in the sequel)

$$\phi \vdash \psi$$
$$\psi \vdash \phi$$

hold; that is, there is a proof of ψ from ϕ and another one going the other way around. As seen earlier, we denote that ϕ and ψ are provably equivalent by $\phi \dashv\vdash \psi$.

Note that, by Remark 1.12, we could just as well have defined $\phi \dashv\vdash \psi$ to mean that $\vdash (\phi \rightarrow \psi) \wedge (\psi \rightarrow \phi)$ holds; it amounts to the same thing.

Examples of provably equivalent formulas are

$$\neg(p \wedge q) \quad \dashv\vdash \quad \neg q \vee \neg p$$
$$\neg(p \vee q) \quad \dashv\vdash \quad \neg q \wedge \neg p$$
$$p \rightarrow q \quad \dashv\vdash \quad \neg q \rightarrow \neg p$$
$$p \rightarrow q \quad \dashv\vdash \quad \neg p \vee q$$
$$p \wedge q \rightarrow p \quad \dashv\vdash \quad r \vee \neg r$$
$$p \wedge q \rightarrow r \quad \dashv\vdash \quad p \rightarrow (q \rightarrow r).$$

The reader should be able to prove all of these equivalences in natural deduction.

1.2.5 An aside: proof by contradiction

Sometimes we can't prove something *directly* in the sense of taking apart given assumptions and reasoning with their constituents in a constructive way. Indeed, the proof system of natural deduction, summarised in Figure 1.2, specifically allows for *indirect* proofs that lack a constructive quality: for example, the rule

allows us to prove ϕ by showing that $\neg\phi$ leads to a contradiction. Although 'classical logicians' argue that this is valid, logicians of another kind, called 'intuitionistic logicians', argue that to prove ϕ you should do it directly, rather than by arguing merely that $\neg\phi$ is impossible. The two other rules on which classical and intuitionistic logicians disagree are

$$\frac{}{\phi \vee \neg\phi} \text{ LEM} \qquad\qquad \frac{\neg\neg\phi}{\phi} \text{ } \neg\neg e.$$

Intuitionistic logicians argue that, to show $\phi \vee \neg\phi$, you have to show ϕ, or $\neg\phi$. If neither of these can be shown, then the putative truth of the disjunction has no justification. The reason why intuitionists reject $\neg\neg e$ is that we have already used this rule to prove LEM and RAA from rules which the intuitionists do accept.

Let us look at a proof that shows up this difference, involving real numbers.

Real numbers are floating point numbers like 23.54721, only some of them might actually be infinitely long such as

$$23.13859274850606327183950734\ldots,$$

with no periodic behaviour after the decimal point.

Given a positive real number a and a *natural* (whole) number b, we can calculate a^b: it is just a times itself, b times, so $2^2 = 2 \cdot 2 = 4$, $2^3 = 2 \cdot 2 \cdot 2 = 8$ and so on. When b is a *real* number, we can also define a^b, as follows. We say that $a^0 \stackrel{\text{def}}{=} 1$ and, for a non-zero rational number $\frac{k}{n}$, where $n \neq 0$, we let $a^{\frac{k}{n}} \stackrel{\text{def}}{=} \sqrt[n]{a^k}$ where $\sqrt[n]{x}$ is the real number y such that $y^n = x$. From real analysis one knows that any real number b is the *limit* of a sequence of rational numbers, so if b is real we define a^b to be the limit of the numbers $a^{\frac{k}{n}}$ where $\frac{k}{n}$ has b as limit. Also, one calls a real number *irrational* if it can't be written in the form $\frac{k}{n}$ for some integers k and $n \neq 0$. In the exercises you will be asked to find a proof showing that $\sqrt{2}$ is irrational.

We now present a proof of a fact about real numbers in the informal style used by mathematicians (this proof can be formalised as a natural deduction proof in the logic presented in Chapter 2). The fact we prove is:

Theorem 1.26 *There exist irrational numbers a and b such that a^b is rational.*

PROOF: We choose b to be $\sqrt{2}$ and proceed by a case analysis. Either b^b is irrational, or it is not. (Thus, our proof uses $\vee$e on an instance of LEM.)

(i). Assume that b^b is rational. Then this proof is easy since we can choose irrational numbers a and b to be $\sqrt{2}$ and see that a^b is just b^b which was assumed to be rational.

(ii). Assume that b^b is *ir*rational. Then we change our strategy slightly and choose a to be $\sqrt{2}^{\sqrt{2}}$. Clearly, a is irrational by the assumption of case (ii). But we know that b is irrational (this was known by the ancient Greeks; see the proof outline in the exercises). So a and b are both irrational numbers and

$$a^b = \left(\sqrt{2}^{\sqrt{2}}\right)^{\sqrt{2}} = \sqrt{2}^{(\sqrt{2} \cdot \sqrt{2})} = \left(\sqrt{2}\right)^2 = 2$$

is rational.

Since the two cases above are exhaustive (*either* b^b is irrational, *or* it isn't) we have proven the theorem. □

This proof is perfectly legitimate and mathematicians use arguments like that all the time. Yet, there is something puzzling about it. Surely, we have secured the fact that there are irrational numbers a and b such that a^b is rational, but are we in a position to specify an actual pair of such numbers satisfying this theorem? More precisely, which of the pairs (a, b) above fulfils the assertion of the theorem, the pair $(\sqrt{2}, \sqrt{2})$, or the pair $(\sqrt{2}^{\sqrt{2}}, \sqrt{2})$? Our proof tells us nothing about *which* of them is the right choice; it just says that at least one of them works.

The exhaustive nature of the case analysis above rests on the use of the rule LEM, which we use to prove that either b is rational or it is not. The so-called intuitionistic logicians would throw out this rule and thereby disallow this proof. They would also throw out the rule ¬¬e, since it was used to prove LEM (page 30), and RAA by the same token; all these rules are inter-derivable, given the others, and all of them encode the non-constructive indirectness which the intuitionists don't like.

Thus, the intuitionists favour a calculus containing the introduction and elimination rules shown in Figure 1.2 and excluding the rule ¬¬e and the derived rules. Intuitionistic logic turns out to have some specialised applications in computer science, such as modelling type-inference systems used in compilers or the staged execution of program code; but in this text we stick to the full so-called classical logic which includes all the rules.

EXERCISES 1.6

1. Find proofs for the following:

   (a) $p \to (q \lor r),\ \neg q,\ \neg r \vdash \neg p$
   (b) $(c \land n) \to t,\ h \land \neg s,\ h \land \neg(s \lor c) \to p \vdash (n \land \neg t) \to p$
   * (c) $\neg(\neg p \lor q) \vdash p$. (Hint: this one and the ones that follow involve using the ¬¬e rule, or perhaps one of the derived rule that depends on ¬¬e.)
   (d) $q \vdash (p \land q) \lor (\neg p \land q)$ (Hint: use LEM.)
   (e) $\neg(p \land q) \vdash \neg p \lor \neg q$
   (f) $p \land q \to r \vdash (p \to r) \lor (q \to r)$.

2. Find proofs for the following:

   * (a) $p \land q \vdash \neg(\neg p \lor \neg q)$
   (b) $\neg(\neg p \lor \neg q) \vdash p \land q$
   (c) Can you prove $p \to q \vdash \neg p \lor q$ without using the law of the excluded middle?
   * (d) $\vdash (p \to q) \lor (q \to r)$ is a theorem. (Hint: use LEM.)
   (e) $p \to q,\ \neg p \to r,\ \neg q \to \neg r \vdash q$
   (f) $p \to q,\ r \to \neg t,\ q \to r \vdash p \to \neg t$

(g) $(p \rightarrow q) \rightarrow r, \ s \rightarrow \neg p, \ t, \ (\neg s \wedge t) \rightarrow q \vdash r$

(h) $(s \rightarrow p) \vee (t \rightarrow q) \vdash (s \rightarrow q) \vee (t \rightarrow p)$

(i) $(p \wedge q) \rightarrow r, \ r \rightarrow s, \ q \wedge \neg s \vdash \neg p$.

3. Prove the following theorems of propositional logic:

    * (a) $((p \rightarrow q) \rightarrow q) \rightarrow ((q \rightarrow p) \rightarrow p)$

    (b) Do you now have a quick argument for $((q \rightarrow p) \rightarrow p) \rightarrow ((p \rightarrow q) \rightarrow q)$?

    (c) $((p \rightarrow q) \wedge (q \rightarrow p)) \rightarrow ((p \vee q) \rightarrow (p \wedge q))$

    * (d) $(p \rightarrow q) \rightarrow ((\neg p \rightarrow q) \rightarrow q)$.

4. Natural deduction is not the only possible formal framework for proofs in propositional logic. As an abbreviation, we write Γ to denote any finite sequence of formulas $\phi_1, \phi_2, \ldots, \phi_n$ $(n \geq 1)$. Thus, any sequent may be written as

$$\Gamma \vdash \psi$$

for an appropriate Γ. In this exercise we propose a different notion of proof, which states rules for transforming valid sequents into valid sequents. For example, if we have already a proof for the sequent

$$\Gamma, \phi \vdash \psi,$$

then we obtain a proof of the sequent

$$\Gamma \vdash \phi \rightarrow \psi$$

by augmenting this very proof with one application of the rule $\rightarrow$i. The new approach expresses this as an inference rule *between sequents*:

$$\frac{\Gamma, \phi \vdash \psi}{\Gamma \vdash \phi \rightarrow \psi} \ \rightarrow i.$$

The rule assumption is written as

$$\frac{}{\phi \vdash \phi} \ \text{assumption},$$

i.e. the premise is empty. Such rules are called *axioms*.

    (a) Express all remaining proof rules of natural deduction in such a form. (Hint: some of the rules may have more than one premise.)

    (b) Explain why proofs of $\Gamma \vdash \psi$ in this new system have a tree-like structure.

    (c) Prove $p \vee (p \wedge q) \vdash p$ in your new proof system.

5. Show that $\sqrt{2}$ cannot be a rational number. Proceed by proof by contradiction: assume that $\sqrt{2}$ is a fraction $\frac{k}{l}$ with integers k and $l \neq 0$. On squaring both sides we get $2 = \frac{k^2}{l^2}$, or equivalently $2l^2 = k^2$. We may assume that any common 2 factors of k and l have been cancelled. Can you now argue that $2l^2$ has a different number of 2 factors from k^2? Why would that be a contradiction and to what?

6. There is an alternative approach to treating negation. One could simply ban the operator $\neg$ from propositional logic and think of $\phi \rightarrow \bot$ as 'being' $\neg\phi$. Naturally, such a logic cannot rely on the natural deduction rules for negation. Which of the rules $\neg i$, $\neg e$, $\neg\neg e$ and $\neg\neg i$ can you simulate with the remaining proof rules by letting $\neg\phi$ be $\phi \rightarrow \bot$?

7. Let us introduce a new connective $\phi \leftrightarrow \psi$ which should abbreviate $(\phi \rightarrow \psi) \wedge (\psi \rightarrow \phi)$. Design introduction and elimination rules for $\leftrightarrow$ and show that they are derived rules if $\phi \leftrightarrow \psi$ is interpreted as $(\phi \rightarrow \psi) \wedge (\psi \rightarrow \phi)$.

1.3 Propositional logic as a formal language

In the previous section we learned about propositional atoms and how they can be used to build more complex logical formulas. We were deliberately informal about that, for our main focus was on trying to understand the precise mechanics of the natural deduction rules. However, it should have been clear that the rules we stated are valid for *any* formulas we can form, as long as they match the pattern required by the respective rule. For example, the rule $\rightarrow e$

1	$p \rightarrow q$	premise
2	p	premise
3	q	$\rightarrow e$ 1, 2

is equally valid if we substitute p with $p \vee \neg r$ and q with $r \rightarrow p$:

1	$p \vee \neg r \rightarrow (r \rightarrow p)$	premise
2	$p \vee \neg r$	premise
3	$r \rightarrow p$	$\rightarrow e$ 1, 2

This is why we expressed such rules as schemes with Greek symbols standing for generic formulas. Yet, it is time that we make precise the notion of 'any formula we may form'. Because this text concerns various logics, we will introduce in (1.2) an easy formalism for specifying well-formed formulas. In general, we need an *unbounded* supply of propositional atoms $p, q, r, \ldots$, or $p_1, p_2, p_3, \ldots$. You should not be too worried about the need for infinitely many such symbols. Although we may only need *finitely many* of these propositions to describe a property of a computer program successfully, we cannot specify how many such atomic propositions we will need in any concrete situation, so having infinitely many symbols at our disposal is a cheap way out. This can be compared with the potentially infinite nature of English: the number of grammatically correct English sentences is infinite, but finitely many such sentences will do in whatever situation you might be in (writing a book, attending a lecture, listening to the radio, having a dinner date, ...).

Formulas in our propositional logic should certainly be strings over the alphabet $\{p, q, r, \ldots\} \cup \{p_1, p_2, p_3, \ldots\} \cup \{\neg, \wedge, \vee, \rightarrow, (,)\}$. This is a trivial observation and as such is not good enough for what we are trying to capture. For example, the string

$$(\neg)() \vee pq \rightarrow$$

is a word over that alphabet, yet, it does not seem to make a lot of sense as far as propositional logic is concerned. So what we have to define are those strings which we want to call formulas. We call such formulas *well-formed*.

Definition 1.27 The well-formed logical formulas of propositional logic are those which we obtain by using the construction rules below, and only those, finitely many times:

atom: Every propositional atom $p, q, r, \ldots$ and $p_1, p_2, p_3, \ldots$ is a well-formed formula.
¬: If ϕ is a well-formed formula, then so is $(\neg\phi)$.
∧: If ϕ and ψ are well-formed formulas, then so is $(\phi \wedge \psi)$.
∨: If ϕ and ψ are well-formed formulas, then so is $(\phi \vee \psi)$.
→: If ϕ and ψ are well-formed formulas, then so is $(\phi \rightarrow \psi)$.

It is most crucial to realize that this definition is the one a computer would expect and that we did not make use of the binding priorities agreed upon in the previous section.

Convention. In this section we act as if we are a rigorous computer and we call formulas well-formed iff they can be deduced to be so using the definition above.

Further, note that the condition 'and only those' in the definition above rules out the possibility of any other means of establishing that formulas are well-formed. Inductive definitions, like the one of well-formed propositional logic formulas above, are so frequent that they are often given by a defining grammar in Backus Naur form (BNF). In that form, the above definition reads more compactly as

$$\phi ::= p \mid (\neg\phi) \mid (\phi \wedge \phi) \mid (\phi \vee \phi) \mid (\phi \rightarrow \phi), \qquad (1.2)$$

where p stands for any atomic proposition and each occurrence of ϕ to the right of ::= stands for any already constructed formula.

So how can we show that a string is a well-formed formula? For example, how do we answer this for ϕ being

$$(((\neg p) \wedge q) \rightarrow (p \wedge (q \vee (\neg r))))?$$

Such reasoning is greatly facilitated by the fact that the grammar in (1.2) satisfies the *inversion principle*, which means that we can invert the process of building formulas: although the grammar rules allow for five different ways of constructing more complex formulas (the five clauses in (1.2)), there is always a unique clause which was used last. For the formula above, this last operation was an application of the fifth clause, for ϕ is an implication with the premise $((\neg p)\wedge q)$ and conclusion $(p\wedge(q\vee(\neg r)))$. By applying the inversion principle to the premise, we see that it is a conjunction of $(\neg p)$ and q. The former has been constructed using the second clause and is well-formed since p is well-formed by the first clause in (1.2). The latter is well-formed for the same reason. Similarly, we can apply the inversion principle to the conclusion $(p \wedge (q \vee (\neg r)))$, inferring that it is indeed well-formed.

For us humans, dealing with brackets is a tedious task. The reason we need them is that formulas really have a tree-like structure, although we prefer to represent them in a linear way. In Figure 1.3 you can see the parse tree[1] of the well-formed formula ϕ. Note how brackets become unnecessary in this parse tree since the paths and the branching structure of this tree remove any possible ambiguity in interpreting ϕ. In representing ϕ as a linear string, the branching structure of the tree is retained by the insertion of brackets as done in the definition of well-formed formulas.

So how would you go about showing that a string of symbols ψ is *not* well-formed? At first sight, this is a bit trickier since we somehow have to make sure that ψ could not have been obtained by *any* sequence of construction rules. Let us look at the formula $(\neg)() \vee pq \rightarrow$ from above. We can decide

---

[1] We will use this name without explaining it any further and are confident that you will understand its meaning through the examples.

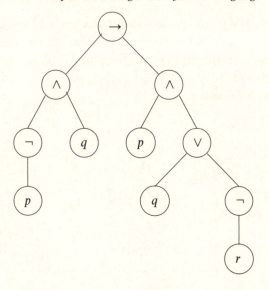

Fig. 1.3. A parse tree representing a well-formed formula.

this matter by being very observant. The string $(\neg)() \vee pq \rightarrow$ contains $\neg)$ and $\neg$ cannot be the rightmost symbol of a well-formed formula (check all the rules to verify this claim!); but the only time we can put a ')' to the right of something is if that something is a well-formed formula (again, check all the rules to see that this is so). Thus, $(\neg)() \vee pq \rightarrow$ is *not* well-formed.

Probably the easiest way to verify whether some formula ϕ is well-formed is by trying to draw its parse tree. In this way, you can verify that the formula $(((\neg p) \wedge q) \rightarrow (p \wedge (q \vee (\neg r))))$ above is well-formed. In Figure 1.3 we see that its parse tree has $\rightarrow$ as its root, expressing that the formula is, at its top level, an implication. Using the grammar clause for implication, it suffices to show that the left and right subtrees of this root node are well-formed. That is, we proceed in a top-down fashion and, in this case, successfully. Note that the parse trees of well-formed formulas have either an atom as root (and then this is all there is in the tree), or the root contains $\neg$, $\vee$, $\wedge$ or $\rightarrow$. In the case of $\neg$ there is only *one* subtree coming out of the root. In all the other cases we must have *two* subtrees, each of which must behave as just described; this is another example of an *inductive* definition.

Thinking in terms of trees will help you understand standard notions in logic, for example, the concept of a *subformula*. Given the well-formed formula ϕ above, its subformulas are just the ones that correspond to the subtrees of its parse tree in Figure 1.3. So we can list all its leaves $p, q, r,$

then $(\neg p)$ and $((\neg p) \wedge q)$ on the left subtree of $\rightarrow$ and $(\neg r)$, $(q \vee (\neg r))$ and $((p \wedge (q \vee (\neg p))))$ on the right subtree of $\rightarrow$. The whole tree is a subtree of itself as well. So we can list all nine subformulas of ϕ as

$$p$$
$$q$$
$$r$$
$$(\neg p)$$
$$((\neg p) \wedge q)$$
$$(\neg r)$$
$$(q \vee (\neg r))$$
$$((p \wedge (q \vee (\neg p))))$$
$$(((\neg p) \wedge q) \rightarrow (p \wedge (q \vee (\neg r)))).$$

Let us consider the tree in Figure 1.4. Why does it represent a well-formed formula? All its leaves are propositional atoms (p twice, q and r), all branching nodes are logical connectives ($\wedge$, $\neg$ twice, $\vee$ and $\rightarrow$) and the numbers of subtrees are correct in all those cases (one subtree for a $\neg$ node and two subtrees for all other non-leaf nodes). How do we obtain the linear representation of this formula? If we ignore brackets, then we are seeking nothing but the *in-order* representation of this tree as a list[1]. The resulting well-formed formula is

$$((\neg(p \vee (q \rightarrow (\neg p)))) \wedge r).$$

The tree in Figure 1.5, however, does *not* represent a well-formed formula for two reasons. First, the leaf $\wedge$ (and a similar argument applies to the leaf $\neg$), the left subtree of the node $\rightarrow$, is not a propositional atom. This could be fixed by saying that we decided to leave the left and right subtree of that node unspecified and that we are willing to provide those now. However, the second reason is fatal. The p node is not a leaf since it has a subtree, the node $\neg$. This cannot make sense if we think of the entire tree as some logical formula. So this tree does not represent a well-formed logical formula.

EXERCISES 1.7
In order to facilitate reading these exercises we assume below the usual conventions about binding priorities agreed upon in Convention 1.3.

---

[1] The other common ways of flattening trees to lists are *preordering* and *postordering*. See any text on binary trees as data structures for further details.

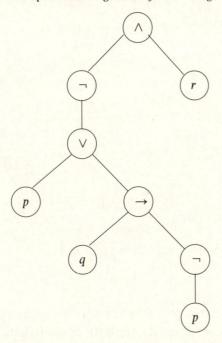

Fig. 1.4. Given: a tree; wanted: its linear representation as a logical formula.

1. Given the following formulas, draw their corresponding parse tree:

    (a) p

  * (b) $p \wedge q$

    (c) $p \wedge \neg q \rightarrow \neg p$

  * (d) $p \wedge (\neg q \rightarrow \neg p)$

    (e) $p \rightarrow (\neg q \vee (q \rightarrow p))$

  * (f) $\neg((\neg q \wedge (p \rightarrow r)) \wedge (r \rightarrow q))$

    (g) $\neg p \vee (p \rightarrow q)$

    (h) $(p \wedge q) \rightarrow (\neg r \vee (q \rightarrow r))$

    (i) $((s \vee (\neg p)) \rightarrow (\neg p))$

    (j) $(s \vee ((\neg p) \rightarrow (\neg p)))$

    (k) $(((s \rightarrow (r \vee l)) \vee ((\neg q) \wedge r)) \rightarrow ((\neg(p \rightarrow s)) \rightarrow r))$

    (l) $(p \rightarrow q) \wedge (\neg r \rightarrow (q \vee (\neg p \wedge r)))$.

* 2. List *all* subformulas of the formula $p \rightarrow (\neg p \vee (\neg \neg q \rightarrow (p \wedge q)))$.

3. List *all* subformulas of the formulas

    (a) $(((s \rightarrow (r \vee l)) \vee ((\neg q) \wedge r)) \rightarrow ((\neg(p \rightarrow s)) \rightarrow r))$

    (b) $(p \rightarrow q) \wedge (\neg r \rightarrow (q \vee (\neg p \wedge r)))$.

* 4. Draw the parse tree of a formula ϕ of propositional logic which is a negation of an implication.

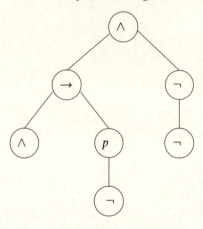

Fig. 1.5. An incorrectly formed tree: its in-order representation is not a well-formed formula.

5. Draw the parse tree of a formula ϕ of propositional logic which is a disjunction whose disjuncts are both conjunctions.

* 6. Draw the parse tree of a formula which is a conjunction of conjunctions.

* 7. Draw the parse tree of the formula $\neg(s \rightarrow (\neg(p \rightarrow (q \vee \neg s))))$ and list all of its subformulas.

8. Draw the parse tree corresponding to $((p \rightarrow \neg q) \vee (p \wedge r) \rightarrow s) \vee \neg r$ and list all its subformulas.

* 9. Consider the parse tree in Figure 1.6. Find the logical formula it represents.

10. Find the linear representation of the tree in Figure 1.12 (shown later) and check whether it is a well-formed formula.

11. Find the linear representation of the tree in Figure 1.7 and check whether it corresponds to a well-formed formula.

* 12. Give two examples of parse trees that do not correspond to well-formed formulas, such that

    (a) one of them could be *extended* by adding one or several subtrees such that the resulting tree corresponds to a well-formed formula;

    (b) the other one is *inherently* ill-formed; i.e. any extension of it could not correspond to a well-formed formula.

13. Determine, by trying to draw parse trees, which of the following formulas are well-formed:

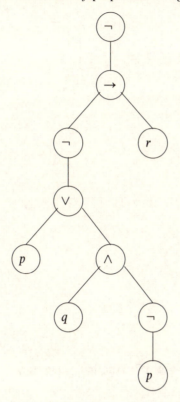

Fig. 1.6. Another parse tree.

(a) $p \wedge \neg(p \vee \neg q) \rightarrow (r \rightarrow s)$
(b) $p \wedge \neg(p \vee q \wedge s) \rightarrow (r \rightarrow s)$
(c) $p \wedge \neg(p \vee \wedge s) \rightarrow (r \rightarrow s)$.

Among the ill-formed formulas above, which ones could you 'fix' by the insertion of brackets only; and in how many ways could you do that?

1.4 Semantics of propositional logic

1.4.1 The meaning of logical connectives

In the second section of this chapter, we developed a calculus of reasoning which could verify sequents of the form

$$\phi_1, \phi_2, \ldots, \phi_n \vdash \psi$$

which means: from the premises $\phi_1, \phi_2, \ldots, \phi_n$, we may conclude ψ.

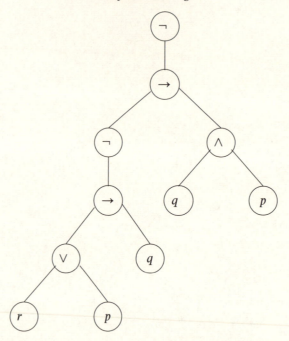

Fig. 1.7. Another parse tree.

In this section we give another account of this relationship between the premises $\phi_1, \phi_2, \ldots, \phi_n$ and the conclusion ψ. To contrast with the sequent above, we define a new relationship, written

$$\phi_1, \phi_2, \ldots, \phi_n \vDash \psi.$$

This account is based on looking at the 'truth values' of the atomic formulas in the premises and the conclusion; and at how the logical connectives manipulate these truth values. What is the truth value of a declarative sentence, like sentence (3) 'Every even natural number is the sum of two prime numbers.'? Well, declarative sentences express a fact about the real world, the physical world we live in, or more abstract ones such as computer models, or our thoughts and feelings. Such facts either match reality (they are *true*), or they don't (they are *false*).

If we combine declarative sentences p and q with a logical connective, say $\wedge$, then the truth value of $p \wedge q$ is determined by three things: the truth value of p, the truth value of q and the meaning of $\wedge$. The meaning of $\wedge$ is captured by the observation that $p \wedge q$ is true iff p *and* q are both true; otherwise $p \wedge q$ is false. Thus, as far as $\wedge$ is concerned, it needs only to know whether p and q are true, it does *not* need to know what p and q are actually saying about

ϕ	ψ	$\phi \wedge \psi$
T	T	T
T	F	F
F	T	F
F	F	F

Fig. 1.8. The truth table for the logical connective '$\wedge$'.

the world out there. This is also the case for all the other logical connectives
and is the reason why we can compute the truth value of a formula just by
knowing the truth values of the atomic propositions occurring in it.

Definition 1.28 The set of truth values contains two elements T and F, where
T represents 'true' and F represents 'false'.

We can think of the meaning of $\wedge$ as a function of two arguments; each
argument is a truth value and the result is again such a truth value. We
specify this function in a table, called the *truth table for conjunction*, which
you can see in Figure 1.8. In the first column, labelled ϕ, we list all possible
truth values of ϕ. Actually we list them *twice* since we also have to deal with
another formula ψ, so the possible number of combinations of truth values
for ϕ and ψ equals $2 \cdot 2 = 4$. Notice that the four pairs of ϕ and ψ values in
the first two columns really exhaust all those possibilities (TT, TF, FT and FF).
In the third column, we list the result of $\phi \wedge \psi$ according to the truth values
of ϕ and ψ. So in the first line, where ϕ and ψ have value T, the result is T
again. In all other lines, the result is F since at least one of the propositions
ϕ or ψ has value F.

In Figure 1.9 you find the truth tables for all logical connectives of
propositional logic. Note that $\neg$ turns T into F and vice versa. Disjunction is
the mirror image of conjunction if we swap T and F, namely, a disjunction
returns F iff both arguments are equal to F, otherwise ($=$ at least one of the
arguments equals T) it returns T. The behaviour of implication is not quite
as intuitive. Think of the meaning of $\rightarrow$ as checking whether *truth is being
preserved*. Clearly, this is not the case when we have T $\rightarrow$ F, since we infer
something that is false from something that is true. So the second entry in
the column $\phi \rightarrow \psi$ equals F. On the other hand, T $\rightarrow$ T obviously preserves
truth, but so are the cases F $\rightarrow$ T and F $\rightarrow$ F, because there is no truth to be
preserved in the first place because the premise is false.

If you feel slightly uncomfortable with the semantics ($=$ the meaning) of
$\rightarrow$, then it might be good to think of $\phi \rightarrow \psi$ as an abbreviation of the

ϕ	ψ	$\phi \wedge \psi$
T	T	T
T	F	F
F	T	F
F	F	F

ϕ	ψ	$\phi \vee \psi$
T	T	T
T	F	T
F	T	T
F	F	F

ϕ	ψ	$\phi \rightarrow \psi$
T	T	T
T	F	F
F	T	T
F	F	T

ϕ	$\neg\phi$
T	F
F	T

$\top$
T

$\bot$
F

Fig. 1.9. The truth tables for all the logical connectives discussed so far.

formula $\neg\phi \vee \psi$ *as far as meaning is concerned*; these two formulas are very different syntactically and natural deduction treats them differently as well. But using the truth tables for $\neg$ and $\vee$ you can check that $\phi \rightarrow \psi$ evaluates to T iff $\neg\phi \vee \psi$ does so. This means that $\phi \rightarrow \psi$ and $\neg\phi \vee \psi$ are *semantically equivalent*; more on that in Section 1.5.

Given a formula ϕ which contains the propositional atoms $p_1, p_2, \ldots, p_n$, we can construct a truth table for ϕ, at least in principle. The caveat is that this truth table has 2^n many lines, each line listing a possible combination of truth values for $p_1, p_2, \ldots, p_n$; and for large n this task is impossible to complete. Our aim is thus to compute the value of ϕ for each of these 2^n cases for moderately small values of n. Let us consider the example ϕ in Figure 1.3. It involves three propositional atoms ($n = 3$) so we have $2^3 = 8$ cases to consider.

We illustrate how things go for one particular case, namely, when q evaluates to F; and p and r evaluate to T. What does $\neg p \wedge q \rightarrow p \wedge (q \vee \neg r)$ evaluate to? Well, the beauty of our semantics is that it is *compositional*. If we know the meaning of the subformulas $\neg p \wedge q$ and $p \wedge (q \vee \neg r)$, then we just have to look up the appropriate line of the $\rightarrow$ truth table to find the value of ϕ, for ϕ is an implication of these two subformulas. Therefore, we can do the calculation by traversing the parse tree of ϕ in a bottom-up fashion. We know what its leaves evaluate to since we stated what the atoms p, q and r evaluated to. Because the meaning of p is T, we see that $\neg p$ computes to F. Now q is assumed to represent F and the conjunction of F and F is F. Thus, the left subtree of the node $\rightarrow$ evaluates to F. As for the right subtree of $\rightarrow$, r stands for T so $\neg r$ computes to F and q means F, so the disjunction of F and F is still F. We have to take that result, F, and compute its conjunction with the meaning of p which is T. Since the conjunction of T and F is F,

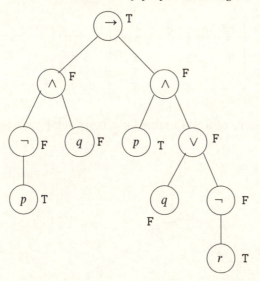

Fig. 1.10. The evaluation of a logical formula given the meanings of its propositional atoms.

we get F as the meaning of the right subtree of →. Finally, to evaluate the meaning of ϕ, we compute F → F which is T. Figure 1.10 shows how the truth values propagate upwards to reach the root whose associated truth value is the truth value of ϕ given the meanings of p, q and r above.

It should now be quite clear how to build a truth table for more complex formulas. Figure 1.11 contains a truth table for the formula $(p \to \neg q) \to (q \lor \neg p)$. To be more precise, the first two columns list all possible combinations of values for p and q. (Such combinations are also called *valuations*, or models of propositional logic.) The next two columns compute the corresponding values for $\neg p$ and $\neg q$. Using these four columns, we may compute the column for $p \to \neg q$ and $q \lor \neg p$. To do so we think of the first and fourth columns as the data for the → truth table and compute the column of $p \to \neg q$ accordingly. For example, in the first line p is T and $\neg q$ is F so the entry for $p \to \neg q$ is T → F = F by definition of the meaning of →. In this fashion, we can fill out the rest of the fifth column. Column 6 works similarly, only we now need to look up the truth table for ∨ with columns 2 and 3 as input. Finally, column 7 results from applying the truth table of → to columns 5 and 6.

EXERCISES 1.8

* 1. Construct the truth table for $\neg p \lor q$ and verify that it coincides with the one for $p \to q$. (By 'coincide' we mean that the respective columns of T and F values are the same.)

p	q	$\neg p$	$\neg q$	$p \to \neg q$	$q \vee \neg p$	$(p \to \neg q) \to (q \vee \neg p)$
T	T	F	F	F	T	T
T	F	F	T	T	F	F
F	T	T	F	T	T	T
F	F	T	T	T	T	T

Fig. 1.11. An example of a truth table for a more complex logical formula.

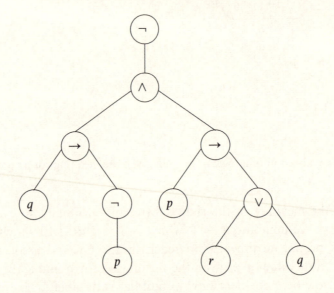

Fig. 1.12. Find the in-order, linear representation of this tree and check whether it is a well-formed formula.

* 2. Compute the complete truth table of the formula

$$((p \to q) \to p) \to p.$$

* 3. Consider the parse tree in Figure 1.12. Assume that q and r evaluate to T and p to F. Compute the truth value of the formula in the figure in a bottom-up fashion.

  4. Given the parse tree in Figure 1.4 assume that q evaluates to T and that p and r evaluate to F. Compute the value of this tree in a bottom-up fashion as done in Figure 1.10.

* 5. We call a formula *valid* if it always computes T, no matter which truth values we choose. We call it *satisfiable* if it computes T for at least one set of truth values. Is the formula of the parse tree in Figure 1.12 above valid? Is it satisfiable?

6. Consider again the tree in Figure 1.7. Compute its truth value under the following assignments of truth values to its leaves:

   (a) Let p be T, q be F and r be T.
   (b) Let p be F, q be T and r be F.

7. Compute the truth table for ϕ in Figure 1.3 (all eight cases please).

1.4.2 Mathematical induction

Here is a little anecdote about the German mathematician Gauss who, as a pupil at age 8, did not pay attention in class (can you imagine?), with the result that his teacher made him sum up all natural numbers from 1 to 100. The story has it that Gauss came up with the correct answer 5050 within seconds, which infuriated his teacher. How did Gauss do it? Well, possibly he knew that

$$1 + 2 + 3 + 4 + \cdots + n = \frac{n \cdot (n+1)}{2}. \tag{1.3}$$

for all natural numbers n. Thus, taking $n = 100$, Gauss could easily calculate:

$$1 + 2 + 3 + 4 + \cdots + 100 = \frac{100 \cdot 101}{2} = 5050.$$

Mathematical induction[1] allows us to prove equations, such as the one in (1.3), for arbitrary n. More generally, it allows us to show that *every* natural number satisfies a certain property. Suppose we have a property M which we think is true of all natural numbers. We write $M(5)$ to say that the property is true of 5, etc. Mathematical induction works like this. Suppose that we know the following two things about the property M:

1. **Base case:** The natural number 1 has property M, i.e. we have a proof of $M(1)$.
2. **Inductive step:** If n is a natural number which *we assume* to have property $M(n)$, then *we can show* that $n + 1$ has property $M(n + 1)$; i.e. we have a proof of $M(n) \rightarrow M(n + 1)$.

------

[1] There is another way of finding the sum $1+2+\cdots+100$, which works like this: write the sum backwards, as $100 + 99 + \cdots + 1$. Now add the forwards and backwards versions, obtaining $101 + 101 + \cdots + 101$ (100 times), which is 10100. Since we added the sum to itself, we now divide by two to get the answer 5050. Gauss probably used this method; but the method of mathematical induction that we explore in this section is much more powerful and can be applied in a wide variety of situations.

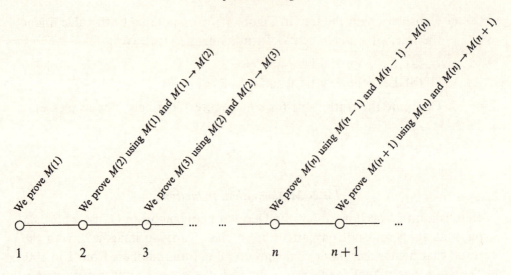

Fig. 1.13. How the principle of mathematical induction works. By proving just two facts, $M(1)$ and $M(n) \rightarrow M(n+1)$ for a formal parameter n, we are able to deduce $M(n)$ for each n.

Then:

Definition 1.29 The principle of mathematical induction says that, on the grounds of these two pieces of information above, every natural number n has property $M(n)$. The assumption of $M(n)$ in the inductive step is called the *induction hypothesis*.

Why does this principle make sense? Well, take *any* natural number k. If k equals 1, then k has property $M(1)$ using the base case and so we are done. Otherwise, we can use the inductive step, applied to $n = 1$, to infer that $2 = 1 + 1$ has property $M(2)$. We can do that using $\rightarrow$e, for we know that 1 has the property in question. Now we use that same inductive step on $n = 2$ to infer that 3 has property $M(3)$ and we repeat this until we reach $n = k$ (see Figure 1.13). Therefore, we should have no objections about using the principle of mathematical induction for natural numbers.

Returning to Gauss' example we claim that the sum

$$1 + 2 + 3 + 4 + \cdots + n$$

equals $\frac{n \cdot (n+1)}{2}$ for all natural numbers n.

Theorem 1.30 *The sum* $1 + 2 + 3 + 4 + \cdots + n$ *equals* $\frac{n \cdot (n+1)}{2}$ *for all natural numbers n.*

PROOF: We use mathematical induction.

In order to reveal the fine structure of our proof we write LHS_n for the expression $1 + 2 + 3 + 4 + \cdots + n$ and RHS_n for $\frac{n \cdot (n+1)}{2}$. Thus, we need to show $\text{LHS}_n = \text{RHS}_n$ for all $n \geq 1$.

Base case: If n equals 1, then LHS_1 is just 1 (there is only one summand), which happens to equal $\text{RHS}_1 = \frac{1 \cdot (1+1)}{2}$.

Inductive step: Let us assume that $\text{LHS}_n = \text{RHS}_n$. Recall that this assumption is called the induction hypothesis; it is the driving force of our argument. We need to show $\text{LHS}_{n+1} = \text{RHS}_{n+1}$, i.e. that the longer sum

$$1 + 2 + 3 + 4 + \cdots + (n+1)$$

equals

$$\frac{(n+1) \cdot ((n+1)+1)}{2}.$$

The key observation is that the sum $1 + 2 + 3 + 4 + \cdots + (n+1)$ is nothing but the sum

$$(1 + 2 + 3 + 4 + \cdots + n) + (n+1)$$

of two summands, where the first one is the sum of our induction hypothesis. The latter says that $1 + 2 + 3 + 4 + \cdots + n$ equals $\frac{n \cdot (n+1)}{2}$, and we are certainly entitled to substitute equals for equals in our reasoning. Thus, we compute

$$
\begin{aligned}
\text{LHS}_{n+1} \\
&= 1 + 2 + 3 + 4 + \cdots + (n+1) \\
&= \text{LHS}_n + (n+1) \quad \text{regrouping the sum} \\
&= \text{RHS}_n + (n+1) \quad \text{by our induction hypothesis} \\
&= \frac{n \cdot (n+1)}{2} + (n+1) \\
&= \frac{n \cdot (n+1)}{2} + \frac{2 \cdot (n+1)}{2} \quad \text{arithmetic} \\
&= \frac{(n+2) \cdot (n+1)}{2} \quad \text{arithmetic} \\
&= \frac{((n+1)+1) \cdot (n+1)}{2} \quad \text{arithmetic} \\
&= \text{RHS}_{n+1}.
\end{aligned}
$$

Since we successfully showed the base case and the inductive step, we can use mathematical induction to infer that all natural numbers n have the property stated in the theorem above. □

Actually, there are numerous variations of this principle. For example, we can think of a version in which the base case is $n = 0$, which would then

cover all natural numbers including 0. Some statements hold only for all
natural numbers, say, greater than 3. So you would have to deal with a base
case 4, but keep the version of the inductive step (see the exercises for such
an example).

Course-of-values induction. There is a variant of mathematical induction
in which the induction hypothesis for proving $M(n+1)$ is not just $M(n)$,
but

$$M(1) \wedge M(2) \wedge \cdots \wedge M(n).$$

In that variant, called *course-of-values* induction, there doesn't have to be an
explicit base case at all — everything can be done in the inductive step.

How can this work without a base case? The answer is that the base case
is implicitly included in the inductive step. Consider the case $n = 3$: the
inductive-step instance is

$$M(1) \wedge M(2) \wedge M(3) \rightarrow M(4).$$

Now consider $n = 1$: the inductive-step instance is

$$M(1) \rightarrow M(2).$$

What about the case when n equals 0? In this case, there are zero formulas
on the left of the $\rightarrow$, so we have to prove $M(1)$ from nothing at all. The
inductive-step instance is simply the obligation to show

$$M(1).$$

Look at how the various cases of $k < n+1$ combine to prove $M(n+1)$. You
might find it useful to modify Figure 1.13 for course-of-values induction.

Having said that the base case is implicit in course-of-values induction,
it frequently turns out that it still demands special attention when you get
inside trying to prove the inductive case. We will see precisely this in the two
applications of course-of-values induction in the following pages.

In computer science, we often deal with finite structures of some kind,
data structures, programs, files etc. Often we need to show that *every* instance
of such a structure has a certain property. For example, the well-formed formulas of Definition 1.27 have the property that the number of '(' brackets
in a particular formula equals its number of ')' brackets. We can use mathematical induction on the domain of natural numbers to prove this. In order
to succeed, we somehow need to connect well-formed formulas to natural
numbers.

Definition 1.31 Given a well-formed formula ϕ, we define its *height* to be 1 plus the length of the longest path of its parse tree.

For example, consider the well-formed formulas in Figures 1.3, 1.4 and 1.12. Their heights are 5, 6 and 5, respectively. In Figure 1.3, the longest path goes from $\to$ to $\wedge$ to $\vee$ to $\neg$ to r, a path of length 4, so the height is $4 + 1 = 5$. Note that the height of atoms is $1 + 0 = 1$.

Since every well-formed formula has finite height, we can show statements about all well-formed formulas by mathematical induction on their height. This trick is most often called *structural induction*, a technique you will encounter a lot in your studies in computer science. Using the notion of the height of a parse tree, we realise that structural induction is just a special case of course-of-values induction.

Theorem 1.32 *For every well-formed propositional logic formula, the number of left brackets is equal to the number of right brackets.*

PROOF: We proceed by course-of-values induction on the height of well-formed formulas ϕ.

Let $M(n)$ mean: all formulas of height n have the same number of left and right brackets. We assume $M(k)$ for each $k < n$ and try to prove $M(n)$. Take a formula ϕ of height n.

- If $n = 1$, then the longest path in ϕ is 0. This means that ϕ is just a propositional atom. So there are no left or right brackets, 0 equals 0.
- If $n > 1$, then the root of the parse tree of ϕ must be $\neg$, $\to$, $\vee$ or $\wedge$, for ϕ is well-formed. We assume that it is $\to$ (the other three cases are argued in a similar way). Then ϕ equals $(\phi_1 \to \phi_2)$ for some well-formed formulas ϕ_1 and ϕ_2 (of course, they are just the left, respectively right, linear representations of the root's two subtrees). It is clear that the heights of ϕ_1 and ϕ_2 are strictly smaller than n. Using the induction hypothesis, we therefore conclude that ϕ_1 has the same number of left and right brackets and that the same is true for ϕ_2. But in $(\phi_1 \to \phi_2)$ we added just two more brackets, one '(' and one ')'. Thus, the number of occurrences of '(' and ')' in ϕ is the same.

□

The formula $p \to (q \wedge \neg r)$ illustrates why we could not prove the above directly with mathematical induction on the height of formulas. While this formula has height 4, its two subtrees have heights 1 and 3, respectively. Thus, an induction hypothesis for height 3 would have worked for the right subtree but failed for the left subtree.

EXERCISES 1.9

    1. This exercise lets you practice proofs using mathematical induction. Make sure that you state your base case and inductive step clearly. You should also indicate where you apply the induction hypothesis.
       Prove that

$$(2 \cdot 1 - 1) + (2 \cdot 2 - 1) + (2 \cdot 3 - 1) + \cdots + (2 \cdot n - 1) = n^2$$

       by mathematical induction on $n \geq 1$.

    2. Let k and l be natural numbers. We say that k is divisible by l if there exists a natural number p such that $k = p \cdot l$. For example, 15 is divisible by 3 because $15 = 5 \cdot 3$. Use mathematical induction to show that $11^n - 4^n$ is divisible by 7 for all natural numbers $n \geq 1$.

    * 3. Use mathematical induction to show that

$$1^2 + 2^2 + 3^2 + \cdots + n^2 = \frac{n \cdot (n+1) \cdot (2n+1)}{6}$$

       for all natural numbers $n \geq 1$.

    * 4. Here is an example of why we need to secure the base case for mathematical induction. Consider the assertion

       'The number $n^2 + 5n + 1$ is even for all $n \geq 1$.'.

       (a) Prove the inductive step of that assertion.
       (b) Show that the base case fails to hold.
       (c) Conclude that the assertion is false.
       (d) Use mathematical induction to show that $n^2 + 5n + 1$ is *odd* for all $n \geq 1$.

    * 5. Prove that $2^n \geq n + 10$ for all natural numbers $n \geq 4$. In this case you need to show the statement for $n = 4$ (the base case) and then you have to show that its validity for n entails its validity for $n + 1$ (the inductive step). Is the statement true for any $n < 4$?

    ——

1.4.3 Soundness of propositional logic

The natural deduction rules make it possible for us to develop rigorous threads of argumentation, in the course of which we arrive at a conclusion ψ assuming certain other propositions $\phi_1, \phi_2, \ldots, \phi_n$. We denoted this by

$$\phi_1, \phi_2, \ldots, \phi_n \vdash \psi.$$

Do we have any evidence that these rules are all *correct* in the sense that they will preserve truth computed by our truth-table semantics? Given a proof of the sequent above, is it conceivable that ψ above is false although all propositions $\phi_1, \phi_2, \ldots, \phi_n$ are true? Fortunately, this is not the case and in this subsection we demonstrate why this is so. Let us suppose that the sequent $\phi_1, \phi_2, \ldots, \phi_n \vdash \psi$ has been established by specifying some proof in our natural deduction calculus. We need to show that *if* all propositions $\phi_1, \phi_2, \ldots, \phi_n$ evaluate to T, then ψ evaluates to T as well.

Definition 1.33 If ψ evaluates to T whenever $\phi_1, \phi_2, \ldots, \phi_n$ evaluate to T, we denote this fact by

$$\phi_1, \phi_2, \ldots, \phi_n \vDash \psi$$

and call $\vDash$ the *semantic entailment* relation.

Let us look at some examples of this notion.

1. Does

$$p \wedge q \vDash p$$

   hold? Well, we have to inspect all assignments of truth values to p and q (there are four of these). Whenever such an assignment computes T for $p \wedge q$ we need to make sure that p is true as well. But $p \wedge q$ computes T only if p and q are true, so $p \wedge q \vDash p$ is indeed the case.

2. What about the relationship

$$p \vee q \vDash p?$$

   There are three assignments for which $p \vee q$ computes T, so p would have to be true for all of these. However, if we assign T to q and F to p, then $p \vee q$ computes T, but p is false. Thus, $p \vee q \vDash p$ does not hold.

3. What if we modify the above to

$$\neg q, p \vee q \vDash p?$$

   Notice that we have to be concerned only about assignments such that $\neg q$ *and* $p \vee q$ compute T. This forces q to be false, which in turn forces p to be true. Hence $\neg q, p \vee q \vDash p$ is the case.

From the discussion above we realize that a soundness argument has to show: $\phi_1, \phi_2, \ldots, \phi_n \vdash \psi$ implies $\phi_1, \phi_2, \ldots, \phi_n \vDash \psi$.

Theorem 1.34 (Soundness) *Let $\phi_1, \phi_2, \ldots, \phi_n$ and ψ be propositional logic formulas. If $\phi_1, \phi_2, \ldots, \phi_n \vdash \psi$, then $\phi_1, \phi_2, \ldots, \phi_n \vDash \psi$.*

PROOF:

Since $\phi_1, \phi_2, \ldots, \phi_n \vdash \psi$ we know there is a proof of ψ from the premises $\phi_1, \phi_2, \ldots, \phi_n$. We now do a pretty slick thing, namely, we reason by *mathematical induction on the length of this proof!* The length of a proof is just the number of lines it involves. So let us be perfectly clear about what it is we mean to show. We intend to show the assertion $M(k)$:

'For all sequents $\phi_1, \phi_2, \ldots, \phi_n \vdash \psi$ ($n \geq 0$) which have a proof of length k, it is the case that $\phi_1, \phi_2, \ldots, \phi_n \vDash \psi$.'

by course-of-values induction on the natural number k. Before we do this, let's slightly reformulate our notation of 'proof' such that each initial segment of proofs constitutes a legal proof (although of different sequents). Note that this is not guaranteed by our notion of proof since chopping off a proof may result in unclosed boxes and therefore only partial proofs. The boxes controlling the scope of assumptions are useful and easy to use when constructing proofs, but, when reasoning about them, it is convenient to use a slightly more bureaucratic notation, in which we explicitly record the assumptions that a line depends upon. Thus, the proof we saw of $p \wedge q \to r \vdash p \to (q \to r)$, namely

1		$p \wedge q \to r$	premise
2		p	assumption
3		q	assumption
4		$p \wedge q$	$\wedge$i 2, 3
5		r	$\to$e 1, 4
6		$q \to r$	$\to$i 3–5
7		$p \to (q \to r)$	$\to$i 2–6

will be noted as

1	$\emptyset$	$p \wedge q \to r$	premise
2	$\{2\}$	p	assumption
3	$\{2,3\}$	q	assumption
4	$\{2,3\}$	$p \wedge q$	$\wedge$i 2, 3
5	$\{2,3\}$	r	$\to$e 1, 4
6	$\{2\}$	$q \to r$	$\to$i 3–5
7	$\emptyset$	$p \to (q \to r)$	$\to$i 2–6

Please observe how the set of assumptions in the second column grows and shrinks like a stack, thus simulating the opening and closing of boxes. So, for the purposes of this section, a proof of $\Gamma \vdash \psi$ is a sequence of pairs

$[(d_1, \phi_1), (d_2, \phi_2), \ldots, (d_k, \phi_k)]$, with d_1 and d_k being $\emptyset$ (all boxes have been closed or not yet opened), each d_i is a subset of $\{1, \ldots, i\}$ and for each i:

- $\phi_i \in \Gamma$ (i.e. ϕ_i is a premise);
- or $i \in d_i$ (i.e. ϕ_i is an assumption);
- or ϕ_i follows from previous lines by an application of our natural deduction rules. Usually, d_i equals d_{i-1}, except when a rule opens or closes a box.

The length of the proof $[(d_1, \phi_1), (d_2, \phi_2), \ldots, (d_k, \phi_k)]$ is k.

Let's proceed with our proof by induction. We assume $M(k')$ for each $k' < k$ and we try to prove $M(k)$. Consider any assignment of truth values to the atoms in $\phi_1, \phi_2, \ldots, \phi_n, \psi$ such that $\phi_1, \phi_2, \ldots, \phi_n$ all compute T.

Base case: a one-line proof. If the proof has length 1 ($k = 1$), then it must be of the form

$$1 \qquad\qquad \phi \quad \text{premise}$$

since all other rules involve more than one line. This is the case when $n = 1$ and ϕ_1 and ψ equal ϕ, i.e. we are dealing with the sequent $\phi \vdash \phi$. Of course, since ϕ evaluates to T so does ϕ. Thus, $\phi \vDash \phi$ holds as claimed.

Course-of-values inductive step. Let us assume that the proof of

$$\phi_1, \phi_2, \ldots, \phi_n \vdash \psi$$

has length k and that the statement we want to prove is true for all numbers less than k. Our proof has the following structure:

$$
\begin{array}{lll}
1 & \phi_1 & \text{premise} \\
2 & \phi_2 & \text{premise} \\
& \vdots & \\
n & \phi_n & \text{premise} \\
& \vdots & \\
k & \psi & \text{justification}
\end{array}
$$

There are two things we don't know at this point. First, what is happening in between those dots? Second, what was the last rule applied, i.e. what is the justification of the last line? The first uncertainty is of no concern; this is where mathematical induction demonstrates its power. The second lack of knowledge is where all the work sits. In this generality, there is simply no way of knowing which rule we applied last, so we need to consider all possible cases.

Propositional logic

1. Let us suppose that this last rule is $\wedge$i. Then we know that ψ is of the form $\psi_1 \wedge \psi_2$ and the justification in line k refers to two lines further up which have ψ_1, respectively ψ_2, as their conclusions. Suppose that these lines are k_1 and k_2. Since k_1 and k_2 are smaller than k, we see that there exist proofs of the sequents

$$\phi_1, \phi_2, \ldots, \phi_n \vdash \psi_1$$
$$\phi_1, \phi_2, \ldots, \phi_n \vdash \psi_2$$

with length *less than* k; just take the first k_1, respectively k_2, lines of our original proof. Using the induction hypothesis, we can conclude that ψ_1 *and* ψ_2 evaluate to T. Now we inspect our truth table for $\wedge$ in Figure 1.9 and realise that $\psi_1 \wedge \psi_2$, i.e. ψ, evaluates to $T \wedge T = T$ as well.

2. If ψ has been shown using the rule $\vee$e, then we must have proved, or assumed, some formula $\eta_1 \vee \eta_2$ before, which was referred to via $\vee$e in the justification of line k. Thus, we have a shorter proof

$$\phi_1, \phi_2, \ldots, \phi_n \vdash \eta_1 \vee \eta_2$$

and so $\eta_1 \vee \eta_2$ evaluates to T by our induction hypothesis. From the truth table of $\vee$ we therefore see that at least one of the formulas η_1 and η_2 computes to T. Assume that η_1 computes to T (the other case is shown in a similar way). In using $\vee$e to conclude ψ, we had to assume η_1 and η_2 and show ψ for each of these cases. Considering that first case, we have a shorter proof of

$$\phi_1, \phi_2, \ldots, \phi_n, \eta_1 \vdash \psi$$

and all formulas on the left-hand side of $\vdash$ evaluate to T. By the induction hypothesis, this implies that ψ computes T as well. The second case is argued in a completely symmetric way.

3. You can guess by now that the rest of the argument checks each possible proof rule in turn and ultimately boils down to verifying that our natural deduction rules behave semantically in the same way as their corresponding truth tables evaluate. We leave the details as an exercise.

□

EXERCISES 1.10

1. Finish the soundness proof above by completing the case analysis ranging over the final proof rule applied. Inspect the summary of

natural deduction rules in Figure 1.2 on page 31 to see which cases are still missing.

2. The soundness of propositional logic is useful in ensuring the *non-existence* of a proof for a given sequent. Suppose that you try to prove $\phi_1, \phi_2, \ldots, \phi_2 \vdash \psi$, but that your best efforts won't succeed. How could you be sure that no such proof can be found? After all, it might just be that you can't find a proof even though there is one. Using soundness, it suffices to find a set of truth values such that all ϕ_i compute to T whereas ψ computes F. Then $\phi_1, \phi_2, \ldots, \phi_2 \nvDash \psi$ holds by the definition of semantic entailment. Using soundness, this means that $\phi_1, \phi_2, \ldots, \phi_2 \nvdash \psi$ holds as well, i.e. this sequent does not have a proof.

   Show that the following sequents are not valid by finding a combination of truth values for the propositional atoms involved such that the truth values of the formulas to the left of $\vdash$ are T and the truth value of the formula to the right of $\vdash$ is F.

   (a) $\neg p \vee (q \rightarrow p) \vdash \neg p \wedge q$
   (b) $\neg r \rightarrow (p \vee q), r \wedge \neg q \vdash r \rightarrow q$
   * (c) $p \rightarrow (q \rightarrow r) \vdash p \rightarrow (r \rightarrow q)$.

3. For each of the following invalid sequents, give examples of natural language declarative sentences for the atoms p, q and r such that the premises are true, but the conclusion false.

   (a) $p \vee q \vdash p \wedge q$
   (b) $\neg p \rightarrow \neg q \vdash \neg q \rightarrow \neg p$
   (c) $p \rightarrow q \vdash p \vee q$
   (d) $p \rightarrow (q \vee r) \vdash (p \rightarrow q) \wedge (p \rightarrow r)$.

1.4.4 Completeness of propositional logic

In this subsection, we hope to convince you that the natural deduction rules of propositional logic are *complete*: whenever $\phi_1, \phi_2, \ldots, \phi_n \vDash \psi$ holds, then there exists a natural deduction proof for the sequent $\phi_1, \phi_2, \ldots, \phi_n \vdash \psi$. Combined with the soundness result of the previous subsection, we then obtain

$$\phi_1, \phi_2, \ldots, \phi_n \vdash \psi \quad \text{iff} \quad \phi_1, \phi_2, \ldots, \phi_n \vDash \psi.$$

This gives you a certain freedom regarding which method you prefer to use. Often it is much easier to show one of these two relationships (although neither of the two is universally better, or easier, to establish). The first method involves a *proof search*, upon which the *logic programming* paradigm is based. The second method typically forces you to compute a truth table which is exponential in the size of occurring propositional atoms. Both methods are intractable in general but particular instances of formulas often respond differently to treatment under these two methods.

The remainder of this section is concerned with an argument saying that $\phi_1, \phi_2, \ldots, \phi_n \vDash \psi$ implies $\phi_1, \phi_2, \ldots, \phi_n \vdash \psi$. Given $\phi_1, \phi_2, \ldots, \phi_n \vDash \psi$, the argument proceeds in three steps:

Step 1: We show that $\vDash \phi_1 \rightarrow (\phi_2 \rightarrow (\phi_3 \rightarrow (\ldots (\phi_n \rightarrow \psi) \ldots)))$.
Step 2: Next, we show that $\vdash \phi_1 \rightarrow (\phi_2 \rightarrow (\phi_3 \rightarrow (\ldots (\phi_n \rightarrow \psi) \ldots)))$.
Step 3: Finally, we show that $\phi_1, \phi_2, \ldots, \phi_n \vdash \psi$.

The first and third steps are quite easy; all the real work is done in the second one.

Step 1:

Definition 1.35 A formula of propositional logic ϕ is called a *tautology* if it is true for all assignments of truth values to its propositional atoms, i.e. if $\vDash \phi$.

Supposing we have $\phi_1, \phi_2, \ldots, \phi_n \vDash \psi$, let us verify that $\phi_1 \rightarrow (\phi_2 \rightarrow (\phi_3 \rightarrow (\ldots (\phi_n \rightarrow \psi) \ldots)))$ is indeed a tautology. Since the latter formula is a nested implication, it can evaluate only to F if all $\phi_1, \phi_2, \ldots, \phi_n$ evaluate to T *and* ψ evaluates to F; see its parse tree in Figure 1.14. But this contradicts the fact that $\phi_1, \phi_2, \ldots, \phi_n \vDash \psi$. Thus, $\vDash \phi_1 \rightarrow (\phi_2 \rightarrow (\phi_3 \rightarrow (\ldots (\phi_n \rightarrow \psi) \ldots)))$ holds.

Step 2:

Theorem 1.36 *If* $\vDash \eta$, *then* $\vdash \eta$. *In other words, if η is a tautology, then η is a theorem.*

This step is the hard one. Assume that $\vDash \eta$ holds. Given that η contains n distinct propositional atoms $p_1, p_2, \ldots, p_n$ we know that η evaluates to T for all 2^n lines in its truth table. How can we use this information to construct a proof for η? In some cases this can be done quite easily by taking a very good look at the concrete structure of η. But here we somehow have to come up with a *uniform* way of building such a proof. The key insight is to 'encode' each line in the truth table of η as a sequent. Then we construct proofs for these 2^n sequents and assemble them into a proof of η.

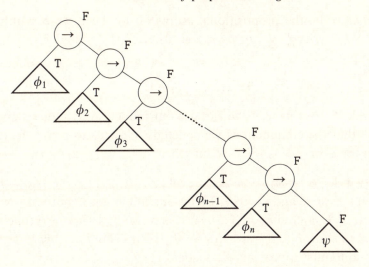

Fig. 1.14. The only way this parse tree can compute F. We represent parse trees for
$\phi_1, \phi_2, \ldots, \phi_n$ as triangles, since their internal structure does not concern us here.

Proposition 1.37 *Let ϕ be a formula such that $p_1, p_2, \ldots, p_n$ are its only propositional atoms. Let l be any line number in ϕ's truth table. For all $1 \le i \le n$ let $\hat{p}_i$ be p_i if the entry in line l of p_i is T, otherwise $\hat{p}_i$ is $\neg p_i$. Then we have*

1. *$\hat{p}_1, \hat{p}_2, \ldots, \hat{p}_n \vdash \phi$ is provable if the entry for ϕ in line l is T*
2. *$\hat{p}_1, \hat{p}_2, \ldots, \hat{p}_n \vdash \neg\phi$ is provable if the entry for ϕ in line l is F*

PROOF: This proof is done by structural induction on the formula ϕ, that is, mathematical induction on the height of the parse tree of ϕ.

1. If ϕ is a propositional atom p, we need to show that $p \vdash p$ and $\neg p \vdash \neg p$. These have one-line proofs.
2. If ϕ is of the form $\neg\phi_1$ we again have two cases to consider. First, assume that ϕ evaluates to T. In this case ϕ_1 evaluates to F. Note that ϕ_1 has the same atomic propositions as ϕ. We may use the induction hypothesis on ϕ_1 to conclude that $\hat{p}_1, \hat{p}_2, \ldots, \hat{p}_n \vdash \neg\phi_1$; but $\neg\phi_1$ is just ϕ, so we are done.

   Second, if ϕ evaluates to F, then ϕ_1 evaluates to T and we get $\hat{p}_1, \hat{p}_2, \ldots, \hat{p}_n \vdash \phi_1$ by induction. Using the rule $\neg\neg$i, we may extend the proof of $\hat{p}_1, \hat{p}_2, \ldots, \hat{p}_n \vdash \phi_1$ to one for $\hat{p}_1, \hat{p}_2, \ldots, \hat{p}_n \vdash \neg\neg\phi_1$; but $\neg\neg\phi_1$ is just $\neg\phi$, so again we are done.

The remaining cases all deal with two subformulas: ϕ equals $\phi_1 \circ \phi_2$, where $\circ$ is $\rightarrow$, $\wedge$ or $\vee$. In all these cases let $q_1, \ldots, q_l$ be the propositional atoms of

ϕ_1 and $r_1, \ldots, r_k$ be the propositional atoms of ϕ_2. Then we certainly have $\{q_1, \ldots, q_l\} \cup \{r_1, \ldots, r_k\} = \{p_1, \ldots, p_n\}$ so $\hat{q}_1, \ldots, \hat{q}_l \vdash \psi_1$ and $\hat{r}_1, \ldots, \hat{r}_k \vdash \psi_2$ together imply

$$\hat{p}_1, \ldots, \hat{p}_n \vdash \psi_1 \wedge \psi_2$$

using the rule $\wedge$i. In this way, we can use our induction hypothesis and only owe proofs that the conjunctions we conclude allow us to prove the desired conclusion for ϕ or $\neg\phi$ as the case may be.

3. To wit, let ϕ be $\phi_1 \rightarrow \phi_2$. If ϕ evaluates to F, then we know that ϕ_1 evaluates to T and ϕ_2 to F. Using our induction hypothesis, we have $\hat{q}_1, \ldots, \hat{q}_l \vdash \phi_1$ and $\hat{r}_1, \ldots, \hat{r}_k \vdash \neg\phi_2$, so $\hat{p}_1, \ldots, \hat{p}_n \vdash \phi_1 \wedge \neg\phi_2$ follows. We need to show $\hat{p}_1, \ldots, \hat{p}_n \vdash \neg(\phi_1 \rightarrow \phi_2)$; but using $\hat{p}_1, \ldots, \hat{p}_n \vdash \phi_1 \wedge \neg\phi_2$, this amounts to proving the sequent

$$\phi_1 \wedge \neg\phi_2 \vdash \neg(\phi_1 \rightarrow \phi_2),$$

which we leave as an exercise.

If ϕ evaluates to T, then we have three cases. First, if ϕ_1 evaluates to F and ϕ_2 to F, then we get, by our induction hypothesis, that $\hat{q}_1, \ldots, \hat{q}_l \vdash \neg\phi_1$ and $\hat{r}_1, \ldots, \hat{r}_k \vdash \neg\phi_2$, so $\hat{p}_1, \ldots, \hat{p}_n \vdash \neg\phi_1 \wedge \neg\phi_2$ follows. Again, we need only to show the sequent $\neg\phi_1 \wedge \neg\phi_2 \vdash \phi_1 \rightarrow \phi_2$, which we leave as an exercise. Second, if ϕ evaluates to F and ϕ_2 to T, we use our induction hypothesis to arrive at $\hat{p}_1, \ldots, \hat{p}_n \vdash \neg\phi_1 \wedge \phi_2$ and have to prove $\neg\phi_1 \wedge \phi_2 \vdash \phi_1 \rightarrow \phi_2$, which we leave as an exercise. Third, if ϕ_1 and ϕ_2 evaluate to T, we arrive at $\hat{p}_1, \ldots, \hat{p}_n \vdash \phi_1 \wedge \phi_2$, using our induction hypothesis, and need to prove $\phi_1 \wedge \phi_2 \vdash \phi_1 \rightarrow \phi_2$, which we leave as an exercise as well.

4. If ϕ is of the form $\phi_1 \wedge \phi_2$, we are again dealing with four entire cases. First, if ϕ_1 and ϕ_2 evaluate to T, we get $\hat{q}_1, \ldots, \hat{q}_l \vdash \phi_1$ and $\hat{r}_1, \ldots, \hat{r}_k \vdash \phi_2$ by our induction hypothesis, so $\hat{p}_1, \ldots, \hat{p}_n \vdash \phi_1 \wedge \phi_2$ follows. Second, if ϕ_1 evaluates to F and ϕ_2 to T, then we get $\hat{p}_1, \ldots, \hat{p}_n \vdash \neg\phi_1 \wedge \phi_2$ using our induction hypothesis and the rule $\wedge$i as above and we need to prove $\neg\phi_1 \wedge \phi_2 \vdash \neg(\phi_1 \wedge \phi_2)$, which we leave as an exercise. Third, if ϕ_1 and ϕ_2 evaluate to F, then our induction hypothesis and the rule $\wedge$i let us infer that $\hat{p}_1, \ldots, \hat{p}_n \vdash \neg\phi_1 \wedge \neg\phi_2$; so we are left with proving $\neg\phi_1 \wedge \neg\phi_2 \vdash \neg\phi_1 \wedge \phi_2$, which we leave as an exercise. Fourth, if ϕ_1 evaluates to T and ϕ_2 to F, we obtain $\hat{p}_1, \ldots, \hat{p}_n \vdash \phi_1 \wedge \neg\phi_2$ by our induction hypothesis and we have to show $\phi_1 \wedge \neg\phi_2 \vdash \neg(\phi_1 \wedge \phi_2)$, which we leave as an exercise.

5. Finally, if ϕ is a disjunction $\phi_1 \vee \phi_2$, we again have four cases.

First, if ϕ_1 and ϕ_2 evaluate to F, then our induction hypothesis and the rule $\wedge$i give us $\hat{p}_1, \ldots, \hat{p}_n \vdash \neg\phi_1 \wedge \neg\phi_2$ and we have to show $\neg\phi_1 \wedge \neg\phi_2 \vdash \neg(\phi_1 \vee \phi_2)$, which we leave as an exercise. Second, if ϕ_1 and ϕ_2 evaluate to T, then we obtain $\hat{p}_1, \ldots, \hat{p}_n \vdash \phi_1 \wedge \phi_2$, by our induction hypothesis, and we need a proof for $\phi_1 \wedge \phi_2 \vdash \phi_1 \vee \phi_2$, which we leave as an exercise. Third, if ϕ_1 evaluates to F and ϕ_2 to T, then we arrive at $\hat{p}_1, \ldots, \hat{p}_n \vdash \neg\phi_1 \wedge \phi_2$, using our induction hypothesis, and need to establish $\neg\phi_1 \wedge \phi_2 \vdash \phi_1 \vee \phi_2$, which we leave as an exercise. Fourth, if ϕ_1 evaluates to T and ϕ_2 to F, then $\hat{p}_1, \ldots, \hat{p}_n \vdash \phi_1 \wedge \neg\phi_2$ results from our induction hypothesis and all we need is a proof for $\phi_1 \wedge \neg\phi_2 \vdash \phi_1 \vee \phi_2$, which we leave as an exercise.

$\square$

We apply this technique to the formula $\vDash \phi_1 \rightarrow (\phi_2 \rightarrow (\phi_3 \rightarrow (\ldots (\phi_n \rightarrow \psi)\ldots)))$. Since it is a tautology it evaluates to T in all 2^n lines of its truth table; thus, the proposition above gives us 2^n many proofs of

$$\hat{p}_1, \hat{p}_2, \ldots, \hat{p}_n \vdash \eta,$$

one for each of the cases that $\hat{p}_i$ is p_i or $\neg p_i$. Our job now is to assemble all these proofs into a single proof for η which does not use any premises. We illustrate how to do this by means of an example. We choose the tautology $p \wedge q \rightarrow p$.

In the example tautology $p \wedge q \rightarrow p$, we have two propositional atoms p and q. By the proposition above, we are guaranteed to have a proof for each of the four sequents

$$
\begin{aligned}
p, q &\vdash p \wedge q \rightarrow p \\
\neg p, q &\vdash p \wedge q \rightarrow p \\
p, \neg q &\vdash p \wedge q \rightarrow p \\
\neg p, \neg q &\vdash p \wedge q \rightarrow p.
\end{aligned}
$$

Ultimately, we want to prove $p \wedge q \rightarrow p$ by appealing to the four proofs of the sequents above. Thus, we somehow need to get rid of the premises on the left-hand sides of these four sequents. This is the place where we rely on the law of the excluded middle which states $r \vee \neg r$, for any r. We use LEM for all propositional atoms (here p and q) and then we separately assume all the four cases, by using $\vee$e. That way we can invoke all four proofs of the sequents above and use the rule $\vee$e repeatedly until we have got rid of all our premises. The combination of these four phases is spelled out schematically on the following page:

1	$p \vee \neg p$					LEM

2	p	ass	$\neg p$		ass

3	$q \vee \neg q$	LEM	$q \vee \neg q$		LEM

Row 4: q (ass) | $\neg q$ (ass) | q (ass) | $\neg q$ (ass)

Row 5: ⋮ | ⋮ | ⋮ | ⋮

Row 7: $p \wedge q \to p$ | $p \wedge q \to p$ | $p \wedge q \to p$ | $p \wedge q \to p$

Row 8: $p \wedge q \to p$ | | Ve | $p \wedge q \to p$ | | Ve

Row 9: $p \wedge q \to p$ | | | | | Ve

As soon as you understand how this particular example works, you will also realise that it will work for an arbitrary tautology with n distinct atoms. Of course, it seems ridiculous to prove $p \wedge q \to p$ using a proof that is this long. But remember that this illustrates a *uniform* method that constructs a proof for every tautology η, no matter how complicated it is.

Step 3: Finally, we need to find a proof for $\phi_1, \phi_2, \ldots, \phi_n \vdash \psi$. Take the proof for $\vdash \phi_1 \to (\phi_2 \to (\phi_3 \to (\ldots(\phi_n \to \psi)\ldots)))$ given by step 2 and augment its proof by introducing $\phi_1, \phi_2, \ldots, \phi_n$ as premises. Then apply $\to$e n times on each of these premises (starting with ϕ_1, continuing with ϕ_2 etc.). Thus, we arrive at the conclusion ψ which gives us a proof for the sequent $\phi_1, \phi_2, \ldots, \phi_n \vdash \psi$.

Corollary 1.38 (Soundness and Completeness) *Let $\phi_1, \phi_2, \ldots, \phi_n, \psi$ be formulas of propositional logic. Then*

$$\phi_1, \phi_2, \ldots, \phi_n \vDash \psi \quad iff \quad \phi_1, \phi_2, \ldots, \phi_n \vdash \psi.$$

EXERCISES 1.11

   1. Let * be a new logical connective such that $p * q$ does *not* hold iff p and q are either both false or both true.

      (a) Write down the truth table for $p * q$.
      (b) Write down the truth table for $(p * p) * (q * q)$.
      (c) Does the table in (b) coincide with a table in Figure 1.9 (page 48)? If so, which one?
      (d) Do you know * already as a logic gate in circuit design? If so, what is it called?

2. * (a) Assume that p evaluates to F and q to T. What does the formula $p \rightarrow (\neg q \vee (q \rightarrow p))$ evaluate to? You may either answer this by computing this value on the formula's parse tree, or you may specify the corresponding line of a truth table.

   * (b) Do the same thing for the formula $\neg((\neg q \wedge (p \rightarrow r)) \wedge (r \rightarrow q))$, where r evaluates to T (and p and q evaluate as in 2(a)).

3. Compute *complete* truth tables for the following formulas:

   * (a) $p \vee (\neg(q \wedge (r \rightarrow q)))$
   (b) $(p \wedge q) \rightarrow (p \vee q)$
   (c) $((p \rightarrow \neg q) \rightarrow \neg p) \rightarrow q$
   (d) $(p \rightarrow q) \vee (p \rightarrow \neg q)$
   (e) $((p \rightarrow q) \rightarrow p) \rightarrow p$
   (f) $((p \vee q) \rightarrow r) \rightarrow ((p \rightarrow r) \vee (q \rightarrow r))$
   (g) $(p \rightarrow q) \rightarrow (\neg p \rightarrow \neg q)$.

4. Find a formula of propositional logic ϕ which contains only the atoms p, q and r and which is true only when p and q are false, or when $\neg q \wedge (p \vee r)$ is true.

5. Show that the following sequents are not valid by finding a combination of truth values for the propositional atoms involved such that the truth value of the formula to the left of $\vdash$ is T and the truth value of the formula to the right of $\vdash$ is F.

   (a) $\neg p, p \vee q \vdash \neg q$
   (b) $p \rightarrow (\neg q \vee r), \neg r \vdash \neg q \rightarrow \neg p$.

6. Suppose a post office sells only 2¢ and 3¢ stamps. Show that any postage of 2¢, or over, can be paid for using only these stamps. Hint: use mathematical induction on n, where n¢ is the postage. In the inductive step consider two possibilities: first, n¢ can be paid for using only 2¢ stamps. Second, paying n¢ requires the use of at least one 3¢ stamp.

* 7. The Fibonacci numbers are most useful in modelling the growth of populations. We define them by $F_1 \stackrel{\text{def}}{=} 1$, $F_2 \stackrel{\text{def}}{=} 1$ and

$$F_{n+1} \stackrel{\text{def}}{=} F_n + F_{n-1}$$

for all $n \geq 2$. So $F_3 \stackrel{\text{def}}{=} F_1 + F_2 = 1 + 1 = 2$ etc. Show the assertion 'F_{3n} *is even*.' by mathematical induction on $n \geq 1$. Note that this assertion is saying that the sequence $F_3, F_6, F_9, \ldots$ consists of even numbers only.

8. Use mathematical induction on n to prove the theorem $((\phi_1 \wedge (\phi_2 \wedge (\cdots \wedge \phi_n) \ldots) \rightarrow \psi) \rightarrow (\phi_1 \rightarrow (\phi_2 \rightarrow (\ldots (\phi_n \rightarrow \psi) \ldots))))$.

9. Consider the function rank, defined by

$$\text{rank}(p) \overset{\text{def}}{=} 1$$
$$\text{rank}(\neg\phi) \overset{\text{def}}{=} 1 + \text{rank}(\phi)$$
$$\text{rank}(\phi \circ \psi) \overset{\text{def}}{=} 1 + \max(\text{rank}(\phi), \text{rank}(\psi)),$$

where p is any atom, $\circ \in \{\rightarrow, \vee, \wedge\}$ and $\max(n, m)$ is n if $n \geq m$ and m otherwise. Recall the concept of the height of a formula defined in Definition 1.31. Use mathematical induction on the height of formulas to show that $\text{rank}(\phi)$ is nothing but the height of ϕ for all propositional formulas ϕ.

10. Prove the following sequents needed to secure the completeness result for propositional logic:

  (a) $\phi_1 \wedge \neg\phi_2 \vdash \neg(\phi_1 \rightarrow \phi_2)$
  (b) $\neg\phi_1 \wedge \neg\phi_2 \vdash \phi_1 \rightarrow \phi_2$
  (c) $\neg\phi_1 \wedge \phi_2 \vdash \phi_1 \rightarrow \phi_2$
  (d) $\phi_1 \wedge \phi_2 \vdash \phi_1 \rightarrow \phi_2$
  (e) $\neg\phi_1 \wedge \phi_2 \vdash \neg(\phi_1 \wedge \phi_2)$
  (f) $\neg\phi_1 \wedge \neg\phi_2 \vdash \neg(\phi_1 \wedge \phi_2)$
  (g) $\phi_1 \wedge \neg\phi_2 \vdash \neg(\phi_1 \wedge \phi_2)$
  (h) $\neg\phi_1 \wedge \neg\phi_2 \vdash \neg(\phi_1 \vee \phi_2)$
  (i) $\phi_1 \wedge \phi_2 \vdash \phi_1 \vee \phi_2$
  (j) $\neg\phi_1 \wedge \phi_2 \vdash \phi_1 \vee \phi_2$
  (k) $\phi_1 \wedge \neg\phi_2 \vdash \phi_1 \vee \phi_2.$

11. Do we have $\vDash (p \rightarrow q) \vee (q \rightarrow r)$? Please give precise reasons for your answer.

12. Do we have $(q \rightarrow (p \vee (q \rightarrow p))) \vee \neg(p \rightarrow q) \vDash p$? Please give precise reasons for your answer.

13. Assuming the soundness and completeness of natural deduction for propositional logic, suppose that you need to show that ϕ is *not* a semantic consequence of $\phi_1, \phi_2, \ldots, \phi_n$, but that you are only allowed to base your argument on the use of natural deduction rules. Which sequent would you need to prove in order to guarantee that $\phi_1, \phi_2, \ldots, \phi_n \nvdash \phi$? Do you need completeness *and* soundness for this to work out?

1.5 Normal forms

In the last section, we showed that our proof system for propositional logic is sound and complete for the semantics of formulas with respect to the truth tables in Figure 1.9. Soundness meant that whatever we prove is going to be a true fact, based on the truth-table semantics. In the exercises, we saw that this can be used to show that a sequent does not have a proof: simply show that $\phi_1, \phi_2, \ldots, \phi_2$ does not semantically entail ψ; then soundness implies that the sequent $\phi_1, \phi_2, \ldots, \phi_2 \vdash \psi$ does not have a proof. Completeness comprised a much more powerful statement: no matter what true sequents there are, they all have syntactic proofs in the proof system of natural deduction. This tight correspondence allows us to freely switch between working with the notion of proofs ($\vdash$) and that of truth tables ($\vDash$).

Using natural deduction to decide instances of $\vdash$ is only one of many possibilities. In Exercise 1.6.4 we already sketched a non-linear, tree-like, notion of proofs for sequents. Likewise, just computing the truth tables and then checking an instance of $\vDash$ by means of Definition 1.33 is only one of many ways of deciding whether $\phi_1, \phi_2, \ldots, \phi_n \vDash \psi$ holds. We now investigate various alternatives for deciding $\phi_1, \phi_2, \ldots, \phi_n \vDash \psi$ which are based on transforming these formulas syntactically into 'equivalent' ones upon which we can then settle the matter by purely syntactic means. This necessitates that we first make clear what exactly we mean by equivalent formulas.

1.5.1 Semantic equivalence, satisfiability and validity

Two formulas ϕ and ψ are said to be equivalent if they have the same 'meaning'. This suggestion is vague and needs to be refined. For example, in Exercise 1.8.1 we saw that $p \to q$ and $\neg p \lor q$ have the same truth table; all four combinations of T and F for p and q return the same result. However, 'coincidence of truth tables' is not good enough for what we have in mind. What about the formulas $p \land q \to p$ and $r \lor \neg r$? At first glance, they seem to have little in common, having different atomic formulas and different connectives. Moreover, the truth table for $p \land q \to p$ is four lines long, whereas the one for $r \lor \neg r$ consists of only two lines. However, both formulas are always true. This suggests that we define the equivalence of formulas ϕ and ψ via $\vDash$: if ϕ entails ψ and vice versa, then these formulas should be the same as far as our semantics of truth values is concerned.

Definition 1.39 Let ϕ and ψ be formulas of propositional logic. We say that

ϕ and ψ are *semantically equivalent* iff

$$\phi \vDash \psi$$
$$\psi \vDash \phi$$

hold. In that case we write $\phi \equiv \psi$. Further, we call ϕ *valid* if

$$\vDash \phi$$

holds.

Note that we could just as well have defined $\phi \equiv \psi$ to mean that $\vDash (\phi \to \psi) \wedge (\psi \to \phi)$ holds; it amounts to the same thing. Indeed, because of soundness and completeness, we see that semantic equivalence is identical to *provable equivalence* (Definition 1.25).

Examples of equivalent formulas are

$$p \to q \;\equiv\; \neg q \to \neg p$$
$$p \to q \;\equiv\; \neg p \vee q$$
$$p \wedge q \to p \;\equiv\; r \vee \neg r$$
$$p \wedge q \to r \;\equiv\; p \to (q \to r).$$

Recall that a formula η is called a tautology if $\vDash \eta$, so the tautologies are exactly the valid formulas. The following lemma says that any decision procedure for tautologies is in fact a decision procedure for the validity of sequents as well.

Lemma 1.40 *Given propositional logic formulas* $\phi_1, \phi_2, \ldots, \phi_n, \psi$, *we have*

$$\phi_1, \phi_2, \ldots, \phi_n \vDash \psi$$

iff

$$\vDash \phi_1 \to (\phi_2 \to (\phi_3 \to \cdots \to (\phi_n \to \psi))).$$

PROOF: First, suppose that $\vDash \phi_1 \to (\phi_2 \to (\phi_3 \to \cdots \to (\phi_n \to \psi)))$ holds. If $\phi_1, \phi_2, \ldots, \phi_n$ are all true under some truth assignment, then ψ has to be true as well for that same assignment. Otherwise, $\vDash \phi_1 \to (\phi_2 \to (\phi_3 \to \cdots \to (\phi_n \to \psi)))$ would not hold (compare this with Figure 1.14). Second, if $\phi_1, \phi_2, \ldots, \phi_n \vDash \psi$, we have already shown that $\vDash \phi_1 \to (\phi_2 \to (\phi_3 \to \cdots \to (\phi_n \to \psi)))$ follows in step 1 of our completeness proof. $\qquad\square$

EXERCISES 1.12

1. Show that a formula ϕ is valid iff $\top \equiv \phi$, where $\top$ is an abbreviation for an instance $p \vee \neg p$ of LEM.

2. Which of the following formulas are semantically equivalent to $p \rightarrow (q \vee r)$?

   (a) $q \vee (\neg p \vee r)$
   (b) $q \wedge \neg r \rightarrow p$
   (c) $p \wedge \neg r \rightarrow q$
   (d) $\neg q \wedge \neg r \rightarrow \neg p$.

3. An *adequate set of connectives* is a set such that for every formula there is an equivalent formula with only connectives from that set. For example, the set $\{\neg, \vee\}$ is adequate for propositional logic, because any occurrence of $\vee$ and $\rightarrow$ can be removed by using the equivalences

$$\phi \rightarrow \psi \ \equiv \ \neg\phi \vee \psi$$
$$\phi \wedge \psi \ \equiv \ \neg(\neg\phi \vee \neg\psi).$$

   (a) Show that $\{\neg, \wedge\}$, $\{\neg, \rightarrow\}$ and $\{\rightarrow, \bot\}$ are adequate sets of connectives. (In the latter case, we are treating $\bot$ as a nullary connective.)
   (b) Show that, if $C \subseteq \{\neg, \wedge, \vee, \rightarrow, \bot\}$ is adequate, then $\neg \in C$ or $\bot \in C$. (Hint: suppose C contains neither $\neg$ nor $\bot$ and consider the truth value of a formula ϕ, formed by using only the connectives in C, for a valuation in which every atom is assigned T.)
   (c) Is $\{\leftrightarrow, \neg\}$ adequate? Prove your answer.

———

For our current purposes, we want to transform formulas into ones which don't contain $\rightarrow$ at all and the occurrences of $\wedge$ and $\vee$ are confined to separate layers such that validity checks are easy. This is being done by

1. using the equivalence $\phi \rightarrow \psi \equiv \neg\phi \vee \psi$ to remove all occurrences of $\rightarrow$ from a formula and
2. by proposing a transformation algorithm that takes a formula without any $\rightarrow$ into a *normal form* (still without $\rightarrow$) for which checking validity is easy.

Naturally, we have to specify which forms of formulas we think of as being 'normal'. Again, there are many such notions, but in this text we study only one important one.

Definition 1.41 A *literal* is either an atom p or the negation of an atom $\neg p$. A formula ϕ is in *conjunctive normal form* (CNF) if it is of the form

$$\psi_1 \wedge \psi_2 \wedge \cdots \wedge \psi_n$$

for some $n \geq 1$, such that ψ_i is a literal, or a disjunction of literals, for all $1 \leq i \leq n$.

Examples of formulas in conjunctive normal form are

$$(\neg q \vee p \vee r) \wedge (\neg p \vee r) \wedge q$$

$$(p \vee r) \wedge (\neg p \vee r) \wedge (p \vee \neg r).$$

In the first case, we have $n = 3$; ψ_1 is $\neg q \vee p \vee r$, ψ_2 is $\neg p \vee r$, so both are disjunctions of literals, ψ_3 is the literal q and ϕ equals $\psi_1 \wedge \psi_2 \wedge \psi_3$. Notice how we made implicit use of the associativity laws for $\wedge$ and $\vee$, saying that $\phi \vee (\psi \vee \eta) \equiv (\phi \vee \psi) \vee \eta$ and $\phi \wedge (\psi \wedge \eta) \equiv (\phi \wedge \psi) \wedge \eta$, since we omitted some parentheses. The formula

$$(\neg(q \vee p) \vee r) \wedge (q \vee r)$$

is not in CNF since $q \vee p$ is not a literal.

Why do we care at all about formulas ϕ in CNF? One of the reasons for their usefulness is that they allow easy checks of validity which otherwise take times exponential in the number of atoms. For example, consider the formula in CNF from above: $(\neg q \vee p \vee r) \wedge (\neg p \vee r) \wedge q$. We have

$$\vDash (\neg q \vee p \vee r) \wedge (\neg p \vee r) \wedge q$$

iff we have

$$\vDash \quad \neg q \vee p \vee r$$
$$\vDash \quad \neg p \vee r$$
$$\vDash \quad q$$

at the same time by the semantics of $\wedge$. But since all of these formulas are disjunctions of literals, or literals, we can settle the matter as follows.

Lemma 1.42 *A disjunction of literals $L_1 \vee L_2 \vee \cdots \vee L_m$ is valid (i.e. $\vDash L_1 \vee L_2 \vee \cdots \vee L_m$) iff there are $1 \leq i, j \leq m$ such that L_i is $\neg L_j$.*

PROOF: Clearly, if L_i equals $\neg L_j$, then $L_1 \vee L_2 \vee \cdots \vee L_m$ computes T for all truth value assignments. For example, the disjunct $p \vee q \vee r \vee \neg q$ can never be made false. To see that the converse holds as well, assume that no literal

L_k has a matching negation ($1 \leq k \leq m$). Then we assign F to it, if L_k is an atom, or T, if L_k is the negation of an atom. For example, the disjunct $\neg q \vee p \vee r$ can be made false by assigning F to p and r and T to q. □

Hence, we have an easy and fast check for $\models \phi$, provided that ϕ is in CNF; inspect all conjuncts ψ_k of ϕ and search for atoms in ψ_k such that ψ_k also contains their negation. If such a match is found for all conjuncts, we have $\models \phi$. Otherwise (= some conjunct contains no pair L_i and $\neg L_i$), we have $\nvDash \phi$ by the lemma above. Thus, the formula $(\neg q \vee p \vee r) \wedge (\neg p \vee r) \wedge q$ above is not valid. Note that the matching literal has to be found in the same conjunct ψ_k. Since there is no free lunch in this universe, we can expect that the computation of a formula ϕ' in CNF, which is equivalent to a given formula ϕ, is a very costly operation indeed.

Before we study how to compute such equivalent conjunctive normal forms, we introduce another semantic concept closely related to that of validity.

Definition 1.43 Given a formula ϕ in propositional logic, we say that ϕ is *satisfiable* if there exists an assignment of truth values to its propositional atoms such that ϕ is true.

For example, the formula $p \vee q \rightarrow p$ is satisfiable since it computes T if we assign T to p. Clearly, $p \vee q \rightarrow p$ is not valid. Thus, satisfiability is a weaker concept since every valid formula is by definition also satisfiable but not vice versa. However, these two notions are just mirror images of each other, the mirror being negation.

Proposition 1.44 *Let ϕ be a formula of propositional logic. Then ϕ is satisfiable iff $\neg \phi$ is not valid.*

PROOF: First, assume that ϕ is satisfiable. By definition, there exists an assignment of truth values to its atoms such that ϕ evaluates to T; but that means that $\neg \phi$ evaluates to F. Thus, $\neg \phi$ cannot be valid.

Second, assume that $\neg \phi$ is not valid. Then there must be an assignment of truth values for its atoms such that $\neg \phi$ computes F. Thus, ϕ evaluates to T and is therefore satisfiable. □

This result is extremely useful since it essentially says that we need provide a decision procedure for only one of these concepts. For example, let us say that we have an algorithm for deciding whether any ϕ is valid. From this we obtain a decision procedure for satisfiability simply by asking whether $\neg \phi$ is valid. If it is, then ϕ is not satisfiable; otherwise ϕ is satisfiable. By the same token, we may transform any decision procedure for satisfiability into one for validity. We will encounter both kinds of procedures in this text.

There is one scenario in which computing an equivalent formula in CNF is really easy; namely, when someone else has already done the work of writing down a full truth table for ϕ. For example, take the truth table of $(p \rightarrow \neg q) \rightarrow (q \vee \neg p)$ in Figure 1.11 (page 50). We simply form a disjunction of literals for all lines where $(p \rightarrow \neg q) \rightarrow (q \vee \neg p)$ computes F. Since there is only one such line, we have only one conjunct ψ_1. That conjunct is now obtained by a disjunction of literals, where we include literals $\neg p$ and q. Note that the literals are just the syntactic opposites of the truth values in that line: here p is T and q is F. The resulting formula in CNF is thus

$$\neg p \vee q$$

which is readily seen to be in CNF and to be equivalent to $(p \rightarrow \neg q) \rightarrow (q \vee \neg p)$.

Why does this always work for any formula ϕ? Well, the constructed formula will be false iff at least one of its conjuncts ψ_i will be false. This means that all the disjuncts in such a ψ_i must be F. Using the de Morgan rule $\neg \phi_1 \vee \neg \phi_2 \vee \cdots \vee \neg \phi_n \equiv \neg(\phi_1 \wedge \phi_2 \wedge \cdots \wedge \phi_n)$, we infer that the conjunction of the syntactic opposites of those literals must be true.

Consider another example, in which ϕ is given by the truth table:

p	q	r	ϕ
T	T	T	T
T	T	F	F
T	F	T	T
T	F	F	T
F	T	T	F
F	T	F	F
F	F	T	F
F	F	F	T

Note that this table is really just a specification of ϕ; it does not tell us what ϕ looks like syntactically, but it does tells us how it ought to 'behave'. Since this truth table has four entries which compute F, we have four conjuncts ψ_i $(1 \leq i \leq 4)$. We read the ψ_i off that table by listing the disjunction of all atoms, where we negate those atoms which are true in those lines:

$$\psi_1 \stackrel{\text{def}}{=} \neg p \lor \neg q \lor r \quad \text{(line 2)}$$
$$\psi_2 \stackrel{\text{def}}{=} p \lor \neg q \lor \neg r \quad \text{(line 5)}$$
$$\psi_3 \stackrel{\text{def}}{=} p \lor \neg q \lor r \quad \text{etc.}$$
$$\psi_4 \stackrel{\text{def}}{=} p \lor q \lor \neg r.$$

The resulting ϕ in CNF is therefore

$$(\neg p \lor \neg q \lor r) \land (p \lor \neg q \lor \neg r) \land (p \lor \neg q \lor r) \land (p \lor q \lor \neg r).$$

If we don't have a full truth table at our disposal, but do know the structure of ϕ, then we would like to compute a version of ϕ in CNF. It should be clear by now that a full truth table of ϕ and an equivalent formula in CNF are pretty much the same thing as far as questions about validity are concerned.

EXERCISES 1.13
1. Show that the relation $\equiv$ is *reflexive*: $\phi \equiv \phi$ holds for all ϕ.
2. Show that the relation $\equiv$ is *symmetric*: $\phi \equiv \psi$ implies $\psi \equiv \phi$.
3. Show that the relation $\equiv$ is *transitive*: $\phi \equiv \psi$ and $\psi \equiv \eta$ imply $\phi \equiv \eta$.
4. Show that $\land$ and $\lor$ are *idempotent* with respect to $\equiv$:

    (a) $\phi \land \phi \equiv \phi$
    (b) $\phi \lor \phi \equiv \phi$.

5. Show that $\land$ and $\lor$ are *commutative*:

    (a) $\phi \land \psi \equiv \psi \land \phi$
    (b) $\phi \lor \psi \equiv \psi \lor \phi$.

6. Show that $\land$ and $\lor$ are *associative*:

    (a) $\phi \land (\psi \land \eta) \equiv (\phi \land \psi) \land \eta$
    (b) $\phi \lor (\psi \lor \eta) \equiv (\phi \lor \psi) \lor \eta$.

7. Show that $\land$ and $\lor$ are *absorptive*:

    * (a) $\phi \land (\phi \lor \eta) \equiv \phi$
    (b) $\phi \lor (\phi \land \eta) \equiv \phi$.

8. Show that $\land$ and $\lor$ are *distributive*:

    (a) $\phi \land (\psi \lor \eta) \equiv (\phi \land \psi) \lor (\phi \land \eta)$
    * (b) $\phi \lor (\psi \land \eta) \equiv (\phi \lor \psi) \land (\phi \lor \eta)$.

9. Show that $\equiv$ allows for *double negation*: $\phi \equiv \neg\neg\phi$.
10. Show that $\equiv$ satisfies the *de Morgan rules*:

(a) $\neg(\phi \wedge \psi) \equiv \neg\phi \vee \neg\psi$

* (b) $\neg(\phi \vee \psi) \equiv \neg\phi \wedge \neg\psi.$

11. Consider the grammar in BNF form

$$L ::= p \mid \neg p,$$

where p ranges over propositional atoms. This grammar defines the syntactic category of *literals* (see Definition 1.41). Specify two more such grammars which define the two syntactic categories *disjunctions of literals* (named D and defined in terms of L) and *conjunctive normal forms* (named C and defined in terms of D).

_____

1.5.2 Conjunctive normal forms and validity

We have already seen the benefits of conjunctive normal forms in that they allow for a fast and easy syntactic test of validity. Therefore, one wonders whether any formula can be transformed into an *equivalent* formula in CNF. This is indeed the case; and we now develop an algorithm doing just that. Note that a formula is valid iff any of its equivalent formulas is valid. This is an immediate consequence of Definition 1.39. By Lemma 1.42, we may reduce the problem of determining whether *any* ϕ is valid to the problem of computing an equivalent $\psi \equiv \phi$ such that ψ is in CNF.

Before we sketch such a procedure, we make some general remarks about its possibilities and its realisability constraints. First of all, there could be more or less efficient ways of computing such normal forms. But even more so, there could be many possible correct outputs, for $\psi_1 \equiv \phi$ and $\psi_2 \equiv \phi$ do not generally imply that ψ_1 is the same as ψ_2, even if ψ_1 and ψ_2 are in CNF. For example, take $\phi \stackrel{\text{def}}{=} p$, $\psi_1 \stackrel{\text{def}}{=} p$ and $\psi_2 \stackrel{\text{def}}{=} p \wedge (p \vee q)$. Note that $\phi \equiv \psi_2$ holds because of the absorption law. Having this ambiguity of equivalent conjunctive normal forms, the computation of a CNF for ϕ with minimal 'cost' (where 'cost' could for example be the number of conjuncts, or the height of ϕ's parse tree) becomes a very important practical problem. We will investigate such issues in the final Chapter 6. Right now, we are content with stating a *deterministic* algorithm which always computes the same CNF for a given ϕ, no matter when, or how often, we call it with ϕ as input.

We call this algorithm CNF. It should satisfy the following design constraints:

(1). it takes (a parse tree of) a formula ϕ of propositional logic as input and rewrites it to another formula of propositional logic; such rewrites might call the algorithm CNF recursively;

(2). each computation, or rewrite step, of CNF results in an equivalent formula;

(3). CNF terminates for all inputs ϕ which are formulas of propositional logic; and

(4). the final formula computed by CNF is in CNF.

So if a call of CNF with a formula ϕ of propositional logic as input terminates, which is enforced by (3), then (2) ensures that the output ψ is equivalent to ϕ: $\psi \equiv \phi$. Thus, (4) guarantees that ψ is an equivalent CNF of ϕ.

What kind of strategy should CNF employ? Note that it will have to function correctly for all, i.e. infinitely many, formulas of propositional logic. This strongly suggests that one should write a procedure that computes a CNF by structural induction over the formula ϕ. For example, if ϕ is of the form $\phi_1 \wedge \phi_2$, then we may simply compute conjunctive normal forms η_i for ϕ_i ($i = 1, 2$), whereupon $\eta_1 \wedge \eta_2$ is a conjunctive normal form which is equivalent to ϕ *provided that* $\eta_i \equiv \phi_i$ ($i = 1, 2$). This strategy also suggests that one should use proof by induction on the height of ϕ to prove that CNF has the properties stated above.

Given a formula ϕ as input, we first do some *preprocessing*.

- Initially, we translate away all implications in ϕ by replacing all subformulas of the form $\psi \rightarrow \eta$ by $\neg \psi \vee \eta$. This is done by a procedure called IMPL_FREE. Note that this procedure has to be recursive, for there might well be nested implications in ψ and η.

- The application of IMPL_FREE might introduce double negations into the output formula. More importantly, negations whose scopes are non-atomic formulas might still be present. For example, the formula $p \wedge \neg(p \wedge q)$ has such a negation with $p \wedge q$ as its scope. Essentially, the question is this: how do we compute a CNF for $\neg \phi$ if we know a CNF for ϕ? This is a nasty question and we circumvent it by translating $\neg \phi$ into an equivalent formula that contains only negations of atoms. Formulas which only negate atoms are said to be in *negation normal form* (NNF). We spell out such a procedure, NNF, in detail later on. The key to its specification for implication-free formulas lies in the de Morgan rules. The second phase of the preprocessing, therefore, calls NNF with the implication-free output of IMPL_FREE to obtain an equivalent formula in NNF.

After these initial preparations, we obtain a formula ϕ' which is the result of the call

$$\text{NNF}\,(\text{IMPL\_FREE}\,(\phi)).$$

Note that $\phi' \equiv \phi$ since both algorithms only transform formulas into equivalent ones. Since ϕ' contains no occurrences of $\rightarrow$ and since only atoms in ϕ' are negated, we may program CNF by an analysis of only *three* cases: literals, conjunctions and disjunctions.

- If ϕ is a literal, then it is by definition in CNF. In that case, we leave ϕ untouched.
- If ϕ equals $\phi_1 \wedge \phi_2$, then we already remarked above that we may compute an equivalent CNF for ϕ by computing equivalent conjunctive normal forms η_i for ϕ_i; then $\eta_1 \wedge \eta_2$ will be an equivalent CNF for ϕ.
- If ϕ equals $\phi_1 \vee \phi_2$, we again compute conjunctive normal forms η_i for ϕ_i; but this time we must not simply return $\eta_1 \vee \eta_2$ since that formula is certainly *not* in CNF, unless η_1 and η_2 happen to be literals. What now? Well, we may resort to the distributivity laws, which entitle us to translate any disjunction of conjunctions into a conjunction of disjunctions. However, for this to result in a CNF, we need to make certain that those disjunctions generated contain only literals. We apply a strategy for using distributivity based on matching patterns in $\phi_1 \vee \phi_2$. This results in an independent algorithm called DISTR which will do all that work for us. Thus, we simply call DISTR with the pair (η_1, η_2) as input and pass along its result.

Assuming that we already have written code for IMPL_FREE, NNF and DISTR, we may now write pseudo code for CNF:

> **function** CNF (ϕ) :
> /* precondition: ϕ implication free and in NNF */
> /* postcondition: CNF (ϕ) computes an equivalent CNF for ϕ */
> **begin function**
>   **case**
> ϕ is a literal : **return** ϕ
> ϕ is $\phi_1 \wedge \phi_2$: **return** CNF $(\phi_1) \wedge$ CNF (ϕ_2)
> ϕ is $\phi_1 \vee \phi_2$: **return** DISTR (CNF (ϕ_1), CNF (ϕ_2))
>   **end case**
> **end function**

Notice how the calling of DISTR is done with the computed conjunctive normal forms of ϕ_1 and ϕ_2. The routine DISTR has η_1 and η_2 as formal input parameters and does a case analysis on whether these inputs are conjunctions. What should DISTR do if none of its input formulas is such a conjunction? Well, since we are calling DISTR for inputs η_1 and η_2 which are in CNF, this can only mean that η_1 and η_2 are literals, or disjunctions of literals. Thus, $\eta_1 \vee \eta_2$ is in CNF.

Otherwise, at least one of the formulas η_1 and η_2 is a conjunction. Since one conjunction suffices for simplifying the problem, we have to decide which conjunct we want to transform if *both* formulas are conjunctions. That way we maintain that our algorithm CNF is deterministic.

So let us suppose that η_1 is of the form $\eta_{11} \wedge \eta_{12}$. Then the distributive law says that

$$\eta_1 \vee \eta_2 \equiv (\eta_{11} \vee \eta_2) \wedge (\eta_{12} \vee \eta_2).$$

Since all participating formulas (η_{11}, η_{12} and η_2) are in CNF, we may call DISTR again for the pairs (η_{11}, η_2) and (η_{12}, η_2), and then simply form their conjunction. This is the key insight for writing the function DISTR. The case when η_2 is a disjunction is symmetric and the structure of the recursive call of DISTR is then dictated by the equivalence

$$\eta_1 \vee \eta_2 \equiv (\eta_1 \vee \eta_{21}) \wedge (\eta_1 \vee \eta_{22}),$$

if $\eta_2 = \eta_{21} \wedge \eta_{22}$.

> **function** DISTR (η_1, η_2) :
> /* precondition: η_1 and η_2 are in CNF */
> /* postcondition: DISTR (η_1, η_2) computes a CNF for $\eta_1 \vee \eta_2$ */
> **begin function**
> > **case**
> > > η_1 is $\eta_{11} \wedge \eta_{12}$: **return** DISTR $(\eta_{11}, \eta_2) \wedge$ DISTR (η_{12}, η_2)
> > > η_2 is $\eta_{21} \wedge \eta_{22}$: **return** DISTR $(\eta_1, \eta_{21}) \wedge$ DISTR (η_1, η_{22})
> > > otherwise (= no conjunctions) : **return** $\eta_1 \vee \eta_2$
> > **end case**
> **end function**

Notice how the three clauses are exhausting all possibilities. Furthermore, the first and second cases overlap if η_1 and η_2 are both conjunctions. It is then our understanding that this code will inspect the clauses of a case statement from the top to the bottom clause. Thus, the first clause would apply.

Having specified the routines CNF and DISTR, this leaves us with the task of writing the functions IMPL_FREE and NNF. We delegate the design of IMPL_FREE to the exercises. The function NNF has to transform any implication-free formula into an equivalent one in negation normal form. Some examples of formulas in NNF are

$$p$$

$$\neg p$$

$$\neg p \wedge (p \wedge q)$$

$$\neg p \wedge (p \rightarrow q),$$

although we won't have to deal with a formula of the last kind since $\rightarrow$ won't occur. Examples of formulas which are not in NNF are $\neg\neg p$ and $\neg(p \wedge q)$. Again, we program NNF recursively by a case analysis over the structure of the input formula ϕ. The last two examples already suggest a solution for two of these clauses. In order to compute a NNF of $\neg\neg\phi$, we simply compute a NNF of ϕ. This is a sound strategy since ϕ and $\neg\neg\phi$ are semantically equivalent. If ϕ equals $\neg(\phi_1 \wedge \phi_2)$, then we use the de Morgan rule

$$\neg(\phi_1 \wedge \phi_2) \equiv \neg\phi_1 \vee \neg\phi_2$$

as a recipe for how NNF should call itself recursively in that case. Dually, the case of ϕ being $\neg(\phi_1 \vee \phi_2)$ appeals to the other de Morgan rule

$$\neg(\phi_1 \vee \phi_2) \equiv \neg\phi_1 \wedge \neg\phi_2$$

and, if ϕ is a conjunction or disjunction, we simply let NNF pass control to those subformulas. Clearly, all literals are in NNF. The resulting code for NNF is thus

function NNF (ϕ) :

/* precondition: ϕ is implication free */

/* postcondition: NNF (ϕ) computes a NNF for ϕ */

begin function

    case

        ϕ is a literal : **return** ϕ

        ϕ is $\neg\neg\phi_1$: **return** NNF (ϕ_1)

        ϕ is $\phi_1 \wedge \phi_2$: **return** NNF $(\phi_1) \wedge$ NNF (ϕ_2)

        ϕ is $\phi_1 \vee \phi_2$: **return** NNF $(\phi_1) \vee$ NNF (ϕ_2)

        ϕ is $\neg(\phi_1 \wedge \phi_2)$: **return** NNF $(\neg\phi_1 \vee \neg\phi_2)$

        ϕ is $\neg(\phi_1 \vee \phi_2)$: **return** NNF $(\neg\phi_1 \wedge \neg\phi_2)$

    end case

    end function

Notice that these cases are exhaustive due to the algorithm's precondition. Given any formula ϕ of propositional logic, we may now convert it into an equivalent CNF by calling

$$\text{CNF (NNF (IMPL\_FREE} (\phi))).$$

In the exercises, you are asked to show that
- all algorithms terminate on input meeting their preconditions,
- the result of $\text{CNF (NNF (IMPL\_FREE} (\phi)))$ is in CNF and
- that result is semantically equivalent to ϕ.

We will return to the important issue of formally proving the correctness of programs in Chapter 4.

Let us now illustrate the programs coded above on some concrete examples. We begin by computing the conjunctive normal form of ϕ, defined to be $\neg p \wedge q \rightarrow p \wedge (r \rightarrow q)$. We show almost all details of this computation and you should compare this with how you would expect the code above to behave. First, we compute IMPL_FREE ϕ:

$$
\begin{aligned}
\text{IMPL\_FREE } \phi &= \neg\text{IMPL\_FREE} (\neg p \wedge q) \vee \text{IMPL\_FREE} (p \wedge (r \rightarrow q)) \\
&= \neg((\text{IMPL\_FREE } \neg p) \wedge (\text{IMPL\_FREE } q)) \vee \text{IMPL\_FREE} (p \wedge (r \rightarrow q)) \\
&= \neg((\neg p) \wedge \text{IMPL\_FREE } q) \vee \text{IMPL\_FREE} (p \wedge (r \rightarrow q)) \\
&= \neg(\neg p \wedge q) \vee \text{IMPL\_FREE} (p \wedge (r \rightarrow q)) \\
&= \neg(\neg p \wedge q) \vee ((\text{IMPL\_FREE } p) \wedge \text{IMPL\_FREE} (r \rightarrow q)) \\
&= \neg(\neg p \wedge q) \vee (p \wedge \text{IMPL\_FREE} (r \rightarrow q)) \\
&= \neg(\neg p \wedge q) \vee (p \wedge (\neg(\text{IMPL\_FREE } r) \vee (\text{IMPL\_FREE } q))) \\
&= \neg(\neg p \wedge q) \vee (p \wedge (\neg r \vee (\text{IMPL\_FREE } q))) \\
&= \neg(\neg p \wedge q) \vee (p \wedge (\neg r \vee q)).
\end{aligned}
$$

Second, we compute NNF (IMPL_FREE ϕ):

$$
\begin{aligned}
\text{NNF (IMPL\_FREE } \phi) &= \text{NNF} (\neg(\neg p \wedge q)) \vee \text{NNF} (p \wedge (\neg r \vee q)) \\
&= \text{NNF} (\neg(\neg p) \vee \neg q) \vee \text{NNF} (p \wedge (\neg r \vee q)) \\
&= (\text{NNF} (\neg\neg p)) \vee (\text{NNF} (\neg q)) \vee \text{NNF} (p \wedge (\neg r \vee q)) \\
&= (p \vee (\text{NNF} (\neg q))) \vee \text{NNF} (p \wedge (\neg r \vee q)) \\
&= (p \vee \neg q) \vee \text{NNF} (p \wedge (\neg r \vee q)) \\
&= (p \vee \neg q) \vee ((\text{NNF } p) \wedge (\text{NNF} (\neg r \vee q))) \\
&= (p \vee \neg q) \vee (p \wedge (\text{NNF} (\neg r \vee q))) \\
&= (p \vee \neg q) \vee (p \wedge ((\text{NNF} (\neg r)) \vee (\text{NNF } q))) \\
&= (p \vee \neg q) \vee (p \wedge (\neg r \vee (\text{NNF } q))) \\
&= (p \vee \neg q) \vee (p \wedge (\neg r \vee q)).
\end{aligned}
$$

Third, we finish it off with

$$
\begin{aligned}
\text{CNF (NNF (IMPL\_FREE } \phi)) \ &= \ \text{CNF} ((p \vee \neg q) \vee (p \wedge (\neg r \vee q))) \\
&= \ \text{DISTR (CNF } (p \vee \neg q), \text{CNF } (p \wedge (\neg r \vee q))) \\
&= \ \text{DISTR } (p \vee \neg q, \text{CNF } (p \wedge (\neg r \vee q))) \\
&= \ \text{DISTR } (p \vee \neg q, p \wedge (\neg r \vee q)) \\
&= \ \text{DISTR } (p \vee \neg q, p) \wedge \text{DISTR } (p \vee \neg q, \neg r \vee q) \\
&= \ (p \vee \neg q \vee p) \wedge \text{DISTR } (p \vee \neg q, \neg r \vee q) \\
&= \ (p \vee \neg q \vee p) \wedge (p \vee \neg q \vee \neg r \vee q).
\end{aligned}
$$

The formula $(p \vee \neg q \vee p) \wedge (p \vee \neg q \vee \neg r \vee q)$ is thus the result of the call CNF (NNF (IMPL_FREE ϕ)) and is in conjunctive normal form and equivalent to ϕ. Note that it is satisfiable (choose p to be true) but not valid (choose p to be false and q to be true); it is also equivalent to the simpler conjunctive normal form $p \vee \neg q$. Observe that our algorithm does not do such optimisations so one would need a separate optimiser running on the output, or one might change the code of our functions to allow for such optimisations 'on the fly'. This could, however, introduce significant computational overhead.

You should realise that we omitted several computation steps in the subcalls CNF $(p \vee \neg q)$ and CNF $(p \wedge (\neg r \vee q))$. They return their input as a result since the input is already in conjunctive normal form. Incidentally, you can show by mathematical induction on the height of ϕ's parse tree that the call CNF (NNF (IMPL_FREE ϕ)) returns ϕ if ϕ is already in CNF.

As a second example, consider $\phi \stackrel{\text{def}}{=} r \to (s \to (t \wedge s \to r))$. We compute

$$
\begin{aligned}
\text{IMPL\_FREE } \phi \ &= \ \neg(\text{IMPL\_FREE } r) \vee \text{IMPL\_FREE } (s \to (t \wedge s \to r)) \\
&= \ \neg r \vee \text{IMPL\_FREE } (s \to (t \wedge s \to r)) \\
&= \ \neg r \vee (\neg(\text{IMPL\_FREE } s) \vee \text{IMPL\_FREE } (t \wedge s \to r)) \\
&= \ \neg r \vee (\neg s \vee \text{IMPL\_FREE } (t \wedge s \to r)) \\
&= \ \neg r \vee (\neg s \vee (\neg(\text{IMPL\_FREE } (t \wedge s)) \vee \text{IMPL\_FREE } r)) \\
&= \ \neg r \vee (\neg s \vee (\neg((\text{IMPL\_FREE } t) \wedge (\text{IMPL\_FREE } s)) \vee \text{IMPL\_FREE } r)) \\
&= \ \neg r \vee (\neg s \vee (\neg(t \wedge (\text{IMPL\_FREE } s)) \vee (\text{IMPL\_FREE } r))) \\
&= \ \neg r \vee (\neg s \vee (\neg(t \wedge s)) \vee (\text{IMPL\_FREE } r)) \\
&= \ \neg r \vee (\neg s \vee (\neg(t \wedge s)) \vee r).
\end{aligned}
$$

$$\text{NNF (IMPL\_FREE } \phi) \;=\; \text{NNF } (\neg r \vee (\neg s \vee \neg(t \wedge s) \vee r))$$

$$= \; (\text{NNF } \neg r) \vee \text{NNF } (\neg s \vee \neg(t \wedge s) \vee r)$$

$$= \; \neg r \vee \text{NNF } (\neg s \vee \neg(t \wedge s) \vee r)$$

$$= \; \neg r \vee (\text{NNF } (\neg s) \vee \text{NNF } (\neg(t \wedge s) \vee r))$$

$$= \; \neg r \vee (\neg s \vee \text{NNF } (\neg(t \wedge s) \vee r))$$

$$= \; \neg r \vee (\neg s \vee (\text{NNF } (\neg(t \wedge s)) \vee \text{NNF } r))$$

$$= \; \neg r \vee (\neg s \vee (\text{NNF } (\neg t \vee \neg s)) \vee \text{NNF } r)$$

$$= \; \neg r \vee (\neg s \vee ((\text{NNF } (\neg t) \vee \text{NNF } (\neg s)) \vee \text{NNF } r))$$

$$= \; \neg r \vee (\neg s \vee ((\neg t \vee \text{NNF } (\neg s)) \vee \text{NNF } r))$$

$$= \; \neg r \vee (\neg s \vee ((\neg t \vee \neg s) \vee \text{NNF } r))$$

$$= \; \neg r \vee (\neg s \vee ((\neg t \vee \neg s) \vee r)) \tag{1.4}$$

which is already in CNF and valid.

EXERCISES 1.14

1. Construct a formula in CNF based on each of the following truth tables:

  * (a)

p	q	ϕ_1
T	T	F
F	T	F
T	F	F
F	F	T

  * (b)

p	q	r	ϕ_2
T	T	T	T
T	T	F	F
T	F	T	F
T	F	F	F
F	T	T	T
F	T	F	F
F	F	T	T
F	F	F	F

(c)

r	s	q	ϕ_3
T	T	T	F
T	T	F	T
T	F	T	F
T	F	F	T
F	T	T	F
F	T	F	F
F	F	T	F
F	F	F	T

* 2. Write a recursive function IMPL_FREE which expects a (parse tree of a) propositional formula as input and produces an equivalent formula as output such that the result contains no implications. How many clauses does your case statement need? Recall Definition 1.27 on page 39.

* 3. Use your algorithm IMPL_FREE together with the functions NNF and CNF to compute CNF (NNF (IMPL_FREE ϕ)), where ϕ is the formula $\neg(p \to (\neg(q \land (\neg p \to q))))$.

4. Use mathematical induction on the height of ϕ to show that the call CNF (NNF (IMPL_FREE ϕ)) returns ϕ if the latter is already in CNF.

5. Why do the functions CNF and DISTR preserve NNF and why is this important?

6. Reason why the result of CNF (NNF (IMPL_FREE (ϕ))) is a formula in CNF.

7. Convince yourself of the fact that CNF (NNF (IMPL_FREE (ϕ))) is semantically equivalent to ϕ.

8. Explain why the call CNF(NNF(IMPL_FREE ϕ)) terminates and computes a formula in CNF which is equivalent to ϕ.

1.5.3 *Horn clauses and satisfiability*

We have already commented on the computational price we pay for transforming a propositional logic formula into an equivalent CNF. The latter class of formulas had a very easy check for validity, but its test for satisfiability is very hard in general. Fortunately, there are practically important subclasses of formulas which have much more efficient ways of deciding their satisfiability. One such example is the class of *Horn formulas*; the name

'Horn' is derived from the logician A. Horn's last name. We shortly define them and give an algorithm for checking their satisfiability.

Recall that the logical constants $\bot$ ('bottom') and $\top$ ('top') denote an unsatisfiable formula, respectively, a tautology.

Definition 1.45 A *Horn formula* is a formula ϕ of propositional logic if it is of the form $\psi_1 \wedge \psi_2 \wedge \cdots \wedge \psi_n$ for some $n \geq 1$ such that each ψ_i is of the form

$$p_1 \wedge p_2 \wedge \cdots \wedge p_{k_i} \to q_i$$

for some $k_i \geq 1$, where $p_1, p_2, \ldots, p_{k_i}, q_i$ are atoms, $\bot$, or $\top$. We call each ψ_i a *Horn clause*.

Examples of Horn formulas are

$$(p \wedge q \wedge s \to p) \wedge (q \wedge r \to p) \wedge (p \wedge s \to s)$$

$$(p \wedge q \wedge s \to \bot) \wedge (q \wedge r \to p) \wedge (\top \to s)$$

$$(p_2 \wedge p_3 \wedge p_5 \to p_{13}) \wedge (\top \to p_5) \wedge (p_5 \wedge p_{11} \to \bot).$$

Examples of formulas which are *not* Horn formulas are

$$(p \wedge q \wedge s \to \neg p) \wedge (q \wedge r \to p) \wedge (p \wedge s \to s)$$

$$(p \wedge q \wedge s \to \bot) \wedge (\neg q \wedge r \to p) \wedge (\top \to s)$$

$$(p_2 \wedge p_3 \wedge p_5 \to p_{13} \wedge p_{27}) \wedge (\top \to p_5) \wedge (p_5 \wedge p_{11} \to \bot)$$

$$(p_2 \wedge p_3 \wedge p_5 \to p_{13} \wedge p_{27}) \wedge (\top \to p_5) \wedge (p_5 \wedge p_{11} \vee \bot).$$

The first formula is not a Horn formula since $\neg p$, the conclusion of the implication of the first conjunct, is not an atom, $\bot$, or $\top$. The second formula does not qualify since the premise of the implication of the second conjunct, $\neg q \wedge r$, is not a conjunction of atoms, $\bot$, or $\top$. The third formula is not a Horn formula since the conclusion of the implication of the first conjunct, $p_{13} \wedge p_{27}$, is not an atom, $\bot$, or $\top$. The fourth formula clearly is not a Horn formula since it is not a conjunction of implications.

The algorithm we propose for deciding the satisfiability of a Horn formula ϕ proceeds like this:

1. It marks all atoms p whenever $\top \to p$ is a subformula of ϕ.

2. If there is a subformula $p_1 \wedge p_2 \wedge \cdots \wedge p_{k_i} \rightarrow \bot$ of ϕ such that all p_j with $1 \leq j \leq k_i$ are marked, then go to 3. Otherwise, if there is a subformula $p_1 \wedge p_2 \wedge \cdots \wedge p_{k_i} \rightarrow q_i$ in ϕ with $q_i \not\equiv \bot$ such that all p_j with $1 \leq j \leq k_i$ are marked, then mark q_i as well and go to 2. Otherwise (= there is no subformula $p_1 \wedge p_2 \wedge \cdots \wedge p_{k_i} \rightarrow \bot$ or $p_1 \wedge p_2 \wedge \cdots \wedge p_{k_i} \rightarrow q_i$ such that all p_j are marked) go to 4.

3. Print out 'The Horn formula ϕ is unsatisfiable.' and stop.

4. Print out 'The Horn formula ϕ is satisfiable.' and stop.

It should be understood that such markings of an atom p are *shared* by all other occurrences of p in the Horn formula. Once we mark p because of one of the criteria above, then all other p are marked as well.

Let us make this algorithm more formal by writing some pseudo-code for it:

function HORN (ϕ):
/* precondition: ϕ is a Horn formula */
/* postcondition: HORN (ϕ) decides the satisfiability for ϕ */
begin function
        mark all atoms p where $\top \rightarrow p$ is a subformula of ϕ;
        while there is a subformula $p_1 \wedge p_2 \wedge \cdots \wedge p_{k_i} \rightarrow q_i$ of ϕ
           such that all p_j are marked but q_i isn't **do**
           if $q_i \equiv \bot$ **then return** 'unsatisfiable'
               else mark q_i for all such subformulas
        end while
      return 'satisfiable'
end function

We need to make sure that this algorithm terminates on all Horn formulas ϕ as input and that its output (= its decision) is correct.

Theorem 1.46 *The algorithm* HORN *is correct for the satisfiability decision problem of Horn formulas and has no more than n cycles in its while-loop if n is the number of atoms in* ϕ. *In particular,* HORN *always terminates on correct input.*

PROOF: Let us first consider the question of program termination. Notice that entering the body of the while-loop has two possible effects: the program terminates with the reply 'unsatisfiable', or an additional atom is marked. Since this marking is done for *all* matching subformulas $p_1 \wedge p_2 \wedge \cdots \wedge p_{k_i} \rightarrow q_i$, the while-loop cannot possibly have more cycles than there are atoms in p.

Since we guaranteed termination, it suffices to show that the answers given by the algorithm HORN are always correct. To that end, it helps to reveal the functional role of those markings. Essentially, marking an atom means that that atom has got to be true if the formula ϕ is ever going to be satisfiable.

We now reason, by mathematical induction on the number of actual cycles of the while-loop above, that all marked atoms have to be true if ϕ ever computes T.

The base case is when the while-loop is never entered since its condition is not true initially. In that case, we need to show that all the markings made in the first line of the algorithm are correct. In that line we mark all atoms p where $\top \to p$ is a subformula of ϕ. Since ϕ is a Horn formula, we conclude that $\top \to p$ must be one of its principal conjuncts ψ_i. Therefore, $\top \to p$ has to be true if ϕ should compute T. Using the truth table for implication together with the understanding that $\top$ is always true, we see that p has to be true as well.

In the inductive step, we assume that all the marked atoms obtained after k cycles of the while-loop are correct in the sense that all marked atoms have to be true whenever ϕ should compute T. Then we need to show that same assertion for atoms after $k+1$ cycles. If we enter the $(k+1)$th cycle, the condition of the while-loop is certainly true. Thus, there exists a subformula $p_1 \wedge p_2 \wedge \cdots \wedge p_{k_i} \to q_i$ of ϕ such that all p_j are marked. By our induction hypothesis, we know that all these p_j have to be true if ϕ is ever going to compute T. The body of that while-loop now consists of two cases. First, if q_i is $\bot$, then we know that $p_1 \wedge p_2 \wedge \cdots \wedge p_{k_i} \to \bot$ is one of the principal conjuncts of ϕ since ϕ is a Horn formula. In particular, it has to be true if ϕ is true; but since all p_j have to be true, we see that $p_1 \wedge p_2 \wedge \cdots \wedge p_{k_i} \to \bot$ is false since $\top \to F = F$. Therefore, ϕ could never be true and the reply 'unsatisfiable' is correct. The other case is, of course, when q_i equals $\top$ or some atom q. Again, since all p_j are marked, they have to be true which forces q_i to be true as well, for $p_1 \wedge p_2 \wedge \cdots \wedge p_{k_i} \to q_i$ has to be true. Thus, marking q_i maintains the property that all marked atoms have to be true under any assignment for which ϕ is true.

This concludes the argument by mathematical induction and we now know that, upon exiting the while-loop based on a false while conditional, all marked atoms have to be true if ϕ is satisfiable, no matter how many cycles that loop went through.

Finally, we need to make sure that ϕ is indeed satisfiable if the condition for (re-)entering the body of the while-loop is not met. This is where the markings turn into an assignment of truth values to atoms. After the call HORN (ϕ) terminates with 'ϕ is satisfiable', we simply assign T to all marked atoms and F to all unmarked atoms. We claim that ϕ has to be true with respect to that assignment. Using the flow of control of the algorithm HORN, we reason by proof by contradiction. If ϕ is *not* true under that assignment, then one of its principal conjuncts $p_1 \wedge p_2 \wedge \cdots \wedge p_{k_i} \to q_i$ has to be false. By the semantics of implication this can only mean that all p_j are true and q_i is false. By the definition of our assignment, we then infer that all p_j are marked, so $p_1 \wedge p_2 \wedge \cdots \wedge p_{k_i} \to q_i$ is a subformula of ϕ that would have been dealt with in one of the cycles of the while-loop; but q_i cannot be $\bot$, for in that case the program would have returned 'unsatisfiable' and stopped. Thus, q_i would have been marked in the body of the while-loop and, by the definition of our assignment of truth values, this means that q_i is true. Therefore, ϕ has to be true under that very assignment.   □

Note that the proof by contradiction employed in the last proof was not really needed. It just made the argument seem more natural to us. The literature is full of such examples where one uses proof by contradiction more out of psychological than proof-theoretical necessity.

EXERCISES 1.15
1. Show that all the algorithms presented in this section terminate on any input meeting their precondition. Can you formalise some of your arguments? Note that such a formal termination proof has to take into account that algorithms might not call themselves again on formulas with *smaller* height. E.g. the call of NNF $(\neg(\phi_1 \wedge \phi_2))$ results in a call NNF $(\neg\phi_1 \vee \neg\phi_2)$ but $\neg(\phi_1 \wedge \phi_2)$ and $\neg\phi_1 \vee \neg\phi_2$ have the same height. Why is this not a problem if you count the nestings of negation instead in an appropriate way?

2. Apply the informal description of the algorithm above to the following Horn formulas:
   (a) $(p \wedge q \wedge w \to \bot) \wedge (t \to \bot) \wedge (r \to p) \wedge (\top \to r) \wedge (\top \to q) \wedge (u \to s) \wedge (\top \to u)$
   (b) $(p \wedge q \wedge w \to \bot) \wedge (t \to \bot) \wedge (r \to p) \wedge (\top \to r) \wedge (\top \to q) \wedge (r \wedge u \to w) \wedge (u \to s) \wedge (\top \to u)$
   (c) $(p \wedge q \wedge s \to p) \wedge (q \wedge r \to p) \wedge (p \wedge s \to s)$
   (d) $(p \wedge q \wedge s \to \bot) \wedge (q \wedge r \to p) \wedge (\top \to s)$
   (e) $(p_5 \to p_{11}) \wedge (p_2 \wedge p_3 \wedge p_5 \to p_{13}) \wedge (\top \to p_5) \wedge (p_5 \wedge p_{11} \to \bot)$
   (f) $(\top \to q) \wedge (\top \to s) \wedge (w \to \bot) \wedge (p \wedge q \wedge s \to \bot) \wedge (v \to s) \wedge (\top \to r) \wedge (r \to p)$
   (g) $(\top \to q) \wedge (\top \to s) \wedge (w \to \bot) \wedge (p \wedge q \wedge s \to v) \wedge (v \to s) \wedge (\top \to r) \wedge (r \to p)$.

3. Explain why the algorithm HORN fails to work correctly if we extend

the concept of Horn formulas such that all atoms in $p_1 \wedge p_2 \wedge \cdots \wedge p_{k_i} \rightarrow q_i$ could be literals?

4. What can you say about the CNF of Horn formulas. More precisely, can you specify syntactic criteria for a CNF that ensure that there is an equivalent Horn formula? Can you describe informally programs which would translate from one form of representation into another?

5. Can you use BNF grammars to formally define the syntactic category of Horn formulas? Which auxiliary syntactic categories do you need?

——

1.6 Bibliographic notes

Logic has a long history stretching back at least 2000 years, but the truth-value semantics of propositional logic presented in this and every logic textbook today was invented only about 160 years ago, by G. Boole [Boo54]. Boole used the symbols $+$ and $\cdot$ for disjunction and conjunction.

Natural deduction was invented by G. Gentzen [Gen69], and further developed by D. Prawitz [Pra65]. Other proof systems existed before then, notably axiomatic systems which present a small number of axioms together with the rule *modus ponens* (which we call $\rightarrow$e). Proof systems often present as small a number of axioms as possible; and only for an adequate set of connectives such as $\rightarrow$ and $\neg$. This makes them hard to use in practice. Gentzen improved the situation by inventing the idea of working with assumptions (used by the rules $\rightarrow$i, $\neg$i and $\vee$e) and by treating all the connectives separately.

Further historical remarks, and also pointers to other contemporary books about propositional and predicate logic, can be found in the bibliographic remarks at the end of Chapter 2. For an introduction to algorithms and data structures see e.g. [Wei98].

2

Predicate logic

2.1 The need for a richer language

In the first chapter, we developed propositional logic by examining it from three different angles: its proof theory (the natural deduction calculus), its syntax (the tree-like nature of formulas) and its semantics (what these formulas actually mean). From the outset, this enterprise was guided by the study of declarative sentences, statements about the world which can, in principle, be given a truth value.

We begin this second chapter by pointing out the limitations of propositional logic with respect to encoding purely declarative sentences. Propositional logic dealt quite satisfactorily with sentence components like *not*, *and*, *or* and *if ... then*, but the logical aspects of natural and artificial languages are much richer than that. What can we do with modifiers like *there exists ... , all ... , among ...* and *only ...* ? Here, propositional logic shows clear limitations and the desire to express more subtle declarative sentences led to the design of *predicate logic*, which is also called *first-order logic*.

Let us consider the declarative sentence

Every student is younger than some instructor.

In propositional logic, we could identify this assertion with a propositional atom *p*. However, that is a rather crude way of reflecting the finer logical structure of this sentence. What is this statement about? Well, it is about *being a student*, *being an instructor* and *being younger than somebody else*. These are all properties of some sort, so we would like to have a mechanism for expressing them together with their logical relationships and dependences. We now use *predicates* for that purpose. For example, we could write

$$S(andy)$$

to denote that Andy is a student and

$$I(paul)$$

to say that Paul is an instructor. Likewise,

$$Y(andy, paul)$$

could mean that Andy is younger than Paul. The symbols S, I and Y are called predicates. Of course, we have to be clear about their meaning. The predicate Y could also mean that the second person is younger than the first one, so we need to specify exactly what these symbols refer to.

Having such predicates at our disposal, we still need to formalise those parts of the sentence above which speak of *every* and *some*. Obviously, this sentence refers to the individuals that make up some academic community (left implicit by the sentence), like Kansas State University or the University of Birmingham, and it says that for each student among them there is an instructor among them such that the student is younger than the instructor.

These predicates are not yet enough to allow us to express the sentence 'Every student is younger than some instructor'. We don't really want to write down all instances of $S(\cdot)$ where $\cdot$ is replaced by every student's name in turn. Similarly, when trying to codify a sentence having to do with the execution of a program, it would be rather laborious to have to write down every state of the computer. Therefore, we employ the concept of a *variable*. Variables are written

$$x, y, z, \ldots \qquad \text{or} \qquad x_1, x_2, x_3, \ldots$$

and can be thought of as *place holders* for concrete values (like a student, or a program state). Using variables, we can now specify the meanings of S, I and Y more formally:

$$S(x): \qquad x \text{ is a student}$$
$$I(x): \qquad x \text{ is an instructor}$$
$$Y(x, y): \qquad x \text{ is younger than } y.$$

Note that the names of the variables are not important, provided that we use them consistently. We can state the intended meaning of I by writing

$$I(y): \qquad y \text{ is an instructor}$$

or, equivalently, by writing

$$I(x): \qquad x \text{ is an instructor.}$$

Variables are mere place holders for objects. The availability of variables is still not sufficient for capturing the essence of the example sentence above. We need to convey the meaning of

> **Every** *student x is younger than* **some** *instructor y.*

This is where we need to introduce *quantifiers*

$$\forall \qquad \text{(read: 'for all')}$$

$$\exists \qquad \text{(read: 'there exists')}$$

which always come attached to a variable, as in $\forall x$ ('for all x') or in $\exists z$ ('there exists z', or 'there is some z'). Now we can write the example sentence in an entirely symbolic way as

$$\forall x\,(S(x) \to (\exists y\,(I(y) \land Y(x,y)))).$$

Actually, this encoding is rather a paraphrase of the original sentence. In our example, the re-translation results in

For every x, if x is a student, then there is some y which is an instructor such that x is younger than y.

Different predicates can have a different number of arguments. The predicates S and I have just one (they are called *unary predicates*), but predicate Y requires two arguments (it is called a *binary predicate*). Predicates with any finite number of arguments are possible in predicate logic.

Another example is the sentence

> *Not all birds can fly.*

For that we choose the predicates B and F which have one argument expressing

$$B(x): \qquad x \text{ is a bird}$$
$$F(x): \qquad x \text{ can fly.}$$

The sentence 'Not all birds can fly' can now be coded as

$$\neg(\forall x\,(B(x) \to F(x)))$$

saying: 'It is not the case that all things which are birds can fly.'. Alternatively, we could code this as

$$\exists x\,(B(x) \land \neg F(x))$$

meaning: 'There is some x which is a bird and cannot fly.'. Note that the first version is closer to the linguistic structure of the sentence above. These two formulas should evaluate to T in the world we currently live in since, for example, penguins are birds which cannot fly. Shortly, we address how such formulas can be given their meaning in general. We will also explain why formulas like the two above are indeed equivalent *semantically*.

Coding up complex facts expressed in English sentences as logical formulas in predicate logic is important and much more care must be taken than in the case of propositional logic. However, once this translation has been accomplished the main objective is to reason symbolically ($\vdash$) or semantically ($\vDash$) about the information expressed in those formulas.

In Section 2.4, we develop the proper notion of models, real or artificial worlds in which these assertions can be true or false, which allows us to define semantic entailment

$$\phi_1, \phi_2, \ldots, \phi_n \vDash \psi.$$

The latter expresses that, given *any* such model in which all $\phi_1, \phi_2, \ldots, \phi_n$ hold, it is the case that ψ holds in that model as well. In that case, one also says that ψ is *semantically entailed* by $\phi_1, \phi_2, \ldots, \phi_n$. Although this definition of semantic entailment closely matches the one for propositional logic in Definition 1.33, the process of *evaluating a predicate formula* is quite different from the computation of truth values for propositional logic. We discuss it in detail in Section 2.4.

In Section 2.3, we extend our natural deduction calculus so that it covers logical formulas of predicate logic as well. In this way we are able to prove sequents

$$\phi_1, \phi_2, \ldots, \phi_n \vdash \psi$$

in a similar way to that in the first chapter. It is outside the scope of this book to show that the natural deduction calculus for predicate logic is sound and complete with respect to semantic entailment; but it is indeed the case that

$$\phi_1, \phi_2, \ldots, \phi_n \vdash \psi \quad \text{iff} \quad \phi_1, \phi_2, \ldots, \phi_n \vDash \psi$$

for formulas of the predicate calculus. The first proof of this was done by the mathematician K. Gödel.

What kind of reasoning must predicate logic be able to support? To get a feel for that, let us consider the following argument:

No books are gaseous. Dictionaries are books. Therefore, no dictionary is gaseous.

The predicates we choose are

$$B(x):\qquad x \text{ is a book}$$
$$G(x):\qquad x \text{ is gaseous}$$
$$D(x):\qquad x \text{ is a dictionary.}$$

Evidently, we need to build a proof theory and semantics that allow us to derive

$$\neg\exists x\,(B(x) \wedge G(x)),\ \forall x\,(D(x) \to B(x)) \vdash \neg\exists x\,(D(x) \wedge G(x))$$

as well as

$$\neg\exists x\,(B(x) \wedge G(x)),\ \forall x\,(D(x) \to B(x)) \vDash \neg\exists x\,(D(x) \wedge G(x)).$$

Verify that this sequent expresses the argument above in a symbolic form.

Predicate symbols and variables allow us to code up much more of the logical structure of declarative sentences than was possible in propositional logic. Predicate logic contains one more concept, that of *function symbols*, that allows us to go even further. Consider the declarative sentence

Every child is younger than its mother.

We could code it using predicates as

$$\forall x\,\forall y\,(C(x) \wedge M(y, x) \to Y(x, y))$$

where $C(x)$ means that x is a child, $M(x, y)$ means that x is y's mother and $Y(x, y)$ means that x is younger than y. (Note that we actually used $M(y, x)$ (y is x's mother), not $M(x, y)$.) As we have coded it, the sentence says that, for all children x and any mother of theirs y, x is younger than y. It is not very elegant to say 'any of x's mothers', since we know that every individual has one and only one mother[1]. The inelegance of coding 'mother' as a predicate is even more apparent if we consider the sentence

Andy and Paul have the same maternal grandmother.

which in predicate logic, using a and p for Andy and Paul and M for mother as before, becomes

$$\forall x\,\forall y\,\forall u\,\forall v\,(M(x, y) \wedge M(y, a) \wedge M(u, v) \wedge M(v, p) \to x = u).$$

This formula says that, if y and v are Andy's and Paul's mothers, respectively, and x and u are *their* mothers (i.e. Andy's and Paul's maternal grandmothers, respectively), then x and u are the same person. Notice that we used a special

---

[1] We assume here that we are talking about genetic mothers, not adopted mothers, step mothers etc.

predicate in predicate logic, *equality*; it is a binary predicate, i.e. it takes two arguments, and is written =. Unlike other predicates, it is usually written in between its arguments rather than before them; that is, we write $x = y$ instead of $= (x, y)$ to say that x and y are equal.

The function symbols of predicate logic give us a way of avoiding this ugly encoding, for they allow us to represent y's mother in a more direct way. Instead of writing $M(x, y)$ to mean that x is y's mother, we simply write $m(y)$ to mean y's mother. The symbol m is a function symbol: it takes one argument and returns the mother of that argument. Using m, the two sentences above have simpler encodings than they had using M:

$$\forall x \, (C(x) \rightarrow Y(x, m(x)))$$

now expresses that every child is younger than its mother. Note that we need only one variable rather than two. Representing that Andy and Paul have the same maternal grandmother is even simpler; it is written

$$m(m(a)) = m(m(p))$$

quite directly saying that Andy's maternal grandmother is the same person as Paul's maternal grandmother.

One can always do without function symbols, by using a predicate symbol instead. However, it is usually neater to use function symbols whenever possible, because we get more compact encodings. However, function symbols can be used only in situations in which we want to denote a single object. We rely on the fact that every individual has a uniquely defined mother, so that we can talk about x's mother without risking any ambiguity (for example, if x had no mother, or two mothers). For this reason, we cannot have a function symbol $b(\cdot)$ for 'brother'. It might not make sense to talk about x's brother, for x might not have any brothers, or he might have several. 'Brother' must be coded as a binary predicate.

To exemplify this point further, if Mary has several brothers, then the claim that 'Ann likes Mary's brother' is ambiguous. It might be that Ann likes one of Mary's brothers, which we would write as

$$\exists x \, (B(m, x) \land L(a, x))$$

(where B and L mean 'is brother of' and 'likes', and a and m mean Ann and Mary) — this sentence says that there exists an x which is a brother of Mary and is liked by Ann. Alternatively, if Ann likes all of Mary's brothers, we write it as

$$\forall x \, (B(m, x) \rightarrow L(a, x))$$

saying that any x which is a brother of Mary is liked by Ann.

Different function symbols may take different numbers of arguments. In a domain involving students and the grades they get in different courses, one might have the binary function symbol $g(\cdot, \cdot)$ taking two arguments: $g(x, y)$ refers to the grade obtained by student x in course y.

2.2 Predicate logic as a formal language

The discussion of the preceding section was intended to give an impression of how we code up sentences as formulas of predicate logic. In this section, we will be more precise about it, giving syntactic rules for the formation of predicate logic formulas. Because of the power of predicate logic, the language is much more complex than that of propositional logic.

The first thing to note is that there are two *sorts* of things involved in a predicate logic formula. The first sort denotes the objects that we are talking about: individuals such as a and p (referring to Andy and Paul) are examples, as are variables such as x and v. Function symbols also allow us to refer to objects: thus, $m(a)$ and $g(x, y)$ are also objects. Expressions in predicate logic which denote objects are called *terms*.

The other sort of things in predicate logic denotes truth values; expressions of this kind are *formulas*. $Y(x, m(x))$ is a formula, though x and $m(x)$ are terms.

A predicate vocabulary consists of three sets: a set of predicate symbols $\mathscr{P}$, a set of function symbols $\mathscr{F}$ and a set of constant symbols $\mathscr{C}$. Each predicate symbol and each function symbol comes with an arity, the number of arguments it expects.

2.2.1 Terms

The terms of our language are made up of variables, constant symbols and functions applied to those. Functions may be nested, as in $m(m(x))$ or $g(m(a), c)$: the grade obtained by Andy's mother in the course c.

Definition 2.1 *Terms* are defined as follows.

- Any variable is a term.
- Any constant in $\mathscr{C}$ is a term.
- If $t_1, t_2, \ldots, t_n$ are terms and $f \in \mathscr{F}$ has arity n, then $f(t_1, t_2, \ldots, t_n)$ is a term.
- Nothing else is a term.

In Backus Naur form we may write

$$t ::= x \mid c \mid f(t, \ldots, t)$$

where x is a variable, $c \in \mathscr{C}$ and $f \in \mathscr{F}$ has arity n.

It is important to note that

- The first building blocks of terms are *constants* and *variables*.
- More complex terms are built from function symbols using as many previously built terms as arguments as the function symbol in question requires.
- The notion of terms is dependent on the sets $\mathscr{C}$ and $\mathscr{F}$. If you change those, you change the set of terms.

We said that a predicate vocabulary is given by three sets, $\mathscr{P}$, $\mathscr{F}$ and $\mathscr{C}$. In fact, constants can be thought of as functions which don't take any arguments (and we even drop the argument brackets) — therefore, constants live in the set $\mathscr{F}$ together with the 'true' functions which do take arguments. From now on, we will drop the set $\mathscr{C}$, since it is convenient to do so, and stipulate that constants are 0-arity functions.

See Figure 2.1 for the parse tree of the term $(2 - (s(x) + y)) * x$, where $+$, $-$ and $*$ are written in infix.

EXERCISES 2.1

1. Let $\mathscr{F}$ be $\{d, f, g\}$, where d is a constant, f a function symbol with two arguments and g a function symbol with three arguments. Which of the following strings are terms over $\mathscr{F}$? Draw the parse tree of those strings which are indeed terms.

   (a) $g(d, d)$

   * (b) $f(x, g(y, z), d)$

   * (c) $g(x, f(y, z), d)$

   (d) $g(x, h(y, z), d)$

   (e) $f(f(g(d, x), f(g(d, x), y, g(y, d)), g(d, d)), g(f(d, d, x), d), z)$.

2. Let $\mathscr{F}$ be as in the last exercise.

   (a) The length of a term over $\mathscr{F}$ is the length of its string representation, where we count all commas and parentheses. For example, the length of $f(x, g(y, z), z)$ is 13. Can you list all terms over $\mathscr{F}$ which do not contain any variables and whose length is less than 10?

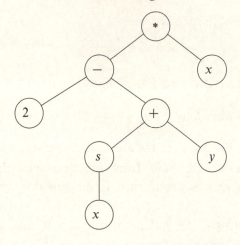

Fig. 2.1. A parse tree representing an arithmetic term.

* (b) The height of a term over $\mathcal{F}$ is defined as 1 plus the length of the longest path in its parse tree, as in Definition 1.31. List all terms over $\mathcal{F}$ which do not contain any variables and whose height is less than 4.

3. Let $\mathcal{F}$ be the set $\{+, -, *, s\}$ where $+, -, *$ are binary functions and s is a unary function. Let $\mathcal{C}$ be the set $\{0, 1, 2, \ldots\}$. We write $+, -, *$ in infix notation rather than prefix notation (that is, we write $x + y$ instead of $+(x, y)$, etc.). Figure 2.1 shows the parse tree of the term $(2 - (s(x) + y)) * x$. Draw the parse tree of the term $(2 - s(x)) + (y * x)$. Compare your solution with the parse tree in Figure 2.1.

2.2.2 Formulas

Suppose that our predicate vocabulary is given by the sets of function symbols $\mathcal{F}$ and predicate symbols $\mathcal{P}$. The choice of predicate, function and constant symbols is driven by what we intend to describe. For example, if we work on a database representing relations between our kin we might want to consider

$$\{M, F, S, D\}$$

referring to *being male, being female, being a son of* ... and *being a daughter of* ... . Naturally, F and M are unary predicates (they take one argument) whereas D and S are binary (taking two).

We already know what the terms over $\mathcal{F}$ are. Given that knowledge, we can now proceed to define the formulas of predicate logic.

Definition 2.2 We define the *set of formulas over* $(\mathcal{F},\mathcal{P})$ inductively, using the already defined set of terms over $\mathcal{F}$:

- If P is a predicate taking n arguments, $n \geq 1$, and if $t_1, t_2, \ldots, t_n$ are terms over $\mathcal{F}$, then $P(t_1, t_2, \ldots, t_n)$ is a formula.
- If ϕ is a formula, then so is $(\neg\phi)$.
- If ϕ and ψ are formulas, then so are $(\phi \wedge \psi)$, $(\phi \vee \psi)$ and $(\phi \to \psi)$.
- If ϕ is a formula and x is a variable, then $(\forall x\, \phi)$ and $(\exists x\, \phi)$ are formulas.
- Nothing else is a formula.

Note how the arguments given to predicates are always terms. Let us stress again that the notion of 'formula' depends on the particular choice of constant, function and predicate symbols. We can condense this definition using Backus Naur form (BNF):

$$\phi ::= P(t_1, t_2, \ldots, t_n) \mid (\neg\phi) \mid (\phi \wedge \phi) \mid (\phi \vee \phi) \mid (\phi \to \phi) \mid (\forall x\, \phi) \mid (\exists x\, \phi) \tag{2.1}$$

where P is a predicate of arity n, t_i are terms and x is a variable. Recall that each occurrence of ϕ on the right-hand side of the $::=$ stands for any formula.

Convention 2.3 For convenience, we retain the usual binding priorities agreed upon in Convention 1.3 and add that $\forall y$ and $\exists y$ bind like $\neg$. Thus, the order is:

- $\neg$, $\forall y$ and $\exists y$ bind most tightly;
- then $\vee$ and $\wedge$;
- then $\to$.

We also often omit brackets around quantifiers, provided that doing so introduces no ambiguities.

Predicate logic formulas can be represented by parse trees. For example, Figure 2.2 represents the formula $\forall x\,((P(x) \to Q(x)) \wedge S(x,y))$.

Example 2.4 Consider translating the sentence

Every son of my father is my brother.

into predicate logic. We use a constant m to represent 'me' (or 'I'). This example illustrates that coding facts about real life in predicate logic can be done in a variety of ways. As before, the design choice is whether we represent 'father' as a predicate or as a function symbol.

1. As a predicate. We choose a constant m for 'me', so m is a term, and we choose further $\{S, F, B\}$ as the set of predicates with meanings

$$S(x, y):\qquad x \text{ is a son of } y$$
$$F(x, y):\qquad x \text{ is the father of } y$$
$$B(x, y):\qquad x \text{ is a brother of } y.$$

Then the symbolic encoding of the sentence above is

$$\forall x\, \forall y\, (F(x, m) \wedge S(y, x) \to B(y, m))$$

saying: 'For all x and all y, if x is a father of m and if y is a son of x, then y is a brother of m.'.

2. As a function. We keep m, S and B as above and write f for the function which, given an argument, returns the corresponding father. Note that this works only because fathers are *unique*, so f really is a function as opposed to a mere relation.

The symbolic encoding of the sentence above is now

$$\forall x\, (S(x, f(m)) \to B(x, m))$$

meaning: 'For all x, if x is a son of the father of m, then x is a brother of m.'. This statement is much less complex insofar as it involves only one quantifier.

EXERCISES 2.2

* 1. Let m be a constant, f a function symbol with one argument and S and B two predicate symbols, each with two arguments. Which of the following strings are formulas in predicate logic? Specify a reason for failure for strings which aren't.

    (a) $S(m, x)$
    (b) $B(m, f(m))$
    (c) $f(m)$
    (d) $B(B(m, x), y)$
    (e) $S(B(m), z)$
    (f) $(B(x, y) \to (\exists z\, S(z, y)))$
    (g) $(S(x, y) \to S(y, f(f(x))))$
    (h) $(B(x) \to B(B(x)))$.

* 2. Use the predicates

$$A(x, y): \quad x \text{ admires } y$$
$$B(x, y): \quad x \text{ attended } y$$
$$P(x): \quad x \text{ is a professor}$$
$$S(x): \quad x \text{ is a student}$$
$$L(x): \quad x \text{ is a lecture}$$

and the function symbol (= constant)

$$m: \quad \text{Mary}$$

to translate the following into predicate logic:

(a) Mary admires every professor.
   (The answer is *not* $\forall x \, A(m, P(x))$; see exercise 1.)
(b) Some professor admires Mary.
(c) Mary admires herself.
(d) No student attended every lecture.
(e) No lecture was attended by every student.
(f) No lecture was attended by any student.

3. Let c and d be constants, f a function symbol with one argument, g a function symbol with two arguments and h a function symbol with three arguments. Further, P and Q are predicate symbols with three arguments. Which of the following strings are formulas in predicate logic? Specify a reason for failure for strings which aren't. Draw parse trees of all strings which are formulas of predicate logic.

(a) $\forall x \, P(f(d), h(g(c, x), d, y))$
(b) $\forall x \, P(f(d), h(P(x, y), d, y))$
(c) $\forall x \, Q(g(h(x, f(d), x), g(x, x)), h(x, x, x), c)$
(d) $\exists z \, (Q(z, z, z) \rightarrow P(z))$
(e) $\forall x \, \forall y \, (g(x, y) \rightarrow P(x, y, x))$
(f) $Q(c, d, c)$.

4. Use the predicate specifications

$$B(x, y): \quad x \text{ beats } y$$
$$F(x): \quad x \text{ is an (American) football team}$$
$$Q(x, y): \quad x \text{ is quarterback of } y$$
$$L(x, y): \quad x \text{ loses to } y$$

and the constant symbols

$$c: \quad \text{Wildcats}$$
$$j: \quad \text{Jayhawks}$$

to translate the following into predicate logic.

   (a) Every football team has a quarterback.
   (b) If the Jayhawks beat the Wildcats, then the Jayhawks do not loose to every football team.
   (c) The Wildcats beat some team, which beat the Jayhawks.

* 5. Find appropriate predicates and their specification to translate the following into predicate logic:

   (a) All red things are in the box.
   (b) Only red things are in the box.
   (c) No animal is both a cat and a dog.
   (d) Every prize was won by a boy.
   (e) A boy won every prize.

6. Let $F(x,y)$ mean that x is the father of y; $M(x,y)$ denotes x is the mother of y. Similarly, $H(x,y)$, $S(x,y)$, and $B(x,y)$ say that x is the husband/sister/brother of y, respectively. You may also use constants to denote individuals, like 'Ed' and 'Patsy'. However, you are not allowed to use any predicate symbols other than the above to translate the following sentences into predicate logic:

   (a) Everybody has a mother.
   (b) Everybody has a father and a mother.
   (c) Whoever has a mother has a father.
   (d) Ed is a grandfather.
   (e) All fathers are parents.
   (f) All husbands are spouses.
   (g) No uncle is an aunt.
   (h) All brothers are siblings.
   (i) Nobody's grandmother is anybody's father.
   (j) Ed and Patsy are husband and wife.
   (k) Carl is Monique's brother-in-law.

7. Formalise the following sentences in predicate logic, defining predicate symbols as appropriate:

   (a) Everybody who visits New Orleans falls in love with it.
   (b) There is a trumpet player who lives in New Orleans, but who does not like crawfish étoufée.
   (c) There are at least two saxophone players who were born in New Orleans and who play better than every sax player in New York city.

(d) At least two piano players from Louisiana other than Elis Marsalis play every week at my favourite club.

(e) If the Superdome is as least as high as the Royal Albert Hall, then every concert hall which is as least as high as the Superdome is as least as high as the Royal Albert Hall.

(f) If you eat a po-boy sandwich which has no chicken, no beef, and no seafood in it, then you are eating alligator nuggets.

(g) Abita Amber is the best beer which is brewed in Louisiana.

(h) Mardi Gras is the biggest party in the world.

(i) Not everybody in Louisiana speaks French, but everybody in Louisiana knows someone from Louisiana who does speak French.

(j) Commander's Palace is not only the best restaurant in New Orleans, but also the best one in the United States of America; however, there are restaurants in France which are even better.

(k) There is only one restaurant where you can get better breakfast than at the Bluebird Café.

(l) If you eat red beans and rice for lunch, then it must be a Monday.

(m) Vaughn's is the coolest bar with the best live jazz in New Orleans.

(n) Everybody who talks about the Crescent City actually refers to New Orleans.

(o) Politics in New Orleans is as least as corrupt as that of all Caribbean islands.

(p) Not every hurricane in New Orleans is a storm; some of them are cocktails, but all of them are dangerous.

2.2.3 Free and bound variables

The introduction of variables and quantifiers allows us to express the notions of *all ...* and *some ...* Intuitively, to verify that $\forall x\, Q(x)$ is true amounts to replacing x by any of its possible values and checking that Q holds for each one of them. There are two important and different senses in which such formulas can be 'true'. First, if we fix a certain meaning of all predicate and function symbols involved, then we can *check* whether a formula is true for this particular scenario. For example, if a formula encodes the specifications of a hardware circuit, then we would want to know whether it is true for the model of the circuit. Second, one sometimes would like to ensure that certain formulas are true *for all models*. Consider $(\forall x\, P(x)) \to (\exists x\, P(x))$; clearly, this formula should be true no matter what model we are looking at. It is this second kind of truth which is the primary focus of this chapter.

Unfortunately, things are more complicated if we want to define formally what it means for a formula to be true in a given model. Ideally, we seek a definition that we could use to write a computer program verifying that a formula holds in a given situation.

To begin with, we need to understand that variables occur in different ways. Consider the formula

$$\forall x\, ((P(x) \to Q(x)) \wedge S(x, y)).$$

We draw its parse tree in the same way as for propositional formulas, but with two additional sorts of nodes:

- The quantifiers $\forall x$ and $\exists y$ form nodes and have, like negation, just one subtree.
- Predicates, which are generally of the form $P(t_1, t_2, \ldots, t_n)$, have the symbol P as a node, but now P has n many subtrees, namely the parse trees of the terms $t_1, t_2, \ldots, t_n$.

So in our particular case above we arrive at the parse tree in Figure 2.2. You can see that variables occur at two different sorts of places. First, they appear next to quantifiers $\forall$ and $\exists$ in nodes like $\forall x$ and $\exists z$; such nodes always have one subtree, subsuming their scope to which the respective quantifier applies.

The other sort of occurrence of variables is *leaf nodes containing variables*. If variables are leaf nodes, then they stand for values that still have to be made concrete. There are two principal such occurrences:

1. In our example in Figure 2.2, we have three leaf nodes x. If we walk up the tree beginning at any one of these x leaves, we run into the quantifier $\forall x$. This means that those occurrences of x are actually *bound* to $\forall x$ so they represent, or stand for, *any possible value of x*.
2. In walking upwards, the only quantifier that the leaf node y runs into is $\forall x$ but that x has nothing to do with y; x and y are different place holders. So y is *free* in this formula. This means that its value has to be specified by some additional information, for example, a location in memory.

Definition 2.5 Let ϕ be a formula in predicate logic. An occurrence of x in ϕ is *free* in ϕ if it is a leaf node in the parse tree of ϕ such that there

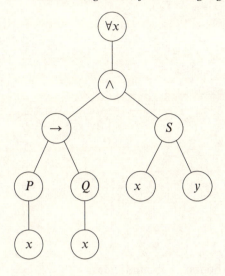

Fig. 2.2. A parse tree of a predicate logic formula.

is no path upwards from that node x to a node $\forall x$ or $\exists x$. Otherwise, that occurrence of x is called *bound*. For $\forall x\,\phi$, or $\exists x\,\phi$, we say that ϕ — minus any of its subformulas $\exists x\,\psi$, or $\forall x\,\psi$ — is the *scope* of $\forall x$, respectively $\exists x$.

Thus, if x occurs in ϕ, then it is bound if, and only if, it is in the scope of $\exists x$ or $\forall x$; otherwise it is free. In terms of parse trees, the scope of a quantifier is just its subtree, minus any subtrees which re-introduce a quantifier for x; e.g. the scope of $\forall x$ in $\forall x\,(P(x) \to \exists x\,Q(x))$ is $P(x)$. It is quite possible, and common, that a variable is bound and free in a formula. Consider the formula

$$(\forall x\,(P(x) \wedge Q(x))) \to (\neg P(x) \vee Q(y))$$

and its parse tree in Figure 2.3. The two x leaves in the subtree of $\forall x$ are bound since they are in the scope of $\forall x$, but the leaf x in the right subtree of $\to$ is free since it is *not* in the scope of any quantifier $\forall x$ or $\exists x$. Note, however, that a single leaf either is under the scope of a quantifier, or it isn't. Hence *individual* occurrences of variables are either free or bound, never both at the same time.

2.2.4 Substitution

Variables are place holders so we must have some means of *replacing* them with more concrete information. On the syntactic side, we often need to

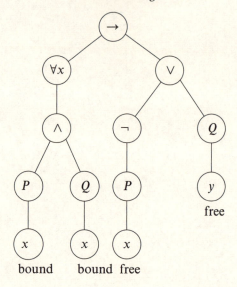

Fig. 2.3. A parse tree of a predicate logic formula illustrating *free* and *bound* occurrences of variables.

replace a leaf node x by the parse tree of an entire term t. Recall from the definition of formulas that any replacement of x may only be a term; it could not be a predicate, or a more complex formula, for x serves as an argument to a predicate one step higher up in the parse tree (see Definition 2.1 and the grammar in (2.1)). In substituting t for x we have to leave untouched the *bound* leaves x since they are in the scope of some $\exists x$ or $\forall x$, i.e. they stand for *some unspecified* or *all* values respectively.

Definition 2.6 Given a variable x, a term t and a formula ϕ we define $\phi[t/x]$ to be the formula obtained by replacing each *free* occurrence of variable x in ϕ with t.

Substitutions are easily understood by looking at some examples. Let f be a function symbol with two arguments and ϕ the formula with the parse tree in Figure 2.2. Then $f(x, y)$ is a term and $\phi[f(x, y)/x]$ is just ϕ again. This is true because *all* occurrences of x are bound in ϕ, so *none* of them gets substituted.

Now consider ϕ to be the formula with the parse tree in Figure 2.3. Here we have one free occurrence of x in ϕ, so we substitute the parse tree of $f(x, y)$ for that free leaf node x and obtain the parse tree in Figure 2.4. Note that the bound x leaves are unaffected by this operation. You can see that

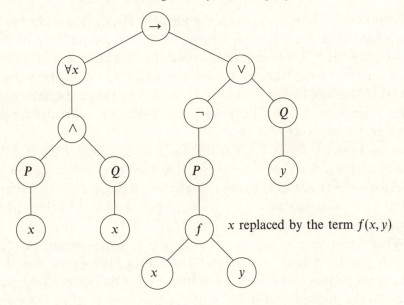

Fig. 2.4. A parse tree of a formula resulting from substitution.

the process of substitution is straightforward, but requires that it be applied *only to the free occurrences* of the variable to be substituted.

A word on notation: in writing $\phi[t/x]$, we really mean this to be the formula *obtained* by performing the operation $[t/x]$ on ϕ. Strictly speaking, the chain of symbols $\phi[t/x]$ is *not* a logical formula, but its *result* will be a formula, provided that ϕ was one in the first place.

Unfortunately, substitutions can give rise to undesired side effects. In performing a substitution $\phi[t/x]$, the term t may contain a variable y, where free occurrences of x in ϕ are under the scope of $\exists y$ or $\forall y$ in ϕ. By carrying out this substitution $\phi[t/x]$, the value y, which might have been fixed by a concrete context, gets caught in the scope of $\exists y$ or $\forall y$. This binding capture overrides the context specification of the concrete value of y, for it will now stand for '*some unspecified*' or '*all*', respectively. Such undesired variable captures are to be avoided at all costs.

Definition 2.7 Given a term t, a variable x and a formula ϕ, we say that t is *free for x* in ϕ if no free x leaf in ϕ occurs in the scope of $\forall y$ or $\exists y$ for any variable y occurring in t.

This definition is maybe hard to swallow. Let us think of it in terms of parse trees. Given the parse tree of ϕ and the parse tree of t, we can perform the substitution $[t/x]$ on ϕ to obtain the formula $\phi[t/x]$. The latter has a parse tree where all free x leaves of the parse tree of ϕ are replaced by the parse tree of t. What 't is free in x for ϕ' means is that the variable leaves of the parse tree of t won't become bound if placed into the bigger parse tree of $\phi[t/x]$. For example, if we consider x, t and ϕ in Figure 2.4, then t is free in x for ϕ since the *new* leaf variables x and y of t are not under the scope of any quantifiers involving x or y.

As an example where t is not free for x in ϕ, consider the ϕ with parse tree in Figure 2.5 and let t be $f(y,y)$. Then we may substitute the leftmost x leaf since it is not in the scope of any quantifier, but, in substituting the x leaf in the left subtree of $\rightarrow$, we introduce a new variable y in t which becomes bound by $\forall y$.

What if there are no free occurrences of x in ϕ? Inspecting the definition of 't is free for x in ϕ', we see that *every* term t is free for x in ϕ in that case, since no free variable x of ϕ is below some quantifier in the parse tree of ϕ. So the problematic situation of variable capture in performing $\phi[t/x]$ cannot occur. Of course, in that case $\phi[t/x]$ is just ϕ again.

It might be helpful to compare 't is free for x in ϕ' with a precondition of calling a procedure for substitution. If you are asked to compute $\phi[t/x]$ in your exercises or exams, then that is what you should do; but any reasonable implementation of substitution used in a theorem prover would have to check whether t is free for x in ϕ and, if not, rename some variables with fresh ones to avoid the undesirable capture of variables.

EXERCISES 2.3
   1. Let ϕ be

$$\exists x\,(P(y,z) \wedge (\forall y\,(\neg Q(y,x) \vee P(y,z))))),$$

where P and Q are predicates with two arguments.

* (a)   Draw the parse tree of ϕ.
* (b)   Identify those variable leaves which occur free and those which occur bound in ϕ.
  (c) Is there a variable in ϕ which has free *and* bound occurrences?
* (d) Consider the terms w (w is a variable), $f(x)$ and $g(y,z)$, where f and g are function symbols with one, respectively two, arguments.

    (i) Compute $\phi[w/x]$, $\phi[w/y]$, $\phi[f(x)/y]$ and $\phi[g(y,z)/z]$.
    (ii) Which of w, $f(x)$ and $g(y,z)$ are free for x in ϕ?
    (iii) Which of w, $f(x)$ and $g(y,z)$ are free for y in ϕ?

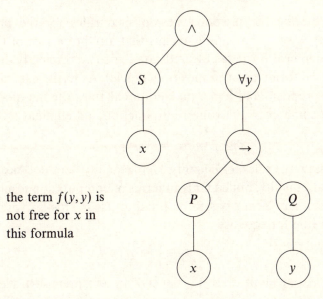

the term $f(y,y)$ is
not free for x in
this formula

Fig. 2.5. A parse tree for which a substitution has dire consequences.

(e) What is the scope of $\exists x$ in ϕ?

* (f) Suppose that we change ϕ to $\exists x\,(P(y,z) \wedge (\forall x\,(\neg Q(x,x) \vee P(x,z))))$. What is the scope of $\exists x$ now?

2.   (a) Draw the parse tree of the following logical formula ψ:

$$\neg(\forall x\,((\exists y\,P(x,y,z)) \wedge (\forall z\,P(x,y,z))))$$

where P is a predicate with three arguments.

(b) Indicate the free and bound variables in that parse tree.

(c) List all variables which occur free *and* bound therein.

(d) Compute $\psi[t/x]$, $\psi[t/y]$ and $\psi[t/z]$, where t equals the term $g(f(g(y,y)),y)$. Is t free for x in ψ? Is t free for y in ψ? Is t free for z in ψ?

2.3 Proof theory of predicate logic

2.3.1 Natural deduction rules

Proofs in the natural deduction calculus for predicate logic are similar to those for propositional logic in Chapter 1, except that we have new rules for dealing with the quantifiers and with the equality symbol. Strictly speaking, we are *overloading* the previously established rules for the propositional connectives ∧, ∨ etc. That simply means that any proof rule of Chapter 1 is still valid for logical formulas of predicate logic (we originally defined those rules for logical formulas of propositional logic). As in the natural deduction calculus for propositional logic, the additional rules for the quantifiers and equality will come in two flavours: introduction and elimination rules.

The proof rules for equality

First, let us state the rules for equality. Here equality does not mean syntactic, or intensional, equality, but equality in terms of computation results. In either of these senses, any term t has to be equal to itself. This is expressed by the introduction rule for equality:

$$\frac{\quad}{t = t} \, =\!i$$

which is an axiom (as it does not depend on any premises). Notice that it may be invoked only if t is a term (our language doesn't permit us to talk about equality between formulas).

This rule is quite evidently sound, but it is not very useful on its own. What we need is a principle that allows us to substitute equals for equals repeatedly. For example, suppose that $y * (w + 2)$ equals $y * w + y * 2$; then it certainly must be the case that $z \geq y * (w + 2)$ implies $z \geq y * w + y * 2$ and vice versa. We may now express this substitution principle as the rule $=\!e$:

$$\frac{t_1 = t_2 \quad \phi[t_1/x]}{\phi[t_2/x]} \, =\!e.$$

Note that t_1 and t_2 have to be free for x in ϕ, whenever we want to apply the rule $=\!e$ (this is an example of a *side condition* of a proof rule).

Convention 2.8 Indeed, throughout this section, when we write a substitution in the form $\phi[t/x]$, we implicitly assume that t is free for x in ϕ; for, as we saw in the last section, a substitution doesn't make sense if this is not the case.

We obtain proof

1	$(x + 1) = (1 + x)$	premise
2	$(x + 1 > 1) \rightarrow (x + 1 > 0)$	premise
3	$(1 + x > 1) \rightarrow (1 + x > 0)$	$=\!e$ 1, 2

establishing the validity of the sequent

$$x + 1 = 1 + x, (x + 1 > 1) \rightarrow (x + 1 > 0) \vdash (1 + x) > 1 \rightarrow (1 + x) > 0.$$

In this particular proof t_1 is $(x+1)$, t_2 is $(1+x)$ and ϕ is $(x > 1) \to (x > 0)$. We used the name =e since it reflects what this rule is doing to data: it eliminates the equality in $t_1 = t_2$ by replacing all t_1 in $\phi[t_1/x]$ with t_2. This is a sound substitution principle, since the assumption that t_1 equals t_2 guarantees that the logical meanings of $\phi[t_1/x]$ and $\phi[t_2/x]$ match.

The principle of substitution, in the guise of the rule =e, is quite powerful. Together with the rule =i, it allows us to show the sequents

$$t_1 = t_2 \quad \vdash \quad t_2 = t_1$$
$$t_1 = t_2, t_2 = t_3 \quad \vdash \quad t_1 = t_3.$$

A proof for the first sequent is:

1	$t_1 = t_2$	premise
2	$t_1 = t_1$	=i
3	$t_2 = t_1$	=e 1, 2

where ϕ is $x = t_1$.

A proof for the second sequent is:

1	$t_2 = t_3$	premise
2	$t_1 = t_2$	premise
3	$t_1 = t_3$	=e 1, 2

where ϕ is $t_1 = x$, so in line 2 we have $\phi[t_2/x]$ and in line 3 we obtain $\phi[t_3/x]$, as given by the rule =e applied to lines 1 and 2. Notice how we applied the scheme =e with several different instantiations.

Our discussion of the rules =i and =e has shown that they force equality to be *reflexive*, *symmetric* and *transitive*. These are minimal and necessary requirements for any sane concept of (extensional) equality. We leave the topic of equality for now to move on to the proof rules for quantifiers.

EXERCISES 2.4
1. Prove the following sequents using, among others, the rules =i and =e. Make sure that you indicate for each application of =e what the rule instances ϕ, t_1 and t_2 are.

   (a) $(y = 0) \wedge (y = x) \vdash 0 = x$
   (b) $t_1 = t_2 \vdash (t + t_2) = (t + t_1)$
   (c) $(x = 0) \vee ((x+x) > 0) \vdash (y = (x+x)) \to ((y > 0) \vee (y = (0+x)))$.

2. Recall that we use $=$ to express the equality of elements in our models. Consider the formula

$$\exists x \, \exists y \, (\neg(x = y) \wedge (\forall z \, ((z = x) \vee (z = y)))).$$

Although we have not yet formally defined what a model $\mathcal{M}$ for predicate logic looks like, can you say intuitively what this formula says about any such model $\mathcal{M}$ in plain English?

* 3. Write down a sentence ϕ_3 of predicate logic which intuitively holds in a model $\mathcal{M}$ if, and only if, that model has exactly three concrete values.

4. Write down a sentence $\phi_{\leq 3}$ of predicate logic which intuitively holds in a model $\mathcal{M}$ iff that model has at most three concrete values.

* 5. Can you find a sentence of predicate logic $\phi_{<\infty}$ which intuitively holds exactly in those models which have only finitely many concrete values? What 'limitation' of predicate logic causes problems in finding such a sentence?

The proof rules for universal quantification

The rule for eliminating $\forall$ is the following:

$$\frac{\forall x \, \phi}{\phi[t/x]} \ \forall x\,\mathrm{e}.$$

It says: if you have $\forall x \, \phi$, then you could replace the x in ϕ by any term t (given, as usual, the side condition that t be free for x in ϕ). The intuitive soundness of this rule is evident: assuming that $\forall x \, \phi$ holds, we should certainly be entitled to maintain that $\phi[t/x]$ holds, where t is some term.

Recall that $\phi[t/x]$ is obtained by replacing all free occurrences of x in ϕ by t. You may think of the term t as a concrete *instance* of x. Since ϕ is assumed to hold for all x, that should also be the case for any term t. To see the necessity of the proviso that t be free for x in ϕ, consider the case that ϕ is

$$\exists y \, (x < y)$$

and the term to be substituted for x is y. Let's suppose we are reasoning about numbers with the usual 'smaller than' relation. The statement $\forall x \, \phi$ then says that for all numbers n there is some bigger number m, which is indeed true of integers or real numbers. However, $\phi[y/x]$ is the formula

$$\exists y \, (y < y)$$

saying that there is a number which is bigger than itself. This is wrong; and we must not allow a proof rule which derives semantically wrong things from semantically valid ones. Clearly, what went wrong was that y became bound in the process of substitution; y is not free for x in ϕ. Thus, in going from $\forall x\, \phi$ to $\phi[t/x]$, we have to enforce the side condition that t be free for x in ϕ.

The rule $\forall x\, i$ is a bit more complicated. It employs a proof box similar to those we have already seen in natural deduction for propositional logic, but this time the box is to stipulate the scope of the 'dummy variable' x_0 rather than the scope of an assumption. The rule $\forall x\, i$ is written

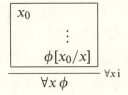

It says: if, starting with a 'fresh' variable x_0, you are able to prove some formula with x_0 in it, then (*because x_0 is fresh*) you can derive $\forall x\, \phi$. The important point is that x_0 is a new variable which doesn't occur *anywhere outside the box*; we think of it as an *arbitrary* term. Since we assumed nothing about this x_0, anything would work in its place; hence the conclusion $\forall x\, \phi$.

It takes a while to understand this rule, since it seems to be going from the particular case of ϕ to the general case $\forall x\, \phi$. The side condition, that x_0 does not occur outside the box, is what allows us to get away with this. In particular, the formula $\phi[x_0/x]$ may only depend on assumptions or premises which occur outside the proof box opened by the dummy variable x_0. These restrictions (a side condition) imply that the case we have for ϕ is, after all, quite general.

To understand this, think of the following analogy. If you want to prove to someone that you can (say) split a tennis ball in your hand by squashing it, you might say 'OK, give me a tennis ball and I'll split it'. So we give you one and you do it. But how can we be sure that you could split *any* tennis ball in this way? Of course, we can't give you *all of them*, so how could we be sure that you could split any one? Well, we assume that the one you did split was an arbitrary, or 'random', one, i.e. that it wasn't special in any way (like a ball which you had 'prepared' beforehand); and that is enough to convince us that you could split *any* tennis ball. Our rule says that if you can prove ϕ about an x_0 that isn't special in any way, then you could prove it for any x whatsoever.

To put it another way, the step from ϕ to $\forall x\, \phi$ is legitimate only if we have arrived at ϕ in such a way that none of its assumptions contain x as a free variable. Any assumption which has a free occurrence of x puts constraints on such an x. For example, the assumption bird(x) confines x to the realm of birds and anything we can prove about x using this formula will have to be a statement restricted to birds and not about anything else we might have had in mind.

It is time we looked at an example of these rules at work. Here is a proof of the sequent

$$\forall x\, (P(x) \to Q(x)), \forall x\, P(x) \vdash \forall x\, Q(x):$$

1		$\forall x\, (P(x) \to Q(x))$	premise
2		$\forall x\, P(x)$	premise
3	x_0	$P(x_0) \to Q(x_0)$	$\forall x\, e\ 1$
4		$P(x_0)$	$\forall x\, e\ 2$
5		$Q(x_0)$	$\to e\ 3, 4$
6		$\forall x\, Q(x)$	$\forall x\, i\ 3{-}5$

The structure of this proof is guided by the fact that the conclusion is a $\forall$ formula. To arrive at this, we will need an application of $\forall x\, i$, so we set up the box controlling the scope of x_0. The rest is now mechanical: we prove $\forall x\, Q(x)$ by proving $Q(x_0)$; but the latter we can prove as soon as we can prove $P(x_0)$ and $P(x_0) \to Q(x_0)$, which themselves are instances of the premises (obtained by $\forall e$ with the term x_0). Note that we wrote the name of the dummy variable to the left of the first proof line in its scope box.

Here is a simpler example which uses only $\forall x\, e$: we show the sequent

$$P(t), \forall x\, (P(x) \to \neg Q(x)) \vdash \neg Q(t)$$

for any term t:

1	$P(t)$	premise
2	$\forall x\, (P(x) \to \neg Q(x))$	premise
3	$P(t) \to \neg Q(t)$	$\forall x\, e\ 2$
4	$\neg Q(t)$	$\to e\ 3, 1$

Note that we invoked $\forall x\, e$ with the same instance t as in the assumption $P(t)$. If we had invoked $\forall x\, e$ with y, say, and obtained $P(y) \to \neg Q(y)$, then that would have been valid, but it would not have been helpful in the case that y was different from t. Thus, $\forall x\,e$ is really a *scheme* of rules, one for each term t (free for x in ϕ), and we should make our choice on the basis of consistent pattern matching. Further, note that we have rules $\forall x\,i$ and $\forall x\,e$ *for each variable* x. In particular, there are rules $\forall y\,i$, $\forall y\,e$ and so on. We will write $\forall i$ and $\forall e$ when we speak about such rules without concern for the actual quantifier variable.

Notice also that, although the square brackets representing substitution appear in the rules $\forall i$ and $\forall e$, they do not appear when we use those rules. The reason for this is that we actually carry out the substitution that is asked for. In the rules, the expression $\phi[t/x]$ means: 'ϕ, but with free occurrences of x replaced by t'. Thus, if ϕ is $P(x, y) \to Q(y, z)$ and the rule refers to $\phi[a/y]$, we carry out the substitution and write $P(x, a) \to Q(a, z)$ in the proof.

A helpful way of understanding the universal quantifier rules is to compare the rules for $\forall$ with those for $\wedge$. The rules for $\forall$ are in some sense generalisations of those for $\wedge$; whereas $\wedge$ has just two conjuncts, $\forall$ acts like it conjoins lots of formulas (one for each substitution instance of its variable). Thus, whereas $\wedge i$ has two premises, $\forall x\,i$ has a premise $\phi[x_0/x]$ for each possible 'value' of x_0. Similarly, where and-elimination allows you to deduce from $\phi \wedge \psi$ whichever of ϕ and ψ you like, forall-elimination allows you to deduce $\phi[t/x]$ from $\forall x\,\phi$, for whichever t you like. To say the same thing another way: think of $\forall x\,i$ as saying: to prove $\forall x\,\phi$, you have to prove $\phi[x_0/x]$ for every possible value x_0; while $\wedge i$ says that to prove $\phi_1 \wedge \phi_2$ you have to prove ϕ_i for every i.

The proof rules for existential quantification

The analogy between $\forall$ and $\wedge$ extends also to $\exists$ and $\vee$; and you could even try to guess the rules for $\exists$ by starting from the rules for $\vee$ and applying the same ideas as those that related $\wedge$ to $\forall$. For example, we saw that the rules for or-introduction were a sort of dual of those for and-elimination; to emphasise this point, we could write them as

$$\frac{\phi_1 \wedge \phi_2}{\phi_k} \wedge e_k \qquad \frac{\phi_k}{\phi_1 \vee \phi_2} \vee i_k,$$

where k can be chosen to be either 1 or 2.

Therefore, given the form of forall-elimination, we can infer that exists-introduction must be simply

$$\frac{\phi[t/x]}{\exists x\,\phi} \exists x\,i.$$

Indeed, this is correct: it simply says that we can deduce $\exists x\,\phi$ whenever we have $\phi[t/x]$ for some term t (naturally, we impose the side condition that t be free for x in ϕ).

In the rule $\exists$i, we see that the formula $\phi[t/x]$ contains, from a computational point of view, more information than $\exists x\,\phi$. The latter merely says that ϕ holds for some, unspecified, value of x; whereas $\phi[t/x]$ has a witness t at its disposal. Recall that the square-bracket notation asks us actually to carry out the substitution. However, the notation $\phi[t/x]$ is somewhat misleading since it suggests not only the right witness t but also the formula ϕ itself. For example, consider the situation in which t equals y such that $\phi[y/x]$ is $y = y$. Then you can check for yourself that ϕ could be a number of things, like $x = x$ or $x = y$. Thus, $\exists x\,\phi$ will depend on which of these ϕ you were thinking of.

Extending the analogy between $\exists$ and $\vee$, the rule $\vee$e leads us to the following formulation of $\exists$e:

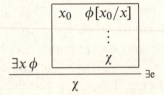

Like $\vee$e, it is a case analysis. The reasoning goes: we know $\exists x\,\phi$, so ϕ is true for at least one 'value' of x. So we do a case analysis over all those possible values, writing x_0 as a generic value representing them all. If assuming $\phi[x_0/x]$ allows us to prove some χ which doesn't mention x_0, then this χ must be true whichever x_0 it was. And that's precisely what the rule $\exists$e allows us to deduce. Of course, we impose the side condition that x_0 can't occur outside the box (therefore, in particular, it cannot occur in χ). The box is controlling two things: the scope of x_0 and also the scope of the assumption $\phi[x_0/x]$.

Just as $\vee$e says that to use $\phi_1 \vee \phi_2$, you have to be prepared for either of the ϕ_i, so $\exists$e says that to use $\exists x\,\phi$ you have to be prepared for any possible $\phi[x_0/x]$. Another way of thinking about $\exists$e goes like this: if you know $\exists x\,\phi$ and you can derive some χ from $\phi[x_0/x]$, i.e. by giving a name to the thing you know exists, then you can derive χ even without giving it the name.

The rule $\exists x\,$e is also similar to $\vee$e in the sense that both of them are elimination rules which don't have to conclude a *subformula* of the formula they are about to eliminate. Please verify that all other elimination rules so far have this *subformula property*[1]. This property is computationally very pleasant, for it allows us to narrow down the search space for a

---

[1] For $\forall x\,$e we perform a substitution $[t/x]$, but it preserves the logical structure of ϕ.

proof dramatically. Unfortunately, $\exists x\,e$, like its cousin $\lor e$, is not of that computationally benign kind.

Let us practice these rules on a couple of examples. Certainly, we should be able to prove

$$\forall x\,\phi \vdash \exists x\,\phi.$$

In the proof

1	$\forall x\,\phi$	premise
2	$\phi[x/x]$	$\forall x\,e\ 1$
3	$\exists x\,\phi$	$\exists x\,i\ 2$

we chose t to be x with respect to both $\forall x\,e$ and to $\exists x\,i$ (and note that x is free for x in ϕ and that $\phi[x/x]$ is simply ϕ again).

A more complicated example is the sequent

$$\forall x\,(P(x) \to Q(x)), \exists x\,P(x) \vdash \exists x\,Q(x)$$

which can be proved by

1		$\forall x\,(P(x) \to Q(x))$	premise
2		$\exists x\,P(x)$	premise
3	x_0	$P(x_0)$	assumption
4		$P(x_0) \to Q(x_0)$	$\forall x\,e\ 1$
5		$Q(x_0)$	$\to e\ 4,3$
6		$\exists x\,Q(x)$	$\exists x\,i\ 5$
7		$\exists x\,Q(x)$	$\exists x\,e\ 2, 3{-}6$

The motivation for introducing the box in line 3 of this proof is the existential quantifier in the premise $\exists x\,P(x)$ which has to be eliminated. Notice that the $\exists$ in the conclusion has to be introduced *within the box* and observe the nesting of these two steps. The formula $\exists x\,Q(x)$ in line 6 is the instantiation of χ in the rule $\exists e$ and it is easy to check that it does not contain an occurrence of x_0, as required by the condition that there be no x_0 outside the box.

The almost identical 'proof'

1	$\forall x\,(P(x) \rightarrow Q(x))$	premise
2	$\exists x\,P(x)$	premise
3	x_0 $P(x_0)$	assumption
4	$P(x_0) \rightarrow Q(x_0)$	$\forall x$ e 1
5	$Q(x_0)$	$\rightarrow$e 4, 3
6	$Q(x_0)$	$\exists x$ e 2, 3–5
7	$\exists x\,Q(x)$	$\exists x$ i 6

is not a legal proof; line 6 allows the fresh parameter x_0 to escape the scope of the box which declares it. This is not permissible and we will see on page 120 an example where such illicit use of proof rules results in unsound arguments.

A sequent with a slightly more complex proof is

$$\forall x\,(Q(x) \rightarrow R(x)),\ \exists x\,(P(x) \wedge Q(x)) \vdash \exists x\,(P(x) \wedge R(x))$$

which could model some argument such as

If all quakers are reformists and if there is a protestant who is also a quaker, then there must be a protestant who is also a reformist.

One possible proof strategy is to assume $P(x_0) \wedge Q(x_0)$, get the instance $Q(x_0) \rightarrow R(x_0)$ from $\forall x\,(Q(x) \rightarrow R(x))$ and use $\wedge$e$_2$ to get our hands on $Q(x_0)$, which gives us $R(x_0)$ via $\rightarrow$e ... :

1	$\forall x\,(Q(x) \rightarrow R(x))$	premise
2	$\exists x\,(P(x) \wedge Q(x))$	premise
3	x_0 $P(x_0) \wedge Q(x_0)$	assumption
4	$Q(x_0) \rightarrow R(x_0)$	$\forall x$ e 1
5	$Q(x_0)$	$\wedge$e$_2$ 3
6	$R(x_0)$	$\rightarrow$e 4, 5
7	$P(x_0)$	$\wedge$e$_1$ 3
8	$P(x_0) \wedge R(x_0)$	$\wedge$i 7, 6
9	$\exists x\,(P(x) \wedge R(x))$	$\exists x$ i 8
10	$\exists x\,(P(x) \wedge R(x))$	$\exists x$ e 2, 3–9

Note the strategy of this proof: We list the two premises. The second premise is of use here only if we apply $\exists x$ e to it. This sets up the proof box in lines 3—9 as well as the fresh parameter name x_0. Since we want to prove $\exists x \, (P(x) \wedge R(x))$, this formula has to be the last one in the box (our goal) and the rest involves $\forall x$ i and $\exists x$ i.

The rules $\forall$i and $\exists$e both have the side condition that the dummy variable cannot occur outside the box in the rule. Of course, these rules may still be nested, by choosing another name (e.g. y_0) for the dummy variable. For example, we will prove the sequent

$$\exists x \, P(x), \ \forall x \, \forall y \, (P(x) \rightarrow Q(y)) \vdash \forall y \, Q(y).$$

(Look how strong the second premise is, by the way: given any x, y, if $P(x)$, then $Q(y)$. This means that, if there is any object with the property P, then all objects shall have the property Q.) The proof goes as follows: we take an arbitrary y_0 and prove $Q(y_0)$; this we do by observing that, since some x satisfies P, so by the second premise any y satisfies Q:

1	$\exists x \, P(x)$	premise
2	$\forall x \forall y \, (P(x) \rightarrow Q(y))$	premise
3	y_0	
4	$x_0 \quad P(x_0)$	assumption
5	$\forall y \, (P(x_0) \rightarrow Q(y))$	$\forall x$ e 2
6	$P(x_0) \rightarrow Q(y_0)$	$\forall y$ e 5
7	$Q(y_0)$	$\rightarrow$e 6, 4
8	$Q(y_0)$	$\exists x$ e 1, 4—7
9	$\forall y \, Q(y)$	$\forall y$ i 3—8

There is no special reason for picking x_0 as a name for the dummy variable we use for $\forall x$ and $\exists x$ and y_0 as a name for $\forall y$ and $\exists y$. We do this only because it makes it easier for us humans. Again, study the strategy of this proof. We ultimately have to show a $\forall y$ formula which requires us to use $\forall y$ i, i.e. we need to open up a proof box (lines 3—8) whose subgoal is to prove a generic instance $Q(y_0)$. Within that box we want to make use of the premise $\exists x \, P(x)$ which results in the proof box set-up of lines 4—7. Notice that, in line 8, we may well move $Q(y_0)$ out of the box controlled by x_0.

We have emphasised the point that the dummy variables in the rules $\exists$e and $\forall$i must not occur outside their boxes. Here is an example which shows how things would go wrong if we didn't have this side condition. We could prove the sequent

$$\exists x\, P(x),\ \forall x\, (P(x) \rightarrow Q(x)) \vdash \forall y\, Q(y)$$

which is intuitively unsound. (Compare it with the previous sequent; the second premise is now much weaker, allowing us to conclude Q only for those objects for which we know P.) Here is an alleged 'proof':

1	$\exists x\, P(x)$	premise
2	$\forall x\, (P(x) \rightarrow Q(x))$	premise
3	x_0	
4	$x_0 \quad P(x_0)$	assumption
5	$P(x_0) \rightarrow Q(x_0)$	$\forall x\, e\ 2$
6	$Q(x_0)$	$\rightarrow e\ 5, 4$
7	$Q(x_0)$	$\exists x\, e\ 1, 4\text{--}6$
8	$\forall y\, Q(y)$	$\forall y\, i\ 3\text{--}7$

The last step introducing $\forall y$ is *not* the bad one; that step is fine. The bad one is the second from last one, concluding $Q(x_0)$ by $\exists x\, e$ and violating the side condition that x_0 may not leave the scope of its box. You can try a few other ways of 'proving' this sequent, but none of them should work (assuming that our proof system is sound with respect to semantic entailment, which we define in the next section). Without this side condition, we would also be able to prove that 'all x satisfy the property P as soon as one of them does so', a semantic disaster of biblical proportions!

2.3.2 Quantifier equivalences

We have already hinted at semantic equivalences between certain forms of quantification. Now we want to provide formal proofs for some of the most commonly used quantifier equivalences. Quite a few of them involve several quantifications over more than just one variable. Thus, this topic is also good practice for using the proof rules for quantifiers in a nested fashion.

For example, the formula $\forall x\, \forall y\, \phi$ should be equivalent to $\forall y\, \forall x\, \phi$ since both say that ϕ should hold for all values of x and y. What about $(\forall x\, \phi) \wedge (\forall x\, \psi)$ versus $\forall x\, (\phi \wedge \psi)$? A moment's thought reveals that they should have the same meaning as well. But what if the second conjunct does not start with $\forall x$? So what if we are looking at $(\forall x\, \phi) \wedge \psi$ in general and want to compare it with $\forall x\, (\phi \wedge \psi)$? Here we need to be careful, since x might be free in ψ and would then become bound in the formula $\forall x\, (\phi \wedge \psi)$.

Here are some quantifier equivalences which you should become familiar with. (Recall that we wrote $\phi_1 \dashv\vdash \phi_2$ in Chapter 1 as an abbreviation for $\phi_1 \vdash \phi_2$ and $\phi_2 \vdash \phi_1$.)

Theorem 2.9 *Let ϕ and ψ be formulas of predicate logic. Then we have the following equivalences:*

1.   (a) $\neg\forall x\, \phi \dashv\vdash \exists x\, \neg\phi$
     (b) $\neg\exists x\, \phi \dashv\vdash \forall x\, \neg\phi.$

2. *Assuming that x is* not *free in ψ:*
     (a) $\forall x\, \phi \wedge \psi \dashv\vdash \forall x\, (\phi \wedge \psi)$
        Remember that $\forall x\, \phi \wedge \psi$ is implicitly bracketed as $(\forall x\, \phi) \wedge \psi$, by virtue of the binding priorities.
     (b) $\forall x\, \phi \vee \psi \dashv\vdash \forall x\, (\phi \vee \psi)$
     (c) $\exists x\, \phi \wedge \psi \dashv\vdash \exists x\, (\phi \wedge \psi)$
     (d) $\exists x\, \phi \vee \psi \dashv\vdash \exists x\, (\phi \vee \psi)$
     (e) $\forall x\, (\psi \rightarrow \phi) \dashv\vdash \psi \rightarrow \forall x\, \phi$
     (f) $\exists x\, (\phi \rightarrow \psi) \dashv\vdash \forall x\, \phi \rightarrow \psi.$

3.   (a) $\forall x\, \phi \wedge \forall x\, \psi \dashv\vdash \forall x\, (\phi \wedge \psi)$
        Remember that $\forall x\, \phi \wedge \forall x\, \psi$ is implicitly bracketed as $(\forall x\, \phi) \wedge (\forall x\, \psi)$, by virtue of the binding priorities.
     (b) $\exists x\, \phi \vee \exists x\, \psi \dashv\vdash \exists x\, (\phi \vee \psi).$

4.   (a) $\forall x\, \forall y\, \phi \dashv\vdash \forall y\, \forall x\, \phi$
     (b) $\exists x\, \exists y\, \phi \dashv\vdash \exists y\, \exists x\, \phi.$

PROOF: We will prove most of these sequents; the proofs for the remaining ones are straightforward adaptations and are left as exercises. Recall that we sometimes write $\bot$ to denote any contradiction.

1.   (a) We will lead up to this by proving two simpler sequents first: $\neg(p_1 \wedge p_2) \vdash \neg p_1 \vee \neg p_2$ and then $\neg\forall x\, P(x) \vdash \exists x\, \neg P(x)$. The reason for proving the first of these is to illustrate the close relationship between $\wedge$ and $\vee$ on the one hand and $\forall$ and $\exists$ on the other — think of a model with just two elements 1 and 2 such that p_i $(i = 1, 2)$ stands for $P(x)$ evaluated at i. The idea is that proving this propositional sequent should give us inspiration for proving the second one of predicate logic. The reason for proving the latter sequent is that it is a special case (in which ϕ equals $P(x)$) of the one we are really after, so

again it should be simpler while providing some inspiration. So, let's go.

| 1 | $\neg(p_1 \wedge p_2)$ | | premise |

$$
\begin{array}{lll}
2 & \neg(\neg p_1 \vee \neg p_2) & & \text{assumption} \\
\end{array}
$$

3	$\neg p_1$	assumption	$\neg p_2$	assumption
4	$\neg p_1 \vee \neg p_2$	$\vee i_1$ 3	$\neg p_1 \vee \neg p_2$	$\vee i_2$ 3
5	$\bot$	$\neg e$ 4, 2	$\bot$	$\neg e$ 4, 2
6	p_1	RAA 3–5	p_2	RAA 3–5
7	$p_1 \wedge p_2$	$\wedge i$ 6, 6		
8	$\bot$	$\neg e$ 7, 1		
9	$\neg p_1 \vee \neg p_2$		RAA 2–8	

You have seen this sort of proof before, in Chapter 1. It is an example of something which requires proof by contradiction, or $\neg\neg e$, or LEM (meaning that it simply cannot be proved in the reduced natural deduction system which discards these three rules) — in fact, we have used the rule RAA three times.

Now we prove $\neg \forall x\, P(x) \vdash \exists x\, \neg P(x)$ similarly, except that where the rules for $\wedge$ and $\vee$ were used we now use those for $\forall$ and $\exists$:

1	$\neg \forall x\, P(x)$	premise
2	$\neg \exists x\, \neg P(x)$	assumption
3	x_0	
4	$\neg P(x_0)$	assumption
5	$\exists x\, \neg P(x)$	$\exists x\, i$ 4
6	$\bot$	$\neg e$ 5, 2
7	$P(x_0)$	RAA 4–6
8	$\forall x\, P(x)$	$\forall x\, i$ 3–7
9	$\bot$	$\neg e$ 8, 1
10	$\exists x\, \neg P(x)$	RAA 2–9

You will really benefit by spending time understanding the way this proof mimics the one above it. This insight is very useful for constructing predicate logic proofs: you first construct a similar propositional proof and then mimic it.

Next we prove $\neg \forall x \, \phi \vdash \exists x \, \neg \phi$:

1	$\neg \forall x \, \phi$	premise
2	$\neg \exists x \, \neg \phi$	assumption
3	x_0	
4	$\neg \phi[x_0/x]$	assumption
5	$\exists x \, \neg \phi$	$\exists x$ i 4
6	$\bot$	$\neg$e 5, 2
7	$\phi[x_0/x]$	RAA 4–6
8	$\forall x \, \phi$	$\forall x$ i 3–7
9	$\bot$	$\neg$e 8, 1
10	$\exists x \, \neg \phi$	RAA 2–9

The reverse sequent $\exists x \, \neg \phi \vdash \neg \forall x \, \phi$ is more straightforward, for it does not involve proof by contradiction, $\neg\neg$e, or LEM. Unlike its converse, it has a constructive proof which the intuitionists do accept. We could again prove the corresponding propositional sequent, but we leave that as an exercise.

1	$\exists x \, \neg \phi$	assumption
2	$\forall x \, \phi$	assumption
3	x_0	
4	$\neg \phi[x_0/x]$	assumption
5	$\phi[x_0/x]$	$\forall x$ e 2
6	$\bot$	$\neg$e 5, 4
7	$\bot$	$\exists x$ e 1, 3–6
8	$\neg \forall x \, \phi$	$\neg$i 2–7

2.   (a) The sequent $\forall x\,\phi \wedge \psi \vdash \forall x\,(\phi \wedge \psi)$ can be proved thus:

1	$(\forall x\,\phi) \wedge \psi$	assumption
2	$\forall x\,\phi$	$\wedge e_1\ 1$
3	ψ	$\wedge e_2\ 1$

4	x_0	
5	$\phi[x_0/x]$	$\forall x\,e\ 2$
6	$\phi[x_0/x] \wedge \psi$	$\wedge i\ 5,3$
7	$(\phi \wedge \psi)[x_0/x]$	identical to 6, since x not free in ψ

| 8 | $\forall x\,(\phi \wedge \psi)$ | $\forall x\,i\ 4\text{--}7$ |

The reverse argument can go like this:

1	$\forall x\,(\phi \wedge \psi)$	assumption

2	x_0	
3	$(\phi \wedge \psi)[x_0/x]$	$\forall x\,e\ 1$
4	$\phi[x_0/x] \wedge \psi$	identical to 3, since x not free in ψ
5	ψ	$\wedge e_2\ 3$
6	$\phi[x_0/x]$	$\wedge e_1\ 3$

7	$\forall x\,\phi$	$\forall x\,i\ 2\text{--}6$
8	$(\forall x\,\phi) \wedge \psi$	$\wedge i\ 7,5$

Notice that the use of $\wedge i$ in the last line is permissible, because ψ was obtained for any instantiation of the formula in line 1.

3.   (b) The sequent $(\exists x\,\phi) \vee (\exists x\,\psi) \vdash \exists x\,(\phi \vee \psi)$ has to be proved using the rule $\vee e$; so we have two principal cases, each of which requires the rule $\exists x\,i$:

1	$(\exists x\,\phi) \vee (\exists x\,\psi)$				premise
2	$\exists x\,\phi$		$\exists x\,\psi$		assumpt.
3	x_0	$\phi[x_0/x]$	x_0	$\psi[x_0/x]$	assumpt.
4		$\phi[x_0/x] \vee \psi[x_0/x]$		$\phi[x_0/x] \vee \psi[x_0/x]$	$\vee i\ 3$
5		$(\phi \vee \psi)[x_0/x]$		$(\phi \vee \psi)[x_0/x]$	identical
6		$\exists x\,(\phi \vee \psi)$		$\exists x\,(\phi \vee \psi)$	$\exists x\,i\ 5$
7	$\exists x\,(\phi \vee \psi)$		$\exists x\,(\phi \vee \psi)$		$\exists x\,e\ 2,3\text{--}6$
8	$\exists x\,(\phi \vee \psi)$				$\vee e\ 1,2\text{--}7$

The converse assumes $\exists x\,(\phi \lor \psi)$ so its proof has to use $\exists x\,e$ as its last rule; for that rule, we need to assume $\phi \lor \psi$ as a temporary assumption and need to conclude $(\exists x\,\phi) \lor (\exists x\,\psi)$ from those data; of course, the assumption $\phi \lor \psi$ requires the usual case analysis:

1		$\exists x\,(\phi \lor \psi)$		premise
2	x_0	$(\phi \lor \psi)[x_0/x]$		assumption
3		$\phi[x_0/x] \lor \psi[x_0/x]$		identical
4		$\phi[x_0/x]$	$\psi[x_0/x]$	assumption
5		$\exists x\,\phi$	$\exists x\,\psi$	$\exists x\,i\,4$
6		$\exists x\,\phi \lor \exists x\,\psi$	$\exists x\,\phi \lor \exists x\,\psi$	$\lor i\,5$
7		$\exists x\,\phi \lor \exists x\,\psi$		$\lor e\,3, 4-6$
8		$\exists x\,\phi \lor \exists x\,\psi$		$\exists x\,e\,1, 2-7$

4.   (b) In assuming $\exists x\,\exists y\,\phi$, we have to nest $\exists x\,e$ and $\exists y\,e$ to conclude $\exists y\,\exists x\,\phi$. Of course, we have to obey the format of these elimination rules as done below:

1		$\exists x\,\exists y\,\phi$	premise
2	x_0	$(\exists y\,\phi)[x_0/x]$	assumption
3		$\exists y\,(\phi[x_0/x])$	identical, since x, y different variables
4	y_0	$\phi[x_0/x][y_0/y]$	assumption
5		$\phi[y_0/y][x_0/x]$	identical, since x, y, x_0, y_0 different variables
6		$\exists x\,\phi[y_0/y]$	$\forall x\,i\,5$
7		$\exists y\,\exists x\,\phi$	$\forall y\,i\,6$
8		$\exists y\,\exists x\,\phi$	$\exists y\,e\,4-7$
9		$\exists y\,\exists x\,\phi$	$\exists x\,e\,2-8$

The converse is proven in the same way by swapping the roles of x and y.

$\square$

EXERCISES 2.5

1. The rules for $\forall$ are very similar to those for $\land$ and those for $\exists$ are just like those for $\lor$.

(a) Find a (propositional) proof for $\phi \rightarrow (q_1 \wedge q_2) \vdash (\phi \rightarrow q_1) \wedge (\phi \rightarrow q_2)$.

(b) Find a (predicate) proof for $\phi \rightarrow \forall x\, Q(x) \vdash \forall x\, (\phi \rightarrow Q(x))$, provided that x is not free in ϕ.

(Hint: whenever you used $\wedge$ rules in the (propositional) proof of the previous item, use $\forall$ rules in the (predicate) proof.)

(c) Find a proof for $\forall x\, (P(x) \rightarrow Q(x)) \vdash \forall x\, P(x) \rightarrow \forall x\, Q(x)$.

(Hint: try $(p_1 \rightarrow q_1) \wedge (p_2 \rightarrow q_2) \vdash p_1 \wedge p_2 \rightarrow q_1 \wedge q_2$ first.)

* (d) Prove $\forall x\, (P(x) \wedge Q(x)) \vdash \forall x\, P(x) \wedge \forall x\, Q(x)$.

* (e) Prove $\forall x\, P(x) \vee \forall x\, Q(x) \vdash \forall x\, (P(x) \vee Q(x))$.

* (f) Prove $\exists x\, (P(x) \wedge Q(x)) \vdash \exists x\, P(x) \wedge \exists x\, Q(x)$.

* (g) Prove $\exists x\, F(x) \vee \exists x\, G(x) \vdash \exists x\, (F(x) \vee G(x))$.

(h) Prove $\forall x\, \forall y\, (S(y) \rightarrow F(x)) \vdash \exists y S(y) \rightarrow \forall x\, F(x)$.

2. What is the propositional logic sequent that corresponds to $\exists x\, \neg \phi \vdash \neg \forall x\, \phi$? Prove it.

3. Provide proofs for the following sequents:

(a) $\forall x\, P(x) \vdash \forall y\, P(y)$; using $\forall x\, P(x)$ as a premise, your proof needs to end with an application of $\forall i$ which requires the formula $P(y_0)$.

(b) $\forall x\, (P(x) \rightarrow Q(x)) \vdash (\forall x\, \neg Q(x)) \rightarrow (\forall x\, \neg P(x))$

(c) $\forall x\, (P(x) \rightarrow \neg Q(x)) \vdash \neg (\exists x\, (P(x) \wedge Q(x)))$.

4. The sequents below look a bit tedious, but in proving them you make sure that you really understand how to nest the rules:

* (a) $\forall x\, \forall y\, P(x, y) \vdash \forall u\, \forall v\, P(u, v)$

(b) $\exists x\, \exists y\, F(x, y) \vdash \exists u\, \exists v\, F(u, v)$

* (c) $\exists x\, \forall y\, P(x, y) \vdash \forall y\, \exists x\, P(x, y)$.

5. In the following exercises, involving the proof rules for quantifiers, whenever you use a rule, you should mention how the relevant syntactic restrictions are satisfied.

(a) Prove one direction of 1(b) of Theorem 2.9: $\neg \exists x\, \phi \vdash \forall x\, \neg \phi$.

(b) Prove 2(b), 2(c), 2(d), 2(e) and 2(f) of Theorem 2.9.

(c) Prove 3(a) of Theorem 2.9: $(\forall x\, \phi) \wedge (\forall x\, \psi) \dashv\vdash \forall x\, (\phi \wedge \psi)$; recall that you have to do two separate proofs.

(d) Prove both directions of 4(a) of the last theorem: $\forall x\, \forall y\, \phi \dashv\vdash \forall y\, \forall x\, \phi$.

6. Prove the following sequents in predicate logic, where P and Q are predicates with one argument:

(a) $\forall x\, (\neg P(x) \wedge Q(x)) \vdash \forall x\, (P(x) \rightarrow Q(x))$

(b) $\forall x\,(P(x) \wedge Q(x)) \vdash \forall x\,(P(x) \rightarrow Q(x))$

(c) $\exists x\,(\neg P(x) \wedge \neg Q(x)) \vdash \exists x\,(\neg(P(x) \wedge Q(x)))$

(d) $\exists x\,(\neg P(x) \vee Q(x)) \vdash \exists x\,(\neg(P(x) \wedge \neg Q(x)))$.

7. Just like natural deduction proofs for propositional logic, certain things that look easy can be hard to prove for predicate logic. Typically, these involve the $\neg\neg$ rule. The patterns are the same as in propositional logic:

   (a) Proving $p \vee q \vdash \neg(\neg p \wedge \neg q)$ is quite easy. Try it.

   (b) Show $\exists x\,P(x) \vdash \neg\forall x\,\neg P(x)$.

   (c) Proving $\neg(\neg p \wedge \neg q) \vdash p \vee q$ is hard; you have to try to prove $\neg\neg(p \vee q)$ first and then use the $\neg\neg$e rule. Do it.

   * (d) Prove $\neg\forall x\,\neg P(x) \vdash \exists x\,P(x)$.

   * (e) Prove $\forall x\,\neg P(x) \vdash \neg\exists x\,P(x)$.

   * (f) Prove $\neg\exists x\,P(x) \vdash \forall x\,\neg P(x)$.

8. The proofs of the sequents below combine the proof rules for equality and quantifiers. We write $\phi \leftrightarrow \psi$ as an abbreviation for $(\phi \rightarrow \psi) \wedge (\psi \rightarrow \phi)$.

   * (a) $P(b) \vdash \forall x\,(x = b \rightarrow P(x))$

   (b) $P(b), \forall x \forall y\,(P(x) \wedge P(y)) \rightarrow x = y) \vdash \forall x\,(P(x) \leftrightarrow x = b)$

   * (c) $\exists x\,\exists y\,(H(x, y) \vee H(y, x)), \neg\exists x\,H(x, x) \vdash \exists x \exists y\,\neg(x = y)$

   (d) $\forall x\,(P(x) \leftrightarrow x = b) \vdash P(b) \wedge \forall x \forall y\,(P(x) \wedge P(y)) \rightarrow x = y)$.

9. Prove the following sequents in predicate logic:

   * (a) $S \rightarrow \forall x\,Q(x) \vdash \forall x\,(S \rightarrow Q(x))$ (S is a predicate with zero arguments.)

   * (b) $\exists x\,(S \rightarrow Q(x)) \vdash S \rightarrow \exists x\,Q(x)$

   (c) $S \rightarrow \exists x\,Q(x) \vdash \exists x\,(S \rightarrow Q(x))$

   (d) $\exists x\,P(x) \rightarrow S \vdash \forall x\,(P(x) \rightarrow S)$

   (e) $\exists x\,P(x) \rightarrow S \vdash \forall x\,(P(x) \rightarrow S)$

   (f) $\exists x\,(P(x) \rightarrow S) \vdash \forall x\,P(x) \rightarrow S$

   * (g) $\forall x\,P(x) \rightarrow S \vdash \exists x\,(P(x) \rightarrow S)$

   (h) $\forall x\,(P(x) \vee Q(x)) \vdash \forall x\,P(x) \vee \exists x\,Q(x)$

   (i) $\forall x\,\exists y\,(P(x) \vee Q(y)) \vdash \exists y\,\forall x\,(P(x) \vee Q(y))$.

10. Show by natural deduction:

   * (a) $\forall x\,P(a, x, x), \forall x\,\forall y\,\forall z\,(P(x, y, z) \rightarrow P(f(x), y, f(z)))$
   $\vdash P(f(a), a, f(a))$

   * (b) $\forall x\,P(a, x, x), \forall x\,\forall y\,\forall z\,(P(x, y, z) \rightarrow P(f(x), y, f(z)))$
   $\vdash \exists z\,P(f(a), z, f(f(a)))$

* (c) $\forall y\, Q(b, y),\ \forall x\, \forall y\, (Q(x, y) \to Q(s(x), s(y)))$
   $\vdash \exists z\, (Q(b, z) \land Q(z, s(s(b)))).$

11. Prove the following sequents in predicate logic:

    (a) $\forall x\, \forall y\, \forall z\, (S(x, y) \land S(y, z) \to S(x, z)),\ \forall x\, \neg S(x, x)$
   $\vdash \forall x\, \forall y\, (S(x, y) \to \neg S(y, x))$

    (b) $\forall x\, (P(x) \lor Q(x)),\ \exists x\, \neg Q(x),\ \forall x\, (R(x) \to \neg P(x)) \vdash \exists x\, \neg R(x)$

    (c) $\forall x\, (P(x) \to (Q(x) \lor R(x))),\ \neg\exists x\, (P(x) \land R(x)) \vdash \forall x\, P(x) \to Q(x)$

    (d) $\exists x\, \exists y\, (S(x, y) \lor S(y, x)) \vdash \exists x\, \exists y\, S(x, y)$

    (e) $(\exists x\, P(x)) \to \forall y\, P(y) \vdash \exists x\, \forall y\, ((P(x) \to P(y)) \land (P(y) \land P(x)))$

    (f) $\exists x\, (P(x) \land Q(x)),\ \forall y\, (P(y) \to R(y)) \vdash \exists x\, R(x) \land Q(x).$

12. Translate the following argument into a sequent in predicate logic using a suitable set of predicate symbols:

If there are any tax payers, then all politicians are tax payers. If there are any philanthropists, then all tax payers are philanthropists. So, if there are any tax-paying philanthropists, then all politicians are philanthropists.

Now come up with a proof of that sequent in predicate logic.

13. Discuss in what sense the equivalences of Theorem 2.9 form the basis of an algorithm which pushes quantifiers to the top of a formula's parse tree.

2.4 Semantics of predicate logic

Having seen how natural deduction of propositional logic can be extended to the predicate case, let's now look at how the semantics of predicate logic works. Just like in the propositional case, the semantics should provide a separate, but ultimately equivalent, characterisation of the logic. By 'separate', we mean that the meaning of the connectives is defined in a different way; in proof theory, they were defined by proof rules providing an *operative* explanation. In semantics, we expect something like truth tables. By 'equivalent', we mean that we should be able to prove soundness and completeness, as we did for propositional logic (although a fully fledged proof of soundness and completeness for predicate logic is beyond the scope of this book).

Before we begin describing the semantics of predicate logic, let us look more closely at the real difference between a semantic and a proof-theoretic account. In proof theory, the basic object which is constructed is a proof. Let us write Γ as a shorthand for lists of formulas $\phi_1, \phi_2, \ldots, \phi_n$. Thus, to show that $\Gamma \vdash \phi$, we need to provide a proof of ϕ from Γ. Yet, how can we show that ϕ is not a consequence of Γ? Intuitively, this is harder; how can you possibly show that *there is no proof* of something? You would have to consider every 'candidate' proof and show it is not one. Thus, proof theory gives a 'positive' characterisation of the logic; it provides convincing evidence for assertions like $\Gamma \vdash \phi$, but it is not very useful for establishing $\Gamma \nvdash \phi$.

Semantics, on the other hand, works in the opposite way. To show that ϕ is *not* a consequence of Γ is the easy bit: you simply give a model of Γ which is not a model of ϕ. Showing that ϕ is a consequence of Γ, on the other hand, is harder in principle. For propositional logic, you need to show that every valuation (an assignment of truth values to all atoms involved) that makes Γ true also makes ϕ true. If there is a small number of valuations, this is not so bad. However, when we look at predicate logic, we will find that there are infinitely many models to consider (the notion corresponding to the valuation in propositional logic is called a model). Thus, in semantics, we have a 'negative' characterisation of the logic. We find establishing assertions of the form $\Gamma \nvDash \phi$ (ϕ is not a semantic entailment of all formulas in Γ) easier than establishing $\Gamma \vDash \phi$ (ϕ is a semantic entailment of Γ), for in the former case we need only talk about one model, whereas in the latter we have to talk about infinitely many.

All this goes to show that it is important to study *both* proof theory *and* semantics. For example, if you are trying to show that ϕ is not a consequence of Γ and you have a hard time doing that, you might want to change your strategy for a while by trying to prove $\Gamma \vdash \phi$. If you find a proof, you know for sure that ϕ is a consequence of Γ. If you can't find a proof, then your attempts at proving it often provide insights which lead you to the construction of a counter example. The fact that proof theory and semantics are equivalent is amazing, but it does not stop them having separate roles in logic, each meriting close study.

2.4.1 Models

Recall how we evaluated formulas in propositional logic. For example, given the propositional formula

$$(p \vee \neg q) \rightarrow (q \rightarrow p)$$

we evaluated this expression by computing a truth value (T or F) for it, based on a given valuation (assumed truth values for p and q). This activity is essentially the construction of one line in the truth table of $(p \vee \neg q) \rightarrow (q \rightarrow p)$. How can we evaluate formulas in predicate logic? We 'enrich' the formula above to

$$\forall x \, \exists y \, ((P(x) \vee \neg Q(y)) \rightarrow (Q(x) \rightarrow P(y))).$$

Could we simply assume truth values for $P(x)$, $Q(y)$, $Q(x)$ and $P(y)$ and compute a truth value as before? Not quite, since we have to reflect the meaning of the quantifiers $\forall x$ and $\exists y$, their *dependences* and the actual parameters of P and Q — a formula $\forall x\, \exists y\, R(x,y)$ generally means something else other than $\exists y\, \forall x\, R(x,y)$; why? The problem is that variables are place holders for any, or some, unspecified concrete value. Such values can be of almost any kind: students, birds, numbers, complicated mathematical objects, data structures, programs and so on.

Thus, if we encounter a formula $\exists y\, \psi$, we try to find some instance of y (some concrete value) such that ψ holds for that particular instance of y. If this succeeds (i.e. there is such a value of y for which ψ holds), then $\exists y\, \psi$ evaluates to T; otherwise (i.e. there is *no* concrete value of y which realises ψ) it returns F. Dually, evaluating $\forall x\, \psi$ amounts to showing that ψ evaluates to T for *all* possible values of x; if this is successful, we know that $\forall x\, \psi$ evaluates to T; otherwise (i.e. there is *some* value of x such that ψ computes F) it returns F. Of course, such evaluations of formulas require a fixed universe of concrete values, the things we are, so to speak, talking about. Thus, the truth value of a formula in predicate logic depends on, and varies with, the actual choice of values and the meaning of the predicate and function symbols involved.

If variables can take on only finitely many values, we can write a program that evaluates formulas in a compositional way. If the root node of ϕ is $\wedge$, $\vee$, $\rightarrow$ or $\neg$, we can compute the truth value of ϕ by using the truth table of the respective logical connective and by computing the truth values of the subtree(s) of that root, as discussed in Chapter 1. If the root is a quantifier, we have sketched above how to proceed. This leaves us with the case of the root node being a predicate symbol P (in propositional logic this was an atom and we were done already). Such a predicate requires n arguments which have to be terms $t_1, t_2, \ldots, t_n$. Therefore, we need to be able to assign truth values to formulas of the form $P(t_1, t_2, \ldots, t_n)$.

For formulas $P(t_1, t_2, \ldots, t_n)$, there is more going on than in the case of propositional logic. For $n = 2$, the predicate P could stand for something like 'the number computed by t_1 is less than, or equal to, the number computed by t_2'. Therefore, we cannot just assign truth values to P in a random fashion. We require a *model* of all function and predicate symbols involved. For example, terms could denote *real numbers* and P could denote the relation 'less than or equal to' on the set of real numbers.

Definition 2.10 Let $\mathscr{F}$ be a set of function symbols and $\mathscr{P}$ a set of predicate symbols, each symbol with a fixed number of required arguments. A *model* $\mathcal{M}$ of the pair $(\mathcal{F}, \mathcal{P})$ consists of the following set of data:

1. A non-empty set A, the *universe of concrete values*;
2. for each $f \in \mathcal{F}$ with n arguments a concrete function

$$f^{\mathcal{M}} : A^n \to A$$

from A^n, the set of n-tuples over A, to A; and
3. for each $P \in \mathcal{P}$ with n arguments a subset $P^{\mathcal{M}} \subseteq A^n$ of n-tuples over A.

The distinction between f and $f^{\mathcal{M}}$ and between P and $P^{\mathcal{M}}$ is most important. The symbols f and P are just that: symbols, whereas $f^{\mathcal{M}}$ and $P^{\mathcal{M}}$ denote a concrete function and relation in a model $\mathcal{M}$, respectively.

Example 2.11 Let $\mathcal{F} \overset{\text{def}}{=} \{+, *, -, s\}$ and $\mathcal{P} \overset{\text{def}}{=} \{=, \leq, <, zero\}$, where $+$, $*$ and $-$ take two arguments and s one; and where $=$, $\leq$ and $<$ are predicates with two arguments and *zero* is a predicate with just one argument. We choose as a model $\mathcal{M}$ the following:

1. The non-empty set A is the set of real numbers.
2. The functions $+^{\mathcal{M}}$, $*^{\mathcal{M}}$ and $-^{\mathcal{M}}$ take two real numbers as arguments and return their *sum*, *product* and *difference*, respectively.
3. The predicates $=^{\mathcal{M}}$, $\leq^{\mathcal{M}}$ and $<^{\mathcal{M}}$ model the relations *equal to*, *less than* and *strictly less than*, respectively. The predicate $zero^{\mathcal{M}}$ holds for r iff r equals 0.

Example 2.12 Let $\mathcal{F} \overset{\text{def}}{=} \{e, \cdot\}$ and $\mathcal{P} \overset{\text{def}}{=} \{\leq\}$, where e is a constant, $\cdot$ is a function of two arguments and $\leq$ is a predicate in need of two arguments as well. Again, we write $\cdot$ and $\leq$ in infix notation as in

$$(t_1 \cdot t_2) \leq (t \cdot t).$$

The model $\mathcal{M}$ we have in mind has as set A all binary strings, finite words over the alphabet $\{0, 1\}$, including the empty string denoted by ϵ. The interpretation $e^{\mathcal{M}}$ of e is just the empty word ϵ. The interpretation $\cdot^{\mathcal{M}}$ of $\cdot$ is the concatenation of words. For example, $0110 \cdot^{\mathcal{M}} 1110$ equals 01101110. In general, if $a_1 a_2 \ldots a_k$ and $b_1 b_2 \ldots b_n$ are such words with $a_i, b_j \in \{0, 1\}$, then $a_1 a_2 \ldots a_k \cdot^{\mathcal{M}} b_1 b_2 \ldots b_n$ equals $a_1 a_2 \ldots a_k b_1 b_2 \ldots b_n$. Finally, we interpret $\leq$ as the *prefix ordering* of words. We say that s_1 is a *prefix* of s_2 if there is a binary word s_3 such that $s_1 \cdot^{\mathcal{M}} s_3$ equals s_2. For example, 011 is a prefix of 011001 and 011, but 010 is not. Thus, $\leq^{\mathcal{M}}$ is the set $\{(s_1, s_2) \mid s_1 \text{ is a prefix of } s_2\}$.

Here are some formulas in predicate logic which we want to check on this model informally:

- In our model, the formula

$$\forall x\,(x \leq x \cdot e) \wedge (x \cdot e \leq x)$$

says that every word is a prefix of itself concatenated with the empty word and conversely. Clearly, this holds in our model, for $s \cdot^{\mathcal{M}} \epsilon$ is just s and every word is a prefix of itself.

- In our model, the formula

$$\exists y\,\forall x\,(y \leq x)$$

says that there exists a word s that is a prefix of every other word. This is true, for we may chose ϵ as such a word (there is no other choice in this case).

- In our model, the formula

$$\forall x\,\exists y\,(y \leq x)$$

says that every word has a prefix. This is clearly the case and there are in general multiple choices for y, which are dependent on x.

- In our model, the formula $\forall x\,\forall y\,\forall z\,((x \leq y) \rightarrow (x \cdot z \leq y \cdot z))$ says that whenever a word s_1 is a prefix of s_2, then $s_1 s$ has to be a prefix of $s_2 s$ for every word s. This is clearly *not* the case. For example, take s_1 as 01, s_2 as 011 and s_3 to be 0.

- In our model, the formula

$$\neg\exists x\,\forall y\,((x \leq y) \rightarrow (y \leq x))$$

says that there is no word s such that whenever s is a prefix of some other word s_1, it is the case that s_1 is a prefix of s as well. This is true since there cannot be such an s. Assume, for the sake of argument, that there were such a word s. Then s is clearly a prefix of $s0$, but $s0$ cannot be a prefix of s since $s0$ contains one more bit than s.

It is crucial to realise that the notion of a model is extremely liberal and open-ended. All it takes is to choose a non-empty set A, whose elements model real-world objects, and a set of concrete functions and relations, one for each function, respectively predicate, symbol. The only mild requirement imposed on all of this is that the concrete functions and relations on A have the same number of arguments as their syntactic counterparts.

However, you, as a designer or implementor of such a model, have the responsibility of choosing your model wisely. Your model should be a sufficiently accurate picture of whatever it is you want to model, but at the same time it should abstract away (= ignore) aspects of the world which are irrelevant from the perspective of your task at hand.

For example, if you build a database of family relationships, then it would be foolish to interpret *father-of*(x, y) by something like 'x is the daughter of y'. By the same token, you probably would not want to have a predicate for 'is taller than', since your focus in this model is merely on relationships defined by birth. Of course, there are circumstances in which you may want to add additional features to your database.

Given a model $\mathcal{M}$ for a pair $(\mathcal{F}, \mathcal{P})$ of function and predicate symbols, we are now almost in a position to formally compute a truth value for all formulas in predicate logic which involve only function and predicate symbols from $(\mathcal{F}, \mathcal{P})$. There is still one thing, though, that we need to discuss. Given a formula $\forall x \, \phi$ or $\exists x \, \phi$, we intend to check whether ϕ holds for all, respectively some, value a in our model. While this is intuitive, we have no way of expressing this in our syntax: the formula ϕ usually has x as a free variable; $\phi[a/x]$ is well-intended, but ill-formed since $\phi[a/x]$ is *not* a logical formula, for a is not a term but an element of our model.

Therefore we are forced to interpret formulas *relative to an environment*. You may think of environments in a variety of ways. Essentially, they are look-up tables for all variables; such a table l associates with every variable x a value $l(x)$ of the model. So you can also say that environments are functions

$$l : \mathsf{var} \to A$$

from the set of variables var to the universe of values A of the underlying model. Given such a look-up table, we can assign truth values to all formulas. However, for some of these computations we need *updated* look-up tables.

Definition 2.13 Let l be a look-up table for a universe of concrete values A and let $a \in A$. We denote by $l[x \mapsto a]$ the look-up table which maps x to a and any other variable y to $l(y)$.

Finally, we are able to give a semantics to formulas of predicate logic. For propositional logic, we did this by computing a truth value. Clearly, it suffices to know in which cases this value is T.

Definition 2.14 Given a model $\mathcal{M}$ for a pair $(\mathcal{F}, \mathcal{P})$ and given an environment l, we define the *satisfaction relation*

$$\mathcal{M} \models_l \phi$$

for each logical formula ϕ over the pair $(\mathcal{F}, \mathcal{P})$ by structural induction on ϕ. The denotation $\mathcal{M} \vDash_l \phi$ says that ϕ computes to T in the model $\mathcal{M}$ with respect to the environment l.

P: If ϕ is of the form $P(t_1, t_2, \ldots, t_n)$, then we interpret the terms $t_1, t_2, \ldots, t_n$ in our set A by replacing all variables with their values according to l. In this way we compute concrete values $a_1, a_2, \ldots, a_n$ of A for each of these terms, where we interpret any function symbol $f \in \mathcal{F}$ by $f^{\mathcal{M}}$. Now $\mathcal{M} \vDash_l P(t_1, t_2, \ldots, t_n)$ holds iff $(a_1, a_2, \ldots, a_n)$ is in the set $P^{\mathcal{M}}$.

$\forall x$: The relation $\mathcal{M} \vDash_l \forall x\, \psi$ holds iff $\mathcal{M} \vDash_{l[x \rightarrow a]} \psi$ holds for all $a \in A$.

$\exists x$: Dually, $\mathcal{M} \vDash_l \exists x\, \psi$ holds iff $\mathcal{M} \vDash_{l[x \rightarrow a]} \psi$ holds for some $a \in A$.

$\neg$: The relation $\mathcal{M} \vDash_l \neg\psi$ holds iff it is not the case that $\mathcal{M} \vDash_l \psi$ holds.

$\vee$: The relation $\mathcal{M} \vDash_l \psi_1 \vee \psi_2$ holds iff $\mathcal{M} \vDash_l \psi_1$ or $\mathcal{M} \vDash_l \psi_2$ holds.

$\wedge$: The relation $\mathcal{M} \vDash_l \psi_1 \wedge \psi_2$ holds iff $\mathcal{M} \vDash_l \psi_1$ and $\mathcal{M} \vDash_l \psi_2$ hold.

$\rightarrow$: The relation $\mathcal{M} \vDash_l \psi_1 \rightarrow \psi_2$ holds iff $\mathcal{M} \vDash_l \psi_2$ holds whenever $\mathcal{M} \vDash_l \psi_1$ holds.

We sometimes write $\mathcal{M} \nvDash_l \phi$ to denote that $\mathcal{M} \vDash_l \phi$ *does not hold*.

There is a straightforward inductive argument on the height of the parse tree of a formula which says that $\mathcal{M} \vDash_l \phi$ holds iff $\mathcal{M} \vDash_{l'} \phi$ holds, whenever l and l' are two environments which are identical on the set of free variables of ϕ. In particular, if ϕ has *no* free variables at all, we then call ϕ a *sentence*; we conclude that $\mathcal{M} \vDash_l \phi$ holds, or does not hold, regardless of the choice of l. Thus, for sentences ϕ we often write

$$\mathcal{M} \vDash \phi$$

since the choice of an environment l is then irrelevant.

Example 2.15 Let us illustrate the definitions above by means of another simple example. Let $\mathcal{F} \stackrel{\text{def}}{=} \{\text{alma}\}$ and $\mathcal{P} \stackrel{\text{def}}{=} \{\text{loves}\}$ where alma is a constant and loves a predicate with two arguments. The model $\mathcal{M}$ we choose here consists of the set $A \stackrel{\text{def}}{=} \{a, b, c\}$, the constant function $\text{alma}^{\mathcal{M}} \stackrel{\text{def}}{=} a$ and the predicate

$$\text{loves}^{\mathcal{M}} \stackrel{\text{def}}{=} \{(a, a), (b, a), (c, a)\},$$

which has two arguments as required. We want to check whether the model $\mathcal{M}$ satisfies

None of Alma's lovers' lovers love her.

First, we need to express the, morally worrying, sentence in predicate logic. Here is such an encoding (one is often able to find other encodings which differ slightly from the one that is closest to the linguistic and semantic structure of the sentence):

$$\forall x \, \forall y \, (\text{loves}(x, \text{alma}) \wedge \text{loves}(y, x) \to \neg\text{loves}(y, \text{alma})).$$

Does the model $\mathcal{M}$ satisfy this formula? Well, it does not; for we may chose a for x and b for y. Since (a, a) is in the set loves$^{\mathcal{M}}$ and (a, a) is in set loves$^{\mathcal{M}}$, we would need that the latter does not hold since it is the interpretation of loves(y, alma); this cannot be.

And what changes if we modify $\mathcal{M}$ to $\mathcal{M}'$, where we keep A and alma$^{\mathcal{M}}$, but redefine the interpretation of loves as

$$\text{loves}^{\mathcal{M}'} \overset{\text{def}}{=} \{(a, a), (b, a), (c, b)\}?$$

Well, now there is exactly one lover of Alma's lovers, namely c; but c is not one of Alma's lovers. Thus, the formula above holds in the model $\mathcal{M}'$.

EXERCISES 2.6
* 1. Consider the formula

$$\phi \overset{\text{def}}{=} \forall x \, \forall y \, Q(g(x, y), g(y, y), z).$$

Obviously, Q is a predicate with three arguments and g a function with two arguments. Find two models $\mathcal{M}$ and $\mathcal{M}'$ with respective environments l and l' such that $\mathcal{M} \vDash_l \phi$ but $\mathcal{M}' \nvDash_{l'} \phi$.

2. Consider the sentence

$$\phi \overset{\text{def}}{=} \forall x \, \exists y \, \exists z \, (P(x, y) \wedge P(z, y) \wedge (P(x, z) \to P(z, x))).$$

Which of the following models satisfies ϕ?

(a) The model $\mathcal{M}$ consists of the set of natural numbers with $P^{\mathcal{M}} \overset{\text{def}}{=} \{(m, n) \mid m < n\}$.

(b) The model $\mathcal{M}'$ consists of the set of natural numbers with $P^{\mathcal{M}'} \overset{\text{def}}{=} \{(m, 2 * m) \mid m \text{ natural number}\}$.

(c) The model $\mathcal{M}''$ consists of the set of natural numbers with $P^{\mathcal{M}''} \overset{\text{def}}{=} \{(m, n) \mid m < n + 1\}$.

3. Let P be a predicate with two arguments. Find a model $\mathcal{M}$ which satisfies the sentence $\forall x \, \neg P(x, x)$. Find also a model $\mathcal{M}'$ such that $\mathcal{M}' \nvDash \forall x \, \neg P(x, x)$.

4. Consider the sentence $\forall x (\exists y P(x,y) \wedge (\exists z P(z,x) \rightarrow \forall y P(x,y)))$. We already noted that its meaning in a given model is independent of the chosen look-up table l. Please simulate the evaluation of this sentence in a model of your choice, focusing on how the initial look-up table l grows and shrinks like a stack when you evaluate its subformulas according to the definition of the satisfaction relation.

5. Let $\mathcal{F} \stackrel{\text{def}}{=} \{d,f,g\}$, where d is a constant symbol, f a function symbol with three arguments and g a function symbol with two arguments. As model $\mathcal{M}$, we choose the set of natural numbers $0,1,2,\dots$. Further, $d^{\mathcal{M}} \stackrel{\text{def}}{=} 2$, $f^{\mathcal{M}}(k,n,m) \stackrel{\text{def}}{=} k*n+m$ and $g^{\mathcal{M}}(k,n) \stackrel{\text{def}}{=} k+n*n$. E.g. $f^{\mathcal{M}}(1,2,3)$ equals 5 and $g^{\mathcal{M}}(2,3)$ equals 11. Assuming a look-up table l with $l(x) \stackrel{\text{def}}{=} 5$ and $l(y) \stackrel{\text{def}}{=} 7$, compute the meaning of the terms below in the model $\mathcal{M}$:

   * (a) $f(d,x,d)$
   (b) $f(g(x,d),y,g(d,d))$
   (c) $g(f(g(d,y),f(x,g(d,d),x),y),f(y,g(d,d),d))$.

6. Let ϕ be the formula

$$\forall x \, \forall y \, \exists z \, (R(x,y) \rightarrow R(y,z)),$$

where R is a predicate symbol of two arguments.

   * (a) Let $A \stackrel{\text{def}}{=} \{a,b,c,d\}$ and $R^{\mathcal{M}} \stackrel{\text{def}}{=} \{(b,c),(b,b),(b,a)\}$. Do we have $\mathcal{M} \models \phi$? Justify your answer, whatever it is.
   * (b) Let $A' \stackrel{\text{def}}{=} \{a,b,c\}$ and $R^{\mathcal{M}'} \stackrel{\text{def}}{=} \{(b,c),(a,b),(c,b)\}$. Do we have $\mathcal{M}' \models \phi$? Justify your answer, whatever it is.

2.4.2 Semantic entailment

Given a model $\mathcal{M}$ for a formula ϕ and an environment l for $\mathcal{M}$, we have learned how to check whether $\mathcal{M}$ satisfies ϕ with respect to l; the affirmative we denoted as $\mathcal{M} \models_l \phi$. This is strikingly different from what happened in propositional logic. There we had a list of *formulas* on the left-hand side of the sign $\models$. We wrote $\phi_1, \phi_2, \dots, \phi_n \models \psi$ to express the semantic entailment of ψ from $\phi_1, \phi_2, \dots, \phi_n$: whenever all $\phi_1, \phi_2, \dots, \phi_n$ evaluate to T, the formula ψ evaluates to T as well. How can we define such a notion for formulas in predicate logic?

Definition 2.16 Let $\phi_1, \phi_2, \dots, \phi_n, \psi$ be formulas in predicate logic. Then $\phi_1, \phi_2, \dots, \phi_n \models \psi$ denotes that, whenever $\mathcal{M} \models_l \phi_i$ for $1 \leq i \leq n$, then $\mathcal{M} \models_l \psi$, *for all* models $\mathcal{M}$ and look-up tables l.

The symbol $\vDash$ is overloaded in predicate logic. We use it to denote satisfiability:

$$\text{there is some model } \mathcal{M} \text{ with } \mathcal{M} \vDash \phi$$

of sentences and semantic entailment:

$$\phi_1, \phi_2, \ldots, \phi_n \vDash \psi$$

of formulas. Computationally, each of these notions means trouble. First, establishing $\mathcal{M} \vDash \phi$ will cause problems, if done on a machine, as soon as the universe of values A of $\mathcal{M}$ is infinite. For example, if ϕ is a sentence of the form $\forall x\, \psi$, then we need to verify $\mathcal{M} \vDash_{[x \to a]} \psi$ for infinitely many elements a.

Second, and much more seriously, in trying to verify $\phi_1, \phi_2, \ldots, \phi_n \vDash \psi$, we have to check things out for *all possible models*, i.e. all models which are equipped with the right structure (i.e. they have functions and predicates with the matching number of arguments). This task is impossible to perform mechanically. This should be contrasted to the situation in propositional logic, where the computation of the truth tables of the propositions involved was the basis for computing this relationship successfully.

However, we can sometimes reason that certain semantic entailments are valid. We do this by providing an argument that does not depend on the actual model at hand. Of course, this works only for a very limited number of cases. The most prominent ones are the *quantifier equivalences* which we already encountered in the section on natural deduction.

Let us look at a couple of examples of semantic entailment.

- The justification of the semantic entailment

$$\forall x\,(P(x) \to Q(x)) \vDash \forall x\, P(x) \to \forall x\, Q(x)$$

is as follows. Let $\mathcal{M}$ be a model satisfying $\forall x\,(P(x) \to Q(x))$. We need to show that $\mathcal{M}$ satisfies $\forall x\, P(x) \to \forall x\, Q(x)$ as well. On inspecting the definition of $\mathcal{M} \vDash \psi_1 \to \psi_2$, we see that we are done if not every element of our model satisfies P. Otherwise, every element does satisfy P. But since $\mathcal{M}$ satisfies $\forall x\,(P(x) \to Q(x))$, the latter fact forces every element of our model to satisfy Q as well. By combining these two cases (i.e. either all elements of $\mathcal{M}$ satisfy P, or not) we have shown that $\mathcal{M}$ satisfies $\forall x\, P(x) \to \forall x\, Q(x)$.

- What about the converse of the above? Is

$$\forall x\, P(x) \to \forall x\, Q(x) \vDash \forall x\,(P(x) \to Q(x))$$

valid as well? Hardly! Suppose that $\mathcal{M}'$ is a model satisfying $\forall x\, P(x) \to \forall x\, Q(x)$. If A' is its underlying set and $P^{\mathcal{M}'}$ and $Q^{\mathcal{M}'}$ are the corresponding interpretations of P and Q, then $\mathcal{M}' \vDash \forall x\, P(x) \to \forall x\, Q(x)$ simply says that, if $P^{\mathcal{M}'}$ equals A', then $Q^{\mathcal{M}'}$ must equal A' as well. However, if $P^{\mathcal{M}'}$ does not equal A', then this implication is vacuously true (remember that $\mathsf{F} \to \cdot = \mathsf{T}$ no matter that $\cdot$ actually is). In this case we do not get any additional constraints on our model $\mathcal{M}'$. After these observations, it is now easy to construct a counter example. Let $A' \stackrel{\text{def}}{=} \{a, b\}$, $P^{\mathcal{M}'} \stackrel{\text{def}}{=} \{a\}$ and $Q^{\mathcal{M}'} \stackrel{\text{def}}{=} \{b\}$. Then $\mathcal{M}' \vDash \forall x\, P(x) \to \forall x\, Q(x)$ holds, but $\mathcal{M}' \vDash \forall x\, (P(x) \to Q(x))$ does not.

2.4.3 The semantics of equality

We have already pointed out the open-ended nature of the semantics of predicate logic. Given a predicate logic over a set of function symbols $\mathcal{F}$ and a set of predicate symbols $\mathcal{P}$, we need only a non-empty set A equipped with concrete functions $f^{\mathcal{M}}$ (for $f \in \mathcal{F}$) and concrete predicates $P^{\mathcal{M}}$ (for $P \in \mathcal{P}$) in A which have the number of arguments agreed upon in our specification. Of course, we also stressed that most models have natural interpretations of functions and predicates, but notions like *semantic entailment*:

$$\phi_1, \phi_2, \ldots, \phi_n \vDash \psi$$

really depend on *all possible models*, even the ones that don't seem to make any sense. Apparently there is no way out of this peculiarity. For example, where would you draw the line between a model that makes sense and one that doesn't? And would any such choice, or such a set of criteria, not be *subjective*? Such constraints could also forbid a modification of your model if this alteration were caused by a slight adjustment of the problem domain you intended to model. You see that there are a lot of good reasons for maintaining such a liberal stance towards the notion of models in predicate logic.

However, there is one famous exception. Often one presents predicate logic such that there is always a special predicate $=$ available to denote equality (recall Section 2.3.1); it has two arguments and

$$t_1 = t_2$$

has the intended meaning that the terms t_1 and t_2 compute the same thing. We discussed its proof rule in natural deduction already in Section 2.3.1. Semantically, one recognises the special role of equality by imposing on an interpretation function $=^{\mathcal{M}}$ to be actual equality on the set A. Thus, (a, b) is in the set $=^{\mathcal{M}}$ iff a and b are the same elements in the set A. For example, given $A \stackrel{\text{def}}{=} \{a, b, c\}$, we are forced to interpret equality such that $=^{\mathcal{M}}$ is just

$$\{(a, a), (b, b), (c, c)\}.$$

Hence the semantics of equality is easy, for it is always modelled *extensionally*.

EXERCISES 2.7

* 1. Consider the three sentences

$$\phi_1 \stackrel{\text{def}}{=} \forall x\, P(x, x)$$
$$\phi_2 \stackrel{\text{def}}{=} \forall x \forall y\, (P(x, y) \to P(y, x))$$
$$\phi_3 \stackrel{\text{def}}{=} \forall x \forall y \forall z\, ((P(x, y) \wedge P(y, z) \to P(x, z)))$$

   which express that the binary predicate P is *reflexive, symmetric and transitive*, respectively. Show that none of these sentences is semantically entailed by the other ones by choosing for each pair of sentences above a model which satisfies these two, but not the third sentence — essentially, you are asked to find three binary relations, each satisfying just two of these properties.

* 2. Show the semantic entailment

$$\forall x\, P(x) \vee \forall x\, Q(x) \vDash \forall x\, (P(x) \vee Q(x)).$$

3. Prove $\forall x \neg\phi \vDash \neg\exists x\, \phi$; for that you have to take any model which satisfies $\forall x \neg\phi$ and you have to reason why this model must also satisfy $\neg\exists x\, \phi$. You should do this in a similar way to the examples in Section 2.4.2.

4. Let ϕ and ψ and η be formulas of predicate logic such that they contain no free variables.

   (a) If ψ is a semantically entailed by ϕ, is it necessarily the case that ψ is *not* semantically entailed by $\neg\phi$?

   * (b) If ψ is semantically entailed by $\phi \wedge \eta$, is it necessarily the case that ψ is semantically entailed by ϕ *and* semantically entailed by η?

   (c) If ψ is semantically entailed by ϕ or by η, is it necessarily the case that ψ is semantically entailed by $\phi \vee \eta$?

   (d) Explain why ψ is semantically entailed by ϕ iff $\phi \to \psi$ is valid, i.e. true in all models.

5. Show

$$\forall x\, (P(x) \vee Q(x)) \nvDash \forall x\, P(x) \vee \forall x\, Q(x).$$

Thus, find a model which satisfies $\forall x\,(P(x) \vee Q(x))$, but not $\forall x\,P(x) \vee \forall x\,Q(x)$.

6. We call a set $\phi_1, \phi_2, \ldots, \phi_n$ of formulas *consistent* if there is a model of all predicate and function symbols involved such that all formulas $\phi_1, \phi_2, \ldots, \phi_n$ evaluate to T for that model. For each set of formulas below show that they are consistent:

   (a) $\forall x\,\neg S(x, x)$, $\exists x\,P(x)$, $\forall x\,\exists y\,S(x, y)$, $\forall x\,(P(x) \rightarrow \exists y\,S(y, x))$
   * (b) $\forall x\,\neg S(x, x)$, $\forall x\,\exists y\,S(x, y)$,
         $\forall x\,\forall y\,\forall z\,((S(x, y) \wedge S(y, z)) \rightarrow S(x, z))$
   (c) $(\forall x\,(P(x) \vee Q(x))) \rightarrow \exists y\,R(y)$, $\forall x\,(R(x) \rightarrow Q(x))$, $\exists y\,(\neg Q(y) \wedge P(y))$
   * (d) $\exists x\,S(x, x)$, $\forall x\,\forall y\,(S(x, y) \rightarrow (x = y))$.

7. Let P and Q be predicate symbols with one argument each. For the formulas below, check whether they are theorems. If not, then you have to find a model of P and Q such that the formula evaluates to F. Otherwise, you should find a proof using no premises:

   (a) $\forall x\,\forall y\,((P(x) \rightarrow P(y)) \wedge (P(y) \rightarrow P(x)))$
   (b) $(\forall x\,((P(x) \rightarrow Q(x)) \wedge (Q(x) \rightarrow P(x)))) \rightarrow ((\forall x\,P(x)) \rightarrow (\forall x\,Q(x)))$
   (c) $((\forall x\,P(x)) \rightarrow (\forall x\,Q(x))) \rightarrow (\forall x\,((P(x) \rightarrow Q(x)) \wedge (Q(x) \rightarrow P(x))))$
   (d) (Difficult.) $(\forall x\,\exists y\,(P(x) \rightarrow Q(y))) \rightarrow (\exists y\,\forall x\,(P(x) \rightarrow Q(y)))$.

8. For each of the formulas of predicate logic below, either find a model which does not satisfy it, or prove it without any premises:

   (a) $(\forall x\,\forall y\,(S(x, y) \rightarrow S(y, x))) \rightarrow (\forall x\,\neg S(x, x))$
   (b) $\exists y\,((\forall x\,P(x)) \rightarrow P(y))$
   (c) $(\forall x\,(P(x) \rightarrow \exists y\,Q(y))) \rightarrow (\forall x\,\exists y\,(P(x) \rightarrow Q(y)))$
   (d) $(\forall x\,\exists y\,(P(x) \rightarrow Q(y))) \rightarrow (\forall x\,(P(x) \rightarrow \exists y\,Q(y)))$
   (e) $\forall x\,\forall y\,(S(x, y) \rightarrow (\exists z\,(S(x, z) \wedge S(z, y))))$
   (f) $(\forall x\,\forall y\,(S(x, y) \rightarrow (x = y))) \rightarrow (\forall z\,\neg S(z, z))$
   (g) $(\forall x\,\exists y\,(S(x, y) \wedge ((S(x, y) \wedge S(y, x)) \rightarrow (x = y)))) \rightarrow (\neg \exists z\,\forall w\,(S(z, w)))$.

2.5 Undecidability of predicate logic

We conclude our introduction to predicate logic with some negative results. Given a formula ϕ in *propositional logic* we can, at least in principle, determine whether $\models \phi$ holds: if ϕ has n propositional atoms, then the truth table of ϕ contains 2^n lines; and $\vDash \phi$ holds if, and only if, the column for ϕ contains only T entries.

The bad news is that such a mechanical procedure, working for all formulas ϕ, cannot be provided if ϕ is a formula in *predicate logic*. We will give a formal proof of this negative result, though we rely on an informal (yet intuitive) notion of computability.

The problem of determining whether a predicate logic formula is valid is known as a *decision problem*. A solution to a decision problem is a program (written in Java, C, or any other common language) that takes problem instances as input and *always* terminates, producing a correct 'yes' or 'no' output. In the case of the decision problem for predicate logic, the input to the program is an arbitrary formula ϕ of predicate logic and the program is correct if it produces 'yes' if the formula is valid and 'no' if it is not. Note that the program which solves a decision problem must terminate for all well-formed input: a program which goes on thinking about it for ever is not allowed.

The decision problem at hand is this:

Validity in predicate logic. *Given a logical formula ϕ in predicate logic, does $\vDash \phi$ hold, yes or no?*

We now show that this problem is not solvable; we cannot write a correct C or Java program that works for all ϕ. It is important to be clear about exactly what we are stating. Naturally, there are some ϕ which can easily be seen to be valid; and others which can easily be seen to be invalid. However, there are also some ϕ for which it is not easy. Every ϕ can, in principle, be discovered to be valid or not, if you are prepared to work arbitrarily hard at it; but there is no uniform mechanical procedure for determining whether ϕ is valid which will work for all ϕ.

We prove this by a well-known technique called *problem reduction*. That is, we take some other problem, of which we already know that it is not solvable, and we then show that the solvability of *our* problem entails the solvability of the other one. This is a beautiful application of the proof rule RAA, since we can then infer that our own problem cannot be solvable as well.

The problem that is known not to be solvable is interesting in its own right and, upon first reflection, does not seem to have a lot to do with predicate logic; it is the *Post correspondence problem*:

The Post correspondence problem. *Given a finite sequence of pairs* (s_1, t_1), $(s_2, t_2), \ldots, (s_k, t_k)$ *such that all* s_i *and* t_i *are binary strings of positive length, is there a sequence of indices* $i_1, i_2, \ldots, i_n$ *with* $n \geq 1$ *such that the concatenation of strings* $s_{i_1} s_{i_2} \ldots s_{i_n}$ *equals* $t_{i_1} t_{i_2} \ldots t_{i_n}$?

Here is an *instance* of the problem which we can solve successfully: the concrete correspondence problem instance C is given by a sequence of three pairs

$$C \stackrel{\text{def}}{=} ((1, 101), (10, 00), (011, 11))$$

so $s_1 \stackrel{\text{def}}{=} 1$, $s_2 \stackrel{\text{def}}{=} 10$ and $s_3 \stackrel{\text{def}}{=} 011$, whereas $t_1 \stackrel{\text{def}}{=} 101$, $t_2 \stackrel{\text{def}}{=} 00$ and $t_3 \stackrel{\text{def}}{=} 11$. A solution to the problem is the sequence of indices $(1, 3, 2, 3)$ since $s_1 s_3 s_2 s_3$ and $t_1 t_3 t_2 t_3$ both equal 101110011. Maybe you think that this problem must surely be solvable; but remember that a computational solution would have to be a program that solves *all* such problem instances. Things get a bit tougher already if we look at this (solvable) problem:

$$s_1 \stackrel{\text{def}}{=} 001 \quad s_2 \stackrel{\text{def}}{=} 01 \quad s_3 \stackrel{\text{def}}{=} 01 \quad s_4 \stackrel{\text{def}}{=} 10$$
$$t_1 \stackrel{\text{def}}{=} 0 \quad t_2 \stackrel{\text{def}}{=} 011 \quad t_3 \stackrel{\text{def}}{=} 101 \quad t_4 \stackrel{\text{def}}{=} 001.$$

You are invited to solve this by hand, or by writing a program for this specific instance.

Note that the same number can occur in the sequence of indices, as happened in the first example in which 3 occurs twice. This means that the search space we are dealing with is infinite, which should give us a strong intuition that the problem is unsolvable. We do not formally prove it in this book.

The proof of the following theorem is due to the mathematician A. Church.

Theorem 2.17 *The decision problem of validity in predicate logic is undecidable: there is no procedure which, given any* ϕ, *decides whether* $\models \phi$ *holds.*

PROOF: As said before, we pretend that validity is decidable for predicate logic and thereby solve the (insoluble) Post correspondence problem. Given a correspondence problem instance C:

$$
\begin{array}{cccc}
s_1 & s_2 & \ldots & s_k \\
t_1 & t_2 & \ldots & t_k
\end{array}
$$

we need to be able to construct, within finite space and time, some formula ϕ of predicate logic such that $\models \phi$ holds iff the correspondence problem instance C above has a solution. As function symbols, we choose a constant e and two function symbols f_0 and f_1 each of which requires one argument. We think of e as the empty string, or word, and f_0 and f_1 symbolically stand for concatenation with 0, respectively 1. So if $b_1 b_2 \ldots b_l$ is a binary string of bits, we can code that up as the term

$$f_{b_l}(f_{b_{l-1}} \ldots (f_{b_2}(f_{b_1}(e))) \ldots).$$

Note that this coding spells that word *backwards*. To facilitate reading those formulas, we abbreviate terms like $f_{b_l}(f_{b_{l-1}} \ldots (f_{b_2}(f_{b_1}(t))) \ldots)$ by $f_{b_1 b_2 \ldots b_l}(t)$.

We also require a predicate symbol P which expects two arguments. The intended meaning of $P(s,t)$ is that there is some sequence of indices $(i_1, i_2, \ldots, i_m)$ such that s is the term representing $s_{i_1} s_{i_2} \ldots s_{i_m}$ and t represents $t_{i_1} t_{i_2} \ldots t_{i_m}$. Thus, s constructs a string using the same sequence of indices as does t; only s uses the s_i whereas t uses the t_i.

Our sentence ϕ has the coarse structure

$$\phi_1 \wedge \phi_2 \rightarrow \phi_3$$

where we set

$$\phi_1 \stackrel{\text{def}}{=} \bigwedge_{i=1}^{k} P(f_{s_i}(e), f_{t_i}(e))$$

$$\phi_2 \stackrel{\text{def}}{=} \forall v \, \forall w \left(P(v,w) \rightarrow \bigwedge_{i=1}^{k} P(f_{s_i}(v), f_{t_i}(w)) \right)$$

$$\phi_3 \stackrel{\text{def}}{=} \exists z \, P(z,z).$$

Our claim is that formula ϕ holds in all models iff the Post correspondence problem C has a solution.

First, let us assume that $\models \phi$. Our strategy is to find a model for ϕ which gives us a solution to the correspondence problem C simply by inspecting what it means for ϕ to satisfy that particular model. The universe of concrete values A of that model is the set of all finite, binary strings (including the empty one). The interpretation $e^{\mathcal{M}}$ of the constant e is just that empty word. The interpretation of f_0 is the unary function $f_0^{\mathcal{M}}$ which appends a 0 to a given word:

$$f_0^{\mathcal{M}}(s) \stackrel{\text{def}}{=} s0;$$

similarly,

$$f_1^{\mathcal{M}}(s) \stackrel{\text{def}}{=} s1$$

appends a 1 to a given word. The interpretation of P on $\mathcal{M}$ is just what we expect it to be:

$$P^{\mathcal{M}} \stackrel{\text{def}}{=} \{(s,t) \mid \text{there is a sequence of indices } (i_1, i_2, \ldots, i_m) \text{ such that}$$
$$s \text{ equals } s_{i_1} s_{i_2} \ldots s_{i_m} \text{ and } t \text{ equals } t_{i_1} t_{i_2} \ldots t_{i_m}\},$$

where s and t are binary strings and the s_i and t_i are the data of the correspondence problem C. Thus, a pair of words (s,t) lies in $P^{\mathcal{M}}$ if, using the same sequence of indices $(i_1, i_2, \ldots, i_m)$, s is built using the corresponding s_i and t is built using the respective t_i.

We now show that the fact that ϕ holds in the model $\mathcal{M}$ implies that C is solvable. First, note that $\mathcal{M}$ satisfies ϕ_1 and ϕ_2. For example, ϕ_2 says about $\mathcal{M}$ that, if the pair (s,t) is in $P^{\mathcal{M}}$, then the pair $(s\,s_i, t\,t_i)$ is also in $P^{\mathcal{M}}$ for $i = 1, 2, \ldots, k$ (you can verify this by inspecting the definition of $P^{\mathcal{M}}$). Now $(s,t) \in P^{\mathcal{M}}$ implies that there is some sequence $(i_1, i_2, \ldots, i_m)$ such that s equals $s_{i_1} s_{i_2} \ldots s_{i_m}$ and t equals $t_{i_1} t_{i_2} \ldots t_{i_m}$. We simply choose the new sequence $(i_1, i_2, \ldots, i_m, i)$ and observe that $s\,s_i$ equals $s_{i_1} s_{i_2} \ldots s_{i_m} s_i$ and $t\,t_i$ equals $t_{i_1} t_{i_2} \ldots t_{i_m} t_i$. (Why does $\mathcal{M} \vDash \phi_1$ hold?)

Since $\mathcal{M} \vDash \phi_1 \wedge \phi_2 \to \phi_3$ and $\mathcal{M} \vDash \phi_1 \wedge \phi_2$, it follows that $\mathcal{M} \vDash \phi_3$. By definition of ϕ_3 and $P^{\mathcal{M}}$, this gives us a solution to C.

Conversely, let us assume that the Post correspondence problem C has some solution, namely the sequence of indices $(i_1, i_2, \ldots, i_n)$. Now we have to show that, if $\mathcal{M}'$ is *any* model having a constant $e^{\mathcal{M}'}$, two unary functions, $f_0^{\mathcal{M}'}$ and $f_1^{\mathcal{M}'}$, and a binary predicate $P^{\mathcal{M}'}$, then that model has to satisfy ϕ. Notice that the root of the parse tree of ϕ is an implication, so this is the crucial clause for the definition of $\mathcal{M}' \vDash \phi$. By that very definition, we are already done if $\mathcal{M}' \not\vDash \phi_1$, or if $\mathcal{M}' \not\vDash \phi_2$. The harder part is therefore the one where $\mathcal{M}' \vDash \phi_1 \wedge \phi_2$, for in that case we need to verify $\mathcal{M}' \vDash \phi_3$ as well. The way we proceed here is by interpreting finite, binary strings in the domain of values A' of the model $\mathcal{M}'$. This is not unlike the coding of an interpreter for one programming language in another. The interpretation is done by a function interpret which is defined inductively on the data structure of finite, binary strings (we write ϵ for the empty word):

$$\text{interpret}(\epsilon) \stackrel{\text{def}}{=} e^{\mathcal{M}'}$$
$$\text{interpret}(s0) \stackrel{\text{def}}{=} f_0^{\mathcal{M}'}(\text{interpret}(s))$$
$$\text{interpret}(s1) \stackrel{\text{def}}{=} f_1^{\mathcal{M}'}(\text{interpret}(s)).$$

Note that interpret(s) is defined inductively on the length of s. This interpretation is, like the coding above, backwards; for example, the binary word

0100110 gets interpreted as

$$f_0^{\mathcal{M}'}(f_1^{\mathcal{M}'}(f_1^{\mathcal{M}'}(f_0^{\mathcal{M}'}(f_0^{\mathcal{M}'}(f_1^{\mathcal{M}'}(f_0^{\mathcal{M}'}(e^{\mathcal{M}'})))))))).$$

Note that

$$\text{interpret}(b_1 b_2 \dots b_l) = f_{b_l}^{\mathcal{M}'}(f_{b_{l-1}}^{\mathcal{M}'}(\dots(f_{b_1}(e^{\mathcal{M}'})\dots)))$$

is just the meaning of $f_s(e)$ in A', where $s \stackrel{\text{def}}{=} b_1 b_2 \dots b_l$. Using that and the fact that $\mathcal{M}' \vDash \phi_1$, we conclude that $(\text{interpret}(s_i), \text{interpret}(t_i)) \in P^{\mathcal{M}'}$ for $i = 1, 2, \dots, k$. Similarly, since $\mathcal{M}' \vDash \phi_2$, we know that for all $(s, t) \in P^{\mathcal{M}'}$ we have that $(\text{interpret}(ss_i), \text{interpret}(tt_i)) \in P^{\mathcal{M}'}$ for $i = 1, 2, \dots, k$. Using these two facts, starting with $(s, t) = (s_{i_1}, t_{i_1})$, we repeatedly use the latter observation to obtain

$$(\text{interpret}(s_{i_1} s_{i_2} \dots s_{i_n}), \text{interpret}(t_{i_1} t_{i_2} \dots t_{i_n})) \in P^{\mathcal{M}'}.$$

Since $s_{i_1} s_{i_2} \dots s_{i_n}$ and $t_{i_1} t_{i_2} \dots t_{i_n}$ together form a solution of C, they are equal; and therefore the elements $\text{interpret}(s_{i_1} s_{i_2} \dots s_{i_n})$ and $\text{interpret}(t_{i_1} t_{i_2} \dots t_{i_n})$ are the same in A', for interpreting the same thing gets you the same result. Hence the pair

$$(\text{interpret}(s_{i_1} s_{i_2} \dots s_{i_n}), \text{interpret}(t_{i_1} t_{i_2} \dots t_{i_n})) \in P^{\mathcal{M}'}$$

verifies $\exists z \, P(z, z)$ in $\mathcal{M}'$ and thus $\mathcal{M}' \vDash \phi_3$. $\square$

There are two more negative results which we now get quite easily. Let us say that a formula ϕ is *satisfiable* if there is some model $\mathcal{M}$ such that $\mathcal{M} \vDash \phi$. This property is not to be taken for granted; the formula

$$\exists x \, (P(x) \wedge \neg P(x))$$

is clearly unsatisfiable. More interesting is the observation that ϕ is unsatisfiable if, and only if, $\neg \phi$ is valid, i.e. holds in *all* models. This is an immediate consequence of the definitional clause $\mathcal{M} \vDash \neg \phi$ for negation. Since we can't compute validity, it follows that we cannot compute satisfiability either.

The other undecidability result comes from the soundness and completeness of predicate logic:

$$\vDash \phi \text{ iff } \vdash \phi \tag{2.2}$$

which we do not prove in this text. Since we can't decide validity, we cannot decide *provability* either, on the basis of (2.2). One might reflect on that last negative result a bit. It means bad news if one wants to implement perfect theorem provers which can mechanically produce a proof of a given formula, or refute it. It means good news, though, if we like the thought that machines still need a little bit of human help. Creativity seems to have limits if we leave it to machines alone.

EXERCISES 2.8

1. Assuming that our proof calculus for predicate logic is sound (see exercise 3), show that the following sequents cannot be proved by finding for each sequent a model such that all formulas to the left of $\vdash$ evaluate to T and the sole formula to the right of $\vdash$ evaluates to F (explain why this guarantees the non-existence of a proof):

   (a) $\forall x\,(P(x) \vee Q(x)) \vdash \forall x\,P(x) \vee \forall x\,Q(x)$
   * (b) $\forall x\,(P(x) \rightarrow R(x)),\ \forall x\,(Q(x) \rightarrow R(x)) \vdash \exists x\,(P(x) \wedge Q(x))$
   (c) $(\forall x\,P(x)) \rightarrow L \vdash \forall x\,(P(x) \rightarrow L)$, where L is a predicate symbol with no arguments
   * (d) $\forall x\,\exists y\,S(x,y) \vdash \exists y\,\forall x\,S(x,y)$
   (e) $\exists x\,P(x),\ \exists y\,Q(y) \vdash \exists z\,(P(z) \wedge Q(z))$.

2. Let P and Q be predicate symbols with one argument each. For the formulas below check whether they are theorems. If not, then you have to find a model of P and Q such that the formula evaluates to F. Otherwise, you should find a proof using no premises:

   (a) $\forall x\,\forall y\,((P(x) \rightarrow P(y)) \wedge (P(y) \rightarrow P(x)))$
   * (b) $(\forall x\,((P(x) \rightarrow Q(x)) \wedge (Q(x) \rightarrow P(x)))) \rightarrow ((\forall x\,P(x)) \rightarrow (\forall x\,Q(x)))$
   (c) $((\forall x\,P(x)) \rightarrow (\forall x\,Q(x))) \rightarrow (\forall x\,((P(x) \rightarrow Q(x)) \wedge (Q(x) \rightarrow P(x))))$
   (d) (Difficult.) $(\forall x\,\exists y\,(P(x) \rightarrow Q(y))) \rightarrow (\exists y\,\forall x\,(P(x) \rightarrow Q(y)))$.

3. To show the soundness of our natural deduction rules for predicate logic, it intuitively suffices to show that the conclusion of a proof rule is true provided that all its premises are true. What additional complication arises due to the presence of variables and quantifiers? Can you precisely formalise the necessary induction hypothesis for proving soundness?

* 4. Assuming that our proof calculus for predicate logic is sound (see exercise 3), show that the following two sequents cannot be proved in predicate logic. Relying on the soundness of our proof calculus, it suffices to do the following: for each sequent you need to specify a model such that the formula on the left of $\vdash$ holds whereas the one to the right of $\vdash$ doesn't.

(a) $\exists x\,(\neg P(x) \wedge Q(x)) \vdash \forall x\,(P(x) \to Q(x))$

(b) $\exists x\,(\neg P(x) \vee \neg Q(x)) \vdash \forall x\,(P(x) \vee Q(x))$.

2.6 Bibliographic notes

Many design decisions have been taken in the development of predicate logic in the form known today. The Greeks and the medievals had systems in which many of the examples and exercises in this book could be represented, but nothing that we would recognise as predicate logic emerged until the work of Gottlob Frege in 1879, printed in [Fre03]. An account of the contributions of the many other people involved in the development of logic can be found in the first few pages of W. Hodges' chapter in [Hod83].

There are many books covering classical logic and its use in computer science; we give a few incomplete pointers to the literature. The books [SA91], [vD89] and [Gal87] cover more theoretical applications than those in this book, including type theory, logic programming, algebraic specification and term-rewriting systems. An approach focusing on automatic theorem proving is taken by [Fit96]. Books which study the mathematical aspects of predicate logic in greater detail, such as completeness of the proof systems and incompleteness of first-order arithmetic, include [Ham78] and [Hod83].

Most of these books present other proof systems besides natural deduction such as axiomatic systems and tableau systems. Although natural deduction has the advantages of elegance and simplicity over axiomatic methods, there are few expositions of it in logic books aimed at a computer science audience. One exception to this is the book [BEKV94], which is the first one to present the rules for quantifiers in the form we used here. A natural deduction theorem prover called Jape has been developed, in which one can vary the set of available rules and specify new ones[1].

A standard reference for computability theory is [BJ80]. A proof for the undecidability of the Post correspondence problem can be found in the text book [Tay98].

The second instance of a Post correspondence problem is taken from [Sch92]. A text on the fundamentals of databases systems is [EN94].

------

[1] www.comlab.ox.ac.uk/oucl/users/bernard.sufrin/jape.shtml

3

Verification by model checking

3.1 Motivation for verification

There is a great advantage in being able to verify the correctness of computer systems (whether they are hardware, software, or a combination). This is most obvious in the case of *safety-critical systems*, but also applies to those that are *commercially critical*, such as mass-produced chips, *mission critical*, etc. Formal verification methods have quite recently become usable by industry and there is a growing demand for professionals able to apply them (witness recent job adverts by BT, Intel, National Semiconductor Corp, etc.). In this chapter, and the next one, we examine two applications of logics to the question of verifying the correctness of computer systems, or programs.

(Formal) verification techniques can be thought of as comprising three parts:

- A *framework for modelling systems*, typically a description language of some sort;
- A *specification language* for describing the properties to be verified;
- A *verification method* to establish whether the description of a system satisfies the specification.

Approaches to verification can be classified according to the following criteria:

Proof-based vs. model-based. In a proof-based approach, the system description is a set of formulas Γ (in a suitable logic) and the specification is another formula ϕ. The verification method consists of trying to find a proof that $\Gamma \vdash \phi$. This typically requires guidance and expertise from the user.

In a model-based approach, the system is represented by a finite

148

model $\mathcal{M}$ for an appropriate logic. The specification is again represented by a formula ϕ and the verification method consists of computing whether a model $\mathcal{M}$ satisfies ϕ ($\mathcal{M} \vDash \phi$). This is usually automatic, though the restriction to finite models limits the applicability.

In Chapters 1 and 2, we could see that logical proof systems are often sound and complete, meaning that $\Gamma \vdash \phi$ (provability) iff $\Gamma \vDash \phi$ (semantic entailment), where the latter is defined as follows: for all models $\mathcal{M}$, if $\mathcal{M} \vDash \Gamma$, then $\mathcal{M} \vDash \phi$. Thus, we see that the model-based approach is potentially simpler than the proof-based approach, for it is based on a single model $\mathcal{M}$ rather than a possibly infinite class of them.

Degree of automation. Approaches differ on how automatic the method is. Extremes are fully automatic and fully manual, with many computer-assisted techniques somewhere in the middle.

Full- vs. property-verification. The specification may describe a single property of the system, or it may describe its full behaviour. The latter is typically expensive to verify.

Intended domain of application, which may be hardware or software; sequential or concurrent; reactive or terminating; etc. A reactive system is one which reacts to its environment and is not meant to terminate (e.g. operating systems, embedded systems and computer hardware).

Pre- vs. post-development. Verification is of greater advantage if introduced early in the course of system development, because errors caught earlier on in the production cycle are less costly to rectify. (Apparently, Intel lost millions of dollars by releasing their Pentium chip with the FDIV error.)

This chapter concerns a verification method called *model checking.* In the terms of the above classification, model checking is an automatic, model-based, property-verification approach. It is intended to be used for *concurrent, reactive* systems and originated as a post-development methodology. Concurrency bugs are among the most difficult to find by *testing* (the activity of running several simulations of important scenarios), since they tend to be non-reproduceable, so it is well worth having a verification technique that can help one to find them.

By contrast, Chapter 4 describes a very different verification technique which in terms of the above classification is a proof-based, computer-assisted, property-verification approach. It is intended to be used for programs which we expect to terminate and produce a result.

Model checking is based on temporal logic. The idea of temporal logic is that a formula is not *statically* true or false in a model, as it is in propositional and predicate logic. Instead, the models of temporal logic contain several states and a formula can be true in some states and false in others. Thus, the static notion of truth is replaced by a *dynamic* one, in which the formulas may change their truth values as the system evolves from state to state. In model checking, the models $\mathcal{M}$ are *transition systems* and the properties ϕ are formulas in temporal logic. To verify that a system satisfies a property, we must do three things:

- Model the system using the description language of a model checker, arriving at a model $\mathcal{M}$.
- Code the property using the specification language of the model checker, resulting in a temporal logic formula ϕ.
- Run the model checker with inputs $\mathcal{M}$ and ϕ.

The model checker outputs the answer 'yes' if $\mathcal{M} \vDash \phi$ and 'no' otherwise; in the latter case, most model checkers also produce a trace of system behaviour which causes this failure. This automatic generation of such 'counter traces' is an important tool in the design and debugging of systems.

Since model checking is a *model-based* approach, in terms of the classification given earlier, it follows that in this chapter, unlike in the previous two, we will not be concerned with semantic entailment ($\Gamma \vDash \phi$), or with proof theory ($\Gamma \vdash \phi$), such as the development of a natural deduction calculus for temporal logic. We will work solely with the notion of satisfaction, i.e. the satisfaction relation between a model and a formula ($\mathcal{M} \vDash \phi$).

There is a whole zoo of temporal logics that people have proposed and used for various things. The abundance of such formalisms may be organised by classifying them according to their particular view of 'time'. *Linear-time* logics think of time as a chain of time instances, *branching-time* logics offer several alternative future worlds at any given point of time; the latter is most useful in modelling non-deterministic systems or computations. Another quality of 'time' is whether we think of it as being *continuous* or *discrete*. The former would be suggested if we study an analogue computer, the latter might be preferred for a synchronous network.

In this chapter, we study a logic where 'time' is branching and discrete. Such a logic has a modal aspect to it since the possible future paths of computations allow us to speak of 'possibilities' and 'necessities'; the study of such modalities is the focus of Chapter 5. The logic we now study is called *computation tree logic* (CTL), due to E. Clarke and E. A. Emerson. This logic has proven to be extremely fruitful in verifying hardware and communication protocols; and people are beginning to apply it even to the verification of software. *Model checking* is the process of computing an answer to the question of whether $\mathcal{M}, s \vDash \phi$ holds, where ϕ is a formula of some logic, $\mathcal{M}$ an appropriate model, s a state of that model and $\vDash$ the underlying satisfaction relation. Of course, ϕ is now a formula of CTL, which we define in a little while, and the model $\mathcal{M}$ is a representation of our 'system'.

You should not confuse such models $\mathcal{M}$ with an actual physical system. Models are abstractions that omit lots of real features of a physical system, which are irrelevant to the checking of ϕ. This is similar to the abstractions that one does in calculus or mechanics. There we talk about *straight* lines, *prefect* circles, or an experiment without *friction*. These abstractions are very powerful, for they allow us to focus on the essentials of our particular concern.

Models of the kind we have in mind are very general indeed. That has the advantage that we may think of a wide spectrum of structures in computer science as having the same *type* of model. So this allows us to develop a unified approach of model checking for the verification of hardware, networks, software, etc. The fundamental constituents of such models are *states*. They could be the current values of variables in a C-like programming language, or actual states of physical devices in a network architecture, for example, the states 'busy' and 'available' of some computing resource. The second kind of constituents of these models expresses the dynamics of the underlying computational process. Such dynamical behaviour is captured in terms of *state transitions*. Thus, one may think of an assignment statement

$$x := x + 1;$$

as a state transition from state s to state s', where the latter state stores the same values for variables as s, but for x, in which it stores a value one bigger than that of s. You may think of the set of possible state transitions in a variety of ways, but it is best for our purposes to think of them in their entirety as a binary relation $\rightarrow$ on the set of states S:

$$\rightarrow \,\subseteq S \times S.$$

We write $s \rightarrow s'$ to express that it is possible for the system to reach state s' from state s *in one computation step*.

The expressive power of such models stems from the fact that there is generally more than one possible successor state from a given state s. For example, if we have a language with *parallel* assignment statements running on a single processor, then we expect to encounter multiple future computation paths depending on the actual scheduler of this parallel activity. See Figure 3.2 (later) for a pictorial representation of such a model.

3.2 The syntax of computation tree logic

Computation tree logic, or CTL for short, is a temporal logic, having connectives that allow us to refer to the future. It is also a *branching-time* logic, meaning that its model of time is a tree-like structure in which the future is not determined; there are different paths in the future, any one of which might be the 'actual' path that is realised.

We work with a fixed set of atomic formulas/descriptions (such as $p, q, r, \ldots$, or $p_1, p_2, \ldots$). These atoms stand for atomic descriptions of a system, like

> *The printer is busy.*

or

> *There are currently no requested jobs for the printer.*

or

> *The current content of register* R1 *is the integer value* 6.

and the choice of atomic descriptions obviously depends on our particular interest in a system at hand.

Definition 3.1 We define CTL formulas inductively via a Backus Naur form (as done for the other logics of Chapters 1 and 2):

$$\phi ::= \quad \perp \mid \top \mid p \mid (\neg\phi) \mid (\phi \wedge \phi) \mid (\phi \vee \phi) \mid (\phi \rightarrow \phi) \mid \text{AX}\,\phi \mid \text{EX}\,\phi \mid$$
$$\text{A}[\phi\ \text{U}\ \phi] \mid \text{E}[\phi\ \text{U}\ \phi] \mid \text{AG}\,\phi \mid \text{EG}\,\phi \mid \text{AF}\,\phi \mid \text{EF}\,\phi.$$

where p ranges over atomic formulas/descriptions.

Thus, the symbols $\top$ and $\perp$ are CTL formulas, as are all atomic descriptions; $\neg\phi$ is a CTL formula if ϕ is one, etc. We will look at the meaning of these formulas, especially the connectives that did not occur in Chapter 1, in the next section; for now, we concentrate on their syntax. The connectives AX, EX, AG, EG, AU, EU, AF and EF are called *temporal connectives*. Notice that each of the CTL temporal connectives is a pair of symbols. The first of the pair is one of A and E. A means 'along All paths' (*inevitably*) and E means 'along at least (there Exists) one path' (*possibly*). The second one of the pair is X, F, G, or U, meaning 'neXt state', 'some Future state', 'all future states (Globally)' and Until, respectively. The pair of operators in $E[\phi_1 \; U \; \phi_2]$, for example, is EU. Notice that AU and EU are binary. The symbols X, F, G and U cannot occur without being preceded by an A or an E; similarly, every A or E must have one of X, F, G and U to accompany it.

Convention 3.2 We assume similar binding priorities for the CTL connectives to what we did for propositional and predicate logic. The unary connectives (consisting of ¬ and the temporal connectives AG, EG, AF, EF, AX and EX) bind most tightly. Next in the order come ∧ and ∨; and after that come →, AU and EU.

Naturally, we use brackets in order to override these priorities. Let us see some examples of well-formed CTL formulas and some examples which are not well-formed, in order to understand the syntax. Suppose that p, q and r are atomic formulas. The following are well-formed CTL formulas:

- EGr;
- AG $(q \rightarrow$ EG$r)$ — note that this is not the same as AG$q \rightarrow$ EGr, for according to the binding priorities the latter formula means (AGq) → (EGr)
- A[r U q]
- EF E[r U q]
- A[p U EFr]
- EF EG$p \rightarrow$ AFr (again, note that this binds as (EF EGp) → AFr, not EF (EG$p \rightarrow$ AFr) or EF EG$(p \rightarrow$ AFr)!)
- AG AFr
- A[p_1 U A[p_2 U p_3]]
- E[A[p_1 U p_2] U p_3]
- AG $(p \rightarrow$ A[p U $(\neg p \wedge$ A[$\neg p$ U q])]).

It is worth spending some time seeing how the syntax rules allow us to construct each of these. The following are not well-formed formulas:

- FGr — since F and G must occur immediately after an E or an A
- A¬G¬p
- F[r U q]
- EF $(r$ U $q)$
- AEFr
- AF $[(r$ U $q) \wedge (p$ U $r)]$.

It is especially worth understanding why the syntax rules don't allow us to construct these. For example, take EF $(r$ U $q)$. EF is an operator and so is

U, so why is this not a well-formed CTL formula? The answer is that U can occur only when paired with an A or an E. The E we have is paired with the F. To make this into a well-formed CTL formula, we would have to write E F E[r U q] or E F A[r U q].

Notice that we use square brackets after the A or E, when the paired operator is a U. There is no strong reason for this; you could use ordinary round brackets instead. However, it often helps one to read the formula (because we can more easily spot where the corresponding close bracket is). Another reason for using the square brackets is that a particular model checker called SMV, which we will study later in this chapter, adopts this notation.

The reason AF $[(r$ U $q) \wedge (p$ U $r)]$ is not a well-formed formula is that the syntax does not allow us to put a boolean connective (like $\wedge$) directly inside A[ ] or E[ ]. Occurrences of A or E must be followed by one of G, F, X or U; when they are followed by U, it must be in the form A[ϕ U ψ]. Now, the ϕ and the ψ *may* contain $\wedge$, since they are arbitrary formulas; so A[$(p \wedge q)$ U $(\neg r \to q)$] *is* a well-formed formula.

Observe that AU and EU are binary connectives which mix infix and prefix notation. In pure infix, we would write ϕ_1 AU ϕ_2, whereas in pure prefix we would write AU(ϕ_1, ϕ_2).

As with any formal language, and as we did in the previous two chapters, it is useful to draw parse trees for well-formed formulas. The parse tree for A[AX $\neg p$ U E[EX $(p \wedge q)$ U $\neg p$]] is shown in Figure 3.1.

Definition 3.3 A subformula of a CTL formula ϕ is any formula ψ whose parse tree is a subtree of ϕ's parse tree.

EXERCISES 3.1
We let $\{p, q, r, s, t\}$ be the set of propositional atoms for all systems of this set of exercises.

1. Write the parse trees for the following CTL formulas:
   * (a) EG r
   * (b) AG $(q \to$ EG $r)$
   * (c) A[p U EF r]
   * (d) EF EG $p \to$ AF r (recall Convention 3.2)
   (e) A[p U A[q U r]]
   (f) E[A[p U q] U r]
   (g) AG $(p \to$ A[p U $(\neg p \wedge$ A[$\neg p$ U q])]).

2. Explain why the following are not well-formed CTL formulas:

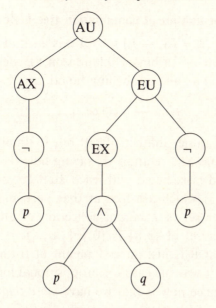

Fig. 3.1. The parse tree of a CTL formula without infix notation.

* (a) FG*r*
  (b) XX*r*
  (c) A¬G¬*p*
  (d) F[*r* U *q*]
  (e) EX X*r*
* (f) AEF*r*
* (g) AF [(*r* U *q*) ∧ (*p* U *r*)].

3. State which of the strings below are well-formed CTL formulas. For those which are well-formed, draw the parse tree. For those which are not well-formed, explain why not.

   (a) ¬(¬*p*) ∨ (*r* ∧ *s*)
   (b) X*q*
* (c) ¬AX *q*
   (d) *p* U (AX ⊥)
* (e) E[(AX *q*) U (¬(¬*p*) ∨ (⊤ ∧ *s*))]
* (f) (F*r*) ∧ (AG *q*)
   (g) ¬(AG *q*) ∨ (EG *q*).

* 4. List all subformulas of the formula AG (*p* → A[*p* U (¬*p* ∧ A[¬*p* U *q*])]).

3.3 Semantics of computation tree logic

Definition 3.4 A model $\mathcal{M} = (S, \rightarrow, L)$ for CTL is a set of states S endowed with a transition relation $\rightarrow$ (a binary relation on S), such that every $s \in S$ has some $s' \in S$ with $s \rightarrow s'$, and a labelling function

$$L : S \rightarrow \mathcal{P}(\text{Atoms}).$$

This definition looks rather mathematical; but it simply means that you have a collection of states S, a relation $\rightarrow$, saying how the system can move from state to state, and, associated with each state s, you have the set of atomic propositions $L(s)$ which are true at that particular state. We write $\mathcal{P}(\text{Atoms})$ for the power set of Atoms, a collection of atomic descriptions. For example, the power set of $\{p, q\}$ is $\{\emptyset, \{p\}, \{q\}, \{p, q\}\}$. A good way of thinking about L is that it is just an assignment of truth values to all the propositional atoms as it was the case for propositional logic (we called that a *valuation*). The difference now is that we have *more than one state*, so this assignment depends on which state s the system is in: $L(s)$ contains all atoms which are true in state s.

We may conveniently express all the information about a (finite) model $\mathcal{M}$ for CTL using directed graphs whose nodes (= the states) contain all propositional atoms that are true in that state. For example, if our system has only three states s_0, s_1 and s_2; if the only possible transitions between states are $s_0 \rightarrow s_1$, $s_0 \rightarrow s_2$, $s_1 \rightarrow s_0$, $s_1 \rightarrow s_2$ and $s_2 \rightarrow s_2$; and if $L(s_0) \stackrel{\text{def}}{=} \{p, q\}$, $L(s_1) \stackrel{\text{def}}{=} \{q, r\}$ and $L(s_2) \stackrel{\text{def}}{=} \{r\}$, then we can condense all this information into the picture in Figure 3.2. We prefer to present models by means of such pictures whenever that is feasible.

The requirement that for every $s \in S$ there is at least one $s' \in S$ such that $s \rightarrow s'$ means that no state of the system can 'deadlock'. This is no severe restriction, because we can always add an extra state s_d representing deadlock, together with new transitions $s \rightarrow s_d$ for each s which was a deadlock in the old system, as well as $s_d \rightarrow s_d$. See Figure 3.3 for such an example.

Let us define the intended meanings of the CTL connectives.

Definition 3.5 Let $\mathcal{M} = (S, \rightarrow, L)$ be a model for CTL. Given any s in S, we define whether a CTL formula ϕ holds in state s. We denote this by

$$\mathcal{M}, s \models \phi.$$

Naturally, the definition of the *satisfaction relation* $\models$ is done by structural induction on all CTL formulas:

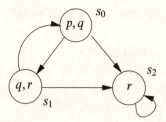

Fig. 3.2. A concise representation of a model $\mathcal{M}$ as a directed graph, whose nodes are states containing all the propositional atoms which are true in that particular state.

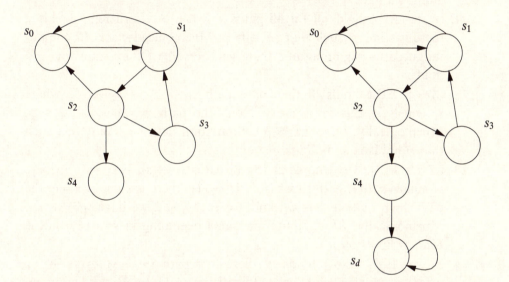

Fig. 3.3. On the left, we have a system with a state s_4 that does not have any further transitions. On the right, we expand that system with a 'deadlock' state s_d such that no state can deadlock; of course, it is then our understanding that reaching the 'deadlock' state corresponds to deadlock in the original system.

1. $\mathcal{M}, s \vDash \top$ and $\mathcal{M}, s \nvDash \bot$ for all $s \in S$.
2. $\mathcal{M}, s \vDash p$ iff $p \in L(s)$.
3. $\mathcal{M}, s \vDash \neg \phi$ iff $\mathcal{M}, s \nvDash \phi$.
4. $\mathcal{M}, s \vDash \phi_1 \wedge \phi_2$ iff $\mathcal{M}, s \vDash \phi_1$ and $\mathcal{M}, s \vDash \phi_2$.
5. $\mathcal{M}, s \vDash \phi_1 \vee \phi_2$ iff $\mathcal{M}, s \vDash \phi_1$ or $\mathcal{M}, s \vDash \phi_2$.
6. $\mathcal{M}, s \vDash \phi_1 \rightarrow \phi_2$ iff $\mathcal{M}, s \nvDash \phi_1$ or $\mathcal{M}, s \vDash \phi_2$.
7. $\mathcal{M}, s \vDash \text{AX}\, \phi$ iff *for all* s_1 such that $s \rightarrow s_1$ we have $\mathcal{M}, s_1 \vDash \phi$. Thus, AX says: 'in every next state'.
8. $\mathcal{M}, s \vDash \text{EX}\, \phi$ iff *for some* s_1 such that $s \rightarrow s_1$ we have $\mathcal{M}, s_1 \vDash \phi$. Thus,

EX says: 'in some next state'. E is dual to A — in exactly the same way that $\exists$ is dual to $\forall$ in predicate logic.

9. $\mathcal{M}, s \vDash \text{AG } \phi$ holds iff for all paths $s_1 \to s_2 \to s_3 \to \ldots$, where s_1 equals s, and all s_i along the path, we have $\mathcal{M}, s_i \vDash \phi$. Mnemonically: *for All* computation paths beginning in s the property ϕ holds *Globally*. Note that 'along the path' includes the path's initial state s.

10. $\mathcal{M}, s \vDash \text{EG } \phi$ holds iff there is a path $s_1 \to s_2 \to s_3 \to \ldots$, where s_1 equals s, and for all s_i along the path, we have $\mathcal{M}, s_i \vDash \phi$. Mnemonically: *there Exists* a path beginning in s such that ϕ holds *Globally* along the path.

11. $\mathcal{M}, s \vDash \text{AF } \phi$ holds iff for all paths $s_1 \to s_2 \to \ldots$, where s_1 equals s, there is some s_i such that $\mathcal{M}, s_i \vDash \phi$. Mnemonically: *for All* computation paths beginning in s there will be some *Future* state where ϕ holds.

12. $\mathcal{M}, s \vDash \text{EF } \phi$ holds iff there is a path $s_1 \to s_2 \to s_3 \to \ldots$, where s_1 equals s, and for some s_i along the path, we have $\mathcal{M}, s_i \vDash \phi$. Mnemonically: *there Exists* a computation path beginning in s such that ϕ holds in some *Future* state;

13. $\mathcal{M}, s \vDash \text{A}[\phi_1 \text{ U } \phi_2]$ holds iff for all paths $s_1 \to s_2 \to s_3 \to \ldots$, where s_1 equals s, that path satisfies $\phi_1 \text{ U } \phi_2$, i.e. there is some s_i along the path, such that $\mathcal{M}, s_i \vDash \phi_2$, and, for each $j < i$, we have $\mathcal{M}, s_j \vDash \phi_1$. Mnemonically: *All* computation paths beginning in s satisfy that ϕ *Until* ψ holds on it.

14. $\mathcal{M}, s \vDash \text{E}[\phi_1 \text{ U } \phi_2]$ holds iff there is a path $s_1 \to s_2 \to s_3 \to \ldots$, where s_1 equals s, and that path satisfies $\phi_1 \text{ U } \phi_2$ as specified in 13. Mnemonically: *there Exists* a computation path beginning in s such that ϕ *Until* ψ holds on it.

For the remainder of this section, we will be concerned with the computational consequences of this definition, and with justifying and explaining its clauses.

The first six clauses are exactly what we expect from our knowledge of propositional logic gained in Chapter 1. Notice that, for example, the truth value of $\neg \phi$ in a state depends on the truth value of ϕ in the *same* state. This contrasts with the clauses for AX and EX. The truth value of AX ϕ in a state s is determined not by the truth value of ϕ in s, but by ϕ in states that are related to s by the relation $\to$; if $s \to s$, then this value also depends on the truth value of ϕ in s.

The next four clauses also exhibit this phenomenon, except more so: for example, to determine the truth value of AG ϕ involves looking at the truth

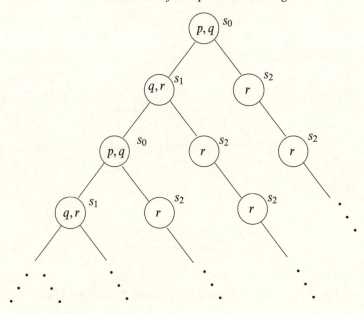

Fig. 3.4. Unwinding the system of Figure 3.2 as an infinite tree of all computation paths beginning in a particular state.

value of ϕ not only in the immediately related states, but in indirectly related states as well. In fact, in the case of AG ϕ, you have to examine the truth value of ϕ in every state related by any number of forward links of $\rightarrow$ to the current state.

Clauses 9–14 above refer to computation paths in models. It is therefore useful to visualise all possible computation paths from a given state s by unwinding the transition system to obtain an infinite computation tree, whence 'computation tree logic'. This greatly facilitates deciding whether a state satisfies a CTL formula[1]. For example, if we unwind the state graph of Figure 3.2 for the designated starting state s_0, then we get the infinite tree in Figure 3.4.

The diagrams in Figures 3.5-3.8 show schematically systems whose starting states satisfy the formulas EF ϕ, EG ϕ, AG ϕ and AF ϕ, respectively. Of course, we could add more ϕ to any of these diagrams and still preserve the satisfaction — although there is nothing to add for AG. The diagrams illustrate a 'least' way of satisfying the formulas.

Remark 3.6 Notice that, in clauses 9–14 above, *the future includes the present.*

---

[1] If this task is done by a computer, then that is a different matter, but *we* seem to benefit from this visualisation of a system as a tree.

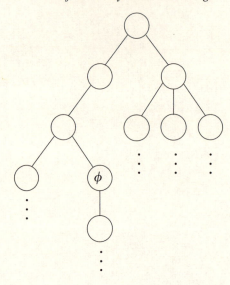

Fig. 3.5. A system whose starting state satisfies EF ϕ.

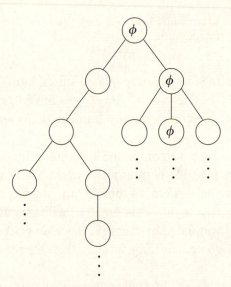

Fig. 3.6. A system whose starting state satisfies EG ϕ.

This means that, when we say 'in all future states', we are including the present state as a future state. It is a matter of convention whether we do this, or not; see the exercises below for an *exclusive* version of CTL. A consequence of adopting the convention that the future shall include the present is that the formulas (AG p) $\rightarrow$ p, $p \rightarrow$ A[q U p] and $p \rightarrow$ EF p are true in every state of every model.

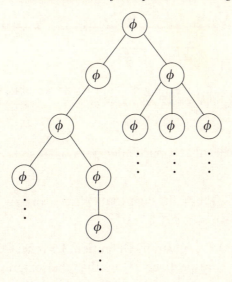

Fig. 3.7. A system whose starting state satisfies AG ϕ.

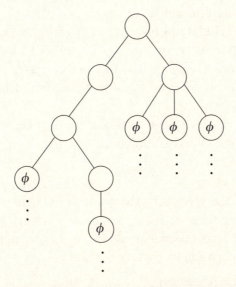

Fig. 3.8. A system whose starting state satisfies AF ϕ.

We now move our discussion to the clauses for AU and EU. The symbol U stands for 'until'. The formula ϕ_1 U ϕ_2 holds on a path if it is the case that ϕ_1 holds continuously *until* the next occurrence of ϕ_2. Moreover, ϕ_1 U ϕ_2 actually demands that ϕ_2 *does* hold in some future state, i.e. it is not enough for ϕ_1 to hold continuously forever. See Figure 3.9 for illustration: each of the states s_3 to s_9 satisfies p U q along the path shown, but s_0 to s_2 don't.

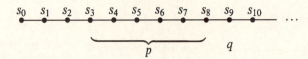

Fig. 3.9. An illustration of the meaning of Until in the semantics of CTL. Each of the states s_3 to s_9 satisfies $p \; U \; q$ along the path shown.

Thus, we defined earlier that a particular path $s_0 \to s_1 \to s_2 \to \ldots$ satisfies $\phi_1 \; U \; \phi_2$ iff:

- there is some s_i along the path, such that $s_i \vDash \phi_2$, and
- for each $j < i$, we have $s_j \vDash \phi_1$.

The clauses for AU and EU given in Definition 3.5 reflect this intuition, for all paths and some path, respectively. Note that the semantics of $\phi_1 \; U \; \phi_2$ is not saying anything about ϕ_1 in state s_i; neither does it say anything about ϕ_2 in states s_j with $j < i$. This might be in contrast to some of the implicit meanings of 'until' in natural language usage. For example, in the sentence 'I smoked until I was 22.' it is not only expressed that the person referred to continually smoked up until he, or she, was 22 years old, but we also would interpret such a sentence as saying that this person gave up smoking from that point onwards. This is different from the semantics of Until in temporal logic.

It should be clear that we have outlined the formal foundations of a procedure that, given ϕ, $\mathcal{M}$ and s, can check whether

$$\mathcal{M}, s \vDash \phi$$

holds. In particular, if the given set of states is finite, then we may compute the set of *all* states satisfying ϕ. If the model $\mathcal{M}$ is clear from the context, we will simply write $s \vDash \phi$ instead of $\mathcal{M}, s \vDash \phi$. Let us now look at some example checks for the system in Figures 3.2 and 3.4.

1. $\mathcal{M}, s_0 \vDash p \wedge q$ holds since the atomic symbols p and q are contained in the node of s_0.
2. $\mathcal{M}, s_0 \vDash \neg r$ holds since the atomic symbol r is *not* contained in node s_0.
3. $\mathcal{M}, s_0 \vDash \top$ holds by definition.
4. $\mathcal{M}, s_0 \vDash EX \, (q \wedge r)$ holds since we have the leftmost computation path $s_0 \to s_1 \to s_0 \to s_1 \to \ldots$ in Figure 3.4, whose second node s_1 contains q and r.
5. $\mathcal{M}, s_0 \vDash \neg AX \, (q \wedge r)$ holds since we have the rightmost computation

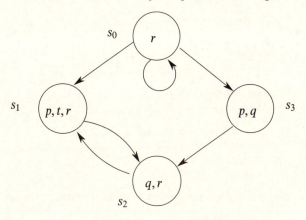

Fig. 3.10. A system with four states.

path $s_0 \rightarrow s_2 \rightarrow s_2 \rightarrow s_2 \rightarrow \dots$ in Figure 3.4, whose second node s_2 only contains r, but *not* q.

6. $\mathcal{M}, s_0 \vDash \neg \text{EF}(p \wedge r)$ holds since there is no computation path beginning in s_0 such that we could reach a state where $p \wedge r$ would hold. This is so, because there is simply no state whatsoever in this system, where p and r hold at the same time.

7. $\mathcal{M}, s_2 \vDash \text{EG}\,r$ (note the s_2 instead of s_0!) holds since there is a computation path $s_2 \rightarrow s_2 \rightarrow s_2 \rightarrow \dots$ beginning in s_2 such that r holds in all future states.

8. $\mathcal{M}, s_2 \vDash \text{AG}\,r$ holds as well, since there is only *one* computation path beginning in s_2 and it satisfies r globally.

9. $\mathcal{M}, s_0 \vDash \text{AF}\,r$ holds since, for all computation paths beginning in s_0, the system reaches a state (s_1 or s_2) such that r holds.

10. $\mathcal{M}, s_0 \vDash \text{E}[(p \wedge q) \text{ U } r]$ holds since we have the rightmost computation path $s_0 \rightarrow s_2 \rightarrow s_2 \rightarrow s_2 \rightarrow \dots$ in Figure 3.4, whose second node s_2 ($i = 1$) satisfies r, but all previous nodes (only $j = 0$, i.e. node s_0) satisfy $p \wedge q$.

11. $\mathcal{M}, s_0 \vDash \text{A}[p \text{ U } r]$ holds since p holds at s_0 and r holds in any possible successor state of s_0, so $p \text{ U } r$ is true for all computation paths beginning in s_0 (so we may choose $i = 1$ independently of the path).

EXERCISES 3.2
We let $\{p, q, r, t\}$ be the set of propositional atoms for all systems of this set of exercises.

1. Consider the system $\mathcal{M}$ in Figure 3.10.

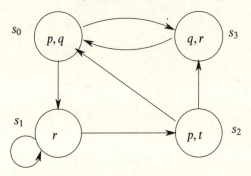

Fig. 3.11. Another system with four states.

(a) Beginning from state s_0, unwind this system into an infinite tree, and draw all computation paths up to length 4 (= the first four layers of that tree).

(b) Make the following checks $\mathcal{M}, s_0 \vDash \phi$, where ϕ is listed below. For that you need to explain why the check holds, or what reasons there are for its failure:

    * (i) $\neg p \rightarrow r$
      (ii) $\text{AF}\, t$
   *(iii) $\neg \text{EG}\, r$
     (iv) $\text{E}(t \text{ U } q)$
      (v) $\text{AF}\, q$
     (vi) $\text{EF}\, q$
    (vii) $\text{EG}\, r$
   (viii) $\text{AG}\, (r \vee q)$.

(c) Make the same checks as in (b) but now for state s_2.

2. Consider the following system $\mathcal{M}$ in Figure 3.11. Check the following CTL formulas ϕ for state s_0, i.e. determine whether $\mathcal{M}, s_0 \vDash \phi$ holds:

(a) $\text{AF}\, q$
(b) $\text{AG}\, (\text{EF}\, (p \vee r))$
(c) $\text{EX}\, (\text{EX}\, r)$
(d) $\text{AG}\, (\text{AF}\, q)$.

3. Do the same as in exercise 2, but for state s_2.

* 4. The meaning of the temporal operators AU, EU, AG, EG, AF and EF was defined to be such that 'the present includes the future'. For example, EF p is true for a state if p is true for that state already. Often one would like corresponding operators such that *the future excludes* *the present.* Use suitable connectives of the grammar in Definition 3.1 to define such (six) modified connectives as derived operators in CTL.

3.3.1 Practical patterns of specifications

What kind of practically relevant properties can we check with formulas of CTL? We list a few of the common patterns. Suppose atomic descriptions include some words such as busy and requested. We may require some of the following properties of real systems:

- It is possible to get to a state where started holds, but ready does not hold:

  EF (started ∧ ¬ready).

- For any state, if a request (of some resource) occurs, then it will eventually be acknowledged:

  AG (requested → AF acknowledged).

- A certain process is enabled infinitely often on every computation path:

  AG (AF enabled).

- Whatever happens, a certain process will eventually be permanently dead-locked:

  AF (AG deadlock).

- From any state it is possible to get to a restart state:

  AG (EF restart).

- An upwards travelling elevator at the second floor does not change its direction when it has passengers wishing to go to the fifth floor:

  AG (floor=2 ∧ direction=up ∧ ButtonPressed5 →

  A[direction=up U floor=5])

  Here, our atomic descriptions are boolean expressions built from system variables, e.g. floor=2.

- The elevator can remain idle on the third floor with its doors closed:

  AG (floor=3 ∧ idle ∧ door=closed → EG (floor=3 ∧ idle ∧ door=closed)).

EXERCISES 3.3

* 1. Express in CTL: Whenever *p* is followed by *q* (after some finite amount of steps), then the system enters an 'interval' in which no *r* occurs until *t*.

 2. Explain in detail why the CTL formulas for the practical specification patterns above capture the stated 'informal' properties expressed in plain English.

3. Consider the CTL formula $AG(p \rightarrow AF(s \wedge AX(AF t)))$. Explain what exactly it expresses in terms of the order of occurrence of events p, s and t.

4. Write down a CTL formula which says that p precedes s and t on all computation paths; you may find it easier to code the negation of that specification first.

5. Represent 'After p, q is never true.' as a CTL formula, where this constraint is meant to apply on all computation paths.

6. Find a CTL formula which expresses the following property on all computation paths:

   (a) 'Between the events q and r, p is never true.'

   (b) 'Transitions to states satisfying p occur at most twice.'.

——

3.3.2 *Important equivalences between CTL formulas*

Definition 3.7 Two CTL formulas ϕ and ψ are said to be *semantically equivalent* if any state in any model which satisfies one of them also satisfies the other; we denote this by $\phi \equiv \psi$.

Note that we wrote $\phi \equiv \psi$ in Chapter 1 if the propositional logic formulas ϕ and ψ had the same meaning no matter what valuation (= assignment of truth values) one considers. We may think of such valuations as $L(s)$ for a CTL model with one state s and one transition $s \rightarrow s$. Therefore, we see how the definition above extends the meaning of $\equiv$ to a larger class of models and formulas.

We have already noticed that A is a universal quantifier on paths and E is the corresponding existential quantifier. Moreover, G and F are also universal and existential quantifiers, ranging over the states along a particular path. In view of these facts, it is not surprising to find that de Morgan rules exist for A and E and also F and G:

$$\neg AF\,\phi \;\equiv\; EG\,\neg\phi \tag{3.1}$$
$$\neg EF\,\phi \;\equiv\; AG\,\neg\phi.$$

On any particular path, each state has a unique successor. Therefore, X is its own dual on computation paths and we have

$$\neg AX\,\phi \;\equiv\; EX\,\neg\phi. \tag{3.2}$$

We also have the equivalences

$$AF \phi \equiv A[\top \ U \ \phi] \qquad\qquad EF \phi \equiv E[\top \ U \ \phi].$$

You can check this by looking back at the meaning of the clause for U. For $\phi_1 \ U \ \phi_2$ to be true in a state along a path, it is necessary that ϕ_2 become true at some future point and that ϕ_1 is true in every state until that point. In the expression above, we let ϕ_1 be $\top$, so that the requirement that ϕ_1 be true in every state until ϕ_2 is vacuously satisfied (since $\top$ is true in every state).

Naturally, any equivalence which holds in propositional logic will also hold in CTL. This is true even if the equivalence involves CTL formulas: e.g. we have that $\top$ and $(AX\,p) \lor \neg AX\,p$ are equivalent since the formula scheme $\phi \lor \neg \phi$ of propositional logic is equivalent to $\top$. Therefore, as in propositional logic, there is some redundancy among the connectives. For example, in Chapter 1 we saw that the set $\{\bot, \land, \neg\}$ forms an adequate set of connectives, since the other connectives $\lor$, $\rightarrow$, $\top$, etc., can be written in terms of those three. (Cf. exercise 3, page 71.)

This is also the case in CTL. Moreover, the connective AX can be written $\neg EX \neg$ by (3.2); and AG, AF, EG and EF can be written in terms of AU and EU as follows: first, write $AG \phi$ as $\neg EF \neg \phi$ and $EG \phi$ as $\neg AF \neg \phi$ (using (3.1)) and then use $AF \phi \equiv A[\top \ U \ \phi]$ and $EF \phi \equiv E[\top \ U \ \phi]$. Therefore AU, EU and EX form an adequate set of temporal connectives.

Also EG, EU, and EX form an adequate set, for we have the equivalence

$$A[p \ U \ q] \equiv \neg(E[\neg q \ U \ (\neg p \land \neg q)] \lor EG \neg q). \qquad (3.3)$$

This equivalence is rather harder to demonstrate than the others; we will do it later (Section 3.8.1).

Similarly, AG, AU and AX form an adequate set. There are many other adequate sets, but we just mention one more, since we will use it later: the set consisting of AF, EU and EX. Since AF can be reduced to EG, this set reduces to EG, EU and EX which we have seen to be adequate.

Theorem 3.8 *The set of operators $\bot$, $\neg$ and $\land$ together with AF, EU and EX are adequate for CTL: any CTL formula can be transformed into a semantically equivalent CTL formula which uses only those logical connectives.*

Some other noteworthy equivalences in CTL are the following:

$$\text{AG}\,\phi \equiv \phi \wedge \text{AX}\,\text{AG}\,\phi$$
$$\text{EG}\,\phi \equiv \phi \wedge \text{EX}\,\text{EG}\,\phi$$
$$\text{AF}\,\phi \equiv \phi \vee \text{AX}\,\text{AF}\,\phi$$
$$\text{EF}\,\phi \equiv \phi \vee \text{EX}\,\text{EF}\,\phi$$
$$\text{A}[\phi\ \text{U}\ \psi] \equiv \psi \vee (\phi \wedge \text{AX}\,\text{A}[\phi\ \text{U}\ \psi])$$
$$\text{E}[\phi\ \text{U}\ \psi] \equiv \psi \vee (\phi \wedge \text{EX}\,\text{E}[\phi\ \text{U}\ \psi]).$$

For example, the intuition for the third one is the following: in order to have AF ϕ in a particular state, ϕ must be true at some point along each path from that state. To achieve this, we either have ϕ true now, in the current state; or we postpone it, in which case we must have AF ϕ in each of the next states. Notice how this equivalence appears to define AF in terms of AX and AF itself — an apparently circular definition. In fact, these equivalences can be used to define the six connectives on the left in terms of AX and EX, in a *non-circular* way. This is called the fixed-point characterisation of CTL; it is the mathematical foundation for the model-checking algorithm developed in Section 3.5; and we return to it later (Section 3.9).

EXERCISES 3.4

1. Which of the following pairs of CTL formulas are equivalent? For those which are not, exhibit a model of one of the pair which is not a model of the other.

    (a) EF ϕ and EG ϕ

  * (b) EF $\phi \vee$ EF ψ and EF $(\phi \vee \psi)$

  * (c) AF $\phi \vee$ AF ψ and AF $(\phi \vee \psi)$

    (d) AF $\neg\phi$ and $\neg$EG ϕ

  * (e) EF $\neg\phi$ and $\neg$AF ϕ

    (f) A[ϕ_1 U A[ϕ_2 U ϕ_3]] and A[A[ϕ_1 U ϕ_2] U ϕ_3] (Hint: it might make it simpler if you think first about models that have just one path.)

    (g) $\top$ and AG $\phi \rightarrow$ EG ϕ

  * (h) $\top$ and EG $\phi \rightarrow$ AG ϕ.

2. Find operators to replace the ? marks, to make the following equivalences.

    (a) EF $\neg\phi \equiv \neg$??ϕ

  * (b) AG $(\phi \wedge \psi) \equiv$ AG ϕ ? AG ψ.

3. Use the definition of $\models$ between states and CTL formulas to explain why $s \models$ AG AF ϕ means that ϕ is true infinitely often along every path starting at s.

4. Prove the Equivalences (3.1) and (3.2).

* 5. Write pseudo-code for a recursive function TRANSLATE which takes as input an arbitrary CTL formula ϕ and returns as output an equivalent CTL formula ψ whose only operators are among the set $\{\bot, \neg, \wedge, AF, EU, EX\}$.

3.4 Example: mutual exclusion

Let us now look at a larger example of verification using CTL, having to do with *mutual exclusion*. When concurrent processes share a resource (such as a file on a disk or a database entry), it may be necessary to ensure that they do not have access to it at the same time. Several processes simultaneously editing the same file would not be desirable.

We therefore identify certain *critical sections* of each process' code and arrange that only one process can be in its critical section at a time. The critical section should include all the access to the shared resource (though it should be as small as possible so that no unnecessary exclusion takes place). The problem we are faced with is to find a *protocol* for determining which process is allowed to enter its critical section at which time. Once we have found one which we think works, we verify our solution by checking that it has some expected properties, such as the following ones:

Safety: The protocol allows only one process to be in its critical section at any time.

This safety property is not enough, since a protocol which permanently excluded every process from its critical section would be safe, but not very useful. Therefore, we should also require:

Liveness: Whenever any process wants to enter its critical section, it will eventually be permitted to do so.

Non-blocking: A process can always request to enter its critical section.

Some rather crude protocols might work on the basis that they cycle through the processes, making each one in turn enter its critical section. Since it might be naturally the case that some of them request accesses to the shared resource more than others, we should make sure our protocol has the property:

No strict sequencing: Processes need not enter their critical section in strict sequence.

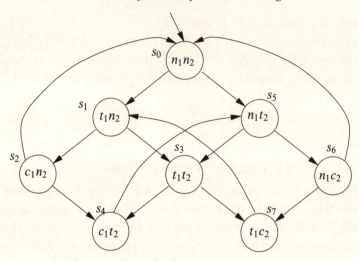

Fig. 3.12. A first-attempt model for mutual exclusion.

3.4.1 *The first modelling attempt*

We will model two processes, each of which is in its non-critical state (n), or trying to enter its critical state (t), or in its critical state (c). Each individual process undergoes transitions in the cycle $n \to t \to c \to n \to \ldots$, but the two processes interleave with each other. Consider the protocol given by the transition system $\mathcal{M}$ in Figure 3.12[1]. The two processes start off in their non-critical sections (global state s_0). State s_0 is the only *initial* state, indicated by the incoming edge with no source. Either of them may now move to its trying state, but only one of them can ever make a transition at a time (asynchronous *interleaving*). So there is a transition arrow from s_0 to s_1 and s_5. From s_1 (i.e. process 1 trying, process 2 non-critical) again two things can happen: either process 1 moves again (we go to s_2), or process 2 moves (we go to s_3). Notice that not every process can move in every state. For example, process 1 cannot move in state s_7, since it cannot go into its critical section until process 2 comes out of its critical section.

We can verify the four properties by first describing them as CTL formulas:

Safety: $\phi_1 \stackrel{\text{def}}{=} \text{AG} \neg(c_1 \wedge c_2)$. Clearly, $\text{AG} \neg(c_1 \wedge c_2)$ is satisfied in the initial state (indeed, in every state).

Liveness: $\phi_2 \stackrel{\text{def}}{=} \text{AG}(t_1 \to \text{AF} c_1)$. This is *not* satisfied by the initial state, for we can find a state accessible from the initial state, namely s_1, in

---

[1] We write $p_1 p_2 \ldots p_m$ in a node s to denote that $p_1, p_2, \ldots, p_m$ are the only propositional atoms true at s.

which t_1 is true but $AF\, c_1$ is false, because there is a computation
path $s_1 \rightarrow s_3 \rightarrow s_7 \rightarrow s_1 \rightarrow \ldots$ on which c_1 is always false.

Non-blocking: $\phi_3 \stackrel{\text{def}}{=} AG\,(n_1 \rightarrow EX\, t_1)$, which is satisfied, since every n_1 state
(i.e. s_0, s_5 and s_6) has an (immediate) t_1 successor.

No strict sequencing: $\phi_4 \stackrel{\text{def}}{=} EF\,(c_1 \wedge E[c_1 \; U \; (\neg c_1 \wedge E[\neg c_2 \; U \; c_1])])$. This is
satisfied; e.g. by the mirror path to the computation path described
for liveness, $s_5 \rightarrow s_3 \rightarrow s_4 \rightarrow s_5 \rightarrow \ldots$.

EXERCISES 3.5

* 1. Observe that the last three specifications have been written from the
  point of view of process 1. Can you modify those specifications such
  that process 2 also meets these constraints? Can you come up with a
  good reason explaining why we did not add the constraints of process
  2?

———

The reason liveness failed in our first attempt at modelling mutual exclusion is that non-determinism means it *might* continually favour one process
over another. The problem is that the state s_3 does not distinguish between
which of the processes *first* went into its trying state. We can solve this by
splitting s_3 into two states.

3.4.2 The second modelling attempt

The two states s_3 and s_9 in Figure 3.13 both correspond to the state s_3 in our
first modelling attempt. They both record that both processes are in their
trying states, but in s_3 it is implicitly recorded that it is process 1's turn,
whereas in s_9 it is process 2's turn. Note that states s_3 and s_9 both have the
labelling $t_1 t_2$. The definition of CTL models does not preclude this. We can
think of there being some other, hidden, variables which are not part of the
initial labelling, which distinguish s_3 and s_9.

Remark 3.9 The four properties of safety, liveness, non-blocking and no
strict sequencing are satisfied by the model in Figure 3.13.

In this second modelling attempt, our transition system is still slightly
over-simplified, because we are assuming that it will move to a different state
on every tick of the clock (there are no transitions to the same state). We
may wish to model that a process can stay in its critical state for several
ticks, but if we include an arrow from s_2, or s_6, to itself, we will again violate

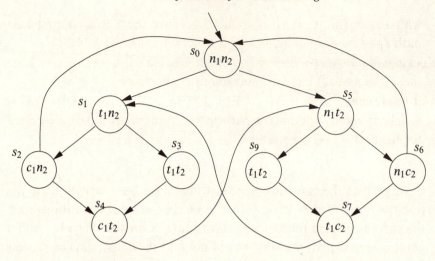

Fig. 3.13. A second-attempt model for mutual exclusion. There are now two states representing $t_1 t_2$, namely s_3 and s_9.

liveness. This problem will be solved later in this chapter when we consider 'fairness constraints' (Section 3.7).

EXERCISES 3.6
    1. Verify Remark 3.9.

____

3.5 A model-checking algorithm

In general, interesting transition systems will have millions of states and the formula we are interested in checking may be quite long. It is therefore well worth trying to find an efficient algorithm.

Our usage of the notion of a 'model' $\mathcal{M}$ has included directed graphs and also their unwindings into infinite trees, given a designated initial state. On doing the exercises, you very probably realised that checks on the infinite tree are easier for you to do, since all possible paths are plainly visible. However, if we think of implementing a model checker on a computer, we certainly cannot unwind transition systems into an infinite tree. We need to do checks on *finite* data structures. This is the reason why we now have to develop new insights into the semantics of CTL. Such a deeper understanding will provide the basis for an efficient algorithm which, given $\mathcal{M}$, $s \in S$ and ϕ, computes whether $\mathcal{M}, s \vDash \phi$ holds. In the latter case, such an algorithm can be augmented to produce an actual path (= run) of the system demonstrating that $\mathcal{M}$ cannot satisfy ϕ. That way, we may *debug* a system by trying to fix what causes that run to refute property ϕ.

There are various ways in which one could consider

$$\mathcal{M}, s_0 \overset{?}{\vDash} \phi$$

as a computational problem. For example, one could have the model $\mathcal{M}$, the formula ϕ and a state s_0 as input; one would then expect a reply of the form 'yes' ($\mathcal{M}, s_0 \vDash \phi$ holds), or 'no' ($\mathcal{M}, s_0 \vDash \phi$ does not hold). Alternatively, the inputs could be just $\mathcal{M}$ and ϕ, where the output would be *all* states s of the model $\mathcal{M}$ which satisfy ϕ.

If we solve the second of these two problems, we automatically have a solution to the first one, since we can simply check whether s_0 is an element of the output set. Conversely, to solve the second problem, given an algorithm for the first, we would simply repeatedly call this algorithm with each state in turn, to decide whether it goes in the output set. We will describe an algorithm to solve the second problem.

3.5.1 The labelling algorithm

We present an algorithm which, given a model and a CTL formula, outputs the set of states of the model that satisfy the formula. The algorithm does not need to be able to handle every CTL connective explicitly, since we have already seen that the connectives $\bot$, $\neg$ and $\wedge$ form an adequate set as far as the propositional connectives are concerned; and AF, EU and EX form an adequate set of temporal connectives. Given an arbitrary CTL formula ϕ, we would simply pre-process ϕ, calling the model-checking algorithm with the output of TRANSLATE (ϕ) as input, where TRANSLATE is the function coded in Exercises 3.4(5), page 169. Here is the algorithm:

INPUT: a CTL model $\mathcal{M} = (S, \rightarrow, L)$ and a CTL formula ϕ.
OUTPUT: the set of states of $\mathcal{M}$ which satisfy ϕ.

First, change ϕ to the output of TRANSLATE (ϕ), i.e. we write ϕ in terms of the connectives AF, EU, EX, $\wedge$, $\neg$ and $\bot$ using the equivalences given earlier in the chapter. Next, label the states of $\mathcal{M}$ with the subformulas of ϕ that are satisfied there, starting with the smallest subformulas and working outwards towards ϕ.

Suppose ψ is a subformula of ϕ and states satisfying all the *immediate* subformulas of ψ have already been labelled. (An immediate subformula of ϕ is any maximal-length subformula other than ϕ itself.) We determine by a case analysis which states to label with ψ. If ψ is

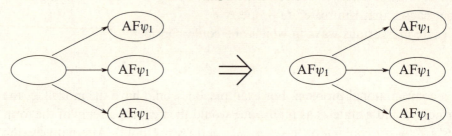

Repeat ...

... until no change.

Fig. 3.14. The iteration step of the procedure for labelling states with subformulas of the form AF ψ_1.

- $\bot$: then no states are labelled with $\bot$.
- p: then label s with p if $p \in L(s)$.
- $\psi_1 \wedge \psi_2$: label s with $\psi_1 \wedge \psi_2$ if s is already labelled both with ψ_1 and with ψ_2.
- $\neg\psi_1$: label s with $\neg\psi_1$ if s is not already labelled with ψ_1.
- AF ψ_1:

    - If any state s is labelled with ψ_1, label it with AF ψ_1.
    - Repeat: label any state with AF ψ_1 if all successor states are labelled with AF ψ_1, until there is no change. This step is illustrated in Figure 3.14.

- E[ψ_1 U ψ_2]:

    - If any state s is labelled with ψ_2, label it with E[ψ_1 U ψ_2].
    - Repeat: label any state with E[ψ_1 U ψ_2] if it is labelled with ψ_1 and at least one of its successors is labelled with E[ψ_1 U ψ_2], until there is no change. This step is illustrated in Figure 3.15.

- EX ψ_1: label any state with EX ψ_1 if one of its successors is labelled with ψ_1.

Having performed the labelling for all the subformulas of ϕ (including ϕ itself), we output the states which are labelled ϕ.

The complexity of this algorithm is $O(f \cdot V \cdot (V + E))$, where f is the number of connectives in the formula, V is the number of states and E is the number of transitions; the algorithm is linear in the size of the formula and quadratic in the size of the model.

Repeat ...

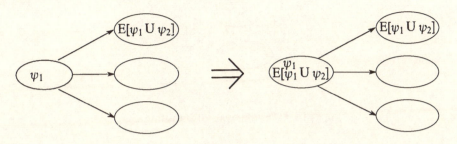

... until no change.

Fig. 3.15. The iteration step of the procedure for labelling states with subformulas of the form E[ψ_1 U ψ_2].

Handling EG *directly*

Instead of using a minimal adequate set of connectives, it would have been possible to write similar routines for the other connectives. Indeed, this would probably be more efficient. The connectives AG and EG require a slightly different approach from that for the others, however. Here is the algorithm to deal with EG ψ_1 *directly*:

- EG ψ_1:
  - Label *all* the states with EG ψ_1.
  - If any state s is *not* labelled with ψ_1, *delete* the label EG ψ_1.
  - Repeat: *delete* the label EG ψ_1 from any state if *none* of its successors is labelled with EG ψ_1; until there is no change.

Here, we label all the states with the subformula EG ψ_1 and then whittle down this labelled set, instead of building it up from nothing as we did in the case for EU. Actually, there is no real difference between this procedure for EG and what you would do if you translated it into ¬AF ¬ as far as the final result is concerned.

A variant which is more efficient

We can improve the efficiency of our labelling algorithm by using a cleverer way of handling EG. Instead of using EX, EU and AF as the adequate set, we use EX, EU and EG instead. For EX and EU we do as before (but take care to search the model by backwards breadth-first searching, for this ensures that we won't have to pass over any node twice). For the EG ψ case:

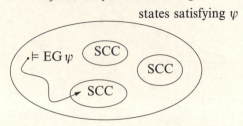

Fig. 3.16. A better way of handling EG.

- restrict the graph to states satisfying ψ, i.e. delete all other states and their transitions;
- find the maximal *strongly connected components* (SCCs); these are maximal regions of the state space in which every state is linked with (= has a finite path to) every other one in that region.
- use backwards breadth-first searching on the restricted graph to find any state that can reach an SCC; see Figure 3.16.

The complexity of this algorithm is $O(f \cdot (V + E))$, i.e. linear both in the size of the model and in the size of the formula.

Example 3.10 We applied the basic algorithm to our second model of mutual exclusion with the formula $E[\neg c_2 \ U \ c_1]$; see Figure 3.17. The algorithm labels all states which satisfy c_1 during phase 1 with $E[\neg c_2 \ U \ c_1]$. This labels s_2 and s_4. During phase 2, it labels all states which do not satisfy c_2 and have a successor state that is already labelled. This labels states s_1 and s_3. During phase 3, we label s_0 because it does not satisfy c_2 and has a successor state (s_1) which is already labelled. Thereafter, the algorithm terminates because no additional states get labelled: all unlabelled states either satisfy c_2, or must pass through such a state to reach a labelled state.

EXERCISES 3.7
* 1. Apply the labelling algorithm to check the formulas ϕ_1, ϕ_2, ϕ_3 and ϕ_4 of the mutual exclusion model in Figure 3.12.
   2. Apply the labelling algorithm to check the formulas ϕ_1, ϕ_2, ϕ_3 and ϕ_4 of the mutual exclusion model in Figure 3.13.
   3. Explain the construction of formula ϕ_4, used to express that the processes need not enter their critical section in strict sequence. Does it rely on the fact that the safety property ϕ_1 holds?
   4. Inspecting the definition of the labelling algorithm, explain what

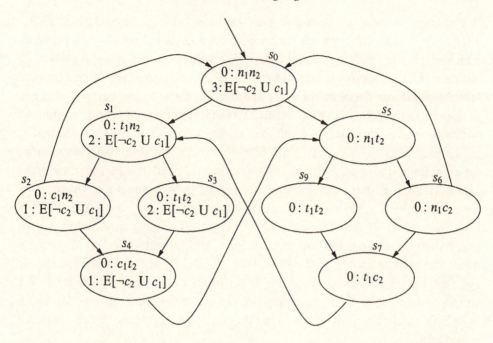

Fig. 3.17. An example run of the labelling algorithm in our second model of mutual exclusion applied to the formula $E[\neg c_2 \ U \ c_1]$.

happens if you perform it on the formula $p \wedge \neg p$ (in any state, in any model).

———

3.5.2 *The pseudo-code of the model checking algorithm*

We present the pseudo-code for the basic labelling algorithm given earlier in this chapter. The main function SAT (for 'satisfies') takes as input a CTL formula, i.e. a formula over the Backus Naur form in Definition 3.1. The program SAT expects a parse tree of some CTL formula constructed by means of the grammar in Definition 3.1. This expectation reflects an important *precondition* on the correctness of the algorithm SAT. For example, the program simply would not know what to do with an input of the form $X(\top \wedge EF \, p_3)$, since this is not a CTL formula (it does not have a parse tree according to the grammar for CTL). Hence, we also need a parser that would make sure that only well-formed CTL formulas are being fed into SAT. However, we merely focus on the development of SAT without such preprocessing because this is the prime objective of this section.

The pseudo-code we write for SAT looks a bit like fragments of FOR-TRAN or Pascal code; we use functions with a keyword **return** that indicates which result the function should return. We will also use natural language to indicate the case analysis over the root node of the parse tree of ϕ. The declaration **local var** declares some fresh variables local to the current instance of the procedure in question, whereas **repeat until** executes the command which follows it repeatedly, until the condition becomes true. Additionally, we employ suggestive notation for the operations on sets, like intersection, set complement and so forth. In reality we would need an abstract data type, called SETS, together with implementations of these operations, but for now we are interested only in the mechanism in principle of the algorithm for SAT; any (correct and efficient) implementation of sets would do and we study such an implementation in Chapter 6. We assume that SAT has access to all the relevant parts of the model: S, $\rightarrow$ and L. In particular, we ignore the fact that SAT would require a description of $\mathcal{M}$ as input as well. We simply assume that SAT operates *directly* on any such given model. Note how SAT implicitly translates ϕ into an equivalent formula of the adequate set chosen.

The algorithm is presented in Figure 3.18 and its subfunctions in Figures 3.19-3.21. They use program variables X, Y, V and W of type SETS. The program for SAT simply handles the easy cases directly and passes more complicated cases on to special procedures, which in turn might call SAT *recursively* on subexpressions.

Of course, we still need to make sure that this algorithm is correct. This will be handled in Section 3.9.

3.5.3 *The 'state explosion' problem*

Although the labelling algorithm (with the clever way of handling EG) is linear in the size of the model, unfortunately the size of the model is itself exponential in the number of variables and the number of components of the system which execute in parallel. This means that, for example, adding a boolean variable to your program will *double* the complexity of verifying a property of it.

The tendency of the state space to become very large is known as the *state explosion* problem. A lot of research has gone into finding ways of overcoming it, including the use of:

- Efficient data structures, called *ordered binary decision diagrams* (OBDDs),

```
function SAT (φ)
 /* determines the set of states satisfying φ */
begin
   case
      φ is ⊤ : return S
      φ is ⊥ : return ∅
      φ is atomic: return {s ∈ S | φ ∈ L(s)}
      φ is ¬φ₁ : return S − SAT (φ₁)
      φ is φ₁ ∧ φ₂ : return SAT (φ₁) ∩ SAT (φ₂)
      φ is φ₁ ∨ φ₂ : return SAT (φ₁) ∪ SAT (φ₂)
      φ is φ₁ → φ₂ : return SAT (¬φ ∨ φ₂)
      φ is AX φ₁ : return SAT (¬EX ¬φ₁)
      φ is EX φ₁ : return SAT_EX(φ₁)
      φ is A(φ₁ U φ₂) : return SAT(¬(E[¬φ₂ U (¬φ₁ ∧ ¬φ₂)] ∨ EG ¬φ₂))
      φ is E(φ₁ U φ₂) : return SAT_EU(φ₁, φ₂)
      φ is EF φ₁ : return SAT (E(⊤ U φ₁))
      φ is EG φ₁ : return SAT(¬AF ¬φ₁)
      φ is AF φ₁ : return SAT_AF (φ₁)
      φ is AG φ₁ : return SAT (¬EF ¬φ₁)
   end case
end function
```

Fig. 3.18. The function SAT. It takes a CTL formula as input and returns the set of states satisfying the formula. It calls the functions $\mathrm{SAT_{EX}}$, $\mathrm{SAT_{EU}}$ and $\mathrm{SAT_{AF}}$, respectively, if EX, EU or AF is the root of the input's parse tree.

```
function SAT_EX (φ)
 /* determines the set of states satisfying EX φ */
local var X, Y
begin
   X := SAT (φ);
   Y := {s₀ ∈ S | s₀ → s₁ for some s₁ ∈ X};
   return Y
end
```

Fig. 3.19. The function $\mathrm{SAT_{EX}}$. It computes the states satisfying ϕ by calling SAT. Then, it looks backwards along $\rightarrow$ to find the states satisfying EX ϕ.

which represent *sets* of states instead of individual states. We study these in Chapter 6 in detail.

- Abstraction: we abstract away variables in the model which are not relevant to the formula being checked.

- Partial order reduction: for asynchronous systems, several interleavings of component traces may be equivalent as far as satisfaction of the formula to be checked is concerned. This can often substantially reduce the size of the model-checking problem.

function SAT$_{AF}$ (ϕ)
/* determines the set of states satisfying AF ϕ */
local var X, Y
begin
    $X := S$;
    $Y := \text{SAT}(\phi)$;
    repeat until $X = Y$
    begin
        $X := Y$;
        $Y := Y \cup \{s \mid \text{for all } s' \text{ with } s \rightarrow s' \text{ we have } s' \in Y\}$
    end
    return Y
end

Fig. 3.20. The function SAT$_{AF}$. It computes the states satisfying ϕ by calling SAT. Then, it accumulates states satisfying AF ϕ in the manner described in the labelling algorithm.

function SAT$_{EU}$ (ϕ, ψ)
/* determines the set of states satisfying E[ϕ U ψ] */
local var W, X, Y
begin
    $W := \text{SAT}(\phi)$;
    $X := S$;
    $Y := \text{SAT}(\psi)$;
    repeat until $X = Y$
    begin
        $X := Y$;
        $Y := Y \cup (W \cap \{s \mid \text{exists } s' \text{ such that } s \rightarrow s' \text{ and } s' \in Y\}$
    end
    return Y
end

Fig. 3.21. The function SAT$_{EU}$. It computes the states satisfying ϕ by calling SAT. Then, it accumulates states satisfying E[ϕ U ψ] in the manner described in the labelling algorithm.

- Induction: model-checking systems with (e.g.) large numbers of identical, or similar, components can often be implemented by 'induction' on this number.
- Composition: break the verification problem down into several simpler verification problems.

The last four issues are beyond the scope of this book, but references may be found at the ends of Chapters 3 and 6.

EXERCISES 3.8

* 1. For mutual exclusion, draw a transition system which forces the two processes to enter their critical section in strict sequence and show that ϕ_4 is false of its initial state.

2. Extend the pseudo-code of Section 3.5.2 so that it can deal with subformulas AG ψ_1, without rewriting it in terms of other formulas. [Question: will your routine be more like the routine for AF, or more like that for EG on page 175? Why?]

* 3. Write the pseudo-code for SAT$_{EG}$, based on the description in terms of deleting labels given in Section 3.5.1.

3.6 The SMV system

So far, this chapter has been quite theoretical; and the sections after this one continue in this vein. However, one of the exciting things about model checking is that it is also a practical subject, for there are several efficient implementations which can check large systems in realistic time. In this section, we look at the best-known of the CTL model checkers, which is called SMV ('symbolic model verifier'). It provides a language for describing the models we have been drawing as diagrams and it directly checks the validity of CTL formulas on those models.

SMV is freely distributed and can be found on the internet. Further details can be found at the end of this chapter. We do not give a full introduction to SMV, but provide just enough information to give the flavour. The serious reader should read more about SMV in the references.

SMV takes as input a text consisting of a program describing a model and some specifications (CTL formulas). It produces as output either the word 'true' *if the specifications hold for all initial states*, or a trace showing why the specification is false for the model determined by our program.

SMV programs consist of one or more modules. As in the programming language C, or Java, one of the modules must be called main. Modules can declare variables and assign to them. Assignments usually give the initial value of a variable and its next value as an expression in terms of the current values of variables. This expression can be non-deterministic (denoted by several expressions in braces, or no assignment at all). Non-determinism is used to model the environment and for abstraction.

The following input to SMV:

```
MODULE main
VAR
  request : boolean;
  status : {ready,busy};
ASSIGN
  init(status) := ready;
  next(status) := case
                     request : busy;
                     1 : {ready,busy};
                  esac;
SPEC
AG(request -> AF status = busy)
```

consists of a program and a specification. The program has two variables, request of type boolean and status of type ready, busy: 0 denotes F and 1 represents T. The variable request is not determined within this program; this means it may be determined by the user, or by the environment. The variable status is partially determined: initially, it is ready; and it becomes busy whenever request is true. If request is false, the next value of status is not determined.

Note that the case 1:   signifies the default case and that case statements are evaluated from the top down: if several expressions to the left of ':' are true, then the command of the first true expression will be executed. The program therefore denotes the transition system shown in Figure 3.22; there are four states, each one corresponding to a possible value of the two binary variables. It takes a while to get used to the syntax of SMV and its meaning. Notice that the program and the transition system are *non-deterministic*, i.e. the 'next state' is not uniquely defined. For example, the state '¬req, busy' has four states it can move to (itself and three others). Note that we wrote 'busy' as a shorthand for 'status=busy' and 'req' for 'request is true'. Observe also how the variable request functions as a genuine environment in this model, for any state transition based on the behaviour of status comes in a pair: to a successor state where request is false, or true, respectively.

Specifications are introduced by the keyword SPEC and are simply CTL formulas. Notice that SMV uses &, |, − > and ! for ∧, ∨, → and ¬, respectively, since they are available on standard keyboards. We may easily verify that the specification of our module main holds of the model in Figure 3.22.

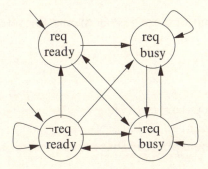

Fig. 3.22. The model corresponding to the SMV program in the text.

EXERCISES 3.9

* 1. Verify that the specification above in the SMV program involving the variables request and busy is satisfied by the model in Figure 3.22.

2. Does E[req U ¬busy] hold in the initial state of the model in Figure 3.22?

3. SMV has the capability of referring to the next value of a declared variable v by writing next(v). Consider the model obtained from Figure 3.22 by removing the loop on state !request & status = busy. Use the SMV feature next(...) to code this model as an SMV program with the same specification as the program for Figure 3.22.

___

3.6.1 Modules in SMV

SMV supports breaking a system description into several *modules*, to aid readability and to verify interaction properties. A module is instantiated when a variable having that module name as its type is declared. This defines a set of variables, one for each one declared in the module description. In the example below, which is one of the ones distributed with SMV, a counter which repeatedly counts from 000 through to 111 is described by three single-bit counters. The module counter is instantiated three times, with the names bit0, bit1 and bit2. The counter module has one formal parameter, carry_in, which is given the actual value 1 in bit0, and bit0.carry_out in the instance bit1. Hence, the carry_in of module bit1 is the carry_out of module bit0. Note that we use the period '.' in m.v to access the variable v in module m. This notation is also used by a host of programming languages to access fields in record structures, or methods in objects. The keyword DEFINE is used to assign the expression value & carry_in to the symbol carry_out (such definitions are just a means for referring to the current value of a certain expression).

```
MODULE main
VAR
  bit0 : counter_cell(1);
  bit1 : counter_cell(bit0.carry_out);
  bit2 : counter_cell(bit1.carry_out);
SPEC
  AG AF bit2.carry_out

MODULE counter_cell(carry_in)
VAR
  value : boolean;
ASSIGN
  init(value) := 0;
  next(value) := value + carry_in mod 2;
DEFINE
  carry_out := value & carry_in;
```

The effect of the DEFINE statement could have been obtained by declaring a new variable and assigning its value thus:

```
VAR
  carry_out : boolean;
ASSIGN
  carry_out := value & carry_in;
```

Notice that, in this assignment, the *current* value of the variable is assigned. Defined symbols are usually preferable to variables, since they don't increase the state space. However, they cannot be assigned non-deterministically since they refer only to another expression.

3.6.2 *Synchronous and asynchronous composition*

By default, modules in SMV are composed *synchronously*: this means that there is a global clock and, each time it ticks, each of the modules executes in parallel. By use of the process keyword, it is possible to compose the modules asynchronously. In that case, they run at different 'speeds', interleaving arbitrarily. At each tick of the clock, *one* of them is non-deterministically chosen and executed for one cycle. Asynchronous interleaving composition is useful for describing communication protocols, asynchronous circuits and other systems whose actions are not synchronised to a global clock.

The bit counter above is synchronous, whereas the examples below of mutual exclusion and the alternating bit protocol are asynchronous.

3.6.3 Mutual exclusion revisited

Figure 3.23 gives the SMV code for a mutual exclusion protocol. This code consists of two modules, main and prc. The module main has the variable turn, which determines whose turn it is to enter the critical section if both are trying to enter (recall the discussion about the states s_3 and s_9 in Section 3.4.2).

The module main also has two instantiations of prc. In each of these instantiations, st is the status of a process (saying whether it is in its critical section, or not, or trying) and other-st is the status of the other process (notice how this is passed as a parameter in the third and fourth lines of main).

The value of st evolves in the way described in a previous section: when it is *n*, it may stay as *n* or move to *t*. When it is *t*, if the other one is *n*, it will go straight to *c*, but if the other one is *t*, it will check whose turn it is before going to *c*. Then, when it is *c*, it may move back to *n*. Each instantiation of prc gives the turn to the other one when it gets to its critical section.

An important feature of SMV is that we can restrict its search tree to execution paths along which an arbitrary CTL formula ϕ is true infinitely often. Because this is often used to model *fair* access to resources, it is called a *fairness constraint* and introduced by the keyword FAIRNESS. Thus, the occurrence of FAIRNESS ϕ means that SMV, when checking a specification ψ, will ignore any path along which ϕ does not occur infinitely often.

In the module prc, we restrict to computation paths along which st is infinitely often not equal to *c*. This is because our code allows the process to stay in its critical section as long as it likes. Thus, there is another opportunity for liveness to fail: if process 2 stays in its critical section forever, process 1 will never be able to enter. Again, we ought not to take this kind of violation into account, since it is patently unfair if a process is allowed to stay in its critical section for ever. We are looking for more subtle violations of the specifications, if there are any. To avoid the one above, we stipulate the fairness constraint !(st=c).

If the module in question has been declared with the process keyword, then at each time point SMV will non-deterministically decide whether or not to select it for execution, as explained earlier. We may wish to ignore

```
MODULE main
  VAR
      pr1: process prc(pr2.st, turn, 0);
      pr2: process prc(pr1.st, turn, 1);
      turn: boolean;
  ASSIGN
      init(turn) := 0;
-- safety
SPEC  AG!((pr1.st = c) & (pr2.st = c))
-- liveness
SPEC  AG((pr1.st = t) -> AF (pr1.st = c))
SPEC  AG((pr2.st = t) -> AF (pr2.st = c))
-- no strict sequencing
SPEC EF(pr1.st=c & E[pr1.st=c U
                  (!pr1.st=c & E[! pr2.st=c U pr1.st=c ])])

MODULE prc(other-st, turn, myturn)
  VAR
      st: {n, t, c};
  ASSIGN
    init(st) := n;
    next(st) :=
      case
          (st = n)                                  : {t,n};
          (st = t) & (other-st = n)                 : c;
          (st = t) & (other-st = t) & (turn = myturn): c;
          (st = c)                                  : {c,n};
          1                                         : st;
      esac;
    next(turn) :=
      case
          turn = myturn & st = c : !turn;
          1                      : turn;
      esac;
  FAIRNESS running
  FAIRNESS  !(st = c)
```

Fig. 3.23. SMV code for mutual exclusion.

paths in which a module is starved of processor time. The reserved word
running can be used instead of a formula in a fairness constraint: writing
FAIRNESS running restricts attention to execution paths along which the
module in which it appears is selected for execution infinitely often.

In prc, we restrict ourselves to such paths, since, without this restriction,
it would be easy to violate the liveness constraint if it were *never* selected
for execution. We assume the scheduler is fair; this assumption is codified
by two FAIRNESS clauses.

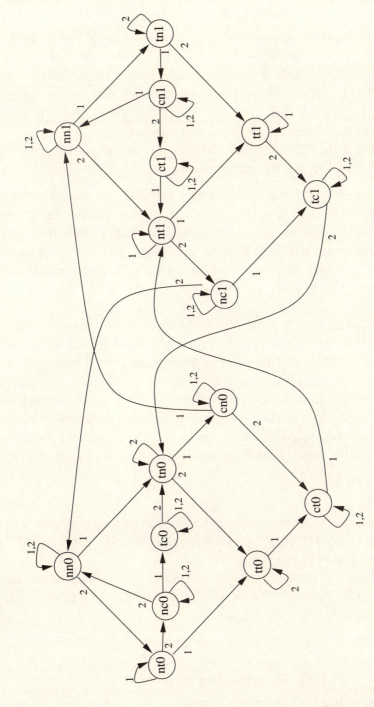

Fig. 3.24. The transition system corresponding to the SMV code in Figure 3.23. The labels on the transitions denote the process which makes the move. The label 1,2 means that either process could make that move.

We return to the issue of fairness, and the question of how our model-checking algorithm copes with it, in the next section.

The transition system corresponding to this program is shown in Figure 3.24. Each state shows the values of the variables; for example, ct1 is the state in which process 1 and 2 are critical and trying, respectively, and turn=1. The labels on the transitions show which process was selected for execution. In general, each state has several transitions, some in which process 1 moves and others in which process 2 moves.

This model is a bit different from the previous model given for mutual exclusion in Figure 3.13, for these two reasons:

- Because the boolean variable turn has been explicitly introduced to distinguish between states s_3 and s_9 of Figure 3.13, we now distinguish between certain states (for example, ct0 and ct1) which were identical before. However, these states are not distinguished if you look just at the transitions *from* them. Therefore, they satisfy the same CTL formulas which don't mention turn. Those states are distinguished only by the way they can arise.
- We have eliminated an over-simplification made in the model of Figure 3.13. Recall that we assumed the system would move to a different state on every tick of the clock (there are no transitions from a state to itself). In Figure 3.24, we allow transitions from each state to itself, representing that a process was chosen for execution and did some local computation, but did not move in or out of its critical section. Of course, by doing this we have introduced paths in which one process gets stuck in its critical section. Hence the need to invoke a fairness constraint to eliminate such paths.

EXERCISES 3.10
* 1. Verify ϕ_1 to ϕ_4 from Section 3.4.1 for the transition system given in Figure 3.24. Which of them require the fairness constraints of the SMV program in Figure 3.23?
* 2. Show that a CTL formula ϕ is true on infinitely many states of a computation path $s_0 \rightarrow s_1 \rightarrow s_2 \rightarrow \dots$ iff for all $n \geq 0$ there is some $m \geq n$ such that $s_m \vDash \phi$.

3.6.4 The alternating bit protocol

The ABP (alternating bit protocol) is a protocol for transmitting messages along a 'lossy line', i.e. a line which may lose or duplicate messages. The protocol guarantees that, providing the line doesn't lose infinitely many messages, communication between the sender and the receiver will be successful. (We allow the line to lose or duplicate messages, but it may not corrupt messages; however; there is no way of guaranteeing successful transmission along a line which can corrupt.)

The ABP works as follows. There are four entities, or agents: the sender, the receiver, the message channel and the acknowledgement channel. The sender transmits the first part of the message together with the 'control' bit 0. If, and when, the receiver receives a message with the control bit 0, it sends 0 along the acknowledgement channel. When the sender receives this acknowledgement, it sends the next packet with the control bit 1. If and when the receiver receives this, it acknowledges by sending a 1 on the acknowledgement channel. By alternating the control bit, both receiver and sender can guard against duplicating messages and losing messages (i.e. they ignore messages that have the unexpected control bit).

If the sender doesn't get the expected acknowledgement, it continually resends the message, until the acknowledgement arrives. If the receiver doesn't get a message with the expected control bit, it continually resends the previous acknowledgement.

Fairness is also important for the ABP. It comes in because, although we want to model the fact that the channel can lose messages, we want to assume that, if we send a message often enough, eventually it will arrive. In other words, the channel cannot lose an infinite sequence of messages. If we did not make this assumption, then the channels could lose all messages and, in that case, the ABP would not work.

Let us see this in the concrete setting of SMV. We may assume that the text to be sent is divided up into single-bit messages, which are sent sequentially. The variable message1 is the current bit of the message being sent, whereas message2 is the control bit. The definition of the module sender is given in Figure 3.25. This module spends most of its time in st=sending, going only briefly to st=sent when it receives an acknowledgement corresponding to the control bit of the message it has been sending. The variables message1 and message2 represent the actual data being sent and the control bit, respectively. On successful transmission, the module obtains a new message to send and returns to st=sending. The new message1 is obtained non-deterministically (i.e. from the environment); message2 alternates in value. We impose FAIRNESS running, i.e. the sender must be selected to run infinitely often. The SPEC tests that we can always succeed in sending the

```
MODULE sender(ack)
VAR
    st        : {sending,sent};
    message1  : boolean;
    message2  : boolean;
ASSIGN
    init(st) := sending;
    next(st) := case
                    ack = message2 & !(st=sent) : sent;
                    1                            : sending;
                esac;
    next(message1) :=
                case
                    st = sent : {0,1};
                    1         : message1;
                esac;
    next(message2) :=
                case
                    st = sent : !message2;
                    1         : message2;
                esac;
FAIRNESS running
SPEC AG AF st=sent
```

Fig. 3.25. The ABP sender in SMV.

current message. The module receiver is programmed in a similar way, in Figure 3.26.

We also need to describe the two channels, in Figure 3.27. The acknowledgement channel is an instance of the one-bit channel one-bit-chan below. Its lossy character is specified by the non-deterministic assignment: the input may be transmitted to the output, but it need not (in which case output retains its old value). However, the second fairness constraint ensures that the channel doesn't continually lose the same message: eventually, a bit will get through (so if input is 1, then eventually output will be 1 too).

The two-bit channel two-bit-chan, used to send messages, is similar. Note, however, that either both parts of the message get through, or neither of them does (the channel is assumed not to corrupt messages). Thus, output2 (the control bit) is non-deterministically assigned to be input2 or output2; and, if the control bit gets through, then so does the message1 part (output1 is forced to take the value input1).

To re-emphasise, we use non-deterministic assignment to model the lossy channels: the new value of output is non-deterministically input, or the old output. Fairness constraints were used to model the fact that, although

```
MODULE receiver(message1,message2)
VAR
   st        : {receiving,received};
   ack       : boolean;
   expected  : boolean;
ASSIGN
   init(st) := receiving;
   next(st) := case
                   message2=expected & !(st=received) : received;
                   1                                   : receiving;
               esac;
   next(ack) :=
               case
                   st = received : message2;
                   1             : ack;
               esac;
   next(expected) :=
               case
                   st = received : !expected;
                   1             : expected;
               esac;
FAIRNESS running
SPEC AG AF st=received
```

Fig. 3.26. The ABP receiver in SMV.

channels can lose messages, we assume that only finitely many are lost in any time interval. More precisely, we ask that the formulas given above, which express that the output will eventually match the input, are infinitely often true along fair computation paths. (If this were not the case, then we could find an uninteresting violation of the liveness constraint, namely a path along which all messages from a certain time onwards get lost.)

Finally, we tie it all together with the module main (Figure 3.28). Its role is to connect together the components of the system, which it does by instantiating the four processes. It also specifies the initial values. Since the first control bit is 0, we also initialise the receiver to expect a 0. The receiver should start off by sending 1 as its acknowledgement, so that sender does not think that its very first message is being acknowledged before anything has happened. For the same reason, the output of the channels is initialised to 1.

The specifications for ABP. Our SMV program satisfies the following specifications:

Safety: If the message bit 1 has been sent and the correct acknowledgement has been returned, then a 1 was received by the receiver:
AG(S.st=sent & S.message1=1 -> msg_chan.output1=1).

```
MODULE one-bit-chan(input)
VAR
    output : boolean;
ASSIGN
    next(output) := {input,output};
FAIRNESS running
FAIRNESS (input=0 -> AF output=0) & (input=1 -> AF output=1)

MODULE two-bit-chan(input1,input2)
VAR
    output1:boolean; output2 : boolean;
ASSIGN
    next(output2) := {input2,output2};
    next(output1) :=
                case
                    input2=next(output2) : input1;
                    1                     : {input1,output1};
                esac;
FAIRNESS running
FAIRNESS (input1=0 -> AF output1=0) & (input1=1 -> AF output1=1) &
         (input2=0 -> AF output2=0) & (input2=1 -> AF output2=1)
```

Fig. 3.27. The ABP channels in SMV.

```
MODULE main
VAR
    S : process sender(ack_chan.output);
    R : process receiver(msg_chan.output1,msg_chan.output2);
    msg_chan : process two-bit-chan(S.message1,S.message2);
    ack_chan : process one-bit-chan(R.ack);
ASSIGN
    init(S.message2)    := 0;
    init(R.expected)    := 0;
    init(R.ack)         := 1;
    init(msg_chan.output2) := 1;
    init(ack_chan.output) := 1;

SPEC  AG(S.st=sent & S.message1=1 -> msg_chan.output1=1)
```

Fig. 3.28. The ABP module.

Liveness: Messages get through eventually. Thus, for any state there is inevitably a future state in which the current message has got through. In the module sender, we specified AG AF st=sent. (This specification could equivalently have been written in the main module, as AG AF S.st=sent.)

Similarly, acknowledgements get through eventually. In the module receiver, we insisted on AG AF st=received.

EXERCISES 3.11

1. Run the SMV system on some examples. Try commenting out, or deleting, some of the fairness constraints, if applicable, and see the counter examples SMV generates. SMV is very easy to run.

* 2. Draw the transition system described by the ABP program.

    Remarks: There are 28 reachable states of the ABP program. (Looking at the program, you can see that the state is described by nine boolean variables, namely S.st, S.message1, S.message2, R.st, R.ack, R.expected, msg_chan.output1, msg_chan.output2 and finally ack_chan.output. Therefore, there are $2^9 = 512$ states in total. However, only 28 of them can be reached from the initial state by following a finite path.)

    If you abstract away from the contents of the message (e.g. by setting S.message1 and msg_chan.output1 to be constant 0), then there are only 12 reachable states. This is what you are asked to draw.

3. In the one-bit channel, there are two fairness constraints. We could have written this as a single one, inserting '&' between running and the long formula, or we could have separated the long formula into two and made it into a total of three fairness constraints.

    In general, what is the difference between the single fairness constraint $\phi_1 \wedge \phi_2 \wedge \cdots \wedge \phi_n$ and the n fairness constraints ϕ_1, ϕ_2, etc., up to ϕ_n? Write an SMV program with a fairness constraint a & b which is not equivalent to the two fairness constraints a and b. (You can actually do it in four lines of SMV.)

3.7 Model checking with fairness

The verification of $\mathcal{M}, s_0 \vDash \phi$ might fail because the model $\mathcal{M}$ may contain behaviour which is unrealistic, or guaranteed not to occur in the actual system being analysed. One technique for avoiding this problem is to refine the model $\mathcal{M}$. However, it may sometimes be better to stick to the original model and to impose a *filter* on the model check. Thus, instead of model checking $s_0 \vDash \phi$, we verify $s_0 \vDash \psi \rightarrow \phi$, where ψ encodes the refinement of our model expressed as a specification. For example, the formula ϕ_4 for no strict sequencing correctly encodes its informal description if we use the safety property ϕ_1 as a filter. However, not all refinements of models for CTL model checking can be done in this way. We saw in the last section that SMV allows us to impose *fairness constraints* on top of the transition system it describes. These assumptions state that a given formula is true infinitely often along every computation path. We call such paths *fair computation paths*. The presence of fairness constraints means that, when evaluating the truth of CTL formulas in specifications, the connectives A and E range only over fair paths.

For example, in the mutual exclusion case, we expressed that the process prc can stay in its critical section (st=c) as long as it needs. We modelled this by the non-deterministic assignment

```
next(st) :=
    case
      ...
      (st = c)    : {c,n};
      ...
    esac;
```

However, if we really allow process 2 to stay in its critical section as long as it likes, then we have a path which violates the liveness constraint $AG(t_1 \to AF c_1)$, since, if process 2 stays forever in its critical section, t_1 can be true without c_1 ever becoming true.

We would like to ignore this path, i.e. we would like to assume that the process can stay in its critical section as long as it needs, *but will eventually exit from its critical section* after some finite time. We therefore impose the fairness constraint that !st=c infinitely often. This means that, whatever state the process is in, there will be a state in the future in which it is not in its critical section. Similar fairness constraints were used for the ABP. Fairness constraints of the form

Property ϕ is true infinitely often.

are known as *simple* fairness constraints. Other types include those of the form

If ϕ is true infinitely often, then ψ is also true infinitely often.

SMV can deal only with simple fairness constraints; but how does it do that? To answer that, we now explain how we may adapt our model-checking algorithm so that A and E are assumed to range only over fair computation paths.

Definition 3.11 Let $C \stackrel{\text{def}}{=} \{\psi_1, \psi_2, \ldots, \psi_n\}$ be a set of n fairness constraints. A computation path $s_0 \to s_1 \to \ldots$ is *fair* with respect to these fairness constraints if for each i there are infinitely many j such that $s_j \models \psi_i$, that is, each ψ_i is true infinitely often along the path. Let us write A_C and E_C for the operators A and E restricted to fair paths.

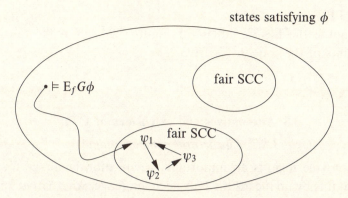

Fig. 3.29. Computing the states satisfying $E_C G \phi$. A state satisfies $E_C G \phi$ iff, in the graph resulting from the restriction to states satisfying ϕ, the state has a fair path from it. A fair path is one which leads to an SCC with a cycle passing through at least one state that satisfies each fairness constraint; in the example, C equals $\{\psi_1, \psi_2, \psi_3\}$.

For example, $\mathscr{M}, s_0 \vDash A_C G \phi$ iff ϕ is true in every state along all fair paths; and similarly for $A_C F$, $A_C U$, etc. Notice that these operators explicitly depend on the chosen set C of fairness constraints. We already know that $E_C U$, $E_C G$ and $E_C X$ form an adequate set; this can be shown in the same manner as was done for the temporal connectives without fairness constraints (Section 3.3.2). We also have that

$$E_C[\phi \, U \, \psi] \equiv E[\phi \, U \, (\psi \wedge E_C G \top)]$$
$$E_C X \phi \equiv EX(\phi \wedge E_C G \top).$$

To see this, observe that a computation path is fair iff any suffix of it is fair. Therefore, we need only provide an algorithm for $E_C G \phi$. It is similar to Algorithm 2 for EG, given earlier in this chapter:

- Restrict the graph to states satisfying ϕ; of the resulting graph, we want to know from which states there is a fair path.
- Find the maximal *strongly connected components* (SCCs) of the restricted graph;
- Remove an SCC if, for some ψ_i, it does not contain a state satisfying ψ_i. The resulting SCCs are the fair SCCs. Any state of the restricted graph that can reach one has a fair path from it.
- Use backwards breadth-first searching to find the states on the restricted graph that can reach a fair SCC.

See Figure 3.29. The complexity of this algorithm is $O(n \cdot f \cdot (V + E))$, i.e. still linear in the size of the model and formula.

EXERCISES 3.12

* 1. Compute the $E_C GT$ labels for Figure 3.24, given the fairness constraints of the code in Figure 3.23.

———

3.8 Alternatives and extensions of CTL

3.8.1 Linear-time temporal logic

Computation tree logic is an important specification language for reactive systems, but it is by no means the only such language. Alternative formalisms include regular expressions, state chart diagrams, graphical interval logics, a modal mu-calculus and linear-time temporal logic (LTL). LTL is closely related to CTL in that it has similar expressive mechanisms, such as an Until connective. Unlike CTL, however, its formulas have meanings on individual computation paths, i.e. there are no explicit path quantifiers E and A. In this sense LTL appears to be less expressive than CTL. However, LTL allows one to nest boolean connectives and modalities in a way not permitted by CTL; in that sense it appears more expressive. In fact it is neither more nor less expressive (as we see later). In the next section, we give a basic introduction to LTL that should allow you to appreciate the commonalities and key differences between CTL and LTL. The main pratical objective of this section is to allow you to compare specification patterns written in LTL with the corresponding ones in CTL.

Definition 3.12 Linear-time temporal logic (LTL) has the following syntax given in Backus Naur form:

$$\phi ::= p \mid (\neg\phi) \mid (\phi \wedge \phi) \mid (\phi \ U \ \phi) \mid (G \phi) \mid (F \phi) \mid (X \phi), \qquad (3.4)$$

where p is any propositional atom.

An LTL formula is evaluated on a path, or a set of paths. A set of paths satisfies ϕ if every path in the set satisfies ϕ. Consider the path $\pi \stackrel{\text{def}}{=} s_1 \rightarrow s_2 \rightarrow \ldots$; we write π^i for the suffix starting at s_i, i.e. π^i is $s_i \rightarrow s_{i+1} \rightarrow \ldots$.

Definition 3.13 Using a model $\mathcal{M} = (S, \rightarrow, L)$ for CTL, we define when a path $\pi = s_1 \rightarrow \ldots$ satisfies an LTL formula via the satisfaction relation $\vDash$ for LTL formulas as follows:

1. $\pi \vDash \top$.
2. $\pi \vDash p$ iff $p \in L(s_1)$.

3. $\pi \vDash \neg \phi$ iff $\pi \nvDash \phi$.
4. $\pi \vDash \phi_1 \wedge \phi_2$ iff $\pi \vDash \phi_1$ and $\pi \vDash \phi_2$.
5. $\pi \vDash X \phi$ iff $\pi^2 \vDash \phi$.
6. $\pi \vDash G \phi$ holds iff, for all $i \geq 1$, $\pi^i \vDash \phi$.
7. $\pi \vDash F \phi$ holds iff, for some $i \geq 1$, $\pi^i \vDash \phi$.
8. $\pi \vDash \phi \ U \ \psi$ holds iff there is some $i \geq 1$ such that $\pi^i \vDash \psi$ and for all $j = 1, \ldots, i - 1$ we have $\pi^j \vDash \phi$.

We say that two LTL formulas ϕ and ψ are *semantically equivalent*, writing $\phi \equiv \psi$, if they are true for the same paths. An LTL formula ϕ is satisfied in a state s of a model $\mathcal{M}$ if ϕ is satisfied on every path starting at s.

These definitions are exactly the ones we would expect from our knowledge of CTL, except that they are expressed in terms of paths. LTL is conceptually simpler than CTL, for it involves thinking about only one path at a time. Of course LTL has the expected equivalences such as $G\phi \equiv \neg F \neg \phi$ and the distribution of F over $\vee$ and G over $\wedge$, i.e.

$$F(\phi \vee \psi) \equiv F\phi \vee F\psi$$
$$G(\phi \wedge \psi) \equiv G\phi \wedge G\psi.$$

Compare this with the quantifier equivalences in Section 2.3.2. It also has an important equivalence, which we met in the context of CTL; we finish this section by proving this fact.

Theorem 3.14 $\phi \ U \ \psi \equiv \neg(\neg \psi \ U \ (\neg \phi \wedge \neg \psi)) \wedge F\psi$ *holds for all LTL formulas ϕ and ψ.*

PROOF: Take any path $s_0 \to s_1 \to s_2 \to \ldots$.

First, suppose $s_0 \vDash \phi \ U \ \psi$ holds. Let n be the smallest number such that $s_n \vDash \psi$; such a number has to exist since $s_0 \vDash \phi \ U \ \psi$; then, for each $k < n$, $s_k \vDash \phi$. We immediately have $s_0 \vDash F\psi$, so it remains to show $s_0 \vDash \neg(\neg \psi \ U \ (\neg \phi \wedge \neg \psi))$, which, if we expand, means:

(∗) for each $i > 0$, if $s_i \vDash \neg \phi \wedge \neg \psi$, then there is some $j < i$ with $s_j \vDash \psi$.

Take any $i > 0$ with $s_i \vDash \neg \phi \wedge \neg \psi$; $i > n$, so we can take $j \stackrel{\text{def}}{=} n$ and have $s_j \vDash \psi$.

Conversely, suppose $s_0 \vDash \neg(\neg \psi \ U \ (\neg \phi \wedge \neg \psi)) \wedge Fq$ holds; we prove $s_0 \vDash \phi \ U \ \psi$. Since $s_0 \vDash F\psi$, we have a minimal n as before. We show that, for any $i < n$, $s_i \vDash \phi$. Suppose $s_i \vDash \neg \phi$; since n is minimal, we know

$s_i \vDash \neg\psi$, so by (*) there is some $j < i < n$ with $s_j \vDash \psi$, contradicting the minimality of n.   □

Recall that we have already used this result in the claim that EG, EU and EX form an adequate set in CTL, where we relied on this equivalence in the following form:

$$A[p \cup q] \equiv \neg(E[\neg q \cup (\neg p \wedge \neg q)] \vee EG \neg q). \tag{3.5}$$

EXERCISES 3.13

1. Express the properties ϕ_1 to ϕ_4 for the mutual exclusion protocol as LTL formulas (with its semantics that it be true on all paths); for some of them you may have to express their negations as LTL formulas.

2. Recall the algorithm NNF from Chapter 1 which computes the negation normal form of propositional logic formulas. Extend this algorithm to LTL: you need to add program clauses for the additional connectives X, F, G and U; these clauses have to animate the semantic equivalences that we presented in this section.

3.8.2 CTL*

What logical formalism do we obtain if we allow nested modalities and boolean connectives before applying the path quantifiers E and A? The resulting logic is CTL* which allows us to write specifications like the following:

- $A[(p \cup r) \vee (q \cup r)]$: along all paths, either p is true until r, or q is true until r.
- $A[X p \vee XX p]$: along all paths, p is true in the next state, or the next but one.
- $E[GF p]$: there is a path along which p is infinitely often true.

These formulas are *not* equivalent to, respectively, $A[(p \vee q) \cup r)]$, $AX p \vee AX AX p$ and $EG EF p$. It turns out that the first of them can be written as a (rather long) CTL formula. The second and third do not have a CTL equivalent.

The syntax of CTL* is given as follows: it divides formulas into two classes:

- *state formulas*, which are evaluated in states:

$$\phi ::= p \mid \top \mid (\neg\phi) \mid (\phi \wedge \phi) \mid A[\alpha] \mid E[\alpha],$$

where p is any atomic formula and α any path formula; and
- *path formulas*, which are evaluated along paths:

$$\alpha ::= \phi \mid (\neg\alpha) \mid (\alpha \wedge \alpha) \mid (\alpha \, U \, \alpha) \mid (G\,\alpha) \mid (F\,\alpha) \mid (X\,\alpha),$$

where ϕ is any state formula. This is an example of an inductive definition which is *mutually recursive* insofar as the definition of each class depends upon the definition of the other.

EXERCISES 3.14
* 1. Find a CTL* path formula which says that p is true for every second state along a path.
  2. Extend the algorithm NNF which computes the negation normal form of propositional logic formulas to CTL*. Since CTL* is defined in terms of two syntactic categories (state formulas and path formulas), this requires two separate versions of NNF which call each other in a way that is reflected by the syntax of CTL* above.

---

*LTL and CTL as subsets of CTL**

Although the syntax of LTL does not include A and E, the semantic viewpoint of LTL is that we consider all paths. Therefore, the LTL formula α is equivalent to the CTL* formula $A[\alpha]$. Thus, LTL can be viewed as a subset of CTL*.

CTL is also a subset of CTL*, since it is the fragment of CTL* in which we restrict the form of path formulas to

$$\alpha ::= (\phi \, U \, \phi) \mid (G\,\phi) \mid (F\,\phi) \mid (X\,\phi).$$

*Examples in various subsets of CTL**

Figure 3.30 shows the relationship among the expressive powers of CTL, LTL and CTL* with the formulas ψ_1 to ψ_4 listed on the following page.

In CTL but not in LTL: $\psi_1 \overset{\text{def}}{=} AG\,EF\,p$, i.e. wherever we have got to, we can always get back to a state in which p is true. This is also useful, e.g. in finding deadlocks in protocols.

    The proof that $AG\,EF\,p$ is not expressible in LTL is as follows. Let ϕ be an LTL formula such that $A[\phi]$ is allegedly equivalent to

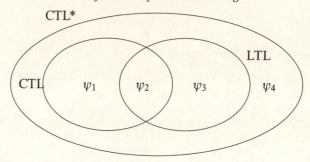

Fig. 3.30. The expressive powers of CTL, LTL and CTL*.

AG EF p. Since $\mathcal{M}, s \vDash$ AG EF p in the left-hand diagram below, we have $\mathcal{M}, s \vDash A[\phi]$. Now let $\mathcal{M}'$ be the submodel of $\mathcal{M}$ shown in the right-hand diagram. The paths from s in $\mathcal{M}'$ are a subset of those from s in $\mathcal{M}$, so we have $\mathcal{M}', s \vDash A[\phi]$. Yet, it is *not* the case that $\mathcal{M}', s \vDash$ AG EF p; a contradiction.

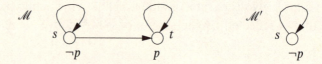

In CTL*, but neither in CTL nor in LTL: $\psi_4 \overset{\text{def}}{=} E[GF\,p]$, saying that there is a path with infinitely many p.

   The proof that this is not expressible in CTL is quite complex and may be found in the papers co-authored by E. A. Emerson with others, given in the references. (Why is it not expressible in LTL?)

In LTL but not in CTL: $\psi_3 \overset{\text{def}}{=} A[GF\,p \rightarrow F\,q]$, saying that if there are infinitely many p along the path, then there is an occurrence of q. This is an interesting thing to be able to say; for example, many fairness constraints are of the form 'infinitely often requested implies eventually acknowledged'.

In LTL and CTL: $\psi_2 \overset{\text{def}}{=}$ AG $(p \rightarrow AF\,q)$ in CTL, or G $(p \rightarrow F\,q)$ in LTL: any p is eventually followed by a q.

Remark 3.15 FG p and AF AG p are not equivalent, since FG p is satisfied, whereas AF AG p is not satisfied, in the model

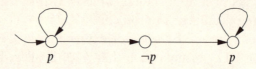

3.8.3 *The expressive power of CTL*

Compared with CTL*, the syntax of CTL is restricted in two ways: it does not allow boolean combinations of path formulas and it does not allow nesting of the path modalities X, F and G. Indeed, we have already seen examples of the inexpressibility in CTL of nesting of path modalities, namely the formulas ψ_3 and ψ_4 above.

In this section, we see that the first of these restrictions is only apparent; we can find equivalents in CTL for formulas having boolean combinations of path formulas. The idea is to translate any formula having boolean combinations of path formulas into one that doesn't. For example, we may see that

$$E[F\,p \wedge F\,q] \;\equiv\; EF\,[p \wedge EF\,q] \vee EF\,[q \wedge EF\,p]$$

since, if we have $F\,p \wedge F\,q$ along any path, then either the p must come before the q, or the other way around, corresponding to the two disjuncts on the right. (If the p and q occur simultaneously, then both disjuncts are true.)

Since U is like F (only with the extra complication of its first argument), we find the following equivalence[1]:

$$
\begin{aligned}
E[(p_1 \text{ U } q_1) \wedge (p_2 \text{ U } q_2)] \;\equiv\; \quad & E[(p_1 \wedge p_2) \text{ U } (q_1 \wedge E[p_2 \text{ U } q_2])] \\
& \vee\, E[(p_1 \wedge p_2) \text{ U } (q_2 \wedge E[p_1 \text{ U } q_1])].
\end{aligned}
$$

And from the CTL equivalence $A[p \text{ U } q] \;\equiv\; \neg(E[\neg q \text{ U } (\neg p \wedge \neg q)] \vee EG\,\neg q)$ we easily obtain

$$E[\neg(p \text{ U } q)] \;\equiv\; E[\neg q \text{ U } (\neg p \wedge \neg q)] \vee EG\,\neg q.$$

Other identities we need in this translation include $E[\neg X\,p] \;\equiv\; EX\,\neg p$.

The 'weak Until' operator in CTL

A useful variant of the Until operator in CTL is known as 'weak Until'. Recall that $A[p \text{ U } q]$ is true in a state if, along all paths from that state, q is true somewhere along the path and p is true from the present state until the state in which q is true. This means that a path in which p is permanently true and q is never true does not satisfy $p \text{ U } q$.

However, sometimes our intuition about Until suggests that we should accept paths in which q never holds, provided that p is permanently true. For example, about an elevator system, we may wish to check that the indicator light stays on until the elevator arrives. Intuitively, a path along

---

[1] Since CTL is syntactically and semantically a 'subset' of CTL*, it actually makes sense to speak of equivalent formulas.

which the elevator never arrives and the indicator light stays on forever is not a violation of this specification, so we should not express it as A[on U arrive].

We therefore introduce the 'weak until', written W. The formula A[p W q] is true in a state if, along all paths from that state, p is true from the present state until the first state in which q is true, *if any*. In particular, if there is no q state on a path, then p needs to hold for all states of that path.

In LTL and CTL*, weak Until may be defined in terms of the ordinary Until, as follows:

$$p \text{ W } q \equiv (p \text{ U } q) \vee \text{G} p.$$

Unfortunately this will not work directly for CTL. The case of EW is simple enough; since E distributes over $\vee$, we have

$$\text{E}[p \text{ W } q] \equiv \text{E}[p \text{ U } q] \vee \text{EG} p.$$

For AW, we have to resort to the translation described above, to finally establish

$$\text{A}[p \text{ W } q] \equiv \neg E[\neg q \text{ U } \neg(p \vee q)].$$

The specification for the elevator then reads as A[on W arrive].

EXERCISES 3.15

1. Find a transition system which distinguishes the following pairs of CTL* formulas (i.e. show that they are *not* equivalent):

   (a) AF G p and AF AG p
   * (b) AG F p and AG EF p
   (c) A[(p U r) $\vee$ (q U r)] and A[($p \vee q$) U r)]
   * (d) A[X p $\vee$ XX p] and AX p $\vee$ AX AX p
   (e) E[GF p] and EG EF p.

2. The translation from CTL with boolean combinations of path formulas to plain CTL introduced in the last section is not complete. Invent CTL equivalents for:

   * (a) E[F p $\wedge$ (q U r)]
   * (b) E[F p $\wedge$ G q].

   In this way, we have dealt with all formulas of the form E[$\phi \wedge \psi$]. Formulas of the form E[$\phi \vee \psi$] can be rewritten as E[ϕ] $\vee$ E[ψ] and A[ϕ] can be written $\neg$E[$\neg\phi$].

   Use this translation to write the following in CTL:

   (c) E[(p U q) $\wedge$ F p]

* (d) $A[(p \cup q) \wedge G p]$
* (e) $A[F p \rightarrow F q]$.

3. The aim of this exercise is to demonstrate the expansion given for AW at the end of the last section, i.e.

$$A[p \ W \ q] \equiv \neg E[\neg q \ U \ \neg(p \vee q)].$$

Show that the following LTL formulas are *valid* (i.e. true in any state of any model):

   (a) $\neg q \ U \ (\neg p \wedge \neg q) \rightarrow \neg G p$
   (b) $G\neg q \wedge F\neg p \rightarrow \neg q \ U \ (\neg p \wedge \neg q)$.

Expand $\neg((p \ U \ q) \vee G p)$ using de Morgan rules and the LTL equivalence $\neg(\phi \ U \ \psi) \equiv (\neg\psi \ U \ (\neg\phi \wedge \neg\psi)) \vee \neg F\psi$. Using your expansion and the facts (a) and (b) above, show

$$\neg((p \ U \ q) \vee G p) \equiv \neg q \ U \ \neg(p \wedge q)$$

and hence show that the desired expansion of AW above is correct.

3.9 The fixed-point characterisation of CTL

Section 3.5.2 presented an algorithm which, given a CTL formula ϕ and a CTL model $\mathcal{M} = (S, \rightarrow, L)$, computes the set of states $s \in S$ satisfying ϕ. We write this set as $[\![\phi]\!]$. The algorithm works recursively on the structure of ϕ. For formulas ϕ of height 1 ($\bot$, $\top$ or p), $[\![\phi]\!]$ is computed directly. Other formulas are composed of smaller subformulas combined by a connective of CTL. For example, if ϕ is $\psi_1 \vee \psi_2$, then the algorithm computes the sets $[\![\psi_1]\!]$ and $[\![\psi_2]\!]$ and combines them in a certain way (in this case, by taking the union) in order to obtain $[\![\psi_1 \vee \psi_2]\!]$.

The more interesting cases arise when we deal with a formula such as $EX \psi$, involving a temporal operator. The algorithm computes the set $[\![\psi]\!]$ and then computes the set of all states which have a transition to a state in $[\![\psi]\!]$. This is in accord with the semantics of $EX \psi$: $\mathcal{M}, s \vDash EX \psi$ iff there is a state s' with $s \rightarrow s'$ and $\mathcal{M}, s' \vDash \psi$.

For most of these logical operators, we may easily continue this discussion to see that the algorithms work just as expected. However, the cases EU, AF and EG, where we needed to iterate a certain labelling policy until it stabilised (= nothing got changed), are not so obvious to reason about. The topic of this section is to develop the semantic insights into these operators that allow us to provide a complete proof for the correctness of the algorithms.

Inspecting the pseudo-code in Figure 3.18, we see that most of these clauses just do the obvious and correct thing according to the semantics of CTL. For example, try out what SAT does when you call it with $\phi_1 \rightarrow \phi_2$. There are less obvious clauses: if the input formula is $A[\phi_1 \ U \ \phi_2]$, then we see that SAT calls itself with a pretty complicated formula as input; yet, this is precisely the formula which we proved to be equivalent to $A[\phi_1 \ U \ \phi_2]$ in our discussion on LTL (see (3.5) on page 198). Therefore, this works correctly provided that SAT works correctly for this new formula. If the input formula is $AF \psi$ for some ψ, then the function SAT_{AF} is called and this uses a while loop. We need to prove that this while statement does the right thing and that it terminates.

EXERCISES 3.16
Let $\mathcal{M} = (S, \rightarrow, L)$ be a model for CTL and recall that $[\![\phi]\!]$ denotes the set of all $s \in S$ such that $\mathcal{M}, s \vDash \phi$. Prove the following set identities by inspecting the clauses of Definition 3.5.

* 1. $[\![\top]\!] = S$,
  2. $[\![\bot]\!] = \emptyset$,
  3. $[\![\neg\phi]\!] = S - [\![\phi]\!]$,
  4. $[\![\phi_1 \wedge \phi_2]\!] = [\![\phi_1]\!] \cap [\![\phi_2]\!]$,
  5. $[\![\phi_1 \vee \phi_2]\!] = [\![\phi_1]\!] \cup [\![\phi_2]\!]$,
* 6. $[\![\phi_1 \rightarrow \phi_2]\!] = (S - [\![\phi_1]\!]) \cup [\![\phi_2]\!]$,
* 7. $[\![AX \phi]\!] = S - [\![EX \neg\phi]\!]$,
  8. $[\![A(\phi_2 \ U \ \phi_2)]\!] = [\![\neg(E(\neg\phi_1 \ U \ (\neg\phi_1 \wedge \neg\phi_2)) \vee EG \neg\phi_2)]\!]$.

In constructing the procedures SAT_{EU} and SAT_{AF} given in Section 3.5.2, we relied on an iterative procedure involving a while statement. What we are still lacking is an account that assures us that all such iterations do indeed terminate and that the computed results are exactly what we would expect, given the semantics of CTL.

Our aim in this section is to prove the correctness of SAT_{AF} and SAT_{EU}. In fact, we will also write a procedure SAT_{EG} and prove its correctness. (Section 3.5.2 handles $EG \phi$ by translating it into $\neg AF \neg\phi$, but we already noted in Section 3.5.1 and exercise 3 on page 181 that EG could be handled directly.)

The procedure SAT_{EG} is given in Figure 3.31. This procedure is based on the intuitions given in Section 3.5.1: note how *deleting* the label if none of the successor states is labelled is coded as *intersecting* the labelled set with the set of states which have a labelled successor.

```
function SAT_EG (φ)
/* determines the set of states satisfying EG φ */
local var X, Y
begin
    Y := SAT (φ);
    X := ∅;
    repeat until X = Y
    begin
        X := Y ;
        Y := Y ∩ {s | exists s' such that s → s' and s' ∈ Y}
    end
    return Y
end
```

Fig. 3.31. The pseudo-code for SAT_EG.

The semantics of $EG\,\phi$ says that $s_0 \vDash EG\,\phi$ holds iff there exists a computation path $s_0 \to s_1 \to s_2 \to \ldots$ such that

$$s_i \vDash \phi \text{ holds } \textit{for all } i \geq 0.$$

We could instead express it as follows: $EG\,\phi$ holds if ϕ holds and $EG\,\phi$ holds in one of the successor states to the current state. This suggests the equivalence

$$EG\,\phi = \phi \wedge EX\,EG\,\phi$$

which can easily be proved from the semantic definitions of the connectives.
    Observing that

$$\llbracket EX\,\psi \rrbracket = \{s \mid \text{exists } s' \text{ such that } s \to s' \text{ and } s' \in \llbracket \psi \rrbracket \},$$

we see that the equivalence above can be written as

$$\llbracket EG\,\phi \rrbracket = \llbracket \phi \rrbracket \cap \{s \mid \text{exists } s' \text{ such that } s \to s' \text{ and } s' \in \llbracket EG\,\phi \rrbracket \}.$$

This does not look like a very promising way of calculating $EG\,\phi$, because we need to know $EG\,\phi$ in order to work out the right-hand side. However, there is a way around this apparent circularity, known as computing fixed points, and that is the subject of this section.

3.9.1 Monotone functions

Definition 3.16 Let S be a set of states and $F : \mathscr{P}(S) \to \mathscr{P}(S)$ a function on the power set of S.

1. We say that F is *monotone* if $X \subseteq Y$ implies $F(X) \subseteq F(Y)$ for all subsets X and Y of S.

2. A subset X of S is called a *fixed point* of F if $F(X) = X$.

For an example, let $S \stackrel{\text{def}}{=} \{s_0, s_1\}$ and $F(Y) \stackrel{\text{def}}{=} Y \cup \{s_0\}$ for all subsets Y of S. Since $Y \subseteq Y'$ implies $Y \cup \{s_0\} \subseteq Y' \cup \{s_0\}$, we see that F is monotone. The fixed points of F are all subsets of S containing s_0. Thus, F has two fixed points, the sets $\{s_0\}$ and $\{s_0, s_1\}$. Notice that F has a least ($= \{s_0\}$) and a greatest ($= \{s_0, s_1\}$) fixed point.

An example of a function $G \colon \mathscr{P}(S) \to \mathscr{P}(S)$, which is *not* monotone, is given by

$$G(Y) \stackrel{\text{def}}{=} \text{if } Y = \{s_0\} \text{ then } \{s_1\} \text{ else } \{s_0\}.$$

So G maps $\{s_0\}$ to $\{s_1\}$ and *all other sets* to $\{s_0\}$. The function G is not monotone since $\{s_0\} \subseteq \{s_0, s_1\}$ but $G(\{s_0\}) = \{s_1\}$ is *not* a subset of $G(\{s_0, s_1\}) = \{s_0\}$. Note also that G does not have *any* fixed points whatsoever.

The reasons for exploring monotone functions on $\mathscr{P}(S)$ in the context of proving the correctness of SAT are

- that monotone functions *always* have a least and a greatest fixed point,
- that the meanings of EG, AF and EU can be expressed via greatest, respectively least, fixed points of monotone functions on $\mathscr{P}(S)$,
- that these fixed-points can be easily computed and
- that the procedures SAT_{EU} and SAT_{AF} code up such fixed-point computations.

Notation 3.17 $F^i(X)$ means

$$\underbrace{F(F(\ldots F(X)\ldots))}_{i \text{ times}}$$

Thus, the function F^i is just 'F applied i many times'.

For example, for the function $F(Y) \stackrel{\text{def}}{=} Y \cup \{s_0\}$, we obtain $F^2(Y) = F(F(Y)) = (Y \cup \{s_0\}) \cup \{s_0\} = Y \cup \{s_0\} = F(Y)$. In this case, $F^2 = F$ and therefore $F^i = F$ for all $i \geq 1$. It is not always the case that the sequence of functions $(F^1, F^2, F^3, \ldots)$ stabilises in such a way. For example, this won't happen for the function G defined above (see the next set of exercises). The following fact is a special case of a fundamental insight, often referred to as the Knaster-Tarski Theorem.

Theorem 3.18 *Let S be a set* $\{s_0, s_1, \ldots, s_n\}$ *with* $n+1$ *elements. If* $F : \mathcal{P}(S) \to \mathcal{P}(S)$ *is a monotone function, then*

$$F^{n+1}(\emptyset)$$

is the least fixed point of F and

$$F^{n+1}(S)$$

is the greatest fixed point of F.

PROOF: Since $\emptyset \subseteq F(\emptyset)$, we get $F(\emptyset) \subseteq F(F(\emptyset))$, i.e. $F^1(\emptyset) \subseteq F^2(\emptyset)$, for F is monotone. We can now use mathematical induction to show that

$$F^1(\emptyset) \subseteq F^2(\emptyset) \subseteq F^3(\emptyset) \subseteq \ldots \subseteq F^i(\emptyset)$$

for all $i \geq 1$. In particular, taking $i \stackrel{\text{def}}{=} n + 1$, we claim that one of the expressions $F^k(\emptyset)$ above is already a fixed point of F. Otherwise, $F^1(\emptyset)$ needs to contain at least one element (for then $\emptyset \neq F(\emptyset)$). By the same token, $F^2(\emptyset)$ needs to have at least two elements since it must be bigger than $F^1(\emptyset)$. Continuing this argument, we see that $F^{n+1}(\emptyset)$ would have to contain at least $n + 2$ many elements. The latter is impossible since S has only $n + 1$ elements. Therefore, $F(F^k(\emptyset)) = F^k(\emptyset)$ for some $0 \leq k \leq n + 1$, which readily implies that $F^{n+1}(\emptyset)$ is a fixed point of F as well.

Now suppose that X is another fixed point of F. We need to show that $F^{n+1}(\emptyset)$ is a subset of X; but, since $\emptyset \subseteq X$, we conclude $F(\emptyset) \subseteq F(X) = X$, for F is monotone and X a fixed point of F. By induction, we obtain $F^i(\emptyset) \subseteq X$ for all $i \geq 0$. So, for $i \stackrel{\text{def}}{=} n + 1$, we get $F^{n+1}(\emptyset) \subseteq X$.

The proof of the statements about the greatest fixed point is dual to the one above. Simply replace $\subseteq$ by $\supseteq$, $\emptyset$ by S and 'bigger' by 'smaller'. $\square$

This theorem about the existence of least and greatest fixed points of monotone functions $F : \mathcal{P}(S) \to \mathcal{P}(S)$ not only asserted the existence of such fixed points; it also provided a recipe for computing them. For example, in computing the least fixed point of F, all we have to do is apply F to the empty set $\emptyset$ and keep applying F to the result until the latter becomes invariant under the application of F. The theorem above further ensures that this process is *guaranteed to terminate*. Moreover, we can specify an upper bound $n + 1$ to the worst-case number of iterations necessary for reaching this fixed point, assuming that S has $n + 1$ elements.

EXERCISES 3.17

Consider the functions

$$H_1, H_2, H_3 : \mathcal{P}(\{1, 2, 3, 4, 5, 6, 7, 8, 9, 10\}) \rightarrow \mathcal{P}(\{1, 2, 3, 4, 5, 6, 7, 8, 9, 10\})$$

defined by

$$H_1(Y) \stackrel{\text{def}}{=} Y - \{1, 4, 7\}$$
$$H_2(Y) \stackrel{\text{def}}{=} \{2, 5, 9\} - Y$$
$$H_3(Y) \stackrel{\text{def}}{=} \{1, 2, 3, 4, 5\} \cap (\{2, 4, 8\} \cup Y).$$

for all $Y \subseteq \{1, 2, 3, 4, 5, 6, 7, 8, 9, 10\}$.

* 1. Which of these functions are monotone; which ones aren't? Justify your answer in each case.
* 2. Compute the least and greatest fixed points of H_3 using the iterations H_3^i with $i = 1, 2, \ldots$ and Theorem 3.18.
  3. Does H_2 have any fixed points?
  4. Recall $G : \mathcal{P}(\{s_0, s_1\}) \rightarrow \mathcal{P}(\{s_0, s_1\})$ with

$$G(Y) \stackrel{\text{def}}{=} \text{if } Y = \{s_0\} \text{ then } \{s_1\} \text{ else } \{s_0\}.$$

Use mathematical induction to show that G^i equals G for all *odd* numbers $i \geq 1$. What does G^i look like for *even* numbers i?

———

3.9.2 *The correctness of SAT$_{EG}$*

We saw at the end of the last section that

$$[\![EG\, \phi]\!] = [\![\phi]\!] \cap \{s \mid \text{exists } s' \text{ such that } s \rightarrow s' \text{ and } s' \in [\![EG\, \phi]\!]\}.$$

This implies that EG ϕ is a fixed point of the function

$$F(X) = [\![\phi]\!] \cap \{s \mid \text{exists } s' \text{ such that } s \rightarrow s' \text{ and } s' \in X\}.$$

In fact, F is monotone, EG ϕ is its greatest fixed point and therefore EG ϕ can be computed using Theorem 3.18.

Theorem 3.19 *Let F be as defined above and $n = |S|$ (the size of the set S).*

1. *F is monotone,*
2. *$[\![EG\, \phi]\!]$ is the greatest fixed-point of F,*
3. *$[\![EG\, \phi]\!] = F^{n+1}(S)$.*

PROOF:

1. In order to show that F is monotone, we take any two subsets X and Y of S such that $X \subseteq Y$ and we need to show that $F(X)$ is a subset of $F(Y)$. Given s_0 such that there is some $s_1 \in X$ with $s_0 \to s_1$, we certainly have $s_0 \to s_1$, where $s_1 \in Y$, for X is a subset of Y. Thus, we showed $\{s_0 \in S \mid s_0 \to s_1 \text{ for some } s_1 \in X\} \subseteq \{s_0 \in S \mid s_0 \to s_1 \text{ for some } s_1 \in Y\}$ from which we readily conclude that

$$
\begin{aligned}
F(X) &= \llbracket \phi \rrbracket \cap \{s_0 \in S \mid s_0 \to s_1 \text{ for some } s_1 \in X\} \\
&\subseteq \llbracket \phi \rrbracket \cap \{s_0 \in S \mid s_0 \to s_1 \text{ for some } s_1 \in Y\} \\
&= F(Y).
\end{aligned}
$$

2. We have already seen that $\llbracket \mathrm{EG}\,\phi \rrbracket$ is a fixed point of F. To show that it is the greatest fixed point, it suffices to show here that any set X with $F(X) = X$ has to be contained in $\llbracket \mathrm{EG}\,\phi \rrbracket$. So let s_0 be an element of such a fixed point X. We need to show that s_0 is in $\llbracket \mathrm{EG}\,\phi \rrbracket$ as well. For that we use the fact that

$$
s_0 \in X = F(X) = \llbracket \phi \rrbracket \cap \{s \in S \mid s \to s_1 \text{ for some } s_1 \in X\}
$$

   to infer that $s_0 \in \llbracket \phi \rrbracket$ and $s_0 \to s_1$ for some $s_1 \in X$; but, since s_1 is in X, we may apply that same argument to $s_1 \in X = F(X) = \llbracket \phi \rrbracket \cap \{s \in S \mid s \to s_2 \text{ for some } s_2 \in X\}$ and we get $s_1 \in \llbracket \phi \rrbracket$ and $s_1 \to s_2$ for some $s_2 \in X$. By mathematical induction, we can therefore construct an infinite path $s_0 \to s_1 \to \cdots \to s_n \to s_{n+1} \to \dots$ such that $s_i \in \llbracket \phi \rrbracket$ for all $i \geq 0$. By the definition of $\llbracket \mathrm{EG}\,\phi \rrbracket$, this entails $s_0 \in \llbracket \mathrm{EG}\,\phi \rrbracket$.
3. The last item is now immediately accessible from the previous one and Theorem 3.18.

$\square$

Now we can see that the procedure $\mathrm{SAT}_{\mathrm{EG}}$ is correctly coded and terminates. First, note that the line

$$
Y := Y \cap \{s \mid \text{exists } s' \text{ such that } s \to s' \text{ and } s' \in Y\}
$$

in the procedure $\mathrm{SAT}_{\mathrm{EG}}$ (Figure 3.31) could be changed to

$$
Y := \mathrm{SAT}(\phi) \cap \{s \mid \text{exists } s' \text{ such that } s \to s' \text{ and } s' \in Y\}
$$

without changing the effect of the procedure. To see this, note that the first time round the loop, Y *is* $\mathrm{SAT}(\phi)$; and in subsequent loops, $Y \subseteq \mathrm{SAT}(\phi)$, so it doesn't matter whether we intersect with Y or $\text{SAT}(\phi)$[1]. With the change, it is clear that SAT_{EG} is calculating the greatest fixed point of F; therefore its correctness follows from Theorem 3.19.

3.9.3 The correctness of SAT_{EU}

Proving the correctness of SAT_{EU} is similar. We start by noting the equivalence

$$E[\phi \; U \; \psi] = \psi \vee (\phi \wedge EX \, E[\phi \; U \; \psi])$$

and we write it as

$$\llbracket E[\phi \; U \; \psi] \rrbracket = \llbracket \psi \rrbracket \cup (\llbracket \phi \rrbracket \cap \{s \mid \text{exists } s'$$
$$\text{such that } s \to s' \text{ and } s' \in \llbracket E[\phi \; U \; \psi] \rrbracket \})$$

That tells us that $\llbracket E[\phi \; U \; \psi] \rrbracket$ is a fixed point of the function

$$G(X) = \llbracket \psi \rrbracket \cup (\llbracket \phi \rrbracket \cap \{s \mid \text{exists } s' \text{ such that } s \to s' \text{ and } s' \in X \}).$$

As before, we can prove that this function is monotone. It turns out that $\llbracket E[\phi \; U \; \psi] \rrbracket$ is its *least* fixed point and that the function SAT_{EU} is actually computing it in the manner of Theorem 3.18.

Theorem 3.20 *Let G be defined as above and $n = |S|$.*

1. *G is monotone,*

---

[1] If you are sceptical, try computing the values $Y_0, Y_1, Y_2, \ldots$, where Y_i represents the value of Y after i iterations round the loop. A useful piece of notation is $\text{pre}_\exists(X) \stackrel{\text{def}}{=} \{s \mid \text{exists } s' \text{ such that } s \to s' \text{ and } s' \in X\}$. The program before the change computes as follows:

$$
\begin{aligned}
Y_0 &= \text{SAT}(\phi) \\
Y_1 &= Y_0 \cap \text{pre}_\exists(Y_0) \\
Y_2 &= Y_1 \cap \text{pre}_\exists(Y_1) \\
    &= Y_0 \cap \text{pre}_\exists(Y_0) \cap \text{pre}_\exists(Y_0 \cap \text{pre}_\exists(Y_0)) \\
    &= Y_0 \cap \text{pre}_\exists(Y_0 \cap \text{pre}_\exists(Y_0)).
\end{aligned}
$$

The last of these equalities follows from the monotonicity of $\text{pre}_\exists$.

$$
\begin{aligned}
Y_3 &= Y_2 \cap \text{pre}_\exists(Y_2) \\
    &= Y_0 \cap \text{pre}_\exists(Y_0 \cap \text{pre}_\exists(Y_0)) \cap \text{pre}_\exists(Y_0 \cap \text{pre}_\exists(Y_0 \cap \text{pre}_\exists(Y_0))) \\
    &= Y_0 \cap \text{pre}_\exists(Y_0 \cap \text{pre}_\exists(Y_0 \cap \text{pre}_\exists(Y_0))).
\end{aligned}
$$

Again the last one follows by monotonicity. Now look at what the program does after the change:

$$
\begin{aligned}
Y_0 &= \text{SAT}(\phi) \\
Y_1 &= \text{SAT}(\phi) \cap \text{pre}_\exists(Y_0) \\
    &= Y_0 \cap \text{pre}_\exists(Y_0) \\
Y_2 &= Y_0 \cap \text{pre}_\exists(Y_1) \\
Y_3 &= Y_0 \cap \text{pre}_\exists(Y_1) \\
    &= Y_0 \cap \text{pre}_\exists(Y_0 \cap \text{pre}_\exists(Y_0)).
\end{aligned}
$$

A formal proof would follow by induction on i.

2. $\llbracket E(\phi \; U \; \psi) \rrbracket$ is the least *fixed-point* of G,
3. $\llbracket E(\phi \; U \; \psi) \rrbracket = G^{n+1}(\emptyset)$.

PROOF:

1. Again, we need to show that $X \subseteq Y$ implies $G(X) \subseteq G(Y)$; but that is essentially the same argument as for F, since the function which sends X to $\{s_0 \in S \mid s_0 \to s_1$ for some $s_1 \in X\}$ is monotone and all that G now does is to perform the intersection and union of that set with constant sets $\llbracket \phi \rrbracket$ and $\llbracket \psi \rrbracket$.

2. If S has $n+1$ elements, then the least fixed point of G equals $G^{n+1}(\emptyset)$ by Theorem 3.18. We show that this set equals $\llbracket E(\phi \; U \; \psi) \rrbracket$. Simply observe what kind of states we obtain by iterating G on the empty set $\emptyset$:

$$
\begin{aligned}
G^1(\emptyset) &= \llbracket \psi \rrbracket \cup (\llbracket \phi \rrbracket \cap \{s_0 \in S \mid s_0 \to s_1 \text{ for some } s_1 \in \emptyset\}) \\
&= \llbracket \psi \rrbracket \cup (\llbracket \phi \rrbracket \cap \emptyset) \\
&= \llbracket \psi \rrbracket \cup \emptyset \\
&= \llbracket \psi \rrbracket,
\end{aligned}
$$

which are all states $s_0 \in \llbracket E(\phi \; U \; \psi) \rrbracket$, where we chose $i = 0$ according to the definition of Until. Now,

$$
G^2(\emptyset) = \llbracket \psi \rrbracket \cup (\llbracket \phi \rrbracket \cap \{s_0 \in S \mid s_0 \to s_1 \text{ for some } s_1 \in G^1(\emptyset)\})
$$

tells us that the elements of $G^2(\emptyset)$ are all those $s_0 \in \llbracket E(\phi \; U \; \psi) \rrbracket$ where we chose $i \leq 1$. By mathematical induction, we see that $G^{k+1}(\emptyset)$ is the set of all states s_0 for which we chose $i \leq k$ to secure $s_0 \in \llbracket E(\phi \; U \; \psi) \rrbracket$. Since this holds for all k, we see that $\llbracket E(\phi \; U \; \psi) \rrbracket$ is nothing but the union of all sets $G^{k+1}(\emptyset)$ with $k \geq 0$; but, since $G^{n+1}(\emptyset)$ is a fixed point of G, we see that this union is just $G^{n+1}(\emptyset)$.

3. We showed this already in the proof of the previous item.

$\square$

The correctness of the coding of SAT_{EU} follows similarly to that of SAT_{EG}. We change the line

$$
Y := Y \cup (W \cap \{s \mid \text{exists } s' \text{ such that } s \to s' \text{ and } s' \in Y\})
$$

into

$$
Y := \text{SAT}(\psi) \cup (W \cap \{s \mid \text{exists } s' \text{ such that } s \to s' \text{ and } s' \in Y\})
$$

and observe that this does not change the result of the procedure, because the first time round the loop, Y is SAT(ψ); and, since Y is always increasing, it makes no difference whether we perform a union with Y or with SAT(ψ). Having made that change, it is then clear that SAT$_{EU}$ is just computing the least fixed point of G using Theorem 3.20.

We illustrate these results about the functions F and G above through an example. Consider the system in Figure 3.32. We begin by computing the set $\llbracket EF\,p \rrbracket$. By the definition of EF this is just $\llbracket E(\top\ U\ p) \rrbracket$. So we have $\phi_1 \stackrel{\text{def}}{=} \top$ and $\phi_2 \stackrel{\text{def}}{=} p$. Taking a look at the system in Figure 3.32, we obtain $\llbracket p \rrbracket = \{s_3\}$ and of course $\llbracket \top \rrbracket = S$. Thus, the function G above equals

$$G(X) = \{s_3\} \cup \{s \in S \mid s \to s' \text{ for some } s' \in X\}.$$

Since $\llbracket E(\top\ U\ p) \rrbracket$ equals the least fixed point of G, we need to iterate G on $\emptyset$ until this process stabilises. First,

$$G^1(\emptyset) = \{s_3\} \cup \{s \in S \mid s \to s' \text{ for some } s' \in \emptyset\} = \{s_3\}.$$

Second,

$$
\begin{aligned}
G^2(\emptyset) &= G(G^1(\emptyset)) \\
&= \{s_3\} \cup \{s \in S \mid s \to s' \text{ for some } s' \in \{s_3\}\} \\
&= \{s_1, s_3\}.
\end{aligned}
$$

Third,

$$
\begin{aligned}
G^3(\emptyset) &= G(G^2(\emptyset)) \\
&= \{s_3\} \cup \{s \in S \mid s \to s' \text{ for some } s' \in \{s_1, s_3\}\} \\
&= \{s_0, s_1, s_2, s_3\}.
\end{aligned}
$$

Fourth,

$$
\begin{aligned}
G^4(\emptyset) &= G(G^3(\emptyset)) \\
&= \{s_3\} \cup \{s \in S \mid s \to s' \text{ for some } s' \in \{s_0, s_1, s_2, s_3\}\} \\
&= \{s_0, s_1, s_2, s_3\}.
\end{aligned}
$$

Therefore, $\{s_0, s_1, s_2, s_3\}$ is the least fixed point of G, which equals $\llbracket E(\top\ U\ p) \rrbracket$ by Theorem 3.20. Since $\llbracket E(\top\ U\ p) \rrbracket = \llbracket EF\,p \rrbracket$ this implies that $\llbracket EF\,p \rrbracket$ equals $\{s_0, s_1, s_2, s_3\}$.

The other example we study is the computation of the set $\llbracket EG\,q \rrbracket$. By Theorem 3.19, that set is the greatest fixed point of the function F above,

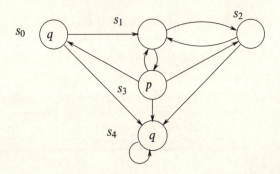

Fig. 3.32. A system for which we compute invariants.

where $\phi \overset{\text{def}}{=} q$. From Figure 3.32 we see that $[\![q]\!] = \{s_0, s_4\}$ and so

$$F(X) = [\![q]\!] \cap \{s \in S \mid s \to s' \text{ for some } s' \in X\}$$
$$= \{s_0, s_4\} \cap \{s \in S \mid s \to s' \text{ for some } s' \in X\}.$$

Since $[\![\text{EG } q]\!]$ equals the greatest fixed point of F, we need to iterate F on S until this process stabilises. First,

$$F^1(S) = \{s_0, s_4\} \cap \{s \in S \mid s \to s' \text{ for some } s' \in S\}$$
$$= \{s_0, s_4\} \cap S \quad \text{since every } s \text{ has some } s' \text{ with } s \to s'$$
$$= \{s_0, s_4\}.$$

Second,

$$F^2(S) = F(F^1(S))$$
$$= \{s_0, s_4\} \cap \{s \in S \mid s \to s' \text{ for some } s' \in \{s_0, s_4\}\}$$
$$= \{s_0, s_4\}.$$

Therefore, $\{s_0, s_4\}$ is the greatest fixed point of F, which equals $[\![\text{EG } q]\!]$ by Theorem 3.19.

EXERCISES 3.18

* 1. Let A and B be two subsets of S and let $F : \mathcal{P}(S) \to \mathcal{P}(S)$ be a monotone function.

    (a) Show that $F_1 : \mathcal{P}(S) \to \mathcal{P}(S)$ with $F_1(Y) \overset{\text{def}}{=} A \cap F(Y)$ is monotone as well.

    (b) Furthermore, show that $F_2 : \mathcal{P}(S) \to \mathcal{P}(S)$ with $F_2(Y) \overset{\text{def}}{=} A \cup (B \cap F(Y))$ is monotone.

2. Use Theorems 3.19 and 3.20 to compute the following sets (the underlying model is in Figure 3.33):

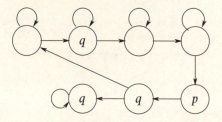

Fig. 3.33. Another system for which we compute invariants.

    (a) $[\![EF\,p]\!]$

    (b) $[\![EG\,q]\!]$.

3. Using the function

$$F(X) = [\![\phi]\!] \cup \{s \mid \text{for all } s' \text{ with } s \to s' \text{ we have } s' \in X\}$$

prove that $[\![AF\,\phi]\!]$ is the least fixed point of F. Hence argue that the procedure SAT_{AF} is correct and terminates.

* 4. One may also compute $AG\,\phi$ directly as a fixed point. Consider the function $H : \mathscr{P}(S) \to \mathscr{P}(S)$ with $H(X) = [\![\phi]\!] \cap \{s_0 \in S \mid s_0 \to s_1 \text{ implies } s_1 \in X\}$. Show that H is monotone and that $[\![AG\,\phi]\!]$ is the greatest fixed point of H. Use that insight to write a procedure SAT_{AG}.

5. Similarly, one may compute $A[\phi_1 \text{ U } \phi_2]$ directly as a fixed point, using $K : \mathscr{P}(S) \to \mathscr{P}(S)$, where $K(X) = [\![\phi_2]\!] \cup ([\![\phi_1]\!] \cap \{s_0 \in S \mid s_0 \to s_1 \text{ implies } s_1 \in X\})$. Show that K is monotone and that $[\![A[\phi_1 \text{ U } \phi_2]]\!]$ is the least fixed point of K. Use that insight to write a procedure SAT_{AU}. Can you use that routine to handle all calls of the form $AF\,\phi$ as well?

6. Prove that $[\![A[\phi_1 \text{ U } \phi_2]]\!] = [\![\phi_2 \vee (\phi_1 \wedge AX (A[\phi_1 \text{ U } \phi_2]))]\!]$.

7. Prove that $[\![AG\,\phi]\!] = [\![\phi \wedge AX (AG\,\phi)]\!]$.

8. Show that the loops in the code for SAT_{EU} and SAT_{EG} always terminate. Use this fact to reason informally that the main program SAT terminates for all valid CTL formulas ϕ. Note that some subclauses, like the one for AU, call SAT recursively and with a more complex formula. Why does this not affect termination?

3.10 Bibliographic notes

The first use of temporal logic for reasoning about concurrent programs was by Amir Pnueli [Pnu81]. His approach involves proving properties of programs represented as a set of axioms. Model checking, which has the advantages of being automatic and often computationally less expensive, was invented by E. Clarke and E. A. Emerson [CE81] and by J. Quielle and J. Sifakis [QS81]. A full history of these ideas can be found in [CGL93], which also provides a survey of the topic.

Historically, LTL was invented first (by the philosopher A. Prior in the 1960s; and worked on by computer scientists A. Pnueli, Z. Manna and others). The logic CTL was invented by E. Clarke and E. A. Emerson (during the early 1980s); and CTL* was invented by E. A. Emerson and J. Halpern (in 1986) to unify the two.

The SMV system was written by K. McMillan [McM93] and is available with source code from Carnegie Mellon University[1]. The examples in this book were developed using this version of SMV. NuSMV[2] is a reimplementation, being developed in Trento by A. Cimatti, E. Clarke, F. Giunchiglia and M. Roveri, and is aimed at being customisable and extensible. Cadence SMV[3] is an entirely new model checker focused on compositional systems. It was also developed by Ken McMillan and its description language resembles but much extends the original SMV.

A WWW site which gathers frequently used specification patterns in various frameworks (such as CTL, LTL and regular expressions) is maintained by Matt Dwyer, George Avrunin, James Corbett and Laura Dillon[4].

Current research in model checking includes attempts to exploit abstractions, symmetries and compositionality [CGL94, Lon83, Dam96] in order to reduce the impact of the state explosion problem.

The model checker Spin, which is geared towards asynchronous systems and is based on the temporal logic LTL, can be found at the Spin website[5]. A model checker called FDR2 based on the process algebra CSP is available[6]. The Edinburgh Concurrency Workbench[7] and the Concurrency Workbench of North Carolina[8] are similar software tools for the design and analysis of concurrent systems.

There are many textbooks about verification of reactive systems; we mention [MP91, MP95, Ros97, Hol90]. The SMV code contained in this chapter can be downloaded from www.cs.bham.ac.uk/research/lics/.

---

[1] www.cs.cmu.edu/~modelcheck/
[2] afrodite.itc.it:1024/~cimatti/
[3] www-cad.eecs.berkeley.edu/~kenmcmil/
[4] www.cis.ksu.edu/~dwyer/spec-patterns.html
[5] netlib.bell-labs.com/netlib/spin/whatispin.html
[6] www.formal.demon.co.uk/FDR2.html
[7] www.dcs.ed.ac.uk/home/cwb
[8] www.csc.ncsu.edu/eos/users/r/rance/WWW/cwb-nc.html

4

Program verification

The methods of the previous chapter are suitable for verifying systems of communicating processes, where control is the main issue, but there are no complex *data*. We relied on the fact that those (abstracted) systems are in a *finite state*. These assumptions are not valid for sequential programs running on a single processor. In those cases, the programs may manipulate non-trivial data and, once we admit variables of type integer, list, or tree, we are in the domain of machines with infinite state space.

In terms of the classification of verification methods given at the beginning of the last chapter, the methods of this chapter are

Proof-based. We do not exhaustively check every state that the system can get in to, as one does with model checking; this would be impossible, given that there are infinitely many states. Instead, we construct a proof that the system satisfies the property at hand, using a proof calculus. This is analogous to the situation in Chapter 2, where use of a suitable proof calculus avoided the problem of having to check infinitely many models of a set of predicate logic formulas in order to establish a sequent.

Semi-automatic. Although many of the steps involved in proving that a program satisfies its specification are mechanical, there are some steps that involve some intelligence and that cannot be carried out algorithmically by a computer. As we will see, there are often good heuristics to help the programmer complete these tasks. This contrasts with the situation of the last chapter, which was fully automatic.

Property-oriented. Just like in the previous chapter, we verify properties of a program rather than a full specification of its behaviour.

Application domain. The domain of application in this chapter is sequential transformational programs. 'Sequential' means that we assume the

216

program runs on a single processor and that there are no concurrency issues. 'Transformational' means that the program takes an input and, after some computation, is expected to terminate with an output. For example, methods of objects in Java are often programmed in this style. This contrasts with the previous chapter which focuses on reactive systems that are not intended to terminate and that react continually with their environment.

Pre/post-development. The techniques of this chapter should be used during the coding process for small fragments of program that perform an identifiable (and hence, specifiable) task and hence should be used during the development process in order to avoid bugs.

4.1 Why should we specify and verify code?

The task of specifying and verifying code is often perceived as an unwelcome addition to the programmer's job and a dispensable one. Arguments in favour of verification include the following:

- The specification of a program is an important component in its documentation. The logical structure of the formal specification, which one writes as a formula in a suitable logic, typically serves as a guiding principle in trying to prove that it holds.
- Experience has shown that verifying programs with respect to formal specifications can significantly cut down the duration of software development and maintenance by eliminating most errors in the planning phase. Verification of system components during the development phase helps clarify their roles and the structure of the system; and reduces the number of bugs found during the testing phase. Debugging big systems is time-consuming and local 'fixes' often introduce new bugs at other places.
- Properly specified and verified software is easier to reuse, since we have a clear specification of what it is meant to do.
- Safety-critical computer systems (such as the control of cooling systems in nuclear power stations, or cockpits of modern aircrafts) demand that their software be specified and verified with as much rigour and formality as possible. Other programs may be commercially critical, such as accountancy software used by banks, and they should be delivered with a warranty: a guarantee for correct performance within proper use. The proof that a program meets its specifications is indeed such a warranty.

The degree to which the software industry accepts the benefits of proper verification of code depends on the perceived extra cost of producing it and the perceived benefits of having it. As verification technology improves, the costs are declining; and as the complexity of software and the extent to which society depends on it increase, the benefits are becoming more important. Texas is the first state of the USA to extend the licensing procedures for engineers to software engineering, thereby enforcing 'due care' methodologies. Thus, we can expect that the importance of verification to industry will continue to increase over the next decades.

Currently, many companies struggle with a legacy of ancient code without proper documentation which has to be adapted to new hardware and network environments, as well as new requirements of users. Often, the original programmers who might still remember what certain pieces of code are for have moved, or died. Software systems now often have a longer life-expectancy than humans, which necessitates a durable, transparent and portable design and implementation process; the year-2000 problem was just one such example. Software verification provides some of this.

4.2 A framework for software verification

Suppose that you are working for a software company and that your task is to write programs which are meant to solve sophisticated problems, or computations. Typically, such a project involves an outside customer, a utility company, for example, who has written up an informal description, in plain English, of the real-world task that is at hand; in this case, it could be the development and maintenance of a database of electricity accounts with all the possible applications of that (automated billing, customer service, etc.). Since the informality of such descriptions may cause ambiguities which eventually could result in serious and expensive design flaws, it is desirable to condense all the requirements of such a project into formal specifications. These formal specifications are usually symbolic encodings of real-world constraints into some sort of logic. Thus, a framework for producing the software could be:

- Convert the informal description D of an application domain into an 'equivalent' formula ϕ_D of some symbolic logic;
- Write a program P which is meant to realise ϕ_D in the programming environment supplied by your company, or wanted by the particular customer;
- *Prove* that the program P satisfies the formula ϕ_D.

This scheme is quite crude — for example, constraints may be actual design decisions for interfaces and data types, or the specification may 'evolve' and may partly be 'unknown' in big projects — but it serves well as a first approximation to trying to define good programming methodology. Several variations of such a sequence of activities are conceivable. For example, you, as a programmer, might have been given only the formula ϕ_D, so you might have little if any insight into the real-world problem which you are supposed to solve. From a technical point of view, this poses no problem, but often it is handy to have both informal and formal descriptions available. Moreover, crafting the informal specification D is often a mutual process between the client and the programmer, whereby the attempt at formalising D can uncover ambiguities or undesired consequences and hence lead to revisions of D. This 'going back and forth' between the realms of informal and formal specifications is necessary since it is hard to 'verify' whether an *informal* description D is equivalent to a *formal* description ϕ_D. The meaning of D as a piece of natural language is grounded in common sense and general knowledge about the real-world domain and often based on heuristics or quantitative reasoning. The meaning of a logic formula ϕ_D, on the other hand, is defined in a precise mathematical, qualitative and compositional way by structural induction on the parse tree of ϕ_D (the first three chapters contain examples of this). It is quite impossible to establish the equivalence of D and ϕ_D by means of a purely formal argument, for how could we reason formally about informal things?

Thus, the process of finding a suitable formalisation ϕ_D of D requires the utmost care; otherwise it is always possible that ϕ_D specifies behaviour which is different from the one described in D. To make matters worse, the description D is often inconsistent; customers usually have a fairly vague conception of what exactly a program should do for them. Thus, producing a clear and coherent description, D, of an application domain is already a crucial step in successful programming; this phase ideally is undertaken by customers and project managers around a table, or in a video conference, talking to each other. We address this first item only implicitly in this text, but you should certainly be aware of its importance in practice.

The next phase of the software development framework involves constructing the program P and after that the last task is to verify that P satisfies ϕ_D. Here again, our framework is oversimplifying what goes on in practice, since often proving that P satisfies its specification ϕ_D goes hand-in-hand with inventing a suitable P. This correspondence between proving and programming can be stated quite precisely, but that is beyond the scope of this book.

4.2.1 A core programming language

The programming language which we set out to study here is the typical core language of most imperative programming languages. Modulo trivial syntactic variations, it is a subset of Pascal, C, C++ and Java. Our language consists of assignment-statements to integer- and boolean-valued variables, if-statements, while-statements and sequential compositions. Everything that can be computed by large languages like C and Java can also be computed by our language, though perhaps not as conveniently, because it does not have any objects, procedures, threads, or recursive data structures. While this makes it seem unrealistic compared with fully blown commercial languages, it allows us to focus our discussion on the process of formal program verification. The features missing from our language could be implemented on top of it; that is the justification for saying that they do not add to the power of the language, but only to the convenience of using it. Verifying programs using those features would require non-trivial extensions of the proof calculus we present here. In particular, dynamic scoping of variables presents hard problems for program-verification methods, but this is beyond the scope of this book.

Our core language has three syntactic domains: integer expressions, boolean expressions and commands which we consider to be our programs. Integer expressions are built in the familiar way from variables $x, y, z, \ldots$, numerals $0, 1, 2, \ldots, -1, -2, \ldots$ and basic operations like addition (+) and multiplication (∗). For example,

$$5$$
$$x$$
$$4 + (x - 3)$$
$$x + (x * (y - (5 + z)))$$

are all valid integer expressions. Our grammar for generating integer expressions is

$$E ::= n \mid x \mid (-E) \mid (E + E) \mid (E - E) \mid (E * E), \qquad (4.1)$$

where n is any numeral in $\{\ldots, -2, -1, 0, 1, 2, \ldots\}$ and x is any variable. Note that we write multiplication in 'mathematics' as $2 \cdot 3$, whereas our core language writes $2 * 3$ instead.

Convention 4.1 In the grammar above, negation $-$ binds more tightly than ∗, which binds more tightly than subtraction $-$ and $+$.

Since if-statements and while-statements contain conditions in them, we also need a syntactic domain B of boolean expressions. In the grammar in Backus Naur form

$$B ::= \texttt{true} \mid \texttt{false} \mid (!B) \mid (B \,\&\, B) \mid (B \,||\, B) \mid (E < E) \qquad (4.2)$$

we write ! for the negation, & for conjunction and || for disjunction of boolean expressions; they may be freely expanded by operators which are definable in terms of the above. For example, the test for equality[1] $E_1 == E_2$ may be expressed via $!(E_1 < E_2) \,\&\, !(E_2 < E_1)$. We generally make use of shorthand notation whenever this is convenient. We also write $(E_1 \,!= E_2)$ to abbreviate $!(E_1 == E_2)$. We will also assume the usual binding priorities for logical operators stated in Convention 1.3. Boolean expressions are built on top of integer expressions since the last clause of (4.2) mentions integer expressions.

Having integer and boolean expressions at hand, we can now define the syntactic domain of commands. Since commands are built from simpler commands using assignments and the control structures, you may think of commands as the actual programs. The grammar for commands we choose is

$$C ::= \texttt{x} = E \mid C;C \mid \texttt{if } B \,\{C\} \texttt{ else } \{C\} \mid \texttt{while } B \,\{C\}.$$

The braces { and } are to mark the extent of the blocks of code in the if-statement and the while-statement, as in languages such as C and Java. They can be omitted if the blocks consist of a single statement. The intuitive meaning of the programming constructs is the following:

1. The atomic command x = E is the usual assignment statement; it evaluates the integer expression E in the current state of the store and then overwrites the current value stored in x with the result of that evaluation.
2. The compound command $C_1; C_2$ is the sequential composition of the commands C_1 and C_2. It begins by executing C_1. If that execution terminates, then it executes C_2 in the storage state resulting from the execution of C_1. Otherwise (if the execution of C_1 does not terminate), the run of $C_1; C_2$ also does not terminate. Sequential composition is

---

[1] In common with languages like C and Java, we use a single equals sign = to mean assignment and a double sign == to mean equality. Earlier languages like Pascal used := for assignment and simple = for equality; it is a great pity that C and its successors did not keep this convention. The reason that = is a bad symbol for assignment is that assignment is not symmetric: $x = y$ interpreted as the assignment x becomes y is not the same thing as $y = x$; yet, $x = y$ and $y = x$ are the same thing if we mean equality. The two dots in := helped remind the reader that this is an asymmetric assignment operation rather than a symmetric assertion of equality. However, the notation = for assignment is now commonplace, so we will use it.

an example of a *control structure* since it implements a certain policy of flow of control in a computation;

3. Another control structure is if B $\{C_1\}$ else $\{C_2\}$. It first evaluates the boolean expression B in the current state; if that result is true, then C_1 is executed; if B evaluated to false, then C_2 is executed.

4. The third control construct while B $\{C\}$ allows us to write statements which are executed repeatedly. Its meaning is that:

   (a) the boolean expression B is evaluated in the current state;
   (b) if B evaluates to false, then the command terminates,
   (c) otherwise, the command C will be executed. If that execution terminates, then we resume at step (a) with a re-evaluation of B.

The point of the while-statement is that it repeatedly executes the command C as long as B evaluates to true. If B never becomes false, or if one of the executions of C does not terminate, then the loop will not terminate. While-statements are the only real source of non-termination in our core programming language.

Example 4.2 The factorial of a natural number n, which is written $n!$, is defined inductively by

$$0! \stackrel{\text{def}}{=} 1 \tag{4.3}$$
$$(n+1)! \stackrel{\text{def}}{=} (n+1) \cdot n!.$$

For example, unwinding this definition for n being 4, we get $4! \stackrel{\text{def}}{=} 4 \cdot 3! = \cdots = 4 \cdot 3 \cdot 2 \cdot 1 \cdot 0! = 24$.

The following program Fac1:

```
y = 1;
z = 0;
while (z != x) {
    z = z + 1;
    y = y * z;
}
```

is intended to compute the factorial[1] of x and to store the result in y. We will prove that Fac1 really does this later in the chapter.

EXERCISES 4.1

* 1. In what circumstances would if B $\{C_1\}$ else $\{C_2\}$ fail to terminate?

---

[1] Please note the difference between the statement $x! = y$, saying that the factorial of x is equal to y, and the piece of code x != y which says that x is not equal to y.

* 2. A familiar command missing from our language is the for-loop. It may be used to sum the elements in an array, for example, by programming as follows:

```
s = 0;
for (i = 0; i <= max; i = i+1) {
    s = s + a[i];
}
```

After performing the initial assignment s = 0, this executes i = 0 first, then executes the body s = s + a[i] and the incrementation i = i + 1 continually until i <= max becomes false. Explain how for ($C_1; B; C_2$) {C_3} can be defined as a derived program in our core language.

3. Suppose that you need a language construct repeat {C} until B which repeats C until B becomes true, i.e.

    i. executes C in the current state;

    ii. evaluates B in the resulting state;

    iii. if B is false, the program resumes with (i); otherwise, the program repeat {C} until B terminates.

    This construct sometimes allows more elegant code than a corresponding while-statement.

    (a) Define repeat C until B as a derived expression using our language.

    (b) Define repeat in terms of the for loop. (You might need the empty command skip which does nothing.)

———

4.2.2 *Hoare triples*

Program fragments, in the syntax described above, commence running in a 'state' of the machine and, after doing some computation, they might terminate. If they do, then the result is another (usually different) state. Since our programming language does not have any procedures or local variables, the 'state' of the machine can be represented simply as a vector of values of all the variables used in the program.

    What syntax should we use for ϕ_D, i.e. the specifications of such programs? Because we are interested in the output of the program, the language should allow us to talk about the variables in the state after the program has executed, using operators like $=$ to express equality and $<$ for less than;

you should be aware of the overloading of $=$ (in code, it represents an assignment instruction; in logical formulas, it stands for equality, which we write $==$ within program code). For example, if the informal description D says that we should

Compute a number y whose square is less than the input x.

then an appropriate specification may be

$$y \cdot y < x.$$

But what if the input x is -4? There is no number whose square is less than a negative number, so it is not possible to write the program in a way that it will work with all possible inputs. If we go back to the client and say this, he or she is quite likely to respond by saying that the requirement is only that the program work for positive numbers; i.e., he or she revises the informal specification so that it now says

If the input x is a positive number, compute a number whose square is less than x.

This means we need to be able to talk not just about the state *after* the program executes, but also about the state *before* it executes. The assertions we make will therefore be triples, typically looking like

$$(\phi) \, P \, (\psi)$$

which (roughly) means: if the program P is run in a state that satisfies ϕ, then the state after it executes will satisfy ψ. The specification of the program P, to calculate a number whose square is less than x, now looks like this:

$$(x > 0) \, P \, (y \cdot y < x). \qquad (4.4)$$

It means that, if we run P in a state such that $x > 0$, then the resulting state will be such that $y \cdot y < x$. It does not tell us what happens if we run P in a state in which $x \leq 0$; thus, the programmer is free to do what he, or she, wants in that case. A program which produces garbage in the case that $x \leq 0$ satisfies the specification, as long as it works correctly for $x > 0$.

The form $(\phi) \, P \, (\psi)$ of our specification is called a *Hoare triple*, after the computer scientist C. A. R. Hoare. The formula ϕ is called the *precondition* of P and ψ is called the *postcondition*.

Often, we do not want to put any constraints on the initial state; we simply wish to say that, no matter what state we start the program in, the resulting state should satisfy ψ. In that case the precondition can be set to ⊤, which is, as in previous chapters, a formula which is true in any state.

Note that the triple in (4.4) does not specify a unique program P, or a unique behaviour. For example, the program which simply does

```
y = 0;
```

satisfies the specification (since $0 \cdot 0$ is less than any positive number), as does the program

```
y = 0;
while (y * y < x) {
    y = y + 1;
    }
y = y - 1;
```

(this program finds the greatest y whose square is less than x; the while-statement overshoots a bit, but then we fix it after the loop[1]). Note that these two programs will result in different values. For example, if x is 22, the first one will compute $y = 0$ and the second will get $y = 4$; but both of them satisfy the specification.

Our agenda, then, is to develop a notion of proof which allows us to prove that a program P satisfies the specification given by a precondition ϕ and a postcondition ψ. Recall that we developed proof calculi for propositional and predicate logic where such proofs could be accomplished by investigating the structure of the formula one wanted to prove. For example, for proving an implication $\phi \rightarrow \psi$ one had to assume ϕ and manage to show ψ, then the proof could be finished with the proof rule for implies-introduction. The proof calculi which we are about to develop follow similar lines. Yet, they are different from the logics we previously studied since they prove triples which are built from two different sorts of things: logical formulas ϕ and ψ versus a piece of code P. Our proof calculi have to address each of these appropriately. Nonetheless, we retain proof strategies which are *compositional*, but now in the structure of P. Note that this is an important advantage in the verification of big projects, where code is built from a multitude of modules such that the correctness of certain parts will depend on the correctness of certain others. Thus, your code might call subroutines which other members of your project are about to code, but you can already check the correctness of your code by assuming that the subroutines meet their own specifications.

---

[1] We could avoid this inelegance by using the `repeat` construct of Exercises 4.1.

4.2.3 Partial and total correctness

Our explanation of what the triple $(\phi)\, P\, (\psi)$ means was rather informal. In particular, it did not say what we should conclude if P does not terminate. In fact there are two ways of handling this situation. *Partial correctness* means that we do not require the program to terminate, whereas in *total correctness* we do require termination.

Definition 4.3 (Partial correctness) We say that the triple $(\phi)\, P\, (\psi)$ is satisfied under *partial correctness* if, for all states which satisfy ϕ, the state resulting from P's execution satisfies the postcondition ψ, *provided that P actually terminates*. In this case, we write

$$\vDash_{\mathsf{par}} (\phi)\, P\, (\psi).$$

We call $\vDash_{\mathsf{par}}$ the satisfaction relation for partial correctness.

Thus, we insist on ψ being true of the resulting state only if the program P has terminated on an input satisfying ϕ. Partial correctness is rather a weak requirement, since any program which does not terminate satisfies its specification. In particular, the program

```
while true { x = 0; }
```

(which endlessly loops and never terminates) satisfies all specifications, since partial correctness only says what must happen *if* the program terminates. *Total correctness*, on the other hand, requires that the program terminates in order for it to satisfy a specification.

Definition 4.4 (Total correctness) We say that the triple $(\phi)\, P\, (\psi)$ is satisfied under *total correctness* if, for all states in which P is executed which satisfy the precondition ϕ, P is guaranteed to terminate and the resulting state satisfies the postcondition ψ. In this case, we write

$$\vDash_{\mathsf{tot}} (\phi)\, P\, (\psi)$$

for the satisfaction relation of total correctness.

The program which loops forever does not satisfy any specification under total correctness. Clearly, total correctness is more useful than partial correctness, so the reader may wonder why partial correctness is introduced at all. The reason is that proving total correctness usually involves proving partial correctness first and then proving termination. So, although our primary interest is in proving total correctness, it often happens that we have to split this into separate proofs of partial correctness and of termination. Most of this chapter is devoted to the proof of partial correctness, though we return to the issue of termination in Section 4.4.

Before we delve into the issue of crafting sound and complete proof calculi for partial and total correctness, let us briefly give examples of typical sorts of specifications which we would like to be able to prove.

Examples 4.5

1. Let Succ be the program

```
a = x + 1;
if (a - 1 == 0 {
    y = 1;
} else {
    y = a;
}
```

The program Succ satisfies the specification

$$(\top) \; \text{Succ} \; (y = (x + 1))$$

under partial and total correctness, so if we think of x as input and y as output, then Succ computes the successor function. Note that this code is far from optimal, in fact, it is a rather roundabout way of implementing the successor function. Although this program seems silly, our proof rules need to be able to prove its simple behaviour.

2. The program Fac1 (Example 4.2) terminates only if x is initially non-negative (why?). Let us look at what properties of Fac1 we expect to be able to prove.

Under total correctness, we should be able to prove that

$$\vDash_{tot} (x \geq 0) \; \text{Fac1} \; (y = x!)$$

holds. It states that, provided $x \geq 0$, Fac1 terminates with the result $y = x!$. However, the stronger statement that

$$\vDash_{tot} (\top) \; \text{Fac1} \; (y = x!)$$

should *not* be provable, because Fac1 does not terminate for negative values of x.

Under partial correctness, both statements

$$\vDash_{par} (x \geq 0) \; \text{Fac1} \; (y = x!) \quad \text{and} \quad \vDash_{par} (\top) \; \text{Fac1} \; (y = x!)$$

should be provable.

EXERCISES 4.2
* 1. For any ϕ, ψ and P explain why $\vDash_{tot} (\phi)\ P\ (\psi)$ implies $\vDash_{par} (\phi)\ P\ (\psi)$.

___

If the partial correctness of triples $(\phi)\ P\ (\psi)$ can be proved in the calculus we develop in this chapter, we write

$$\vdash_{par} (\phi)\ P\ (\psi),$$

using a single turnstile. Similarly, if it can be proved under total correctness, we write

$$\vdash_{tot} (\phi)\ P\ (\psi).$$

Thus, $\vDash_{par} (\phi)\ P\ (\psi)$ means that P is partially correct, while $\vdash_{par} (\phi)\ P\ (\psi)$ means that P can be proved to be (partially) correct by our calculus. The first one means it is actually correct, while the second one means it is provably correct in our calculus.

If our calculus is any good, the notions $\vdash_{par}$ and $\vDash_{par}$ should coincide! More precisely, we will say that our calculus is *sound* if, whenever it tells us something can be proved, that thing is indeed true. Thus, it is sound if it doesn't tell us that false things can be proved. Formally, we write that $\vdash_{par}$ is sound if

$$\vdash_{par} (\phi)\ P\ (\psi) \text{ implies } \vDash_{par} (\phi)\ P\ (\psi)$$

for all ϕ, ψ and P; and, similarly, $\vdash_{tot}$ is sound if

$$\vdash_{tot} (\phi)\ P\ (\psi) \text{ implies } \vDash_{tot} (\phi)\ P\ (\psi)$$

for all ϕ, ψ and P. We say that a calculus is *complete* if it is able to prove everything that is true. Formally, $\vdash_{par}$ is complete if

$$\vDash_{par} (\phi)\ P\ (\psi) \text{ implies } \vdash_{par} (\phi)\ P\ (\psi);$$

and similarly for $\vdash_{tot}$ being complete.

We said (in Chapters 1 and 2) that soundness is relatively easy to show, since typically the soundness of individual proof rules can be established independently of the others. Completeness, on the other hand, is harder to show since it depends on the entire set of proof rules cooperating together. The same situation holds for the program logic we introduce in this chapter. Establishing its soundness is simply a matter of considering each rule in turn (done in Exercises 4.9), whereas establishing its completeness is harder and is beyond the scope of this book.

4.2.4 Program variables and logical variables

The variables which we have seen so far in the programs that we verify are called *program variables*. They can also appear in the preconditions and post-conditions of specifications. Sometimes, in order to formulate specifications, we need to use other variables which do not appear in the program.

Examples 4.6

1. Another version of the factorial program might have been this one, Fac2:

   ```
   y = 1;
   while (x != 0) {
       y = y * x;
       x = x - 1;
   }
   ```

   Unlike the previous version, it 'consumes' the input x. Nevertheless, it correctly calculates the factorial of x and stores the value in y; and we would like to express that as a Hoare triple. However, it is not a good idea to write

   $$(x \geq 0) \; \text{Fac2} \; (y = x!)$$

   because, if the program terminates, then x will be 0 and y will be the factorial of the *initial* value of x.

   We need a way of remembering the initial value of x, to cope with the fact that it is 'destroyed' by the program. This is where logical variables come in: we write the specification as

   $$(x = x_0 \wedge x \geq 0) \; \text{Fac2} \; (y = x_0!).$$

   Here, x_0 is a logical variable and we read it as being universally quantified. That is, the specification is read as: for all integers x_0, if x equals x_0, $x \geq 0$ and we run the program such that it terminates, then the resulting state will satisfy y equals $x_0!$.

2. Consider the program Sum:

   ```
   z = 0;
   while (x > 0) {
       z = z + x;
       x = x - 1;
   }
   ```

This program adds up the first x integers and stores the result in z. Thus, $(x = 3)$ Sum $(z = 6)$, $(x = 8)$ Sum $(z = 36)$, etc. We know from Chapter 1 (Theorem 1.30) that

$$1 + 2 + \cdots + x = \frac{x(x + 1)}{2},$$

so we would like to express, as a Hoare triple, that the value of z upon termination is $\frac{x_0(x_0+1)}{2}$ where x_0 is the initial value of x. Thus, we write

$$(x = x_0 \wedge x \geq 0) \text{ Sum } \left(z = \frac{x_0(x_0 + 1)}{2}\right).$$

Variables like x_0 in these examples are called *logical variables*, because they occur only in the logical formulas that constitute the precondition and postcondition; they do not occur in the code to be verified. The state of the system gives a value to each program variable, but not for the logical variables. Logical variables take a similar role to the dummy variables of the rules for $\forall i$ and $\exists e$ in Chapter 2.

4.3 Proof calculus for partial correctness

The proof calculus which we now present goes back to R. Floyd and C. A. R. Hoare. In the next subsection, we specify proof rules for each of the grammar clauses for commands. We could go on to use these proof rules directly, but it turns out to be more convenient to present them in a different form, suitable for the construction of proofs known as *proof tableaux*. This is what we do in the subsection following the next one.

4.3.1 *Proof rules*

The proof rules for our calculus are given in Figure 4.1. They should be interpreted as rules that allow us to pass from simple assertions of the form $(\phi) P (\psi)$ to more complex ones. The rule for assignment has no premises, which allows us to construct some triples out of nothing, to get the proof going. A complete proof takes the form of a tree (we will see one later in the chapter, in Figure 4.2).

Composition. Given specifications for the program fragments C_1 and C_2, say

$$(\phi) C_1 (\eta) \qquad \text{and} \qquad (\eta) C_2 (\psi),$$

$$\frac{(\phi)\; C_1\; (\eta) \qquad (\eta)\; C_2\; (\psi)}{(\phi)\; C_1; C_2\; (\psi)} \quad \text{Composition}$$

$$\frac{}{(\psi[E/x])\; x = E\; (\psi)} \quad \text{Assignment}$$

$$\frac{(\phi \wedge B)\; C_1\; (\psi) \qquad (\phi \wedge \neg B)\; C_2\; (\psi)}{(\phi)\; \texttt{if } B\; \{C_1\}\; \texttt{else}\; \{C_2\}\; (\psi)} \quad \text{If-statement}$$

$$\frac{(\psi \wedge B)\; C\; (\psi)}{(\psi)\; \texttt{while } B\; \{C\}\; (\psi \wedge \neg B)} \quad \text{Partial-while}$$

$$\frac{\vdash \phi' \rightarrow \phi \qquad (\phi)\; C\; (\psi) \qquad \vdash \psi \rightarrow \psi'}{(\phi')\; C\; (\psi')} \quad \text{Implied}$$

Fig. 4.1. Proof rules for program logic

the proof rule for sequential composition shown in Figure 4.1 allows us to derive a specification for $C_1; C_2$, namely

$$(\phi)\; C_1; C_2\; (\psi).$$

Thus, if we know that C_1 takes ϕ-states to η-states and C_2 takes η-states to ψ-states, then running C_1 and C_2 in that sequence will take ϕ-states to ψ-states.

Using this rule in program verification, we have to read it bottom-up: in order to prove $(\phi)\; C_1; C_2\; (\psi)$, we need to find an appropriate η and prove $(\phi)\; C_1\; (\eta)$ and $(\eta)\; C_2\; (\psi)$. If $C_1; C_2$ runs on input satisfying ϕ and we need to show that the store satisfies ψ after its execution, then we hope to show this by splitting the problem into two. After the execution of C_1, we have a store satisfying η which, considered as input for C_2, should result in an output satisfying ψ.

Assignment. The rule for assignment has no premises and is therefore an axiom of our logic. It tells us that, if we wish to show that ψ holds in the state after the assignment $x = E$, we must show that $\psi[E/x]$ holds before the assignment; $\psi[E/x]$ means the formula obtained by taking ψ and replacing all occurrences of x with E. We read the stroke as 'in place of'; thus, $\psi[E/x]$ is ψ with E in place of x. Several explanations may be required to understand this rule.

- At first sight, it looks as if the rule has been stated in reverse; one might expect that, if ψ holds in a state in which we perform the assignment x = E, then surely $\psi[E/x]$ holds in the resulting state, i.e. we just replace x by E. This is wrong. It is true that the assignment x = E replaces the value of x in the starting state by E, but that does not mean that we replace occurrences of x in a *condition on* the starting state by E.

  The right way to understand this rule is to think about what you would have to prove about the initial state in order to prove that ψ holds in the resulting state. Since ψ will (in general) be saying something about the value of x, whatever it says about that value must have been true of E, since in the resulting state the value of x is E. Thus, ψ with E in place of x — which says whatever ψ says about x but applied to E — must be true in the initial state.

- The axiom $(\psi[E/x])\, x = E\, (\psi)$ is best applied backwards than forwards in the verification process. That is to say, if we know ψ and we wish to find ϕ such that $(\phi)\, x = E\, (\psi)$, it is easy: we simply set ϕ to be $\psi[E/x]$; but, if we know ϕ and we want to find ψ such that $(\phi)\, x = E\, (\psi)$, there is no easy way of getting a suitable ψ. This backwards characteristic of the assignment and the composition rule will be important when we look at how to construct proofs; we will work from the end of the program to the beginning.

- If we apply this axiom in this backwards fashion, then it is completely mechanical to apply. It just involves doing a substitution. That means we could get a computer to do it for us. Unfortunately, that is not true for all the rules; application of the rule for while-statements, for example, requires ingenuity. Therefore a computer can at best assist us in performing a proof by carrying out the mechanical steps, such as application of the assignment axiom, while leaving the steps that involve ingenuity to the programmer.

- Observe that, in computing $\psi[E/x]$ from ψ, we replace all the occurrences of x in ψ. Note that there cannot be problems caused by *bound* occurrences, as seen in Definition 2.6 in Chapter 2, because *any quantifiers that occur in ψ are applied to logical variables, not to program variables.*

Examples 4.7

1. Suppose P is the program x = 2. The following are instances of the assignment axiom:

   (a) $(2 = 2)\,P\,(x = 2)$
   (b) $(2 = 4)\,P\,(x = 4)$

(c) $(2 = y)P(x = y)$

(d) $(2 > 0)P(x > 0)$.

These are all correct statements. Reading them backwards, we see that they say:

(a) If you want to prove $x = 2$ after the assignment x = 2, then we must be able to prove that $2 = 2$ before it. (Of course, 2 is equal to 2, so proving it shouldn't present a problem.)

(b) If you wanted to prove that $x = 4$ after the assignment, the only way in which it would work is if $2 = 4$; however, unfortunately it is not. More generally, $(\bot) x = E (\psi)$ holds for any E and ψ (why?).

(c) If you want to prove $x = y$ after the assignment, you will need to prove that $2 = y$ before it.

(d) To prove $x > 0$, we'd better have $2 > 0$.

2. Suppose P is x = x + 1. By choosing various postconditions, we obtain the following instances of the assignment axiom:

(a) $(x + 1 = 2)P(x = 2)$

(b) $(x + 1 = y)P(x = y)$

(c) $(x + 1 + 5 = y)P(x + 5 = y)$

(d) $(x + 1 > 0 \wedge y > 0)P(x > 0 \wedge y > 0)$.

Note that the precondition obtained by performing the substitution can often be simplified. The proof rule for implications below will allow such modifications of conditions.

If-statements. The proof rule for if-statements allows us to prove a triple of the form

$$(\phi) \text{ if } B \{C_1\} \text{ else } \{C_2\} (\psi)$$

by decomposing it into two triples, corresponding to the cases of B evaluating to true and to false. Typically, the precondition ϕ will not tell us anything about the value of the boolean expression B, so we have to consider both cases. If B is true in the state we start in, then C_1 is executed and hence C_1 will have to translate ϕ states to ψ states; alternatively, if B is false, then C_2 will be executed and will have to do that job. Thus, we have to prove that $(\phi \wedge B) C_1 (\psi)$ and $(\phi \wedge \neg B) C_2 (\psi)$. Note that the preconditions are augmented by the knowledge that B is true and false, respectively.

This additional information is often crucial for completing the respective subproofs.

While-statements. The rule for while-statements given in Figure 4.1 is arguably the most complicated one. The reason is that the while-command is the most complicated construct in our language. It is the only command that loops, i.e. executes the same piece of code several times; and, unlike the for command in languages like Java, we cannot predict how many times it will loop around, or even whether it will terminate at all.

The idea behind the rule for while is the 'invariant' ψ. In general, the body C of the command while (B) $\{C\}$ changes the values of the variables it manipulates; but the invariant expresses a relationship between those values which is preserved by execution of C. In the proof rule, ψ expresses this invariant; the rule's premise, $(\psi \wedge B) C (\psi)$, states that (provided B is true), if ψ is true before we execute C, and C terminates, then it will be true after it. The conclusion states that, no matter how many times we go around the loop, if ψ is true initially and the while-statement terminates, then ψ will be true at the end. Moreover, since the while-statement has terminated, B will be false.

Implied. One final rule is required in our calculus: the rule 'Implied' of Figure 4.1. It tells us that, if we have proved $(\phi) P (\psi)$ and we have a formula ϕ' which implies ϕ and another one ψ' which is implied by ψ, then we should also be allowed to prove that $(\phi') P (\psi')$. Note that the rule allows the precondition to be strengthened (thus, we *assume* more than we need to), while the postcondition is weakened (i.e. we *conclude* less than we are entitled to). (If we tried to do it the other way around, weakening the precondition or strengthening the postcondition, then we would conclude things which are incorrect — why?)

The rule 'Implied' acts as a link between program logic and (a suitable extension of) predicate logic. It allows us to import proofs in predicate logic enlarged with the basic facts of arithmetic, which are required for reasoning about integer expressions, into the proofs in program logic.

4.3.2 *Proof tableaux*

The proof rules presented in Figure 4.1 are not in a form which is easy to use in examples. To illustrate this point, we present an example of a proof

$$\dfrac{(1 = 1)y = 1(y = 1)}{(\top)y = 1(y = 1)} \; i \qquad \dfrac{(y = 1 \wedge 0 = 0)z = 0(y = 1 \wedge z = 0)}{(y = 1)z = 0(y = 1 \wedge z = 0)} \; i$$

$$\dfrac{(\top)y = 1(y = 1) \qquad (y = 1)z = 0(y = 1 \wedge z = 0)}{(\top)y = 1; \, z = 0(y = 1 \wedge z = 0)} \; c$$

$$\dfrac{(y \cdot (z + 1) = (z + 1)!)z = z{+}1(y \cdot z = z!)}{(y = z! \wedge z \neq x)z = z{+}1(y \cdot z = z!)} \; i \qquad (y \cdot z = z!)y = y*z\,(y = z!)$$

$$\dfrac{(y = z!)\, \text{while } (z \mathrel{!=} x) \; \{z = z{+}1; \; y = y*z\} \; (z \mathrel{!=} x) \; \{z = z{+}1; \; y = y*z\} \; (y = z! \wedge z = x)}{(y = 1 \wedge z = 0)\, \text{while } (z \mathrel{!=} x) \; \{z = z{+}1; \; y = y*z\} \; (y = x!)} \; \begin{array}{l} w \\[2pt] i \end{array}$$

$$(y = x!) \quad c$$

Fig. 4.2. The proof of correctness of Fac1 in tree form.

in Figure 4.2; it is a proof of the triple

$$(\top) \; \text{Fac1} \; (y = x!)$$

where Fac1 is the factorial program given in Example 4.2; we abbreviated rule names and dropped the bars and names for Assignment. We have not yet presented enough information for the reader to complete such a proof on her own, but you can at least use the proof rules in Figure 4.1 to check whether all rule instances of that proof are permissible, i.e. match the required pattern. It should be clear that proofs in this form are unwieldy to work with. They will tend to be very wide and a lot of information is copied from one line to the next. Proving properties of programs which are longer than Fac1 would be very difficult in this style; in Chapters 1, 2 and 5 we abandon representation of proofs as trees for similar reasons.

The rule for sequential composition suggests a more convenient way of presenting proofs in program logic, called *proof tableaux*. We can think of any program of our core programming language as a sequence

$$C_1;$$
$$C_2;$$
$$.$$
$$.$$
$$.$$
$$C_n$$

where none of the commands C_i is a composition of smaller programs, i.e. all of the C_i above are either assignments, if-statements or while-statements. (We allow the if-statements, or while-statements, to have embedded compositions.) Let P stand for the program $C_1; C_2; \ldots; C_{n-1}; C_n$. Suppose that we want to show

$$\vdash_{par} (\phi_0) \; P \; (\phi_n)$$

for a precondition ϕ_0 and a postcondition ϕ_n. Then, we may split this problem into smaller ones by trying to find formulas ϕ_j $(0 < j < n)$ such that $\vdash_{par} (\phi_i) \; C_{i+1} \; (\phi_{i+1})$ holds for $i = 0, 1, \ldots, n - 1$. This suggests that we should design a proof calculus which presents a proof of $\vdash_{par} (\phi_0) \; P \; (\psi_n)$ by interleaving formulas with code as in

$$(\!|\phi_0|\!)$$
$$C_1;$$
$$(\!|\phi_1|\!) \qquad \text{justification}$$
$$C_2;$$

$$\cdot$$
$$\cdot$$
$$\cdot$$

$$(\!|\phi_{n-1}|\!) \qquad \text{justification}$$
$$C_n;$$
$$(\!|\phi_n|\!) \qquad \text{justification}$$

Against each formula, we write a justification (whose nature will be clarified shortly). Proof tableaux thus consist of the program code interleaved with formulas, which we call *midconditions*, that should hold at the point they are written.

Each of the transitions

$$(\!|\phi_i|\!)$$
$$C_{i+1}$$
$$(\!|\phi_{i+1}|\!)$$

will appeal to one of the rules of Figure 4.1, depending on whether C_{i+1} is an assignment, an if-statement or a while-statement. Note that this notation for proofs makes the proof rule for composition in Figure 4.1 implicit.

How should the intermediate formulas ϕ_i be found? In principle, it seems as though one could start from ϕ_0 and, using C_1, obtain ϕ_1 and continue working downwards. However, because the assignment rule works backwards, it turns out that it is more convenient to start with ϕ_n and work upwards, using C_n to obtain ϕ_{n-1}, etc. The process of obtaining ϕ_i from C_{i+1} and ϕ_{i+1} is called computing the *weakest precondition* of C_{i+1}, given the postcondition ϕ_{i+1}. That is to say, we are looking for the logically weakest formula whose truth at the beginning of the execution of C_{i+1} is enough to guarantee ϕ_{i+1}[1].

The construction of a proof tableau for $(\!|\phi|\!) \, C_1;\ldots;C_n \, (\!|\psi|\!)$ typically consists of starting with the postcondition ψ and pushing it upwards through

---

[1] ϕ is weaker than ψ means that ϕ is implied by ψ in predicate logic enlarged with the basic facts about arithmetic. We want the weakest formula, because we want to impose as few constraints as possible on the preceding code. In some cases, especially those involving the `while` command, it might not be possible to extract the logically *weakest* formula. We just need one which is sufficiently weak to allow us to complete the proof at hand.

C_n, then $C_{n-1}, \dots$, until a formula ϕ' emerges at the top. Ideally, the formula ϕ' represents the weakest precondition which guarantees that the ψ will hold if the program is executed and terminates. The weakest precondition ϕ' is then checked to see whether it follows from the given precondition ϕ (thus, we appeal to the 'Implied' rule of Figure 4.1).

Before a discussion of how to find invariants for while-statement, we now look at the assignment and the if-statement to see how the weakest precondition is calculated for each one.

Assignment. The assignment axiom is easily adapted to work for proof tableaux. We write it thus:

$$\left(\psi[E/x]\right)$$
$$x \;=\; E$$
$$\left(\psi\right) \qquad \qquad \text{Assignment}$$

The justification is written against the ψ, since, once the proof has been constructed, we want to read it in a forwards direction. The construction itself proceeds in a backwards direction, because that is the way the assignment axiom facilitates.

Implied. In tableau form, the 'Implied' rule allows us to write one formula ϕ_2 directly underneath another one ϕ_1 with no code in between, provided that ϕ_1 logically implies ϕ_2. Since the midconditions in tableaux are formulas of predicate logic, when we say 'logically implies' we mean 'Implies in (a suitable extension[1] of) predicate logic'. The 'Implied' rule acts as an interface between predicate logic and program logic. This is a surprising and crucial insight. Our proof calculus for partial correctness is a hybrid system which interfaces with another proof calculus via the 'Implied' proof rule. It is important to keep the two calculi apart.

When we appeal to the 'Implied' rule, we will not explicitly write out the proof of the implication in predicate logic, for this chapter focuses on the program logic. Moreover, the implications we typically encounter will be easy to verify.

The 'Implied' rule is often used to simplify formulas that are generated by applications of the other rules. It is also used when the weakest precondition

---

[1] Our programs compute over integer expressions, so we will often have to reason about them using the laws of arithmetic. These laws have to be added to the proof rules for predicate logic. Thus, we speak of an extension of this logic.

ϕ' emerges by pushing the postcondition upwards through the whole program. We use the 'Implied' rule to show that the given precondition implies the weakest precondition. Let's look at some examples of this.

Examples 4.8

1. We show $\vdash_{par} (y = 5) \; x \; = \; y \; + \; 1 \; (x = 6)$:

$$(y = 5)$$
$$(y + 1 = 6) \quad \text{Implied}$$
$$x = y + 1$$
$$(x = 6) \quad \text{Assignment}$$

The proof is constructed from the bottom upwards. We start with $(x = 6)$ and, using the assignment axiom, we push it upwards through $x = y + 1$. This means substituting $y + 1$ for all occurrences of x, resulting in $(y + 1 = 6)$. Now, we compare this with the given precondition $(y = 5)$. The given precondition implies it, so we have finished the proof.

   Although the proof is constructed bottom-up, we may read it top-down. The justifications make sense when read top-down. Thus, the second line is implied by the first and the fourth follows from the second by the intervening assignment.

2. We prove $\vdash_{par} (y < 3) \; y \; = \; y \; + \; 1 \; (y < 4)$:

$$(y < 3)$$
$$(y + 1 < 4) \quad \text{Implied}$$
$$y = y + 1;$$
$$(y < 4) \quad \text{Assignment}$$

Notice that Implied always refers to the immediately preceding line. As already remarked, proofs in program logic generally combine two logical levels: the first level is directly concerned with proof rules for programming constructs such as the assignment statement; the second level is ordinary entailment familiar to us from Chapters 1 and 2. We may use ordinary logical implications to change a certain condition ϕ to any condition ϕ' which is implied by ϕ for reasons which have nothing to do with the given code. In the example above, ϕ was $y < 3$ and the implied formula ϕ' was then $y + 1 < 4$. The validity of this implication is rooted in general facts about integers and the relation $<$ defined on them. Completely formal proofs would require separate proofs attached to all instances of the rule Implied. However, as already remarked, we won't do that since we chose to focus our attention in this chapter on those parts of proofs which reason directly with code.

3. Our next example is a sequential composition of assignment statements:

```
z = x;

z = z + y;

u = z;
```

Our goal is to show that u stores the sum of x and y after this sequence of assignments terminates. Let us write P for the code above. Thus, we mean to prove $\vdash_{par} (\top) P (u = x + y)$.

We construct the proof by starting with the postcondition $u = x+y$ and pushing it up through the assignments, in reverse order, using the assignment rule.

- Pushing it up through u = z involves replacing all occurrences of u by z, resulting in $z = x + y$. We thus have the proof fragment

$$(z = x + y)$$
```
u = z;
```
$$(u = x + y) \qquad \text{Assignment}$$

- Pushing $z = x + y$ upwards through z = z + y involves replacing z by $z + y$, resulting in $z + y = x + y$.
- Pushing that upwards through z = x involves replacing z by x, resulting in $x + y = x + y$. The proof fragment now looks like this:

$$(x + y = x + y)$$
```
z = x;
```
$$(z + y = x + y) \qquad \text{Assignment}$$
```
z = z + y;
```
$$(z = x + y) \qquad \text{Assignment}$$
```
u = z;
```
$$(u = x + y) \qquad \text{Assignment}$$

The weakest precondition that thus emerges is $x + y = x + y$; we have to check that this follows from the given precondition, $\top$. This means checking that any state that satisfies $\top$ also satisfies $x + y = x + y$. Well, $\top$ is satisfied in *all* states, but so is $x + y = x + y$, so the implication $\top \rightarrow x + y = x + y$ holds.

The final completed proof therefore looks like this:

$$(\top)$$
$$(x + y = x + y) \qquad \text{Implied}$$
$$\text{z = x;}$$
$$(z + y = x + y) \qquad \text{Assignment}$$
$$\text{z = z + y;}$$
$$(z = x + y) \qquad \text{Assignment}$$
$$\text{u = z;}$$
$$(u = x + y) \qquad \text{Assignment}$$

and we can now read it from the top down.

The application of the proof rule for assignment requires some care. We describe two pitfalls which the unwary may fall into, if the rule is not applied correctly.

• Consider the example 'proof'

$$(x + 1 = x + 1)$$
$$\text{x = x + 1;}$$
$$(x = x + 1) \qquad \text{Assignment}$$

which uses the rule for assignment incorrectly. Pattern matching with the assignment axiom means that ψ has to be $x = x + 1$, the expression E is $x + 1$ and $\psi[E/x]$ is $x + 1 = x + 1$. However, $\psi[E/x]$ is obtained by replacing *all* occurrences of x in ψ by E, thus, $\psi[E/x]$ would have to be equal to $x + 1 = x + 1 + 1$. Therefore, the corrected proof

$$(x + 1 = x + 1 + 1)$$
$$\text{x = x + 1;}$$
$$(x = x + 1) \qquad \text{Assignment}$$

shows $\vdash_{par} (x + 1 = x + 1 + 1) \text{ x = x + 1 } (x = x + 1)$.

As an aside, note that this corrected proof is not very useful. The triple says that, if $x+1 = (x+1)+1$ holds in a state and the assignment x = x+1 is executed and terminates, then the resulting state satisfies $x = x+1$; but, since the precondition $x+1 = x+1+1$ can never be true, this triple tells us nothing informative about the assignment.

- Another way of using the proof rule for assignment incorrectly is by allowing additional assignments to happen in between $\psi[E/x]$ and x = E, as in the 'proof'

$$\left(x+2 = y+1\right)$$
$$\text{y = y + 1000001;}$$
$$\text{x = x + 2;}$$
$$\left(x = y+1\right) \qquad\qquad \text{Assignment}$$

This is not a correct application of the assignment rule, since an additional assignment happens in line 2 right before the actual assignment to which the inference in line 4 applies. This additional assignment makes this reasoning unsound: line 2 overwrites the current value in y to which the equation in line 1 is referring. Clearly, $x+2 = y+1$ won't be true any longer. Therefore, we are allowed to use the proof rule for assignment only if there is no additional code between the precondition $\psi[E/x]$ and the assignment x = E.

EXERCISES 4.3

* 1. Use the proof rule for assignment and logical implication as appropriate to show the following partial correctness proofs:

  (a) $\vdash_{par} \left(x > 0\right)$ y = x + 1 $\left(y > 1\right)$
  (b) $\vdash_{par} \left(\top\right)$ y = x; y = x + x + y $\left(y = 3 \cdot x\right)$
  (c) $\vdash_{par} \left(x > 1\right)$ a = 1; y = x; y = y - a $\left(y > 0 \wedge x > y\right)$.

* 2. Write down a program P such that:

  (a) $\left(\top\right) P \left(y = x+2\right)$
  (b) $\left(\top\right) P \left(z > x+y+4\right)$

  and prove it.

3. We already discussed that the rule for assignment has to be applied consistently. However, there is a safe way of relaxing the format of the proof rule for assignment: as long as no variable occurring in E gets updated in between the assertion $\psi[E/x]$ and the assignment x = E we may conclude ψ right after this assignment. Explain why such a proof rule would be sound.

If-statements. We now consider how to push a midcondition upwards through an if-statement. Suppose we are given a condition ψ and a program fragment if (B) $\{C_1\}$ else $\{C_2\}$. We wish to calculate the weakest ϕ such that

$$(\phi)\, \text{if } (B)\, \{C_1\} \text{ else } \{C_2\}\, (\psi).$$

This ϕ may be calculated as follows.

1. Push ψ upwards through C_1; let's call the result ϕ_1. (Note that, since C_1 may be a sequence of other commands, this will involve appealing to other rules. If C_1 contains another if-statement, then this step will involve a 'recursive call' to the rule for if-statements.)

2. Similarly, push ψ upwards through C_2; call the result ϕ_2.

3. Set ϕ to be $(B \rightarrow \phi_1) \wedge (\neg B \rightarrow \phi_2)$.

Example 4.9 Let us see this proof rule at work on the contrived code for Succ given earlier in the chapter. Here is the code again:

```
a = x + 1;
if (a - 1 == 0)  {
y = 1;
} else {
y = a;
}
```

The partial correctness assertion we want to show is $\vdash_{par} (\top)\, \text{Succ}\, (y = x + 1)$. Note that this program is the sequential composition of an assignment and an if-statement. Thus, we need to obtain a suitable midcondition to put between the if-statement and the assignment.

We push the postcondition $y = x + 1$ upwards through the two branches of the if-statement, obtaining

- ϕ_1 is $1 = x + 1$;
- ϕ_2 is $a = x + 1$;

and obtain the midcondition $(a - 1 = 0 \rightarrow 1 = x + 1) \wedge (\neg(a - 1 = 0) \rightarrow a = x + 1)$. The partial proof now looks like this:

$(\top)$
$(?)$?

```
a = x + 1;
```
$((a - 1 = 0 \rightarrow 1 = x + 1) \wedge (\neg(a - 1 = 0) \rightarrow a = x + 1))$?
```
if (a - 1 == 0) {
```
$(1 = x + 1)$ If-Statement
```
        y = 1;
```
$(y = x + 1)$ Assignment
```
} else {
```
$(a = x + 1)$ If-Statement
```
        y = a;
```
$(y = x + 1)$ Assignment
```
}
```
$(y = x + 1)$ If-Statement

Note that we referred to a slightly different version of the rule If-statement:

$$\frac{(\phi_1)\, C_1\, (\psi) \qquad (\phi_2)\, C_2\, (\psi)}{((B \rightarrow \phi_1) \wedge (\neg B \rightarrow \phi_2))\; \texttt{if } B\; \{C_1\}\; \texttt{else}\; \{C_2\}\; (\psi)} \quad \text{If-Statement} \quad (4.5)$$

However, this rule can be derived using the proof rules discussed so far; this is left as an exercise below.

EXERCISES 4.4

    1. Explain why the modified rule If-Statement in (4.5) is sound with respect to the partial and total satisfaction relation.

* 2. Show that any instance of the modified rule If-Statement in a proof can be replaced by an instance of the original If-statement and instances of the rule Implied.

Continuing this example, we push the long formula above the if-statement through the assignment, to obtain

$$(x + 1 - 1 = 0 \rightarrow 1 = x + 1) \wedge (\neg(x + 1 - 1 = 0) \rightarrow x + 1 = x + 1).$$

We need to show that this is implied by the given precondition, $\top$, i.e. that it is true in any state. Indeed, simplifying it gives

$$(x = 0 \rightarrow 1 = x + 1) \wedge (\neg(x = 0) \rightarrow x + 1 = x + 1)$$

and both these implications are true. (The second one is true because its conclusion is true, regardless of the premise.) The above proof now is completed as:

$$\left(\top \right)$$
$$\big((x + 1 - 1 = 0 \to 1 = x + 1) \wedge (\neg (x + 1 - 1 = 0) \to x + 1 = x + 1) \big) \qquad \text{Implied}$$

`a = x + 1;`
$$\big((a - 1 = 0 \to 1 = x + 1) \wedge (\neg (a - 1 = 0) \to a = x + 1) \big) \qquad \text{Assignment}$$

`if (a - 1 == 0) {`

$$\left(1 = x + 1 \right) \qquad \text{If-Statement}$$

 `y = 1;`

$$\left(y = x + 1 \right) \qquad \text{Assignment}$$

`} else {`

$$\left(a = x + 1 \right) \qquad \text{If-Statement}$$

 `y = a;`

$$\left(y = x + 1 \right) \qquad \text{Assignment}$$

`}`

$$\left(y = x + 1 \right) \qquad \text{If-Statement}$$

EXERCISES 4.5

Use the proof rules for assignments, if-statements and logical implication as appropriate to show the following partial correctness proofs:

* 1. $\vdash_{par} \left(\top \right) P \left(z = \min(x, y) \right)$, where $\min(x, y)$ is the smallest number of x and y (e.g. $\min(7, 3) = 3$) and the code of P is given by

```
if (x > y) {
    z = y;
} else {
    z = x;
}
```

2. For each of the specifications below, write code for P and prove the correctness of the specified input/output behaviour:

* (a) $\left(\top \right) P \left(z = \max(w, x, y) \right)$, where $\max(w, x, y)$ denotes the largest of w, x and y.
* (b) $\left(\top \right) P \left(((x = 5) \to (y = 3)) \wedge ((x = 3) \to (y = -1)) \right)$.

3. Prove $\left(\top \right) \mathrm{Succ} \left(y = x + 1 \right)$ *without* using the modified proof rule for if-statements.

While-statements. Recall that the proof rule for partial correctness of while-statements was presented in the following form in Figure 4.1 (here we have written η instead of ψ):

$$\frac{\left(\eta \wedge B \right) C \left(\eta \right)}{\left(\eta \right) \text{ while } B \ \{ C \} \left(\eta \wedge \neg B \right)} \qquad \text{Partial-while.} \qquad (4.6)$$

Before we look at how that will be represented in proof tableaux, let us look in more detail at the ideas behind the rule. The formula η is chosen to be an invariant of the body C of the while-statement; this means that, provided the boolean guard B is true, if η is true before we start C, and C terminates, then it is also true at the end. This is what the premise $(\eta \wedge B)\, C\, (\eta)$ expresses.

Now suppose we embark on the while-statement in a state that satisfies η and that (4.6) holds. We do not know how many times we will execute C; but we check the truth of B each time we start.

- If B is false as soon as we embark on the while-statement, then we do not execute C at all. Nothing has happened to change the truth value of η, so we end the while-statement with $\eta \wedge \neg B$.
- If B is true when we embark on the while-statement, we execute C. By the premise of the rule in (4.6), we know η is true at the end of C.
  - if B is now false, we stop with $\eta \wedge \neg B$.
  - if B is true, we execute C again; η is again re-established. No matter how many times we execute C in this way, η is re-established at the end of each one. We terminate if, and only if, we find B to be false at the end of an execution of C, in which case we have $\eta \wedge \neg B$.

This argument shows that the while-rule is sound with respect to the satisfaction relation for partial correctness, in the sense that anything we prove using it is indeed true. However, as it stands it allows us to prove only things of the form $(\eta)\, \texttt{while}\ (B)\ \{C\}\, (\eta \wedge \neg B)$, i.e. triples in which the postcondition is the same as the precondition together with $\neg B$. Suppose that we are required to prove

$$(\phi)\, \texttt{while}\ (B)\ \{C\}\, (\psi),$$

for some ϕ and ψ which are not related in that way. How can we use the while-rule in a situation like this?

The answer is that we must *discover* a suitable η, such that

- $\vdash \phi \rightarrow \eta$,
- $\vdash \eta \wedge \neg B \rightarrow \psi$ and
- $(\eta)\, \texttt{while}\ (B)\ \{C\}\, (\eta \wedge \neg B)$ hold.

Then, by the 'Implied' rule, our requirement $(\phi)\, \texttt{while}\ (B)\ \{C\}\, (\psi)$ is implied by $(\eta)\, \texttt{while}\ (B)\ \{C\}\, (\eta \wedge \neg B)$ and we can prove triples of that form using the while-rule.

The crucial thing, then, is the discovery of a suitable invariant η. It is a necessary step in order to use the while-rule and in general it requires intelligence and ingenuity. This contrasts markedly with the case of the if-rule and the assignment-rule, which are purely mechanical in nature: their usage is just a matter of symbol-pushing and does not require any insight.

Discovery of a suitable invariant requires careful thought about what the while-statement is really doing; indeed, the eminent computer scientist E. Dijkstra says that to understand a while-statement is tantamount to knowing what its invariant is (given fixed preconditions and postconditions for that while-statement).

This is because a suitable invariant can be interpreted as saying that the intended computation performed by the while-statement is correct up to the current step of the execution. It then follows that, when the execution terminates, the entire computation is correct. Let us discuss invariants and how to discover them.

Definition 4.10 An *invariant* of the while-statement while (B) $\{C\}$ having guard B and body C is a formula η such that $\vDash_{\mathrm{par}} (\eta \wedge B) \, C \, (\eta)$; i.e., if η and B are true in a state and C is executed and terminates, then η is again true in the resulting state.

Note that η does not have to be true continuously during the execution of C; in general, it will not be. All we require is that, if it is true before C is executed, then it is true (if and) when C terminates.

For a given while-statement there are several invariants. For example, $\top$ is an invariant for *any* loop; so, indeed, is $\bot$, since the premise of 'if $\bot \wedge B$ is true, then ... ' is false, so the implication is true. The formula $\neg B$ is also an invariant of while (B) do $\{C\}$; but most of these invariants are useless to us, because we are looking for one which has the properties

$$\vdash \phi \to \eta \qquad \text{and} \qquad \vdash \eta \wedge \neg B \to \psi,$$

where ϕ and ψ are the preconditions and postconditions of the while-statement. Usually, this will single out just one of all the possible invariants (up to equivalence).

A useful invariant expresses a relationship between the variables manipulated by the body of the while-statement which is preserved by the loop, even though the values of the variables themselves may change. The invariant can often be found by constructing a trace of the program in action.

Example 4.11 Consider the program Fac1 seen earlier in the chapter:

```
y = 1;
z = 0;
while (z != x) {
    z = z + 1;
    y = y * z;
}
```

Suppose program execution begins with $x = 6$. When the program flow first encounters the while-statement, $z = 0$ and $y = 1$, so the condition $z \neq x$ is true and the body is executed. Thereafter, $z = 1$ and $y = 1$ and the boolean guard is still true, so it is executed again. Continuing in this way, we obtain the following trace:

iteration	z	y	B
0	0	1	true
1	1	1	true
2	2	2	true
3	3	6	true
4	4	24	true
5	5	120	true
6	6	720	false

We stop when the guard becomes false.

The invariant of this example is easy to see: it is '$y = z!$'. Every time we complete an execution of the body of the while-statement, this fact is true, even though the values of y and z have been changed. Moreover, this invariant has the properties that we need; it is *weak enough* that it is implied by the precondition of the while-statement, which is $y = 1 \wedge z = 0$ (established by the initial assignments; recall that $0! \stackrel{\text{def}}{=} 1$), but also *strong enough* that, together with the negation of the guard, it implies the postcondition '$y = x!$'. That is to say, we have the implications

$$\vdash (y = 1 \wedge z = 0) \rightarrow (y = z!) \qquad \text{and} \qquad \vdash (y = z! \wedge x = z) \rightarrow (y = x!).$$

Informally, these implications follow from the fact that the invariant says that the intended computation performed by the while-statement is correct up to the current step of the execution.

As in this example, a suitable invariant is often discovered by looking at the form of the postcondition. A complete proof of the factorial example in tree form, using this invariant, was given in Figure 4.2.

How should we use the while-rule in proof tableaux? We need to think about how to push an arbitrary postcondition ψ upwards through a while-statement to meet the precondition ϕ. The steps are:

1. Guess a formula η which you hope is a suitable invariant.
2. Prove that $\vdash \eta \wedge \neg B \rightarrow \psi$, where B is the boolean guard of the while-statement. This proves that η is strong enough to imply the desired postcondition.
3. Push η upwards through the body C of the loop; this involves applying other rules dictated by the form of C. Let us name the formula that emerges η'.
4. Prove that $\eta \wedge B \rightarrow \eta'$; this proves that η is indeed an invariant.
5. Now write η above the while-statement; this is the result of pushing ψ up through the while-statement (and it better be the case that we can prove $\vdash \phi \rightarrow \eta$).

If item 2, 4, or 5 fails you need to try a better η; or re-assess your code.

Example 4.12 We continue the example of the factorial. The partial proof obtained by pushing $y = x!$ upwards through the while-statement (thus checking the hypothesis that $y = z!$ is an invariant) is as follows:

```
y = 1;
z = 0;
```
$$\left(y = z! \right) \qquad\qquad ?$$
```
while (z != x) {
```
$$\left(y = z! \wedge z \neq x \right) \qquad \text{Invariant Hyp.} \wedge \text{guard}$$
$$\left(y \cdot (z+1) = (z+1)! \right) \qquad \text{Implied}$$
```
        z = z + 1;
```
$$\left(y \cdot z = z! \right) \qquad\qquad \text{Assignment}$$
```
        y = y * z;
```
$$\left(y = z! \right) \qquad\qquad \text{Assignment}$$
```
}
```
$$\left(y = x! \right) \qquad\qquad ?$$

Whether $y = z!$ is a suitable invariant depends on three things:

- The ability to prove that it is indeed *an* invariant, i.e. that $y = z!$ implies $y \cdot (z+1) = (z+1)!$. This is indeed the case, since we just multiply each side of $y = z!$ by $z + 1$ and appeal to the inductive definition of $(z + 1)!$ in Example 4.2.

- The ability to prove that it is strong enough that it and the negation of the boolean guard together imply the postcondition; this is also the case, for $y = z!$ and $x = z$ imply $y = x!$.

- The ability to prove that it is weak enough to be established by the code leading up to the while-statement. This is what we prove by continuing to push the result upwards through the code preceding the loop.

Continuing, then: pushing $y = z!$ through $z = 0$ results in $y = 0!$ and pushing that through $y = 1$ results in $1 = 0!$. This is indeed true because $0!$ is defined to be 1, i.e. it is implied by $\top$, and our completed proof is:

$$(\top)$$
$$(1 = 0!) \qquad\qquad\qquad \text{Implied}$$
```
y = 1;
```
$$(y = 0!) \qquad\qquad\qquad \text{Assignment}$$
```
z = 0;
```
$$(y = z!) \qquad\qquad\qquad \text{Assignment}$$
```
while (z != x) {
```
$$(y = z! \wedge z \neq x) \qquad\qquad \text{Invariant Hyp.} \wedge \text{guard}$$
$$(y \cdot (z + 1) = (z + 1)!) \quad \text{Implied}$$
```
    z = z + 1;
```
$$(y \cdot z = z!) \qquad\qquad\qquad \text{Assignment}$$
```
    y = y * z;
```
$$(y = z!) \qquad\qquad\qquad \text{Assignment}$$
```
}
```
$$(y = z! \wedge \neg(z \neq x)) \qquad \text{Partial-while}$$
$$(y = x!) \qquad\qquad\qquad \text{Implied}$$

EXERCISES 4.6

* 1. Show $\vdash_{par} (x \geq 0) \, \texttt{Copy1} \, (x = y)$, where $\texttt{Copy1}$ denotes the code on the following page:

```
a = x;
y = 0;
while (a != 0) {
    y = y + 1;
    a = a - 1;
}
```

* 2. Let Multi1 denote the following code:

```
a = 0;
z = 0;
while (a != y) {
    z = z + x;
    a = a + 1;
}
```

Show $\vdash_{par} (y \geq 0)$ Multi1 $(z = x \cdot y)$.

3. Let Multi2 be the 'counting down' version of Multi1; it also overwrites the variable y:

```
z = 0;
while (y != 0) {
    z = z + x;
    y = y - 1;
}
```

Show $\vdash_{par} (y = y_0 \wedge y \geq 0)$ Multi2 $(z = x \cdot y_0)$.

4. Another version of Copy1 is Copy2:

```
y=0;
while (y != x) {
    y = y + 1;
}
```

What is a suitable invariant? Show that $\vdash_{par} (x \geq 0)$ Copy2 $(x = y)$.

5. The program Div is supposed to compute the dividend of x by y;
this is defined to be the unique integer d such that there exists some
$r < y$ (r is the remainder) with $x = d \cdot y + r$. For example, if $x = 15$
and $y = 6$, then $d = 2$ because $15 = 2 \cdot 6 + 3$, where $3 < 6$. Let Div be
given by:

```
        r = x;
        d = 0;
        while (r >= y) {
            r = r - y;
            d = d + 1;
        }
```

Give a proof for $\vdash_{par} (\neg(y = 0)) \; \texttt{Div} \; ((x = d \cdot y + r) \wedge (r < y))$.

* 6. Consider the following variation $\texttt{Downfac}$ of the program which computes the factorial of x:

```
        a = x;
        y = 1;
        while (a > 0) {
            y = y * a;
            a = a - 1;
        }
```

Show $\vdash_{par} (x \geq 0) \; \texttt{Downfac} \; (y = x!)$.

7. Can you prove $\vdash_{par} (\top) \; \texttt{Copy1} \; (x = y)$?

4.3.3 A case study: minimal-sum section

We practice the proof rule for while-statements once again by verifying a program which computes the minimal-sum section of an array of integers. Let us extend our core programming language with arrays of integers[1]. For example, we may declare an array

```
    int a[n];
```

whose name is a and whose fields are accessed by a[1], a[2], ..., a[n], where n is some constant. Generally, we allow any integer expression E to compute the field index, as in a[E]. It is the programmer's responsibility to make sure that the value computed by E is always within the array bounds.

Definition 4.13 Let $a[1], \ldots, a[n]$ be an array of integer values. A *section* of a is a continuous piece $a[i], \ldots, a[j]$, where $1 \leq i \leq j \leq n$. A *minimal-sum section* is a section $a[i], \ldots, a[j]$ such that the sum

$$a[i] + a[i+1] + \cdots + a[j]$$

is minimal over all sections of a.

---

[1] We only *read* from arrays in the program Min_Sum which follows. Writing to arrays introduces additional problems because an array element can have several syntactically different names and this has to be taken into account by the calculus.

Example 4.14 Let us illustrate these concepts on the example integer array $[-1, 3, 15, -6, 4, -5]$. Both $[3, 15, -6]$ and $[-6]$ are sections, but $[3, -6, 4]$ isn't since 15 is missing. A minimal-sum section for this particular array is $[-6, 4, -5]$ with sum -7; it is the only minimal-sum section in this case.

In general, minimal-sum sections need not be unique. For example, the array $[4, -8, 3, -4, 8, -6, -3, 5]$ has two minimal-sum sections, namely $[-8, 3, -4]$ and $[-6, -3]$, each of which sums to -9.

The task at hand is to

- write a program Min_Sum, written in our core programming language (extended with integer arrays), which computes a minimal-sum section of a given array;
- make the informal description of this problem into a formal specification about the behaviour of Min_Sum;
- use our proof calculus for partial correctness to show that Min_Sum satisfies those formal specifications provided that it terminates.

There is an obvious program to do the job: we could list all the possible sections of a given array, then traverse that list to compute the sum of each section and keep the recent minimal sum in a storage location. For the example array $[-1, 3, -2]$, this results in the list

$$[-1], \quad [-1, 3], \quad [-1, 3, -2], \quad [3], \quad [3, -2], \quad [-2]$$

and we see that only the last section $[-2]$ produces the minimal sum -2. This idea can easily be coded in our core programming language, but it has a serious drawback: the number of sections of a given array of size n is proportional to the square of n; if we also have to sum all those, then our task has complexity $O(n^3)$. Computationally, this is an expensive price to pay, so we should inspect the problem more closely in order to see whether we can do better.

Can we compute the minimal sum in time proportional to n, by passing through the array just once? Intuitively, this seems difficult, since if we store just the minimal sum seen so far as we pass through the array, we may miss the opportunity of some large negative numbers later on because of some large numbers we encounter en route. For example, suppose the array is

$$[-8, 3, -65, 20, 45, -100, -8, 17, -4, -14].$$

Should we settle for $-8 + 3 - 65$, or should we try to take advantage of the -100 (remembering that we can pass through the array only once)? In this case, the whole array gives us the smallest sum, but it is difficult to see how a program which passes through the array just once could detect this.

The solution is to store two values during the pass: the minimal sum seen so far (s in the program below) and also the minimal sum seen so far of *all* the sections which end at the current point in the array (t below). Here is a program that is intended to do this:

```
k = 2;
t = a[1];
s = a[1];
while (k != n + 1) {
    t = min(t + a[k], a[k]);
    s = min(s,t);
    k = k + 1;
}
```

where min is a function which computes the minimum of its two arguments. The variable k proceeds through the array and t stores the minimal sum of sections that end at $a[k]$. As each new value is examined, we can either add it to the current minimal sum, or decide that a lower minimal sum can be obtained by starting a new section. The variable s stores the minimal sum seen so far; it is computed as the minimum we have seen so far in the last step, or the minimal sum of sections that end at the current point.

EXERCISES 4.7
Given $n = 5$ and the arrays below, simulate the code above for each of these arrays and check that the computed result actually gives us a minimal-sum section:

*   1. $[-3, 1, -2, 3, -8]$
     2. $[1, 45, -1, 23, -1]$
*   3. $[-1, -2, -3, -4, 1097]$.

———

Testing the program with a few examples is not sufficient to find all mistakes, however, and the reader would rightly not be convinced that this program really does compute the minimal-sum section in all cases. So let us try to use the program logic calculus introduced in this chapter to prove it.

Notation 4.15 Let $S_{i,j}$ mean the sum of the array between i and j, i.e. $a[i] + a[i + 1] + \cdots + a[j]$.

We formalise our requirement of the program as two specifications[1].

S1. $\big(\top\big)\,\texttt{Min\_Sum}\,\big(\forall i,j\,(1 \le i \le j \le n \to s \le S_{i,j})\big).$

It says that, after the program terminates, s is less than, or equal to, the sum of any section of the array. Note that i and j are logical variables in that they don't occur in the program at all.

S2. $\big(\top\big)\,\texttt{Min\_Sum}\,\big(\exists i,j\,(1 \le i \le j \le n \land s = S_{i,j})\big),$

which says that there is a section whose sum is s.

If there is a section whose sum is s and no section has a sum less than s, then s is the sum of a minimal-sum section. So, together, **S1** and **S2** give us the property we want.

Let us prove **S1**. The first task is to find a suitable invariant. As always, the following characteristics of an invariant are a useful guide:

- It expresses the fact that the computation performed so far by the while-statement is correct.
- It typically has the same form as the desired postcondition of the while-statement.
- It expresses a relationship between the variables manipulated by the while-statement which is re-established each time we go round the loop.

A suitable invariant in this case appears to be

$$\forall i,j\,(i \le j \le k+1 \to s \le S_{i,j}),$$

since it says that s is less than, or equal to, the minimal sum observed up to the current stage of the computation (represented by k). Note that it has the same form as the desired postcondition: we replaced the n by $k+1$, since the final value of n is $k+1$. We can now simplify slightly, since $j \le k+1$ is equivalent to $j < k$ (remembering that j and k are integers), obtaining

$$\forall i,j\,(i \le j < k \to s \le S_{i,j}),$$

Notice that i and j are quantified in the formula, because they are logical variables; k is a program variable.

If we start work on producing a proof tableau with this invariant, we will soon find that it is not strong enough. Intuitively, this is because it ignores the value of t, which stores the minimal sum of a section ending just before $a[k]$, which is crucial in the idea behind the program. A suitable invariant expressing that t is correct up to the current point of the computation is

$$\forall i\,(i < k \to t \le S_{i,k-1}).$$

[1] The notation $\forall i,j$ abbreviates $\forall i \forall j$, and similarly for $\exists i,j$.

$(\top)$

$\big((a[1] \leq S_{1,1}) \wedge (a[1] \leq S_{1,1})\big)$ Implied

$\big((i < 2 \rightarrow a[1] \leq S_{i,1}) \wedge (i \leq j < 2 \rightarrow a[1] \leq S_{i,j})\big)$ Implied

```
k = 2;
```
$\big((i < k \rightarrow a[1] \leq S_{i,k-1}) \wedge (i \leq j < k \rightarrow a[1] \leq S_{i,j})\big)$ Assignment

```
t = a[1];
```
$\big((i < k \rightarrow t \leq S_{i,k-1}) \wedge (i \leq j < k \rightarrow a[1] \leq S_{i,j})\big)$ Assignment

```
s = a[1];
```
$\big((i < k \rightarrow t \leq S_{i,k-1}) \wedge (i \leq j < k \rightarrow s \leq S_{i,j})\big)$ Assignment

```
while (k != n + 1) {
```
$\big((i < k \rightarrow t \leq S_{i,k-1}) \wedge (i \leq j < k \rightarrow s \leq S_{i,j}) \wedge k \neq n+1\big)$ Invariant Hyp. $\wedge$ guard

$\big(((i < k+1 \rightarrow \min(t + a[k], a[k]) \leq S_{i,k}) \wedge$

      $i \leq j < k+1 \rightarrow \min(s, \min(t + a[k], a[k])) \leq S_{i,j})\big)$ Implied (Lemma 4.16)

```
    t = min(t + a[k], a[k]);
```
$\big((i < k+1 \rightarrow t \leq S_{i,k}) \wedge (i \leq j < k+1 \rightarrow \min(s, t) \leq S_{i,j})\big)$ Assignment

```
    s = min(s,t);
```
$\big((i < k+1 \rightarrow t \leq S_{i,k}) \wedge (i \leq j < k+1 \rightarrow s \leq S_{i,j})\big)$ Assignment

```
    k = k + 1;
```
$\big((i < k \rightarrow t \leq S_{i,k-1}) \wedge (i \leq j < k \rightarrow s \leq S_{i,j})\big)$ Assignment

```
}
```
$\big((i < k \rightarrow t \leq S_{i,k-1}) \wedge (i \leq j < k \rightarrow s \leq S_{i,j}) \wedge (k = n+1)\big)$ Partial-while

$\big(i \leq j \leq n \rightarrow s \leq S_{i,j}\big)$ Implied

Fig. 4.3. Tableau for specification **S1** of Min_Sum.

Our invariant is the conjunction of these formulas, namely

$$\forall i, j \, (i \leq j < k \rightarrow s \leq S_{i,j}) \wedge \forall i \, (i < k \rightarrow t \leq S_{i,k-1}).$$

The completed proof tableau of **S1** for Min_Sum is given in Figure 4.3. (We do not include the quantification on i and j, for this would make it even harder to read.) The tableau is constructed by

- Proving that the candidate invariant is indeed an invariant. This involves pushing it upwards through the body of the while-statement and showing that what emerges follows from the invariant and the boolean guard. This implication is shown in the proof of Lemma 4.16.
- Proving that the invariant, together with the negation of the guard, is strong enough to prove the desired postcondition. This is the last implication of the proof tableau.
- Proving that the invariant is established by the code before the while-statement. We simply push it upwards through the three initial assignments.

As so often the case, in constructing the tableau, we find that two formulas meet; and we have to prove that the first one implies the second one. Sometimes this is easy and we can just note the implication in the tableau. In this case, however, the proof is tricky enough to need to be taken off-line and proved as a lemma:

Lemma 4.16 *Let k, s and t be any numbers and $S_{i,j}$ denote the sum of a fixed array between indices i and j, as above.*

1. *If: $\forall i\,(1 \leq i < k \rightarrow t \leq S_{i,k-1})$,*
   then: $\forall i\,(1 \leq i < k+1 \rightarrow \min(t + a[k], a[k]) \leq S_{i,k})$.
2. *If: $\forall i\,(1 \leq i < k \rightarrow t \leq S_{i,k-1}) \wedge \forall i, j\,(1 \leq i \leq j < k \rightarrow s \leq S_{i,j})$,*
   then: $\forall i, j\,(1 \leq i \leq j < k+1 \rightarrow \min(s, t + a[k], a[k]) \leq S_{i,j})$.

PROOF:

1. Take any i with $1 \leq i < k+1$; we will prove that $\min(t + a[k], a[k]) \leq S_{i,k}$.

   - If $i < k$, then $S_{i,k} = S_{i,k-1} + a[k]$, so what we have to prove is $\min(t + a[k], a[k]) \leq S_{i,k-1} + a[k]$; but we know $t \leq S_{i,k-1}$, so the result follows by adding $a[k]$ to each side.
   - Otherwise, $i = k$, $S_{i,k} = a[k]$ and the result follows.

2. Take any i and j with $1 \leq i \leq j < k+1$; we prove that $\min(s, t + a[k], a[k]) \leq S_{i,j}$.

   - If $i \leq j < k$, then the result is immediate.
   - Otherwise, $i \leq j = k$ and the result follows from part 1 of the lemma.

$\square$

EXERCISES 4.8

* 1. Prove **S2** for Min_Sum.
  2. Our algorithm for Min_Sum computes the *sum* of a minimal section, but it does not inform us where such a section may be located in the input array. Adapt the algorithm (it should still pass through the array only once) to fix that.

———

4.4 Proof calculus for total correctness

In the preceding section, we developed a calculus for proving *partial* correctness of triples $(\phi)\,P\,(\psi)$. In that setting, proofs come with a disclaimer: *only if* the program P terminates does a proof of $\vdash_{\mathsf{par}} (\phi)\,P\,(\psi)$ tell us anything about the behaviour of P. Partial correctness does not tell us anything if P loops indefinitely. In this section, we extend the proof calculus so that it also proves that programs terminate. In the previous section, we already pointed out that only the syntactic construct while B $\{C\}$ could be responsible for non-termination. Therefore, the proof calculus for total correctness is the same as for partial correctness for all the rules except the rule for while-statements. A proof of total correctness for a while-statement will consist of two parts:

- the proof of partial correctness and
- a proof that the given while-statement terminates.

Usually, it is a good idea to prove partial correctness first since this often provides helpful insights for a termination proof.

The proof of termination usually has the following form. We identify an integer expression whose value can be shown to *decrease* every time we go around the loop, but which is always non-negative. If we can find an expression with these properties, it follows that the loop must terminate; because the expression can only be decremented a finite number of times before it becomes 0. That is because there is only a finite number of integer values between 0 and the initial value of the expression.

The integer expression is called the *variant*. As an example consider Downfac in Exercise 4.6.6. A suitable variant expression is simply the variable a, since we can easily prove that a is decremented every time we go around the loop, yet, thanks to the guard a > 0, it is never negative. For the program Fac1 of Example 4.2, a suitable variant is $x - z$.

We can codify this intuition in the following rule for total correctness which replaces the rule for the while statement:

$$\frac{\left(\eta \wedge B \wedge 0 \leq E = E_0\right) C \left(\eta \wedge 0 \leq E < E_0\right)}{\left(\eta \wedge 0 \leq E\right) \text{ while } B \ \{C\} \left(\eta \wedge \neg B\right)} \text{ Total-while.} \qquad (4.7)$$

In this rule, E is the expression whose value decreases with each execution of the loop (this is coded by saying that, if its value is E_0 before the loop, then it is strictly less than E_0 after it), yet still it remains non-negative. As before, η is the loop invariant.

We use the rule Total-while in tableaux similarly to how we use Partial-while, but note that the body of the rule C must be shown to satisfy

$$\left(\eta \wedge B \wedge 0 \leq E = E_0\right) C \left(\eta \wedge 0 \leq E < E_0\right).$$

When we push $\eta \wedge 0 \leq E < E_0$ upwards through the body, we have to prove that what emerges from the top is implied by $\eta \wedge B \wedge 0 \leq E = E_0$; and the weakest precondition for the whole loop, which gets written above the while statement, is $\eta \wedge 0 \le E$.

Let us illustrate this rule by proving

$$\vdash_{tot} (x \ge 0) \; \text{Fac1} \; (y = x!).$$

Fac1 is given in Example 4.2, as follows:

```
y = 1;
z = 0;
while (x != z) {
        z = z + 1;
        y = y * z;

}
```

As already mentioned, $x - z$ is a suitable variant. The invariant $(y = z!)$ of the partial correctness proof is retained. We obtain the following complete proof for total correctness:

$(x \ge 0)$
$(1 = 0! \wedge 0 \le x - 0)$ Implied
`y = 1;`
$(y = 0! \wedge 0 \le x - 0)$ Assignment
`z = 0;`
$(y = z! \wedge 0 \le x - z)$ Assignment
`while (x != z) {`
       $(y = z! \wedge x \ne z \wedge 0 \le x - z = E_0)$ Invariant Hyp. $\wedge$ guard
       $(y \cdot (z + 1) = (z + 1)! \wedge 0 \le x - (z + 1) < E_0)$ Implied
   `z = z + 1;`
       $(y \cdot z = z! \wedge 0 \le x - z < E_0)$ Assignment
   `y = y * z;`
       $(y = z! \wedge 0 \le x - z < E_0)$ Assignment
`}`
$(y = z! \wedge x = z)$ Total-while
$(y = x!)$ Implied

Notice that the precondition $x \ge 0$ is crucial in securing the fact that $0 \le x - z$ holds right before the while-statements gets executed. In fact, a moment's thought reveals that our program does not terminate if $x < 0$.

One may wonder whether there is a way of uniformly coming up with an expression E that successfully proves termination, in cases that the while-statement indeed terminates. Like most other such universal problems discussed in this text, the wish to completely mechanise the construction of E

cannot be realised. Hence, finding a working variant E is a creative activity which requires skill, intuition and practice.

EXERCISES 4.9

* 1. Prove $\vdash_{tot} (x \geq 0)$ Copy1 $(x = y)$.
* 2. Prove $\vdash_{tot} (y \geq 0)$ Multi1 $(z = x \cdot y)$.
  3. Prove $\vdash_{tot} ((y = y_0) \wedge (y \geq 0))$ Multi2 $(z = x \cdot y_0)$.
* 4. Prove $\vdash_{tot} (x \geq 0)$ Copy2 $(x = y)$. Does your invariant have an active part in this?
  5. Prove **S2** for Min_Sum, ensuring total correctness.
* 6. Prove $\vdash_{tot} (x \geq 0)$ Downfac $(y = x!)$.
  7. Prove $\vdash_{tot} (\neg(y = 0))$ Div $((x = d \cdot y + r) \wedge (r < y))$. Which expression E does the job?
  8. Prove that $\vdash_{par}$ is sound for $\vDash_{par}$. Just like in Section 1.4.3, it suffices to assume that the premises of proof rules are instances of $\vDash_{par}$. Then, you need to prove that its conclusion must be an instance of $\vDash_{par}$ as well.
  9. Prove that $\vdash_{tot}$ is sound for $\vDash_{tot}$.

4.5 Bibliographic notes

An early exposition of the program logics for partial and total correctness of programs written in an imperative while-language can be found in [Hoa69]. The text [Dij76] contains a formal treatment of weakest preconditions. Backhouse's book [Bac86] describes program logic and weakest preconditions and also contains numerous examples and exercises. Other books giving more complete expositions of program verification than we can in this chapter are [AO91, Fra92]; they also extend the basic core language to include features such as procedures and parallelism. The issue of writing to arrays and the problem of array cell aliasing are described in [Fra92]. The original article describing the minimal-sum section problem is [Gri82]. A gentle introduction to the mathematical foundations of functional programming is [Tur91]. Some web sites deal with software liability and possible standards for intellectual property rights applied to computer programs [1][2]. Text books on systematic programming language design by uniform extensions of the core language we presented at the beginning of this chapter are [Ten91, Sch94]. A text on functional programming on the freely available language Standard ML of New Jersey is [Pau91].

[1] www.opensource.org
[2] www.sims.berkeley.edu/~pam/papers.html

5

Modal logics and agents

5.1 Modes of truth

In propositional or predicate logic, formulas are either true, or false, in any model. Propositional logic and predicate logic do not allow for any further possibilities. From many points of view, however, this is inadequate. In natural language, for example, we often distinguish between various 'modes' of truth, such as *necessarily true, known to be true, believed to be true* and *true in the future.* For example, we would say that, although the sentence

Bill Clinton is president of the USA.

is currently true, it will not be true at some point in the future. Equally, the sentence

There are nine planets in the solar system.

while true, and maybe true for ever in the future, is not necessarily true, in the sense that it could have been a different number. However, the sentence

The cube root of 27 is 3.

as well as being true is also necessarily true and true in the future. It does not enjoy all modes of truth, however. It may not be known to be true by some people (children, for example); it may not be believed by others (if they are mistaken).

In computer science, it is often useful to reason about modes of truth. In Chapter 3, we studied the logic CTL in which we could distinguish not only between truth at different points in the future, but also between different futures. Temporal logic is thus a special case of modal logic. The modalities of CTL allowed us to express a host of computational behaviour of systems. Modalities are also extremely useful in modelling other domains of computer science. In artificial intelligence, for example, scenarios with

261

several interacting agents are developed. Each agent may have different knowledge about the environment and also about the knowledge of other agents. In this chapter, we will look in depth at modal logics applied to reasoning about knowledge.

Modal logic adds unary connectives to express one, or more, of these different modes of truth. The simplest modal logics just deal with one concept, such as knowledge, necessity, or time. More sophisticated modal logics have connectives for expressing several modes of truth in the same logic; we will see some of these towards the end of this chapter.

We take a *logic engineering* approach in this chapter, in which we address the following question: given a particular mode of truth, how may we develop a logic capable of expressing and formalising that concept? To answer this question, we need to decide what properties the logic should have and what examples of reasoning it should be able to express. Our main case study will be the logic of *knowledge in a multi-agent system*. But first, we look at the syntax and semantics of basic modal logic.

5.2 Basic modal logic

5.2.1 Syntax

The language of basic modal logic is that of propositional logic with two extra connectives, $\Box$ and $\Diamond$. They are *unary* connectives; i.e., they apply themselves to a single formula. Another such unary connective is negation ($\neg$). As done in Chapters 1 and 3, we write $p, q, r, \ldots$ to denote atomic formulas.

Definition 5.1 The *formulas* of basic modal logic ϕ are defined by the following Backus Naur form (BNF):

$$\phi ::= \bot \mid \top \mid p \mid \neg\phi \mid (\phi \wedge \phi) \mid (\phi \vee \phi) \mid (\phi \rightarrow \phi) \mid (\phi \leftrightarrow \phi) \mid \Box\phi \mid \Diamond\phi,$$

where p is any atomic formula.

Example formulas of basic modal logic are $(p \wedge \Diamond(p \rightarrow \Box\neg r))$ and $\Box((\Diamond q \wedge \neg r) \rightarrow \Box p)$, having the parse trees shown in Figure 5.1. The following strings are *not* formulas, because they cannot be constructed using the grammar for formulas: $(p\Box \rightarrow q)$ and $(p \rightarrow \Diamond(q \Diamond r))$. Please explain why (compare this with the discussion in Chapter 1.3).

Convention 5.2 As done in Chapter 1, we assume that the unary connectives ($\neg$, $\Box$ and $\Diamond$) bind most closely, followed by $\wedge$ and $\vee$ and then followed by $\rightarrow$ and $\leftrightarrow$.

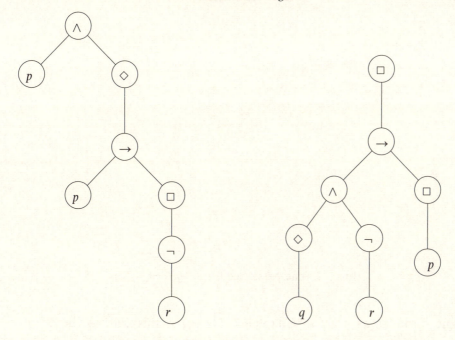

Fig. 5.1. Parse trees for $(p \wedge \Diamond(p \rightarrow \Box\neg r))$ and $\Box((\Diamond q \wedge \neg r) \rightarrow \Box p)$.

This allows us to remove many sets of brackets, retaining them only to avoid ambiguity, or to override these binding priorities. For example, $\Box((\Diamond q \wedge \neg r) \rightarrow \Box p)$ can be written $\Box(\Diamond q \wedge \neg r \rightarrow \Box p)$. We cannot omit the remaining brackets, however, for $\Box\Diamond q \wedge \neg r \rightarrow \Box p$ has quite a different parse tree (see Figure 5.2) from the one in Figure 5.1.

In basic modal logic, $\Box$ and $\Diamond$ are read 'box' and 'diamond', but, when we apply modal logics to express various modes of truth, we may read them appropriately. For example, in the logic that studies necessity and possibility, $\Box$ is read 'necessarily' and $\Diamond$ 'possibly'; in the logic of agent Q's knowledge, $\Box$ is read 'agent Q knows' and $\Diamond$ is read 'it is consistent with agent Q's knowledge that', or more colloquially, 'for all Q knows'. We will see why these readings are appropriate later in the chapter.

5.2.2 Semantics

A model in propositional logic is simply an assignment of truth values to each of the atomic formulas present in a formula (we called that a valuation in Chapter 1). That way, we may compute the truth values of all propositional

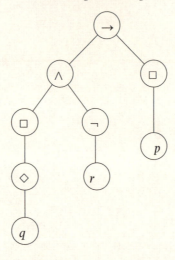

Fig. 5.2. The parse tree for $\Box \Diamond q \wedge \neg r \to \Box p$.

logic formulas as done in Chapter 1. However, this will not be adequate for modal logic, since we want to distinguish between different modes, or degrees, of truth.

Definition 5.3 A *model* $\mathcal{M}$ of basic modal logic is specified by three things:

1. A set W, whose elements are called *worlds*;
2. A relation R on W $(R \subseteq W \times W)$, called the *accessibility relation*;
3. A function $L : W \to \mathcal{P}(\text{Atoms})$, called the *labelling function*.

These models are often called Kripke models, in honour of S. Kripke who invented them and worked extensively in modal logic in the 1950s and 1960s. Intuitively, $w \in W$ stands for a possible world and wRw' means that w' is a world *related* to world w. The actual nature of that relationship depends on what we intend to model. Although the definition of models looks quite complicated, we can use an easy graphical notation to depict them in cases when they are finite. We illustrate the graphical notation by an example. Suppose W equals $\{x_1, x_2, x_3, x_4, x_5, x_6\}$ and the relation R is given as follows:

- $R(x_1, x_2)$, $R(x_1, x_3)$, $R(x_2, x_2)$, $R(x_2, x_3)$, $R(x_3, x_2)$, $R(x_4, x_5)$, $R(x_5, x_4)$, $R(x_5, x_6)$; and no other pairs are related by R.

Suppose further that the labelling function behaves as follows:

x	$L(x)$
x_1	$\{q\}$
x_2	$\{p, q\}$
x_3	$\{p\}$
x_4	$\{q\}$
x_5	$\emptyset$
x_6	$\{p\}$

Then, the Kripke model is illustrated in Figure 5.3. The set W is drawn as a set of circles, with arrows between them showing the relation R. Within each circle is the value of the labelling function in that world. (If you have read Chapter 3, then you might have noticed that Kripke structures are also the models for CTL, where W is S, the set of states; R is $\rightarrow$, the relation of state transitions; and L is the labelling function.)

Definition 5.4 Let $\mathcal{M} = (W, R, L)$ be a model of basic modal logic. Suppose $x \in W$ and ϕ is a formula. We will define when formula ϕ *is true in the world* x. This is done via a satisfaction relation $x \Vdash \phi$ by structural induction on ϕ:

$$x \Vdash \top$$
$$x \nVdash \bot$$
$$x \Vdash p \quad \text{iff } p \in L(x)$$
$$x \Vdash \neg\phi \quad \text{iff } x \nVdash \phi$$
$$x \Vdash \phi \wedge \psi \quad \text{iff } x \Vdash \phi \text{ and } x \Vdash \psi$$
$$x \Vdash \phi \vee \psi \quad \text{iff } x \Vdash \phi \text{, or } x \Vdash \psi$$
$$x \Vdash \phi \rightarrow \psi \quad \text{iff } x \Vdash \psi \text{, whenever we have } x \Vdash \phi$$
$$x \Vdash \phi \leftrightarrow \psi \quad \text{iff } x \Vdash \phi \text{ iff } x \Vdash \psi$$
$$x \Vdash \Box\psi \quad \text{iff, for each } y \in W \text{ with } R(x, y), \text{ we have } y \Vdash \psi$$
$$x \Vdash \Diamond\psi \quad \text{iff there is a } y \in W \text{ such that } R(x, y) \text{ and } y \Vdash \psi.$$

When $x \Vdash \phi$, we say 'x satisfies ϕ', or 'ϕ is true in world x'. We write $\mathcal{M}, x \Vdash \phi$ if we want to stress that $x \Vdash \phi$ holds in the model $\mathcal{M}$.

The first two clauses just express the fact that $\top$ is always true, while $\bot$ is always false. Next, we see that $L(x)$ is the set of all the atomic formulas that are true at x. The clauses for the boolean connectives ($\neg$, $\wedge$, $\vee$, $\rightarrow$ and $\leftrightarrow$) should also be straightforward: they mean that we apply the usual understanding of these connectives in the current world x. The interesting cases are those for $\Box$ and $\Diamond$. For $\Box\phi$ to be true at x, we require that ϕ be true in all the worlds related by R to x. For $\Diamond\phi$, it is required that there

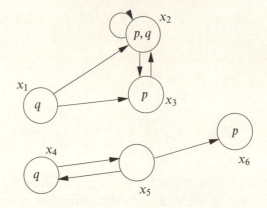

Fig. 5.3. A Kripke model.

is at least one related world[1] in which ϕ is true. Thus, $\Box$ and $\Diamond$ are a bit like the quantifiers $\forall$ and $\exists$ of predicate logic, except that they do not take variables as arguments. This fact makes them conceptually much simpler than quantifiers. The modal operators $\Box$ and $\Diamond$ are also rather like AX and EX in CTL (see Section 3.2). Note that the meaning of $\phi_1 \leftrightarrow \phi_2$ coincides with that of $(\phi_1 \to \phi_2) \wedge (\phi_2 \to \phi_1)$; we called it 'iff', or 'if and only if'.

Definition 5.5 A model $\mathcal{M} = (W, R, L)$ of basic modal logic is said to satisfy a formula if every state in the model satisfies it. Thus, we write $\mathcal{M} \vDash \phi$ iff, for each $x \in W$, $x \Vdash \phi$.

Examples 5.6 Consider the Kripke model of Figure 5.3. We find the following:

- $x_1 \Vdash q$, since $q \in L(x_1)$.
- $x_1 \Vdash \Diamond q$, for there is a world related to x_1 (namely, x_2) which satisfies q. In mathematical notation: $R(x_1, x_2)$ and $x_2 \Vdash q$.
- $x_1 \nVdash \Box q$, however. This is because $x_1 \Vdash \Box q$ says that all worlds related to x_1 (i.e. x_2 and x_3) satisfy q; but x_3 does not.
- $x_5 \nVdash \Box p$ and $x_5 \nVdash \Box q$. Moreover, $x_5 \nVdash \Box p \vee \Box q$. However, $x_5 \Vdash \Box (p \vee q)$.

  To see these facts, note that the worlds related to x_5 are x_4 and x_6. Since $x_4 \nVdash p$, we have $x_5 \nVdash \Box p$; and since $x_6 \nVdash q$, we have $x_5 \nVdash \Box q$. Therefore, we get that $x_5 \nVdash \Box p \vee \Box q$. However, $x_5 \Vdash \Box (p \vee q)$ holds because, in each of x_4 and x_6, we find p or q.

---

[1] Note that 'related world' suggests a symmetry which is not present in this semantics. The meaning of the box and diamond modalities at x is defined via all worlds y with xRy rather than the other way around.

- The worlds which satisfy $\Box p \to p$ are x_2, x_3, x_4, x_5 and x_6; for x_2, x_3 and x_6 this is so since they already satisfy p; for x_4 this is true since it does not satisfy $\Box p$ (we have $R(x_4, x_5)$ and x_5 does not satisfy p); a similar reason applies to x_5. As for x_1, it cannot satisfy $\Box p \to p$ since it satisfies $\Box p$ but not p itself.

Worlds like x_6 that have nothing related to them deserve special attention in modal logic. Observe that $x_6 \nVdash \Diamond \phi$, no matter what ϕ is, because $\Diamond \phi$ says '*there is* a related world which satisfies ϕ'. In particular, '*there is a related world*', which in the case of x_6 there is not. Even when ϕ is $\top$, we have $x_6 \nVdash \Diamond \top$. So, although $\top$ is satisfied in every world, $\Diamond \top$ is not necessarily. In fact, $x \Vdash \Diamond \top$ holds iff x has at least one related world.

A dual situation exists for the satisfaction of $\Box \phi$ in worlds with no related world. No matter what ϕ is, we find that $x_6 \Vdash \Box \phi$. That is because $x_6 \Vdash \Box \phi$ says that ϕ is true in *all the worlds related to* ϕ. There are no such worlds, so ϕ is vacuously true in all of them: there is simply nothing to check. This reading of 'for all related worlds' may seem surprising, but it secures the de Morgan rules for the box and diamond modalities shown below. Even $\Box \bot$ is true in x_6. If you wanted to convince someone that $\Box \bot$ was not true in x_6, you'd have to show that there is a world related to x_6 in which $\bot$ is not true; but you can't do this, for there are no worlds related to x_6. So again, although $\bot$ is false in every world, $\Box \bot$ might not be false. In fact, $x \Vdash \Box \bot$ holds iff x has no related worlds.

Formulas and formula schemes

The grammar in Definition 5.1 specifies exactly the formulas of basic modal logic, given a set of atomic formulas. For example, $p \to \Box \Diamond p$ is such a formula. It is sometimes useful to talk about a whole family of formulas which have the same 'shape'; these are called *formula schemes*. For example, $\phi \to \Box \Diamond \phi$ is a formula scheme. Any formula which has the shape of a certain formula scheme is called an *instance* of the scheme. For example,

- $p \to \Box \Diamond p$,
- $q \to \Box \Diamond q$ and
- $(p \wedge \Diamond q) \to \Box \Diamond (p \wedge \Diamond q)$

are instances of the scheme $\phi \to \Box \Diamond \phi$. An example of a formula scheme of propositional logic is $\phi \wedge \psi \to \psi$. We may think of a formula scheme as an open, or under-specified, parse tree, where certain portions of the tree still need to be supplied. E.g. the tree of the formula scheme $\phi \to \Box \Diamond \phi$ is depicted in Figure 5.4.

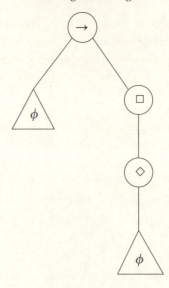

Fig. 5.4. The parse tree of the formula scheme $\phi \rightarrow \Box\Diamond\phi$.

Semantically, a scheme can be thought of as the conjunction of all its instances (since there are generally infinitely many such instances, this cannot be carried out syntactically!). We say that a world/model satisfies a scheme if it satisfies all its instances. Note that an instance being satisfied in a Kripke model does not imply that the whole scheme is satisfied. For example, we may have a Kripke model in which all worlds satisfy $\neg p \vee q$, but at least one world does not satisfy $\neg q \vee p$; the scheme $\neg\phi \vee \psi$ is not satisfied.

Equivalences between modal formulas

Definition 5.7 We say that a set of formulas Γ of basic modal logic *semantically entails* a formula ϕ of basic modal logic if, in any world x of any model $\mathcal{M} = (W, R, L)$, we have $x \Vdash \phi$ whenever $x \Vdash \psi$ for all $\psi \in \Gamma$. In that case, we write $\Gamma \vDash \phi$. We say that ϕ and ψ are *semantically equivalent* if $\phi \vDash \psi$ and $\psi \vDash \phi$ hold. We denote this by $\phi \equiv \psi$.

Note that $\phi \equiv \psi$ holds iff any world in any model which satisfies one of them also satisfies the other. The definition of semantic equivalence is based on semantic entailment in the same way as the corresponding one for formulas of propositional logic. However, the underlying notion of semantic entailment for modal logic quite different, as we will see shortly.

Any equivalence in propositional logic is also an equivalence in modal logic. Indeed, if we take any equivalence in propositional logic and substitute the atoms uniformly for any modal logic formula, the result is also an equivalence in modal logic. For example, take the equivalent formulas $p \rightarrow \neg q$ and $\neg(p \wedge q)$ and now perform the substitution

$$p \mapsto \Box p \wedge (q \rightarrow p)$$
$$q \mapsto r \rightarrow \Diamond (q \vee p).$$

The result of this substitution is the pair of formulas

$$\Box p \wedge (q \rightarrow p) \rightarrow \neg (r \rightarrow \Diamond (q \vee p))$$
$$\neg((\Box p \wedge (q \rightarrow p)) \wedge (r \rightarrow \Diamond (q \vee p)))$$

which are equivalent as formulas of unary modal logic.

We have already noticed that $\Box$ is a universal quantifier on worlds and $\Diamond$ is the corresponding existential quantifier. In view of these facts, it is not surprising to find that de Morgan rules apply for $\Box$ and $\Diamond$:

$$\neg \Box \phi \equiv \Diamond \neg \phi \text{ and } \neg \Diamond \phi \equiv \Box \neg \phi.$$

Moreover, $\Box$ distributes over $\wedge$ and $\Diamond$ distributes over $\vee$:

$$\Box(\phi \wedge \psi) \equiv \Box \phi \wedge \Box \psi \text{ and } \Diamond(\phi \vee \psi) \equiv \Diamond \phi \vee \Diamond \psi.$$

It is also not surprising to find that $\Box$ does *not* distribute over $\vee$ and $\Diamond$ does *not* distribute over $\wedge$, i.e. we do not have equivalences between $\Box(\phi \vee \psi)$ and $\Box \phi \vee \Box \psi$, or between $\Diamond(\phi \wedge \psi)$ and $\Diamond \phi \wedge \Diamond \psi$. For example, in the fourth item of Example 5.6 we had $x_5 \Vdash \Box(p \vee q)$ and $x_5 \nVdash \Box p \vee \Box q$. These equivalences correspond closely to the quantifier equivalences discussed in Section 2.3.2.

Note that $\Box \top$ is equivalent to $\top$, but *not* to $\Diamond \top$, as we saw earlier. Similarly, $\Diamond \bot \equiv \bot$ but they are not equivalent to $\Box \bot$.

Another equivalence is $\Diamond \top \equiv \Box p \rightarrow \Diamond p$. For suppose $x \Vdash \Diamond \top$ (i.e. x has a related world, say y) and suppose $x \Vdash \Box p$; then $y \Vdash p$, so $x \Vdash \Diamond p$. Conversely, suppose $x \Vdash \Box p \rightarrow \Diamond p$; we must show it satisfies $\Diamond \top$. Let us distinguish between the cases $x \Vdash \Box p$ and $x \nVdash \Box p$; in the former, we get $x \Vdash \Diamond p$ so x must have a related world; and in the latter, x must again have a related world in order to avoid satisfying $\Box p$. Either way, x has a related world, i.e. satisfies $\Diamond \top$. Naturally, this argument works for any formula ϕ, not just an atom p.

Valid formulas

Definition 5.8 A formula of basic modal logic is said to be *valid* if it is true in every world of every model, i.e. iff $\vDash \phi$.

Any propositional tautology is a valid formula and so is any substitution instance of it. (A substitution instance of a formula is the result of uniformly substituting the atoms of the formula by other formulas.) For example, since $p \vee \neg p$ is a tautology, we may perform the substitution

$$p \mapsto \Box p \wedge (q \to p)$$

and obtain the valid formula $(\Box p \wedge (q \to p)) \vee \neg(\Box p \wedge (q \to p))$.

As we may expect from equivalences above, the following are valid formulas:

- $\neg\Box\phi \leftrightarrow \Diamond\neg\phi$
- $\Box(\phi \wedge \psi) \leftrightarrow \Box\phi \wedge \Box\psi$
- $\Diamond(\phi \vee \psi) \leftrightarrow \Diamond\phi \vee \Diamond\psi$.

To prove that the first of these is valid, we reason as follows. Suppose x is a world in a model $\mathcal{M} = (W, R, L)$. We want to show $x \Vdash \neg\Box\phi \leftrightarrow \Diamond\neg\phi$, i.e. that $x \Vdash \neg\Box\phi$ iff $x \Vdash \Diamond\neg\phi$. Well, using Definition 5.4,

> $x \Vdash \neg\Box\phi$
>> iff it isn't the case that $x \Vdash \Box\phi$
>> iff it isn't the case that, for all y such that $R(x, y)$, $y \Vdash \phi$
>> iff there is some y such that $R(x, y)$ and not $y \Vdash \phi$
>> iff there is some y such that $R(x, y)$ and $y \Vdash \neg\phi$
>> iff $x \Vdash \Diamond\neg\phi$.

Proofs that the other two are valid are similarly routine and left as exercises.

Another important formula which can be seen to be valid is the following:

$$\Box(\phi \to \psi) \wedge \Box\phi \to \Box\psi.$$

It is sometimes written in the equivalent (but slightly less intuitive) form

$$\Box(\phi \to \psi) \to (\Box\phi \to \Box\psi).$$

This formula scheme is called K in most books about modal logic, honouring the logician S. Kripke who, as we mentioned earlier, invented the so-called 'possible worlds semantics' which we described.

To see that K is valid, again suppose we have some world x in some model $\mathcal{M} = (W, R, L)$. We have to show that $x \Vdash \Box(\phi \to \psi) \wedge \Box\phi \to \Box\psi$. Again referring to Definition 5.4, we assume that $x \Vdash \Box(\phi \to \psi) \wedge \Box\phi$ and try to prove that $x \Vdash \Box\psi$:

> $x \Vdash \Box(\phi \to \psi) \wedge \Box\phi$
>> iff $x \Vdash \Box(\phi \to \psi)$ and $x \Vdash \Box\phi$
>>> iff for all y with $R(x, y)$, we have $y \Vdash \phi \to \psi$ and $y \Vdash \phi$
>> implies that, for all y with $R(x, y)$, we have $y \Vdash \psi$
>>> iff $x \Vdash \Box\psi$.

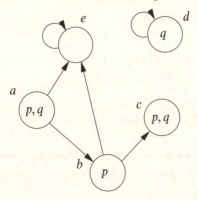

Fig. 5.5. Another Kripke model.

There aren't any other interesting valid formulas in the basic system of modal logic. Later, we will see additional valid formulas in particular extended systems of interest.

EXERCISES 5.1

1. Consider the Kripke model $\mathcal{M}$ depicted in Figure 5.5. For each of the following, calculate whether it is true, or false:

      (a) $a \Vdash p$

      (b) $a \Vdash \Box\neg q$

  * (c) $a \Vdash q$

  * (d) $a \Vdash \Box\Box q$

      (e) $a \Vdash \Diamond p$

  * (f) $a \Vdash \Box\Diamond\neg q$

      (g) $c \Vdash \Diamond\top$

      (h) $d \Vdash \Diamond\top$

      (i) $d \Vdash \Box\Box q$

  * (j) $c \Vdash \Box\bot$

      (k) $b \Vdash \Box\bot$

      (l) $a \Vdash \Diamond\Diamond(p \wedge q) \wedge \Diamond\top$.

2. Using the same model, find for each of the following a world which satisfies it:

      (a) $\Box\neg p \wedge \Box\Box\neg p$

      (b) $\Diamond q \wedge \neg\Box q$

  * (c) $\Diamond p \vee \Diamond q$

  * (d) $\Diamond(p \vee \Diamond q)$

      (e) $\Box p \vee \Box\neg p$

      (f) $\Box(p \vee \neg p)$.

3. Like the previous question, but find a world which does *not* satisfy the formula.

4. Find a Kripke model $\mathcal{M}$ and a formula scheme which is not satisfied in $\mathcal{M}$, but which has true instances in $\mathcal{M}$.

5. Consider the Kripke model given thus: $\mathcal{M} = (W, R, L)$, where $W = \{a, b, c, d, e\}$ and $R = \{(a, c), (a, e), (b, a), (b, c), (d, e), (e, a)\}$, with $L(a) = \{p\}$, $L(b) = \{p, q\}$, $L(c) = \{p, q\}$, $L(d) = \{q\}$ and $L(e) = \emptyset$. Investigate which of the formulas in Exercise 2 have a world which satisfies it.

6.   (a) Think about what you have to do to decide whether $p \to \Box \Diamond q$ is true in a model.

   * (b) Find a model in which it is true and one in which it is false.

7. For each of the following pairs of formulas, can you find a model and a world in it which *distinguishes them*, i.e. makes one of them true and one false? (Thus, you are showing that they do not entail each other.) If you cannot, it might mean that the formulas are equivalent. Justify your answer.

   (a) $\Box p$ and $\Box \Box p$
   (b) $\Box \neg p$ and $\neg \Diamond p$
   (c) $\Box (p \wedge q)$ and $\Box p \wedge \Box q$
   * (d) $\Diamond (p \wedge q)$ and $\Diamond p \wedge \Diamond q$
   (e) $\Box (p \vee q)$ and $\Box p \vee \Box q$
   * (f) $\Diamond (p \vee q)$ and $\Diamond p \vee \Diamond q$
   (g) $\Box (p \to q)$ and $\Box p \to \Box q$
   (h) $\Diamond \top$ and $\top$
   (i) $\Box \top$ and $\top$
   (j) $\Diamond \bot$ and $\bot$.

8. Show that the following formulas of basic modal logic are valid:

   * (a) $\Box (\phi \wedge \psi) \leftrightarrow (\Box \phi \wedge \Box \psi)$
   (b) $\Diamond (\phi \vee \psi) \leftrightarrow (\Diamond \phi \vee \Diamond \psi)$
   * (c) $\Box \top \leftrightarrow \top$
   (d) $\Diamond \bot \leftrightarrow \bot$.

9. Inspect Definition 5.4. We said that we defined $x \Vdash \phi$ by structural induction on ϕ. Is this really correct? Note the implicit definition of a second relation $x \nVdash \phi$. Why is this definition still correct and in what sense does it still rely on structural induction?

5.3 Logic engineering

Having looked at the framework for basic modal logic, we turn now to how one may formalise the different modes of truth discussed at the beginning of this chapter. The basic framework is quite general and can be refined in various ways to give us the properties appropriate for the intended applications. Logic engineering is the subject of engineering logics to fit new applications. It is potentially a very broad subject, drawing on all branches of logic, computer science and mathematics. In this chapter, however, we are restricting ourselves to the particular engineering of modal logics.

We will consider how to engineer the basic framework for modal logic to fit the following readings of $\Box\phi$:

- It is necessarily true that ϕ
- It will always be true that ϕ
- It ought to be that ϕ
- Agent Q believes that ϕ
- Agent Q knows that ϕ
- After any execution of program P, ϕ holds.

As modal logic automatically gives us the connective $\Diamond$, which is equivalent to $\neg\Box\neg$, we can find out what the corresponding readings of $\Diamond$ in our system will be. For example, 'it is *not* necessarily true that *not* ϕ' means that it is possibly true that ϕ. You could work this out in steps:

> It is *not* necessarily true that ϕ
> $=$ it is possible that *not* ϕ.

Therefore,

> It is *not* necessarily true that *not* ϕ
> $=$ it is possible that *not not* ϕ
> $=$ it is possible that ϕ.

Let us work it out with the reading 'agent Q knows ϕ' for $\Box\phi$. Then, $\Diamond\phi$ is read as

> agent Q does *not* know *not* ϕ
> $=$ as far as Q's knowledge is concerned, ϕ could be the case
> $=$ ϕ is consistent with what agent Q knows
> $=$ for all agent Q knows, ϕ.

The readings for $\Diamond$ for the other modes are given in Table 5.6.

$\Box\phi$	$\Diamond\phi$
It is necessarily true that ϕ	It is possibly true that ϕ
It will always be true that ϕ	Sometime in the future ϕ
It ought to be that ϕ	It is permitted to be that ϕ
Agent Q believes that ϕ	ϕ is consistent with Q's beliefs
Agent Q knows that ϕ	For all Q knows, ϕ
After any execution of program P, ϕ holds	After some execution of P, ϕ holds

Table 5.6. *The readings of $\Diamond$ corresponding to each reading of $\Box$.*

5.3.1 The stock of valid formulas

We saw in the last section some valid formulas of basic modal logic, such as instances of the axiom scheme K:

$$\Box(\phi \to \psi) \to (\Box\phi \to \Box\psi)$$

and of the schemes

$$\neg\Box\phi \leftrightarrow \Diamond\neg\phi$$
$$\Box(\phi \wedge \psi) \leftrightarrow \Box\phi \wedge \Box\psi$$
$$\Diamond(\phi \vee \psi) \leftrightarrow \Diamond\phi \vee \Diamond\psi.$$

Many other formulas, such as these ones:

- $\Box p \to p$
- $\Box p \to \Box\Box p$
- $\neg\Box p \to \Box\neg\Box p$
- $\Diamond\top$

are *not* valid. For example, for each one of these, there is a world in the Kripke model of Figure 5.3 which does not satisfy the formula. The world x_1 satisfies $\Box p$, but it does not satisfy p, so it does not satisfy $\Box p \to p$. If we add $R(x_1, x_2)$ to our model, then x_1 also does not satisfy $\Box\Box p$, it also fails to satisfy $\Box p \to \Box\Box p$. If we set $L(x_4) = \{p, q\}$, then x_4 does not satisfy $\neg\Box p \to \Box\neg\Box p$, because it satisfies $\neg\Box p$, but it does not satisfy $\Box\neg\Box p$ (the path $x_4 R x_5 R x_4$ serves as a counter example). Finally, x_6 does not satisfy $\Diamond\top$, for this formula states that there is a related world satisfying $\top$. However, there is no world related to x_6.

If we are to build a logic capturing the concept of necessity, however, we must surely have that $\Box p \to p$ is valid; for anything which is *necessarily true* is also simply true. Similarly, we would expect $\Box p \to p$ to be valid in the case that $\Box p$ means 'agent Q knows p', for anything which is known must

$\Box\phi$	$\Box\phi \to \phi$	$\Box\phi \to \Box\Box\phi$	$\Diamond\phi \to \Box\Diamond\phi$	$\Box\top$	$\Box\phi \to \Diamond\phi$	$\Diamond\phi \lor \Box\neg\phi$	$\Box(\phi\to\psi) \land \Box\phi \to \Box\psi$	$\Box\phi \land \Box\psi \to \Box(\phi\land\psi)$
It is necessarily true that ϕ	√	√	√	√	√	×	√	×
It will always be true that ϕ	×	√	×	×	×	×	√	×
It ought to be that ϕ	×	×	×	√	√	×	√	×
Agent Q believes that ϕ	×	√	√	√	√	×	√	×
Agent Q knows that ϕ	√	√	√	√	√	×	√	×
After any execution of program P, ϕ holds	×	×	×	×	×	×	√	×

Table 5.7. *Which formula schemes are valid for the various readings of* $\Box$?

also be true. We cannot *know* something which is false. We can, however, *believe* falsehoods, so in the case of a logic of belief, we would *not* expect $\Box p \to p$ to be valid.

Part of the job of logic engineering is to determine what formula schemes should be valid and to craft the logic in such a way that precisely those ones are valid.

Table 5.7 shows six interesting readings for $\Box$ and eight formula schemes. For each reading and each formula scheme, we decide whether we should expect the scheme to be valid. Notice that we should only put a tick if the formula should be valid for all cases of ϕ and ψ. If it could be valid for some cases, but not for others, we put a cross.

There are many points worth noting about Table 5.7. First, observe that it is rather debatable whether to put a tick, or a cross, in some of the cells. We need to be precise about the concept of truth we are trying to formalise, in order to resolve any ambiguity.

Necessity. When we ask ourselves whether $\Box\phi \to \Box\Box\phi$ and $\Diamond\phi \to \Box\Diamond\phi$ should be valid, it seems to depend on what notion of necessity we are referring to. These formulas are valid if that which is necessary is *necessarily* necessary. If we are dealing with *physical necessity*, then this amounts to: are the laws of the universe themselves physically necessary, i.e. do they entail that they should be the laws of the universe? The answer seems to be no. However, if we meant *logical necessity*, it seems that we should give the answer yes, for the laws of logic are meant to be those assertions whose truth cannot be denied. The row is filled on the understanding that we mean logical necessity.

Always in the future. We must be precise about whether or not the future includes the present; this is precisely what the formula $\Box\phi \rightarrow \phi$ states. It is a matter of convention whether the future includes the present, or not. In Chapter 3, we saw that CTL adopts the convention that it does. For variety, therefore, let us assume that the future does not include the present in this row of the table. That means that $\Box\phi \rightarrow \phi$ fails. What about $\Diamond\top$? It says that there is a future world in which $\top$ is true. In particular, then, there is a future world, i.e. time has no end. Whether we regard this as true or not depends on exactly what notion of 'the future' we are trying to model. We assumed the validity of $\Diamond\top$ in Chapter 3 on CTL since this resulted in an easier presentation of our model-checking algorithms, but we might choose to model it otherwise, as in Figure 5.7.

Ought. In this case the formulas $\Box\phi \rightarrow \Box\Box\phi$ and $\Diamond\phi \rightarrow \Box\Diamond\phi$ state that the moral codes we adopt are themselves forced upon us by morality. This seems not to be the case; for example, we may believe that *It ought to be the case that we wear a seat-belt*, but this does not compel us to believe that *It ought to be the case that we ought to wear a seat-belt*. However, anything which ought to be so should be permitted to be so; therefore, $\Box\phi \rightarrow \Diamond\phi$.

Belief. To decide whether $\Diamond\top$, let us express it as $\neg\Box\bot$, for this is semantically equivalent. It says that agent Q does not believe any contradictions. Here we must be precise about whether we are modelling human beings, with all their foibles and often plainly contradictory beliefs, or whether we are modelling idealised agents that are logically omniscient (i.e. capable of working out the logical consequences of their beliefs). We opt to model the latter concept. The same issue arises when we consider, for example, $\Diamond\phi \rightarrow \Box\Diamond\phi$, which (when we rewrite it as $\neg\Box\psi \rightarrow \Box\neg\Box\psi$) says that, if agent Q doesn't believe something, then he believes that he doesn't believe it. Validity of the formula $\Box\phi \vee \Box\neg\phi$ would mean that Q has an opinion on every matter; we suppose this is unlikely. What about $\Diamond\phi \wedge \Diamond\psi \rightarrow \Diamond(\phi \wedge \psi)$? Let us rewrite it as $\neg\Diamond(\phi \wedge \psi) \rightarrow \neg(\Diamond\phi \wedge \Diamond\psi)$, i.e. $\Box(\neg\phi \vee \neg\psi) \rightarrow (\Box\neg\phi \vee \Box\neg\psi)$, or, if we subsume the negations into the ϕ and ψ, $\Box(\phi \vee \psi) \rightarrow (\Box\phi \vee \Box\psi)$. This seems not to be valid, for agent Q could find herself or himself in a situation in which she or he believes that there is a key in the red box, or in the green box, without believing that it is in the red box and also without believing that it is in the green box.

Knowledge. It seems to differ from belief only in respect of the first formula in Table 5.7; while agent Q can have false beliefs, he can only *know* that which is true. In the case of knowledge, the formulas $\Box\phi \to \Box\Box\phi$ and $\neg\Box\psi \to \Box\neg\Box\psi$ are called *positive introspection* and *negative introspection*, respectively, since they state that the agent can introspect upon her knowledge; if she knows something, she knows that she knows it; and if she does not know something, she again knows that she doesn't know it. Clearly, this represents *idealised* knowledge, since most humans (with all their hang-ups and infelicities) do not satisfy these properties. The formula scheme K is sometimes referred to as *logical omniscience* in the logic of knowledge, since it says that the agent's knowledge is closed under logical consequence. This means that the agent knows all the consequences of anything he knows, which is unfortunately (or fortunately?) true only for idealised agents, not humans.

Execution of programs. Not many of our formulas seem to hold in this case. The scheme $\Box\phi \to \Box\Box\phi$ says that running the program twice is the same as running it once, which is plainly wrong in the case of a program which deducts money from your bank account. $\Diamond\top$ says that there is an execution of the program which terminates; this is false for some programs.

The formulas $\Diamond\top$ and $\Box\phi \to \Diamond\phi$ were seen to be equivalent in the preceding section and, indeed, we see that they get the same pattern of ticks and crosses. We can also show that $\Box\phi \to \phi$ entails $\Diamond\top$ (i.e. $(\Box\phi \to \phi) \to \Diamond\top$ is valid), so whenever the former gets a tick, so should the latter. This is indeed the case, as you can verify in Table 5.7.

EXERCISES 5.2

1. Show that $\Diamond\top \to (\Box\phi \to \Diamond\phi)$ is a valid formula of basic modal logic.
2. For which of the readings of $\Box$ in Table 5.7 are the formulas below valid?

* (a) $(\phi \to \Box\phi) \to (\phi \to \Diamond\phi)$;
  (b) $(\Box\phi \to (\phi \land \Box\Box\phi \land \Diamond\phi)) \to ((\Box\phi \to (\phi \land \Box\Box\phi)) \land (\Diamond\phi \to \Box\Diamond\phi))$.

5.3.2 Important properties of the accessibility relation

So far, we have been engineering logics at the level of deciding what formulas should be valid for the various readings of $\Box$. We can also engineer at the level of Kripke models. For each of our seven readings of $\Box$, there is a corresponding reading of the accessibility relation R. Moreover, for some

$\Box\phi$	$R(x,y)$
It is necessarily true that ϕ	y is possible according to the information at x
It will always be true that ϕ	y is in the future of x
It ought to be that ϕ	y is acceptable according to the information at x
Agent Q believes that ϕ	y could be the actual world according to Q's beliefs at x
Agent Q knows that ϕ	y could be the actual world according to Q's knowledge at x
After any execution of P, ϕ holds	y is a possible resulting state after execution of P at x

Table 5.8. *For each reading of $\Box$, the meaning of R is given.*

readings it will make sense to stipulate that R is reflexive, or transitive, or has some other properties.

Let us start with necessity. The clauses

$$x \Vdash \Box\psi \quad \text{iff for each } y \in W \text{ with } R(x,y) \text{ we have } y \Vdash \psi$$
$$x \Vdash \Diamond\psi \quad \text{iff there is a } y \in W \text{ such that } R(x,y) \text{ and } y \Vdash \psi$$

from Definition 5.4 tell us that ϕ is necessarily true at x if ϕ is true in all worlds y related to x in a certain way; but related in what way? Intuitively, necessarily ϕ is true if ϕ is true in all *possible* worlds; so $R(x,y)$ should be interpreted as meaning that y is a possible world according to the information in x.

In the case of knowledge, we think of $R(x,y)$ as saying: y could be the actual world according to agent Q's knowledge at x. In other words, if the actual world is x, then agent Q (who is not omniscient) cannot rule out the possibility of it being y. If we plug this definition into the clause above for $x \Vdash \Box\phi$, we find that agent Q knows ϕ iff ϕ is true in all the worlds that, for all he knows, could be the actual world. The meaning of R for each of the seven readings of $\Box$ is shown in Table 5.8.

Recall that a given binary relation R may be:

- *reflexive*: if, for every $x \in W$, we have $R(x,x)$.
- *symmetric*: if, for every $x,y \in W$, we have $R(x,y)$ implies $R(y,x)$.
- *serial*: if, for every x there is a y such that $R(x,y)$.

- *transitive*: if, for every $x, y, z \in W$, we have $R(x, y)$ and $R(y, z)$ imply $R(x, z)$.
- *Euclidean*: if, for every $x, y, z \in W$ with $R(x, y)$ and $R(x, z)$, we have $R(y, z)$).
- *functional*: if, for each x there is a unique y such that $R(x, y)$.
- *linear*: if, for every $x, y, z \in W$, we have that $(R(x, y)$ and $R(x, z))$ together imply that $R(y, z)$, or y equals z, or $R(z, y)$.
- *total*: if for every $x, y \in W$ we have $R(x, y)$ or $R(y, x)$.
- (an *equivalence relation*, if it is reflexive, symmetric and transitive.)

Now, let us consider this question: according to the various readings of R, which of these properties do we expect R to have?

Example 5.9 If $\Box\phi$ means 'agent Q knows ϕ', then $R(x, y)$ means y could be the actual world according to Q's knowledge at x.

- Should R be reflexive? This would say: x could be the actual world according to Q's knowledge at x. In other words, Q cannot know that things are different from how they really are — i.e., *Q cannot have false knowledge*. This is a desirable property for R to have. Moreover, it seems to rest on the same intuition (i.e. the impossibility of false knowledge) as the validity of the formula $\Box\phi \to \phi$. Indeed, the validity of this formula and the property of reflexivity are closely related, as we see in the next section.
- Should R be transitive? It would say: if y is possible according to Q's knowledge at x and z is possible according to her knowledge at y, then z is possible according to her knowledge at x.

  Well, this seems to be true. For suppose it was not true, i.e. at x she knew something preventing z from being the real world. Then, *she would know she knew this thing* at x; therefore, she would know something at y which prevented z from being the real world; which contradicts our premise.

  In this argument, we relied on positive introspection, i.e. the formula $\Box\phi \to \Box\Box\phi$. Again, we will shortly see that there is a close correspondence between R being transitive and the validity of this formula.

EXERCISES 5.3
* 1. Let R be the relation *strictly less than* on the set of all natural numbers $n \geq 1$. Determine which of the properties *reflexive* through to *total* apply to this R.
  2. Repeat exercise 1. with the following choices of sets and relations:

(a) Let xRy mean that x divides y, where x and y range over integers (e.g. 5 divides 15, whereas 7 does not).

(b) Let xRy mean that x is a brother of y.

(c) Let xRy mean that there exist positive real numbers a and b such that x equals $a \cdot y + b$, where x and y range over real numbers.

———

5.3.3 Correspondence theory

We saw in the preceding section that there appeared to be a correspondence between the validity of $\Box\phi \rightarrow \phi$ and the property that the accessibility relation R is reflexive. The connection between them is that both relied on the intuition that anything which is known by an agent is true. Moreover, there also seemed to be a correspondence between $\Box\phi \rightarrow \Box\Box\phi$ and R being transitive; they both seem to assert the property of *positive introspection*, i.e. that which is known is known to be known.

In this section, we will see that there is a precise mathematical relationship between these formulas and properties of R. Indeed, to every formula scheme there corresponds a property of R. From the point of view of logic engineering, it is important to see this relationship, because it helps one to understand the logic being studied. For example, if you believe that a certain formula scheme should be accepted in the system of modal logic you are engineering, then it is well worth looking at the corresponding property of R and checking that that makes sense for the application, too. Alternatively, for some formulas it may seem difficult to understand what they are really saying, so looking at the corresponding property of R can help.

To state the relationship between formula schemes and their corresponding properties, we need the notion of a (modal) frame.

Definition 5.10 A *frame* $\mathscr{F} = (W, R)$ is a set W (of worlds) and a binary relation R on W.

A frame is like a Kripke model (Definition 5.3), except that it has no labelling function. From any model we can extract a frame, by just forgetting about the labelling function; for example, Figure 5.9 shows the frame extracted from the Kripke model of Figure 5.3. A frame is just a set of 'points' and the relationship between them. It has no information about what atomic formulas are true at the various points. However, it is useful to say sometimes that the frame, as a whole, satisfies a formula. This is defined as follows.

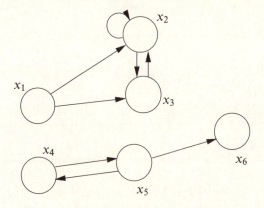

Fig. 5.9. The frame of the model in Figure 5.3.

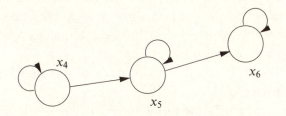

Fig. 5.10. Another frame.

Definition 5.11 A frame $\mathscr{F} = (W, R)$ satisfies a formula of basic modal logic ϕ, written $\mathscr{F} \vDash \phi$, if, for each labelling function L and each $w \in W$, we have $\mathscr{M}, w \Vdash \phi$, where $\mathscr{M} = (W, R, L)$ (recall Definition 5.4 for $\mathscr{M}, w \Vdash \phi$).

One can show that, if a frame satisfies a formula, then it also satisfies every substitution instance of that formula. Indeed, if a frame satisfies an instance of a formula scheme, then it satisfies the whole scheme. This contrasts markedly with models. For example, the model of Figure 5.3 satisfies $p \vee \Diamond p \vee \Diamond \Diamond p$, but it does not satisfy every instance of $\phi \vee \Diamond \phi \vee \Diamond \Diamond \phi$; for example, x_6 does not satisfy $q \vee \Diamond q \vee \Diamond \Diamond q$; but because frames do not contain any information about the truth or falsity of propositional atoms, they can't distinguish between different atoms; so, if a frame satisfies a formula, it also satisfies the formula scheme obtained by substituting the p, q etc. by ϕ, ψ etc.

Examples 5.12 Consider the frame $\mathscr{F}$ in Figure 5.10.

- $\mathscr{F}$ satisfies the formula $\Box p \rightarrow p$. To see this, we have to consider any

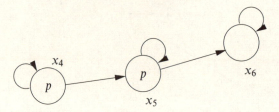

Fig. 5.11. A model.

labelling function of the frame (there are eight such labelling functions, since p could be true or false in each of the three worlds) and show that each world satisfies the formula for each labelling. Rather than really doing this literally, let us give a generic argument: let x be any world. Suppose that $x \Vdash \Box p$; we want to show $x \Vdash p$. We know that $R(x, x)$ because each x is related to itself in the diagram; so, it follows from the clause for $\Box$ in Definition 5.4 that $x \Vdash p$.

- Therefore, our frame $\mathscr{F}$ satisfies any formula of this shape, i.e. it satisfies the formula scheme $\Box \phi \to \phi$.
- The frame does not satisfy the formula $\Box p \to \Box \Box p$. For suppose we take the labelling of Figure 5.11; then $x_4 \Vdash \Box p$, but $x_4 \not\Vdash \Box \Box p$.

If you think about why the frame of Figure 5.10 satisfied $\Box p \to p$ and why it did not satisfy $\Box p \to \Box \Box p$, you will probably guess the following:

Theorem 5.13 *Let $\mathscr{F} = (W, R)$ be a frame.*

1. *The following statements are equivalent:*
   - R *is reflexive;*
   - $\mathscr{F}$ *satisfies* $\Box \phi \to \phi$*;*
   - $\mathscr{F}$ *satisfies* $\Box p \to p$*;*

2. *The following statements are equivalent:*
   - R *is transitive;*
   - $\mathscr{F}$ *satisfies* $\Box \phi \to \Box \Box \phi$*;*
   - $\mathscr{F}$ *satisfies* $\Box p \to \Box \Box p$*.*

PROOF: For each of the cases, there are three things to prove: (a) that, if R has the property, then the frame satisfies the formula scheme; and (b) that, if the frame satisfies the formula scheme then it satisfies the instance of it; and (c) that, if the frame satisfies the formula, then R has the property.

1. (a) Suppose R is reflexive. Let L be a labelling function, so now $\mathcal{M} = (W, R, L)$ is a model of basic modal logic. We need to show $\mathcal{M} \models \Box\phi \to \phi$. That means we need to show $x \Vdash \Box\phi \to \phi$ for any $x \in W$, so pick any x. Use the clause for implication in Definition 5.4. Suppose $x \Vdash \Box\phi$; since $R(x, x)$, it immediately follows from the clause for $\Box$ in Definition 5.4 that $x \Vdash p$. Therefore, we have shown $x \Vdash \Box\phi \to \phi$.

   (b) We just set ϕ to be p.

   (c) Suppose the frame satisfies $\Box p \to p$. Take any x; we're going to show $R(x, x)$.

   Take a labelling function L such that $p \notin L(x)$ and $p \in L(y)$ for all worlds y except x. Suppose we don't have $R(x, x)$. Then, $x \Vdash \Box p$, since all the worlds related to x satisfy p (this is because all the worlds except x satisfy p); but since $\mathscr{F}$ satisfies $\Box p \to p$, it follows that $x \Vdash \Box p \to p$; therefore, putting $x \Vdash \Box p$ and $x \Vdash \Box p \to p$ together, we get $x \Vdash p$. This is a contradiction, since we said that $p \notin L(x)$. We got this contradiction just by assuming that we didn't have $R(x, x)$. So this assumption cannot be made. It must be that $R(x, x)$ holds in our frame!

2. (a) Suppose R is transitive. Let L be a labelling function and $\mathcal{M} = (W, R, L)$. We need to show $M \Vdash \Box\phi \to \Box\Box\phi$. That means we need to show $x \Vdash \Box\phi \to \Box\Box\phi$ for any $x \in W$, so pick any x. Suppose $x \Vdash \Box\phi$; we need to show $x \Vdash \Box\Box\phi$. That is, using the clause for $\Box$ in Definition 5.4, that any y such that $R(x, y)$ satisfies $\Box\phi$; that is, for any y, z with $R(x, y)$ and $R(y, z)$, we have $z \Vdash \phi$.

   Well, suppose we did have y and z with $R(x, y)$ and $R(y, z)$. By the fact that R is transitive, we obtain $R(x, z)$. But we're supposing that $x \Vdash \Box\phi$, so (clause for $\Box$) that means $z \Vdash \phi$, which is what we needed to prove.

   (b) Again, just set ϕ to be p.

   (c) Suppose the frame satisfies $\Box p \to \Box\Box p$. Take any x, y and z with $R(x, y)$ and $R(y, z)$; we are going to show $R(x, z)$.

   Take a labelling function L such that $p \notin L(z)$ and $p \in L(w)$ for all worlds w except z. Suppose we don't have $R(x, z)$; then $x \Vdash \Box p$, since $w \Vdash p$ for all $w \neq z$. Using the axiom $\Box p \to \Box\Box p$, it follows that $x \Vdash \Box\Box p$; i.e., $y \Vdash \Box p$ (since $R(x, y)$), i.e., $z \Vdash p$ (since $R(y, z)$). So we get a contradiction. Thus, we must have $R(x, z)$. □

This picture is completed in Table 5.12, which shows, for a collection of

name	formula scheme	property of R
T	$\Box\phi \rightarrow \phi$	reflexive
B	$\phi \rightarrow \Box\Diamond\phi$	symmetric
D	$\Box\phi \rightarrow \Diamond\phi$	serial
4	$\Box\phi \rightarrow \Box\Box\phi$	transitive
5	$\Diamond\phi \rightarrow \Box\Diamond\phi$	Euclidean
	$\Box\phi \leftrightarrow \Diamond\phi$	functional
	$\Box(\phi \wedge \Box\phi \rightarrow \psi) \vee \Box(\psi \wedge \Box\psi \rightarrow \phi)$	linear

Table 5.12. *The property of R corresponding to some formulas.*

formulas, the corresponding property of R. What this table means mathematically is the following:

Theorem 5.14 *A frame* $\mathscr{F} = (W, R)$ *satisfies a formula scheme in Table 5.12 iff R has the corresponding property in that table.*

The names of the formulas in the left-hand column are historical, but have stuck and are still used widely in books.

5.3.4 Some modal logics

The logic engineering approach of this section encourages us to build a logic by picking and choosing among formula schemes, according to the application at hand. Some examples of formula schemes that we can consider for the given application are those in Tables 5.7 and 5.12.

Definition 5.15 A modal logic[1] L is a subset of formulas of basic modal logic, as specified in Definition 5.1, with the following properties:

1. L is closed under propositional logic. That is, anything which can be derived from members of L using propositional logic is itself a member of L.
2. L contains all instances of the formula scheme K:

$$\Box(\phi \rightarrow \psi) \rightarrow (\Box\phi \rightarrow \Box\psi).$$

3. L is closed under the *rule of necessitation*; this says that, if $\phi \in L$, then also $\Box\phi \in L$.
4. L is closed under taking substitution instances; meaning that, if ϕ is in L, then any substitution instance of ϕ is also in L.

---

[1] In the technical literature this is called a *normal* modal logic.

To build a modal logic, choose the formula schemes which you would like to have inside it. These are called the *axioms* of the logic. Then, 'close' it under the conditions of the definition.

The modal logic K

The weakest modal logic doesn't have any 'optional' formula schemes, like those of Tables 5.7 and 5.12. It just contains propositional logic and all instances of the formula scheme K, together with other formulas which come from applying conditions 3 and 4 of Definition 5.15. The name K is given to this logic (as well as being given to the formula scheme K).

The modal logic KT45

A well-known modal logic is KT45 (also called S5 in the literature), which adds three extra axioms. This is used to reason about knowledge; $\Box\phi$ means that the agent Q knows ϕ. The axioms T, 4 and 5 (see Table 5.12), respectively, tell us that

T. Truth: the agent Q knows only true things.
4. Positive introspection: if the agent Q knows something, then she knows that she knows it.
5. Negative introspection: if the agent Q doesn't know something, then she knows that she doesn't know it.

In this application, the formula scheme K means logical omniscience: the agent's knowledge is closed under logical consequence. Note that these properties represent idealisations of knowledge. Human knowledge has none of these properties! Even computer agents may not have them all. There are several attempts in the literature to define logics of knowledge that are more realistic, but we will not consider them here.

The semantics of the logic KT45 must consider only relations R which are: reflexive (T), transitive (4) and Euclidean (5). Indeed,

Fact 5.16 A relation is reflexive, transitive and Euclidean iff it is reflexive, transitive and symmetric, i.e. if it is an equivalence relation.

KT45 is simpler than K in the sense that it has few essentially different ways of composing modalities.

Theorem 5.17 *Any sequence of modal operators and negations in KT45 is equivalent to one of the following:* $-, \Box, \Diamond, \neg, \neg\Box$ *and* $\neg\Diamond$, *where* $-$ *indicated the absence of any negation or modality.*

EXERCISES 5.4

* 1. Prove the Fact 5.16.
  2. Prove Theorem 5.17. Use mathematical induction on the length of the sequence of negations and modal operators. Note that this requires a case analysis over the topmost operator other than a negation, or a modality.
  3. Prove Theorem 5.14, but for the case in which R is reflexive, or transitive.

The modal logic KT4

The modal logic KT4 is also called S4 in the literature. Correspondence theory tells us that its models are precisely the Kripke models $\mathcal{M} = (W, R, L)$, where R is reflexive and transitive. Such structures are often very useful in computer science. For example, if ϕ stands for the type of a piece of code (ϕ could be int $\times$ int $\to$ bool, indicating some code which expects a pair of integers as input and outputs a boolean value), then $\Box\phi$ could stand for *residual code* of type ϕ. Thus, in the current world x this code would not have to be executed, but could be saved (= residualised) for execution at a later computation stage. The formula scheme $\Box\phi \to \phi$, the axiom T, then means that code may be executed right away, whereas the formula scheme $\Box\phi \to \Box\Box\phi$ (the axiom 4) allows that residual code remain residual, i.e. we can repeatedly postpone its execution in future computation stages. Such type systems have important applications in the specialisation and partial evaluation of code. We refer the interested reader to the bibliographic notes at the end of the chapter.

Theorem 5.18 *Any sequence of modal operators and negations in KT4 is equivalent to one of the following: $-$, $\Box$, $\Diamond$, $\Box\Diamond$, $\Diamond\Box$, $\Box\Diamond\Box$, $\Diamond\Box\Diamond$, $\neg$, $\neg\Box$, $\neg\Diamond$, $\neg\Box\Diamond$, $\neg\Diamond\Box$, $\neg\Box\Diamond\Box$ and $\neg\Diamond\Box\Diamond$.*

Intuitionistic propositional logic

In Chapter 1, we gave a natural deduction system for propositional logic which was sound and complete with respect to semantic entailment based on truth tables. We also pointed out that the proof rules RAA, LEM and $\neg\neg$e are questionable in certain computational situations. If we disallow their usage in natural deduction proofs, we obtain a logic, called *intuitionistic propositional logic*, together with its own proof theory. So far so good; but it is less clear what sort of semantics one could have for such a logic (again with soundness and completeness in mind). This is where certain models of KT4 will do the job quite nicely. Recall that correspondence theory implies that a model $\mathcal{M} = (W, R, L)$ of KT4 is such that R is reflexive and transitive. The only additional requirement we impose on a model for intuitionistic propositional logic is that its labelling function L be *monotone* in R: xRy implies that $L(x)$ is a subset of $L(y)$. This models that atomic positive formulas persist throughout the worlds that are reachable from a given world.

Definition 5.19 A *model of intuitionistic propositional logic* is a model $\mathcal{M} = (W, R, L)$ of KT4 such that xRy always implies $L(x) \subseteq L(y)$. Given a propositional logic formula without negation, we define $x \Vdash \phi$ as in Definition 5.4 *with the exception of the interpretation of implication and negation.* For $\phi_1 \rightarrow \phi_2$ we define $x \Vdash \phi_1 \rightarrow \phi_2$ iff for all y with xRy we have $y \Vdash \phi_2$ whenever we have $y \Vdash \phi_1$. For $\neg\phi$ we define $x \Vdash \neg\phi$ iff for all y with xRy we have $y \nVdash \phi$.

As an example of such a model consider $W = \{x, y\}$, the relation R given by $R(x, x)$, $R(x, y)$ and $R(y, y)$. Note that R is indeed reflexive and transitive. The labelling function L satisfies $L(x) = \emptyset$ and $L(y) = \{p\}$. We claim that $x \nVdash p \vee \neg p$ (recall that $p \vee \neg p$ is an instance of LEM which we proved in Chapter 1 with the full natural deduction calculus). Clearly, we do not have $x \Vdash p$, for p is not in the set $L(x)$ which is empty. Thus, Definition 5.4 for the case $\vee$ implies that $x \Vdash p \vee \neg p$ can hold only if $x \Vdash \neg p$ holds. But $x \Vdash \neg p$ simply does not hold, since there is a world y with xRy such that $y \Vdash p$ holds, for $p \in L(y)$. Here you can see that the availability of possible worlds in the models of KT4 together with a 'modal interpretation' of implications and negations broke down the validity of the theorem LEM in classical logic.

One can now define semantic entailment in the same manner as for modal logics. Then, one can prove soundness and completeness of the reduced natural deduction system with respect to this semantic entailment, but those proofs are beyond the scope of this book.

EXERCISES 5.5

1. Below you find a list of sequents $\Gamma \vdash \phi$ in propositional logic. Find out whether you can prove them without the use of the rules RAA, LEM and $\neg\neg$e. If you cannot succeed, then try to construct a model $\mathcal{M} = (W, R, L)$ for intuitionistic propositional logic such that one of its worlds satisfies all formulas in Γ, but does not satisfy ϕ. (Assuming soundness, this would guarantee that the sequent in question does not have a proof in intuitionistic propositional logic.)

    (a) $\vdash (p \rightarrow q) \vee (q \rightarrow r)$

    (b) The proof rule MT: $p \rightarrow q, \neg q \vdash \neg p$

    (c) $\neg p \vee q \vdash p \rightarrow q$

    (d) $p \rightarrow q \vdash \neg p \vee q$

    (e) The proof rule $\neg\neg$e: $\neg\neg p \vdash p$

    (f) The proof rule $\neg\neg$i: $p \vdash \neg\neg p$.

2. Prove that the natural deduction rules for propositional logic *without* the rules $\neg\neg$e, LEM and RAA are sound for the possible world semantics of intuitionistic propositional logic. Why does this show that the excluded rules cannot be implemented using the remaining ones?

5.3.5 *Semantic entailment*

Definition 5.20 Let L be a modal logic. With Definition 5.15 in mind, such a logic is completely given by a collection of formula schemes, the axioms of L. Given a set Γ of basic modal formulas and ϕ a formula of basic modal logic, we say that Γ *semantically entails* ϕ in L and write

$$\Gamma \vDash_L \phi$$

iff $\Gamma \cup L$ semantically entails ϕ in basic modal logic.

    Thus, we have $\Gamma \vDash_L \phi$ if every Kripke model and every world x satisfying $\Gamma \cup L$ therein also satisfies ϕ. Note that for $L = \emptyset$ this definition is consistent with the one of Definition 5.7, since we then have $\Gamma \cup L = \Gamma$.

EXERCISES 5.6

1. Interpreting $\square \phi$ as 'agent Q believes ϕ', explain the meaning of the following formula schemes:

    (a) $\square \phi \rightarrow \Diamond \phi$

  * (b) $\square \phi \vee \square \neg \phi$

    (c) $\square(\phi \rightarrow \psi) \wedge \square \phi \rightarrow \square \psi$.

2. In the second row of Table 5.7, we adopted the convention that the future excludes the present. Which formula schemes would be satisfied in that row if instead we adopted the (more common) convention that the future *includes* the present?

3. * (a) Reading $\square$ as knowledge, should we accept symmetry of R? totality?

(b) What properties of R should we accept for $\square$ modelling belief?
(Hint: nearly the same as those for 'knowledge'.)
* (c) What about the case of $\square$ modelling 'always in the future'?

4. Find a frame which is reflexive, transitive, but not symmetric. Show that your frame does not satisfy the formula $p \to \square\Diamond p$, by providing a suitable labelling function and choosing a world which refutes $p \to \square\Diamond p$. Can you find a labelling function and world which does satisfy $p \to \square\Diamond p$ in your frame?

5. Give two examples of frames which are Euclidean (i.e. their accessibility relation is Euclidean) and two which are not. Explain intuitively why $\Diamond p \to \square\Diamond p$ holds on the first two, but not on the latter two.

6. For each of the following formulas, find the property of R which corresponds to it.

(a) $\phi \to \square\phi$
* (b) $\square\bot$
* (c) $\Diamond\square\phi \to \square\Diamond\phi$.

* 7. Find a formula whose corresponding property is *density*: for all $x, z \in W$ such that $R(x, z)$, there exists $y \in W$ such that $R(x, y)$ and $R(y, z)$.

8. The modal logic KD45 is used to model belief (see Table 5.12 for the axiom schemes D, 4, and 5).

(a) Explain how it differs from KT45.
(b) Show that $\vDash_{KT45} \square p \to \Diamond p$. What is the significance of this, in terms of knowledge and belief?
(c) Explain why the condition of seriality is relevant to belief.

9. Recall Definition 5.7. How would you define $\equiv_L$ for a modal logic L?

5.4 Natural deduction

Computing semantic entailment would be rather difficult if we had only Definition 5.20. We would have to consider every Kripke model and every world in it. Fortunately, we have a much more usable approach, which is an extension, respectively adaptation, of the systems of natural deduction met in Chapters 1 and 2. Recall that we presented natural deduction proofs as linear representations of proof trees which may involve proof boxes which control the scope of assumptions, or quantifiers. The proof boxes have formulas and/or other boxes inside them. There are rules which dictate how to construct proofs. Boxes open with an *assumption*; when a box is closed (in accordance with a rule) we say that its assumption is *discharged*. Formulas may be repeated and brought into boxes, but may not be brought out of boxes. Every formula must have some justification to its right: a justification can be the name of a rule, or the word 'assumption', or an instance of the proof rule copy (see Section 1.2.1).

Natural deduction works in a very similar way for modal logic. The main difference is that we introduce a new kind of proof box, to be drawn with dashed lines. This is required for the rules for the connective $\Box$. The dashed proof box has a completely different role from the solid one. As we saw in Chapter 1, going into a solid proof box means making an assumption. Going into a dashed box means *reasoning in an arbitrary related world*. If at any point in a proof we have $\Box\phi$, we could open a dashed box and put ϕ in it. Then, we could work on this ϕ, to obtain, for example, ψ. Now we could come out of the dashed box and, since we have shown ψ in an arbitrary related world, we may deduce $\Box\psi$ in the world outside the dashed box.

Thus, the rules for bringing formulas into dashed boxes and taking formulas out of them are the following:

- If $\Box\phi$ occurs somewhere in a proof, ϕ may be put into a subsequent dashed box.
- If ψ occurs at the end of a dashed box, then $\Box\psi$ may be put after the dashed box.

We have thus added two rules, $\Box$ introduction and $\Box$ elimination:

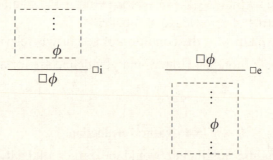

In modal logic, natural deduction proofs contain both solid and dashed boxes, nested in any way. Note that there are no explicit rules for $\Diamond$, which must be written $\neg\Box\neg$ in proofs.

The extra rules for KT45

The rules $\Box$i and $\Box$e are sufficient for the modal logic K. Stronger modal logics such as KT45 require some extra rules if one wants to capture semantic entailment via proofs. In the case of KT45, this extra strength is coded up by rule forms of the axioms T, 4 and 5, as follows:

$$\frac{\Box \phi}{\phi}\ T \qquad\qquad \frac{\Box \phi}{\Box \Box \phi}\ 4 \qquad\qquad \frac{\neg \Box \phi}{\Box \neg \Box \phi}\ 5$$

An equivalent alternative to the rules 4 and 5 would be to stipulate relaxations of the rules about moving formulas in and out of dashed boxes. Since rule 4 allows us to double-up boxes, we could instead think of it as allowing us to move formulas beginning with $\Box$ into dashed boxes. Similarly, axiom 5 has the effect of allowing us to move formulas beginning with $\neg \Box$ into dashed boxes; since it is a scheme, we could write $\neg \phi$ instead of ϕ. We write $\vdash_L \phi$ if ϕ has a proof in the natural deduction system for basic modal logic extended with the axioms from L.

Examples 5.21 Some examples of natural deduction proofs:

1. $\vdash_K \Box p \wedge \Box q \rightarrow \Box(p \wedge q)$.

1	$\Box p \wedge \Box q$	assumption
2	$\Box p$	$\wedge e_1$ 1
3	$\Box q$	$\wedge e_2$ 1
4	p	$\Box e$ 2
5	q	$\Box e$ 3
6	$p \wedge q$	$\wedge i$ 4,5
7	$\Box(p \wedge q)$	$\Box i$ 4–6
8	$\Box p \wedge \Box q \rightarrow \Box(p \wedge q)$	$\rightarrow i$ 1–7

2. $\vdash_{KT45} p \rightarrow \Box \Diamond p$.

1	p	assumption
2	$\Box \neg p$	assumption
3	$\neg p$	T 2
4	$\bot$	$\neg e$ 1, 3
5	$\neg \Box \neg p$	$\neg i$ 2–4
6	$\Box \neg \Box \neg p$	axiom 5 on line 5
7	$p \rightarrow \Box \neg \Box \neg p$	$\rightarrow i$ 1–6

3. $\vdash_{KT45} \Box\Diamond\Box p \to \Box p$.

1	$\Box\neg\Box\neg\Box p$	assumption
2	$\neg\Box\neg\Box p$	$\Box$e 1
3	$\neg\Box p$	assumption
4	$\Box\neg\Box p$	axiom 5 on line 3
5	$\bot$	$\neg$e 4, 2
6	$\neg\neg\Box p$	$\neg$i 3–5
7	$\Box p$	$\neg\neg$e 6
8	p	T 7
9	$\Box p$	$\Box$i 2–8
10	$\Box\neg\Box\neg\Box p \to \Box p$	$\to$i 1–9

Note that our proofs don't really have to use pointers such as 3–5, 2–8 and 1–9 since the rule name below the respective box binds to that entire box.

EXERCISES 5.7

1. Find natural deduction proofs for the following, in the basic modal logic K.

  * (a) $\Box(p \to q) \vdash \Box p \to \Box q$
    (b) $\Box(p \to q) \vdash \Diamond p \to \Diamond q$
  * (c) $\vdash \Box(p \to q) \wedge \Box(q \to r) \to \Box(p \to r)$
    (d) $\Box(p \wedge q) \vdash \Box p \wedge \Box q$
    (e) $\vdash \Diamond\top \to (\Box p \to \Diamond p)$
  * (f) $\Diamond(p \to q) \vdash \Box p \to \Diamond q$
    (g) $\Diamond(p \vee q) \vdash \Diamond p \vee \Diamond q$.

2. Find natural deduction proofs for the following, in modal logic KT45.

    (a) $p \to \Box\Diamond p$
    (b) $\Box\Diamond p \leftrightarrow \Diamond p$
  * (c) $\Diamond\Box p \leftrightarrow \Box p$
    (d) $\Box(\Box p \to \Box q) \vee \Box(\Box q \to \Box p)$
    (e) $\Box(\Diamond p \to q) \leftrightarrow \Box(p \to \Box q)$.

3. Study the proofs you gave for the previous exercise to see whether any of these formula schemes could be valid in basic modal logic. Inspect where and how these proofs used the axioms T, 4 and 5 to see whether you can find a counter example, i.e. a Kripke model and a world which does not satisfy the formula.

4. Provide a sketch of an argument which shows that the natural deduction rules for basic modal logic are sound with respect to the semantics over Kripke structures given earlier on.

———

5.5 Reasoning about knowledge in a multi-agent system

In a *multi-agent system,* different agents have different knowledge of the world. An agent may need to reason about its own knowledge about the world; it may also need to reason about what other agents know about the world. For example, in a bargaining situation, the seller of a car must consider what a buyer knows about the car's value. The buyer must also consider what the seller knows about what the buyer knows about the value and so on.

Reasoning about knowledge refers to the idea that agents in a group take into account not only the facts of the world, but also the knowledge of other agents in the group. Applications of this idea include: games, economics, cryptography and protocols. It is not very easy for humans to follow the thread of such nested sentences as

Dean doesn't know whether Nixon knows that Dean knows that Nixon knows that McCord burgled O'Brien's office at Watergate.

However, computer agents are better than humans in this respect.

5.5.1 *Some examples*

We start with some classic examples about reasoning in a multi-agent environment. Then, in the next section, we engineer a modal logic which allows for a formal representation of these examples via sequents and which solves them by proving them in a natural deduction system.

The wise-men puzzle

There are three wise men. It's common knowledge — known by everyone and known to be known by everyone, etc. — that there are three red hats and two white hats. The king puts a hat on each of the wise men in such a way that they are not able to see their own hat, and asks each one in turn whether they know the colour of the hat on their head. Suppose the first man says he does not know; then the second says he does not know either.

It follows that the third man must be able to say that he knows the colour of his hat. Why is this? What colour has the third man's hat?

To answer these questions, let us enumerate the seven possibilities which exist: they are

$$R \ R \ R$$
$$R \ R \ W$$
$$R \ W \ R$$
$$R \ W \ W$$
$$W \ R \ R$$
$$W \ R \ W$$
$$W \ W \ R$$

where (for example) R W W refers to the situation that the first, second and third men have red, white and white hats, respectively. The eighth possibility, W W W, is ruled out by the fact that there are only two white hats.

Now let's think of it from the second and third men's point of view. When they hear the first man speak, they can rule out the possibility of the true situation being R W W, because if it were this situation, then the first man, seeing that the others were wearing white hats and knowing that there are only two white hats, would have concluded that his hat must be red. As he said that he did not know, the true situation cannot be R W W. Notice that the second and third men must be intelligent in order to perform this reasoning; and they must know that the first man is intelligent and truthful as well. In the puzzle, we assume the truthfulness and intelligence and perceptiveness of the men are common knowledge — known by everyone and known to be known by everyone, etc.

When the third man hears the second man speak, he can rule out the possibility of the true situation being W R W, for similar reasons: if it were that, the second man would have said that he knew his hat was red, but he did not say this. Moreover, the third man can also rule out the situation R R W when he hears the second man's answer, for this reason: if the second man had seen that the first was wearing red and the third white, he would have known that it must be R W W or R R W; but he would have known from the first man's answer that it couldn't be R W W, so he would have concluded it was R R W and that he was wearing a red hat; but he did not draw this conclusion, so, reasons the third man, it cannot be R R W.

Having heard the first and second men speak, the third man has eliminated R W W, W R W and R R W, leaving only R R R, R W R, W R R and W W R. In all of these he is wearing a red hat, so he concludes that he must be wearing a red hat.

Notice that the men learn a lot from hearing the other men speak. We emphasise again the importance of the assumption that they tell the truth about their state of knowledge and are perceptive and intelligent enough to come to correct conclusions. Indeed, it is not enough that the three men are truthful, perceptive and intelligent; they must be known to be so by the others and (in later examples) this fact must also be known, etc. Therefore, we assume that all this is common knowledge.

The muddy-children puzzle

This is one of the many variations on the wise-men puzzle; a difference is that the questions are asked in parallel rather than sequentially. There is a large group of children playing in the garden (their perceptiveness, truthfulness and intelligence being common knowledge, it goes without saying). A certain number of children (say k) get mud on their foreheads. Each child can see the mud on others, but not on his own forehead. If $k > 1$, then each child can see another with mud on its forehead, so each one knows that at least one in the group is muddy. Consider these two scenarios:

Scenario 1. The father repeatedly asks the question 'Does any of you know whether you have mud on your own forehead?'. The first time they all answer 'no'; but, unlike in the wise-men example, they don't learn anything by hearing the others answer 'no', so they go on answering 'no' to the father's repeated questions.

Scenario 2. The father first announces that at least one of them is muddy (which is something they know already); and then, as before, he repeatedly asks them 'Does any of you know whether you have mud on your own forehead?'. The first time they all answer 'no'. Indeed, they go on answering 'no' to the first $k - 1$ repetitions of that same question; but at the kth those with muddy foreheads are able to answer 'yes'.

At first sight, it seems rather puzzling that the two scenarios are different, given that the only difference in the events leading up to them is that in the second one the father announces something that they already know. It would be wrong, however, to conclude that the children learn nothing from this announcement. Although everyone knows the content of the announcement, the father's saying it makes it common knowledge among them, so now they all know that everyone else knows it, etc. This is the crucial difference between the two scenarios.

To understand scenario 2, consider a few cases of k.

$k = 1$, i.e. just one child has mud. That child is immediately able to answer 'yes', since she has heard the father and doesn't see any other child with mud.

$k = 2$, say only the children a and b have mud. Everyone answers 'no' the first time. Now a thinks: since b answered 'no' the first time, he must see someone with mud. Well, the only person I can see with mud is b, so if b can see someone else it must be me. So a answers 'yes' the second time. Child b reasons symmetrically about a and also answers 'yes' the second time round.

$k = 3$, say only the children a, b and c have mud. Everyone answers 'no' the first two times. But now a thinks: if it was just b and c with mud, they would have answered 'yes' the second time, making the argument for $k = 2$ above. So there must be a third person with mud; since I can see only b and c having mud, the third person must be me. So a answers 'yes' the third time. For symmetrical reasons, so do b and c.

And similarly for other cases of k.

To see that it was not common knowledge before the father's announcement that one of the children was muddy, consider again $k = 2$, with children a and b. Of course, a and b both know someone is muddy (they see each other); but, for example, a doesn't know that b knows that someone is dirty. For all a knows, b might be the only dirty one and therefore not be able to see a dirty child.

5.5.2 *The modal logic KT45^n*

We now generalise the modal logic KT45 given in Section 5.3.4. Instead of having just one $\Box$, it will have many, one for each agent i from a fixed set $\mathscr{A} = \{1, 2, \ldots, n\}$ of agents. We write those modal connectives as K_i (for each agent $i \in \mathscr{A}$); the K is to emphasise the application to *knowledge*. We assume a collection $p, q, r, \ldots$ of atomic formulas. The formula $K_i p$ means that agent i knows p; so, for example,

$$K_1 p \wedge K_1 \neg K_2 K_1 p$$

means that agent 1 knows p, but knows that agent 2 doesn't know he knows it. We also have the modal connectives E_G, where G is any subset of $\mathscr{A}$. The formula $E_G p$ means everyone in the group G knows p. If $G = \{1, 2, 3, \ldots, n\}$, then $E_G p$ is equivalent to

$$K_1 p \wedge K_2 p \wedge \cdots \wedge K_n p.$$

We assume similar binding priorities to those put forward in Convention 5.2.

Convention 5.22 The binding priorities of KT45^n are the ones of basic modal logic, if we think of each modality K_i, E_G and C_G as 'being $\Box$'.

One might think that ϕ could not be more widely known than everyone knowing it, but this is not the case. It could be, for example, that everyone knows ϕ, but they might not know that they all know it. If ϕ is supposed to be a secret, it might be that you and your friend both know it, but your friend does not know that you know it and you don't know that your friend knows it. Thus, $E_G E_G \phi$ is a state of knowledge even greater than $E_G \phi$ and $E_G E_G E_G \phi$ is greater still. We say that ϕ is *common knowledge among G*, written $C_G \phi$, if everyone knows ϕ and everyone knows that everyone knows it; and everyone knows that; and knows *that*, etc., i.e. we may think of $C_G \phi$ as an infinite conjunction

$$E_G \phi \wedge E_G E_G \phi \wedge E_G E_G E_G \phi \wedge \dots.$$

However, since our logics only have finite conjunctions, we cannot reduce C_G to something which is already in the logic. We have to express the infinite aspect of C_G via its semantics and retain it as an additional modal connective. Finally, $D_G \phi$ means the knowledge of ϕ is distributed among the group G; although no-one in G may know it, they would be able to work it out if they put their heads together and combined the information distributed among them.

Definition 5.23 A *formula* ϕ in the multi-modal logic of KT45^n is defined by the following grammar:

$$\phi ::= \bot \mid \top \mid p \mid \neg\phi \mid (\phi \wedge \phi) \mid (\phi \vee \phi) \mid (\phi \to \phi) \mid (\phi \leftrightarrow \phi) \mid$$
$$K_i\phi \mid E_G\phi \mid C_G\phi \mid D_G\phi$$

where p is any atomic formula, $i \in \mathcal{A}$ and $G \subseteq \mathcal{A}$. We simply write E, C and D without subscripts if we refer to $E_{\mathcal{A}}$, $C_{\mathcal{A}}$ and $D_{\mathcal{A}}$.

Compare this definition with Definition 5.1. Instead of $\Box$, we have several modalities K_i and we also have E_G, C_G and D_G for each $G \in \mathcal{A}$. Actually, all of these connectives will shortly be seen to be 'box-like' rather than 'diamond-like', in the sense that they distribute over $\wedge$ rather than over $\vee$ (compare the discussion of equivalences inside Section 5.2.2). The 'diamond-like' correspondents of these connectives are not explicitly in the language, but may of course be obtained using negations (i.e. $\neg K_i \neg$, $\neg C_G \neg$, etc.).

Definition 5.24 A *model* $\mathcal{M} = (W, (R_i)_{i\in\mathcal{A}}, L)$ of the multi-modal logic KT45^n with the set $\mathcal{A}$ of n agents is specified by three things:

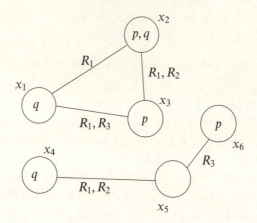

Fig. 5.13. A KT45^n model.

1. a set W, of *worlds*;
2. for each $i \in \mathscr{A}$, an *equivalence relation* R_i on W ($R_i \subseteq W \times W$), called the *accessibility relations*;
3. a labelling function $L : W \rightarrow \mathscr{P}(\text{Atoms})$.

Compare this with Definition 5.3. The difference is that, instead of just one accessibility relation, we now have a family, one for each agent in $\mathscr{A}$; and we assume the accessibility relations are equivalence relations.

We exploit these properties of R_i in the graphical illustrations of Kripke models for KT45^n. For example, a model with worlds $\{x_1, x_2, x_3, x_4, x_5, x_6\}$ is shown in Figure 5.13. The links between the worlds have to be labelled with the name of the relation, since we have several relations. For example, x_1 and x_2 are R_1-related, whereas x_4 and x_5 are related both by R_1 and by R_2. We simplify by no longer requiring arrows on the links. This is because we know that the relations are symmetric, so the links are bi-directional. Moreover, the relations are also reflexive, so there should be loops like the one on x_4 in Figure 5.11 in all the worlds and for all of the relations. We can simply omit these from the diagram, since we don't need to distinguish between worlds which are self-related and those which are not.

Definition 5.25 Take a model $\mathscr{M} = (W, (R_i)_{i \in \mathscr{A}}, L)$ of KT45. We define when ϕ *is true in* x via a satisfaction relation $x \Vdash \phi$ by induction on ϕ:

$$x \Vdash p \quad \text{iff } p \in L(x)$$
$$x \Vdash \neg\phi \quad \text{iff } x \nVdash \phi$$
$$x \Vdash \phi \wedge \psi \quad \text{iff } x \Vdash \phi \text{ and } x \Vdash \psi$$

$x \Vdash \phi \vee \psi$ iff $x \Vdash \phi$ or $x \Vdash \psi$

$x \Vdash \phi \rightarrow \psi$ iff $x \Vdash \psi$ whenever we have $x \Vdash \phi$

$x \Vdash K_i \psi$ iff, for each $y \in W$, $R_i(x,y)$ implies $y \Vdash \psi$

$x \Vdash E_G \psi$ iff, for each $i \in G$, $x \Vdash K_i \psi$

$x \Vdash C_G \psi$ iff, for each $k = 1, 2, \ldots$, we have $x \Vdash E_G^k \psi$,

$\qquad$ where E_G^k means $E_G E_G \ldots E_G$ (k times)

$x \Vdash D_G \psi$ iff, for each $y \in W$, we have $y \Vdash \psi$,

$\qquad$ whenever $R_i(x,y)$ for all $i \in G$.

Again, we write $\mathcal{M}, x \Vdash \phi$ if we want to emphasise the model $\mathcal{M}$.

Compare this with Definition 5.4. The cases for the boolean connectives are the same as for basic modal logic. Each K_i behaves like a $\Box$, but refers to its own accessibility relation R_i. There are no equivalents of $\Diamond$, but, as already stated, we can recover them as $\neg K_i \neg$. The connective E_G is defined in terms of the K_i and C_G is defined in terms of E_G.

Many of the results we had for basic modal logic (with a single accessibility relation) also hold in this more general setting of several accessibility relations. Summarising,

- a *frame* $\mathcal{F}$ for KT45^n $(W, (R_i)_{i \in \mathcal{A}})$ for the modal logic KT45^n is a set W (of worlds) and, for each $i \in \mathcal{A}$, a relation R_i on W.
- a frame $\mathcal{F} = (W, (R_i)_{i \in \mathcal{A}})$ for KT45^n is said to satisfy ϕ, written $\mathcal{F} \vDash \phi$, if, for each labelling function L and each $w \in W$, we have $\mathcal{M}, w \Vdash \phi$, where $\mathcal{M} = (W, (R_i)_{i \in \mathcal{A}}, L)$.

The following theorem is useful for answering questions about formulas involving E and C. Let $\mathcal{M} = (W, (R_i)_{i \in \mathcal{A}}, L)$ be a model for KT45^n and $x, y \in W$. We say that y is *G-reachable in k steps* from x if there are $w_1, w_2, \ldots, w_{k-1} \in W$ and $i_1, i_2, \ldots, i_k$ in G such that

$$x \, R_{i_1} \, w_1 \, R_{i_2} \, w_2 \, \ldots \, R_{i_{k-1}} \, w_{k-1} \, R_{i_k} \, y.$$

We also say that y is *G-reachable* from x if there is some k such that it is G-reachable in k steps.

Theorem 5.26

1. $x \Vdash E_G^k \phi$ *iff, for all y that are G-reachable from x in k steps, we have* $y \Vdash \phi$.

2. $x \Vdash C_G \phi$ *iff, for all y that are G-reachable from x, we have* $y \Vdash \phi$.

PROOF:

1. First, suppose $y \Vdash \phi$ for all y G-reachable from x in k steps. We will prove that $x \Vdash E_G^k \phi$. It is sufficient to show that $x \Vdash K_{i_1} K_{i_2} \ldots K_{i_k} \phi$ for any $i_1, i_2, \ldots, i_k \in G$. Take any $i_1, i_2, \ldots, i_k \in G$ and any $w_1, w_2, \ldots, w_{k-1}$ and y such that $x R_{i_1} w_1 R_{i_2} w_2 \ldots R_{i_{k-1}} w_{k-1} R_{i_k} y$. Since y is G-reachable from x in k steps, we have $y \Vdash \phi$ by our assumption, so $x \Vdash K_{i_1} K_{i_2} \ldots K_{i_k} \phi$ as required.

   Conversely, suppose $x \Vdash E_G^k \phi$ and y is G-reachable from x in k steps. We must show $y \Vdash \phi$. Take $i_1, i_2, \ldots, i_k$ by G-reachability; since $x \Vdash E_G^k \phi$ implies $x \Vdash K_{i_1} K_{i_2} \ldots K_{i_k} \phi$, we have $y \Vdash \phi$.

2. This argument is similar.

Some valid formulas in KT45^n

The formula K holds for the connectives K_i, E_G, C_G and D_G, i.e. we have the corresponding formula schemes

$$K_i \phi \wedge K_i(\phi \to \psi) \to K_i \psi$$
$$E_G \phi \wedge E_G(\phi \to \psi) \to E_G \psi$$
$$C_G \phi \wedge C_G(\phi \to \psi) \to C_G \psi$$
$$D_G \phi \wedge D_G(\phi \to \psi) \to D_G \psi.$$

This means that these different 'levels' of knowledge are closed under logical consequence. For example, if certain facts are common knowledge and some other fact follows logically from them, then that fact is also common knowledge.

Observe that E, C and D are 'box-like' connectives, in the sense that they quantify universally over certain accessibility relations. That is to say, we may define the relations R_{E_G}, R_{D_G} and R_{C_G} in terms of the relations R_i, as follows:

$$
\begin{array}{llll}
R_{E_G}(x, y) & \text{iff} & R_i(x, y) & \text{for some } i \in G \\
R_{D_G}(x, y) & \text{iff} & R_i(x, y) & \text{for all } i \in G \\
R_{C_G}(x, y) & \text{iff} & R_{E_G}^k(x, y) & \text{for each } k \geq 1.
\end{array}
$$

It follows from this that E_G, D_G and C_G satisfy the K formula with respect to the accessibility relations R_{E_G}, R_{D_G} and R_{C_G}, respectively.

What about other valid formulas? Since we have stipulated that the relations R_i are equivalence relations, it follows from the multi-modal analogues of Theorem 5.13 and Table 5.12 that the following formulas are valid in KT45^n (for each agent i):

$$
\begin{array}{ll}
K_i \phi \to K_i K_i \phi & \text{positive introspection} \\
\neg K_i \phi \to K_i \neg K_i \phi & \text{negative introspection} \\
K_i \phi \to \phi & \text{truth.}
\end{array}
$$

These formulas also hold for D_G, since R_{D_G} is also an equivalence relation, but these don't automatically generalise for E_G and C_G. For example, $E_G\phi \to E_G E_G\phi$ is not valid; if it were valid, it would imply that common knowledge was nothing more than knowledge by everybody. The scheme $\neg E_G\phi \to E_G\neg E_G\phi$ is also not valid. The failure of these formulas to be valid can be traced to the fact that R_{E_G} is not necessarily an equivalence relation, even though each R_i is an equivalence relation.

However, R_{E_G} is reflexive, so $E_G\phi \to \phi$ is valid, provided that $G \neq \emptyset$ (if $G = \emptyset$, then $E_G\phi$ holds vacuously, even if ϕ is false).

Since R_{C_G} is an equivalence relation, the formulas T, 4 and 5 above do hold for C_G, although the third one still requires the condition that $G \neq \emptyset$.

EXERCISES 5.8

1. This exercise is about the wise-men puzzle.

   (a) Each man is asked the question 'do you know the colour of your hat?'. Suppose that the first man says 'no', but the second one says 'yes'. Given this information (together with the common knowledge), can we infer the colour of his hat?

   (b) Can we predict whether the third man will now answer 'yes' or 'no'?

   (c) What would be the situation if the third man were blind? What about the first man?

2. This exercise is about the muddy-children puzzle. Suppose $k = 4$, say children a, b, c and d have mud on their foreheads. Explain why, before the father's announcement, it is not common knowledge that someone is dirty.

3. Write formulas for the following:

   (a) Agent 1 knows that p.

   (b) Agent 1 knows that p or q.

   * (c) Agent 1 knows p or agent 1 knows q.

   (d) Agent 1 knows whether p.

   (e) Agent 1 doesn't know whether p or q.

   (f) Agent 1 knows whether agent 2 knows p.

   * (g) Agent 1 knows whether agent 2 knows whether p.

   (h) No-one knows p.

   (i) Not everyone knows whether p.

   (j) Anyone who knows p knows q.

   * (k) Some people know p but don't know q.

   (l) Everyone knows someone who knows p.

4. Determine which of the following hold in the Kripke model of Figure 5.13:

    (a) $x_1 \Vdash K_1 p$
    (b) $x_3 \Vdash K_1 (p \vee q)$
    (c) $x_1 \Vdash K_2 q$
    * (d) $x_3 \Vdash E(p \vee q)$
    (e) $x_1 \Vdash Cq$
    (f) $x_1 \Vdash D_{\{1,3\}} p$
    (g) $x_1 \Vdash D_{\{1,2\}} p$
    (h) $x_6 \Vdash E \neg q$
    * (i) $x_6 \Vdash C \neg q$
    (j) $x_6 \Vdash C_{\{3\}} \neg q$.

5. For each of the following formulas, show that it is not valid by finding a Kripke model with a world not satisfying the formula:

    (a) $E_G \phi \rightarrow E_G E_G \phi$
    (b) $\neg E_G \phi \rightarrow E_G \neg E_G \phi$.

* 6. Explain why $C_G \phi \rightarrow C_G C_G \phi$ and $\neg C_G \phi \rightarrow C_G \neg C_G \phi$ are valid.

7. Prove the second part of Theorem 5.26.

8. Recall Section 3.9. Can you specify a monotone function over the power set of possible worlds which computes the set of worlds satisfying $C_G \phi$? Is this a least, or a greatest, fixed point?

———

5.5.3 Natural deduction for $KT45^n$

The proof system for $KT45$ is easily extended to $KT45^n$ (but for simplicity, we omit reference to the connective D).

1. The dashed boxes now come in different 'flavours' for different modal connectives; we'll indicate the modality in the top left corner of the dashed box.

2. The axioms T, 4 and 5 can be used for any K_i, whereas axioms 4 and 5 can be used for C_G, but not for E_G (recall the discussion in Section 5.5.2).

3. From $C_G \phi$ we may deduce $E_G^k \phi$, for any k (we call this rule CE); or we could go directly to $K_{i_1} \ldots K_{i_k} \phi$ for any agents $i_1, \ldots, i_k$. This rule is called CK. Strictly speaking, it is a whole set of such rules, one for each choice of $i_1, \ldots, i_k$, but we refer to all of them as CK.

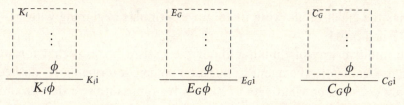

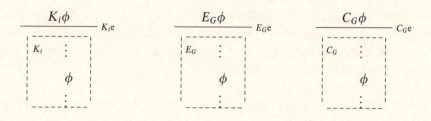

$$\frac{K_i\phi \text{ for each } i \in G}{E_G\phi}\, KE \qquad \frac{E_G\phi \quad i \in G}{K_i\phi}\, EK_i \qquad \frac{C_G\phi}{E_G\ldots E_G\phi}\, CE$$

$$\frac{C_G\phi}{K_{i_1}\ldots K_{i_k}\phi}\, CK \qquad \frac{C_G\phi}{C_G C_G\phi}\, C4 \qquad \frac{\neg C_G\phi}{C_G\neg C_G\phi}\, C5$$

$$\frac{K_i\phi}{\phi}\, KT \qquad \frac{K_i\phi}{K_i K_i\phi}\, K4 \qquad \frac{\neg K_i\phi}{K_i\neg K_i\phi}\, K5$$

Fig. 5.14. Natural deduction rules for KT45^n.

4. From $E_G\phi$ we may deduce $K_i\phi$ for any $i \in G$ (called EK_i). From $\bigwedge_{i \in G} K_i\phi$ we may deduce $E_G\phi$ (rule KE). Note that the proof rule EK_i is like a generalised and-elimination rule, whereas KE behaves like an and-introduction rule.

The proof rules for KT45^n are summarised in Figure 5.14. As before, we can think of the rules $K4$ and $K5$ and $C4$ and $C5$ as relaxations of the rules about moving formulas in and out of dashed proof boxes. Since rule $K4$ allows us to double-up K_i, we could instead think of it as allowing us to move formulas beginning with K_i into K_i-dashed boxes. Similarly, rule

$C5$ has the effect of allowing us to move formulas beginning with $\neg C_G$ into C_G-dashed boxes.

An intuitive way of thinking about the dashed boxes is that formulas in them are known to the agent in question. When you open a K_i-dashed box, you are considering what agent i knows. It's quite intuitive that an ordinary formula ϕ cannot be brought into such a dashed box, because the mere truth of ϕ does not mean that agent i knows it. Note that this means, for example, that you can't use the rule $\neg i$ if one of the premises of the rule is outside the dashed box you're working in.

Observe the power of $C\,\phi$ in the premises: we can bring ϕ into *any* dashed box (by rules CK and $K_i e$), no matter how deeply nested. $E^k\,\phi$, on the other hand, means ϕ can be brought into any dashed box with nesting $\leq k$. (Compare this with Theorem 5.26.)

Example 5.27 We show that the sequent $C(p \vee q)$, $K_1(K_2 p \vee K_2 \neg p)$, $K_1 \neg K_2 q$ $\vdash K_1 p$ is provable in the modal logic KT45^{n}[1]. That means: if it is common knowledge that $p \vee q$; and agent 1 knows that agent 2 knows whether p is the case and also knows that agent 2 doesn't know that q is true; then agent 1 knows that p is true. See Figure 5.15. In line 12, we derived q from $\neg p$ and $p \vee q$. Rather than show the full derivation in propositional logic (which is not the focus here), we summarise by writing 'prop' (for an inference in propositional logic) as the justification.

5.5.4 Formalising the examples

Now that we have set up the modal logic KT45^n, we can turn our attention to the question of how to represent the wise-men and muddy-children puzzles in this logic. Unfortunately, in spite of its sophistication, our logic is too simple to capture all the nuances of those examples. Although it has connectives for representing different items of knowledge held by different agents, it does not have any temporal aspect, so it cannot directly capture the way in which the agents' knowledge changes as time proceeds. We will overcome this limitation by considering several 'snapshots' during which time is fixed.

The wise-men puzzle

Recall that there are three wise men; and it's common knowledge that there are three red hats and two white hats. The king puts a hat on each of the wise men and asks them sequentially whether they know the colour of the hat on their head — they are unable to see their own hat. We suppose the

---

[1] In this section we simply write $\vdash$ for proofs in the logic KT45^n, unless indicated otherwise.

1	$C(p \vee q)$	premise
2	$K_1(K_2p \vee K_2\neg p)$	premise
3	$K_1 \neg K_2 q$	premise
4	$K_1 K_2(p \vee q)$	CK 1

5	K_1	$K_2(p \vee q)$		K_1e 4
6		$K_2p \vee K_2\neg p$		K_1e 2
7		$\neg K_2 q$		K_1e 3

8		K_2p assumption	$K_2\neg p$ assumption	
9		p axiom T 8	K_2 $\neg p$ K_2e 8	
10			$p \vee q$ K_2e 5	
11			q prop 9, 10	
12			K_2q K_2i 9–11	
13			$\bot$ $\neg e$ 12, 7	
14			p $\bot e$ 13	

15		p		Ve 6, 8–14, 8–14

16	$K_1 p$	$K_1 i$ 5–15

Fig. 5.15. A proof of $C(p \vee q), K_1(K_2p \vee K_2\neg p), K_1\neg K_2q \vdash K_1p$.

first man says he does not know; then the second says he does not know. We want to prove that, whatever the distribution of hats, the third man now knows his hat is red.

Let p_i mean that man i has a red hat; so $\neg p_i$ means that man i has a white hat. Let Γ be the set of formulas

$$\{C(p_1 \vee p_2 \vee p_3),$$
$$C(p_1 \to K_2p_1), \quad C(\neg p_1 \to K_2\neg p_1),$$
$$C(p_1 \to K_3p_1), \quad C(\neg p_1 \to K_3\neg p_1),$$
$$C(p_2 \to K_1p_2), \quad C(\neg p_2 \to K_1\neg p_2),$$
$$C(p_2 \to K_3p_2), \quad C(\neg p_2 \to K_3\neg p_2),$$
$$C(p_3 \to K_1p_3), \quad C(\neg p_3 \to K_1\neg p_3),$$
$$C(p_3 \to K_2p_3), \quad C(\neg p_3 \to K_2\neg p_3)\}.$$

This corresponds to the initial set-up: it is common knowledge that one of the hats must be red and that each man can see the colour of the other men's hats.

The announcement that the first man doesn't know the colour of his hat amounts to the formula

$$C(\neg K_1 p_1 \wedge \neg K_1 \neg p_1)$$

and similarly for the second man.

A naive attempt at formalising the wise-men problem might go something like this: we simply prove

$$\Gamma, \; C(\neg K_1 p_1 \wedge \neg K_1 \neg p_1), \; C(\neg K_2 p_2 \wedge \neg K_2 \neg p_2) \vdash K_3 p_3,$$

i.e. if Γ is true and the announcements are made, then the third man knows his hat is red. However, this fails to capture the fact that time passes between the announcements. The fact that $C \neg K_1 p_1$ is true after the first announcement does not mean it is true after some subsequent announcement. For example, if someone announces p_1, then $C p_1$ becomes true.

The reason that this formalisation is incorrect, then, is that, although knowledge accrues with time, *lack* of knowledge does not accrue with time. If I know ϕ, then (assuming that ϕ doesn't change) I will know it at the next time-point; but if I do *not* know ϕ, it may be that I *do* know it at the next time point, since I may acquire more knowledge.

To formalise the wise-men problem correctly, we need to break it into two entailments, one corresponding to each announcement. When the first man announces he does not know the colour of his hat, a certain *positive* formula ϕ becomes common knowledge. Our informal reasoning explained that all men could then rule out the state RWW which, given $p_1 \vee p_2 \vee p_3$, led them to the common knowledge of $p_2 \vee p_3$. Thus, ϕ is just $p_2 \vee p_3$ and we need to prove the entailment

Entailment 1.

$$\Gamma, \; C(\neg K_1 p_1 \wedge \neg K_1 \neg p_1) \vdash C(p_2 \vee p_3). \tag{5.1}$$

A proof of this sequent can be found in Figure 5.16.

Since $p_2 \vee p_3$ is a positive formula, it persists with time and can be used in conjunction with the second announcement to prove the desired conclusion:

Entailment 2.

$$\Gamma, \; C(p_2 \vee p_3), \; C(\neg K_2 p_2, \wedge \neg K_2 \neg p_2) \vdash K_3 p_3. \tag{5.2}$$

This method requires some careful thought: given an announcement of negative information (such as a man declaring that he does not know what the colour of his hat is), we need to work out what positive knowledge formula can be derived from this and such knowledge has to be sufficient to allow us to proceed to the next round (= make even more progress towards solving the puzzle).

Routine proof segments like those in lines 12-16 of Figure 5.16 may be abbreviated into one step as long as all participating proof rules are recorded. The resulting shorter representation can bee seen in Figure 5.17.

In Figure 5.16, notice that the premises in lines 2 and 5 are not used. The premises in lines 2 and 3 stand for any such formula for a given value of i and j, provided $i \neq j$; this explains the inference made in line 8. In Figure 5.18, again notice that the premises in lines 1 and 5 are not used. Observe also that axiom T in conjunction with CK allows us to infer ϕ from any $C\phi$, although we had to split this up into two separate steps in lines 16 and 17. Practical implementations would probably allow for hybrid rules which condense such reasoning into one step.

The muddy-children puzzle

Suppose there are n children. Let p_i mean that the ith child has mud on its forehead. We consider Scenario 2, in which the father announces that one of the children is muddy. Similarly to the case for the wise men, it is common knowledge that each child can see the other children, so it knows whether the others have mud, or not. Thus, for example, we have that $C(p_1 \rightarrow K_2 p_1)$, which says that it is common knowledge that, if child 1 is muddy, then child 2 knows this and also $C(\neg p_1 \rightarrow K_2 \neg p_1)$. Let Γ be the collection of formulas:

$$C(p_1 \lor p_2 \lor \cdots \lor p_n)$$

$$\bigwedge_{i \neq j} C(p_i \rightarrow K_j p_i)$$

$$\bigwedge_{i \neq j} C(\neg p_i \rightarrow K_j \neg p_i).$$

Note that $\bigwedge_{i \neq j} \psi_{(i,j)}$ is a shorthand for the conjunction of all formulas $\psi_{(i,j)}$, where i is different from j. Let G be any set of children. We will require formulas of the form

$$\alpha_G \stackrel{\text{def}}{=} \bigwedge_{i \in G} p_i \land \bigwedge_{i \notin G} \neg p_i.$$

1	$C(p_1 \lor p_2 \lor p_3)$	premise
2	$C(p_i \to K_j p_i)$	premise, $(i \neq j)$
3	$C(\neg p_i \to K_j \neg p_i)$	premise, $(i \neq j)$
4	$C \neg K_1 p_1$	premise
5	$C \neg K_1 \neg p_1$	premise

6   C

     7      $\neg p_2 \land \neg p_3$ assumption

     8      $\neg p_2 \to K_1 \neg p_2$ $Ce\ 3\ (i, j) = (2, 1)$

     9      $\neg p_3 \to K_1 \neg p_3$ $Ce\ 3\ (i, j) = (3, 1)$

     10      $K_1 \neg p_2 \land K_1 \neg p_3$ prop $7, 8, 9$

     11      $K_1 \neg p_2$ $\land e_1\ 10$

     12      $K_1 \neg p_3$ $\land e_2\ 10$

     13   K_1

       14      $\neg p_2$ $K_1 e\ 11$

       15      $\neg p_3$ $K_1 e\ 12$

       16      $\neg p_2 \land \neg p_3$ $\land i\ 14, 15$

       17      $p_1 \lor p_2 \lor p_3$ $Ce\ 1$

       18   p_1 prop $16, 17$

     19      $K_1 p_1$ $K_1 i\ 11-18$

     20      $\neg K_1 p_1$ $Ce\ 4$

     21      $\bot$ $\neg e\ 19, 20$

     22      $\neg(\neg p_2 \land \neg p_3)$ $\neg i\ 7-21$

     23      $p_2 \lor p_3$ prop 22

24      $C(p_2 \lor p_3)$ $Ci\ 6-23$

Fig. 5.16. Proof of the sequent 'Entailment 1' for the wise-men puzzle.

The formula α_G states that it is precisely the children in G that have muddy foreheads.

Suppose now that $k = 1$, i.e. that one child has mud on its forehead. We would like to show that that child knows that it is the one. We prove the following entailment.

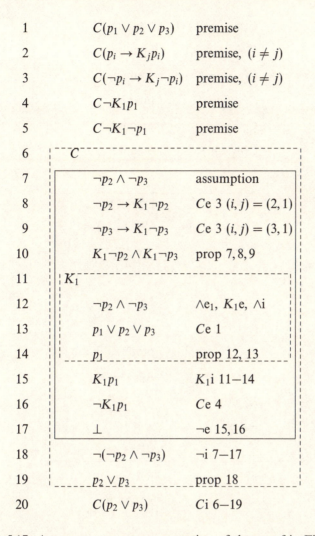

1	$C(p_1 \lor p_2 \lor p_3)$	premise
2	$C(p_i \to K_j p_i)$	premise, $(i \neq j)$
3	$C(\neg p_i \to K_j \neg p_i)$	premise, $(i \neq j)$
4	$C \neg K_1 p_1$	premise
5	$C \neg K_1 \neg p_1$	premise
6	C	
7	$\neg p_2 \land \neg p_3$	assumption
8	$\neg p_2 \to K_1 \neg p_2$	$Ce\ 3\ (i, j) = (2, 1)$
9	$\neg p_3 \to K_1 \neg p_3$	$Ce\ 3\ (i, j) = (3, 1)$
10	$K_1 \neg p_2 \land K_1 \neg p_3$	prop $7, 8, 9$
11	K_1	
12	$\neg p_2 \land \neg p_3$	$\land e_1, K_1 e, \land i$
13	$p_1 \lor p_2 \lor p_3$	$Ce\ 1$
14	p_1	prop $12, 13$
15	$K_1 p_1$	$K_1 i\ 11{-}14$
16	$\neg K_1 p_1$	$Ce\ 4$
17	$\bot$	$\neg e\ 15, 16$
18	$\neg(\neg p_2 \land \neg p_3)$	$\neg i\ 7{-}17$
19	$p_2 \lor p_3$	prop 18
20	$C(p_2 \lor p_3)$	$Ci\ 6{-}19$

Fig. 5.17. A more compact representation of the proof in Figure 5.16.

Entailment 1.

$$\Gamma, \alpha_{\{i\}} \vdash K_i p_i. \tag{5.3}$$

This says that, if the actual situation is one in which only one child (called i) has mud, then that agent will know it. Our proof follows exactly the same lines as the intuition: i sees that no other children have mud, but knows that at least one has mud, so knows it must be itself who has a muddy forehead. The proof is given in Figure 5.19.

Note that the comment 'for each $j \neq i$' means that we supply this argument

1	$C(p_1 \vee p_2 \vee p_3)$	premise
2	$C(p_i \rightarrow K_j p_i)$	premise, $(i \neq j)$
3	$C(\neg p_i \rightarrow K_j \neg p_i)$	premise, $(i \neq j)$
4	$C \neg K_2 p_2$	premise
5	$C \neg K_2 \neg p_2$	premise
6	$C(p_2 \vee p_3)$	premise

7	K_3		
8		$\neg p_3$	assumption
9		$\neg p_3 \rightarrow K_2 \neg p_3$	CK 3 $(i,j) = (3,2)$
10		$K_2 \neg p_3$	$\rightarrow e$ 9, 8
11		K_2	
12		$\neg p_3$	$K_2 e$ 10
13		$p_2 \vee p_3$	Ce 6
14		p_2	prop 12, 13
15		$K_2 p_2$	$K_2 i$ 11–14
16		$K_i \neg K_2 p_2$	CK 4, for each i
17		$\neg K_2 p_2$	KT 16
18		$\bot$	$\neg e$ 15, 17
19		p_3	RAA 8–18
20	$K_3 p_3$		$K_3 i$ 7–19

Fig. 5.18. Proof of the sequent 'Entailment 2' for the wise-men puzzle.

for any such j. Thus, we can form the conjunction of all these inferences which we left implicit in the inference on line 10.

Suppose, however, that it is not the case that there is only one child with mud. In this case, the children all announce in the first parallel round that they do not know whether they are muddy or not, corresponding to the formula

$$A \stackrel{\text{def}}{=} C(\neg K_1 p_1 \wedge \neg K_1 \neg p_1) \wedge \cdots \wedge C(\neg K_n p_n \wedge \neg K_n \neg p_n).$$

We saw in the wise-men example that it is dangerous to put the announce-

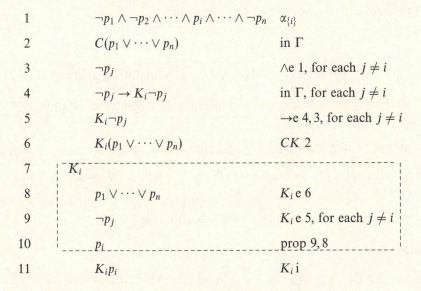

1	$\neg p_1 \wedge \neg p_2 \wedge \cdots \wedge p_i \wedge \cdots \wedge \neg p_n$	$\alpha_{\{i\}}$
2	$C(p_1 \vee \cdots \vee p_n)$	in Γ
3	$\neg p_j$	$\wedge$e 1, for each $j \neq i$
4	$\neg p_j \to K_i \neg p_j$	in Γ, for each $j \neq i$
5	$K_i \neg p_j$	$\to$e 4, 3, for each $j \neq i$
6	$K_i(p_1 \vee \cdots \vee p_n)$	CK 2
7	K_i	
8	$p_1 \vee \cdots \vee p_n$	K_i e 6
9	$\neg p_j$	K_i e 5, for each $j \neq i$
10	p_i	prop 9, 8
11	$K_i p_i$	K_i i

Fig. 5.19. Proof of the sequent 'Entailment 1' for the muddy-children puzzle.

ment A alongside the premises Γ, because the truth of A (which has negative claims about the children's knowledge) cannot be guaranteed to persist with time. So we seek some positive formula which represents what the children learn upon hearing the announcement. As in the wise-men example, this formula is implicit in the informal reasoning about the muddy children given in Section 5.5.1: if it is common knowledge that there are at least k muddy children, then, after an announcement of the form A, it will be common knowledge that there are at least $k + 1$ muddy children.

Therefore, after the first announcement A, the set of premises is

$$\Gamma, \bigwedge_{1 \le i \le n} C \neg \alpha_{\{i\}}.$$

This is Γ together with the common knowledge that the set of muddy children is not a singleton set.

After the second announcement A, the set of premises becomes

$$\Gamma, \bigwedge_{1 \le i \le n} C \neg \alpha_{\{i\}}, \bigwedge_{i \neq j} C \neg \alpha_{\{i,j\}},$$

which we may write as

$$\Gamma, \bigwedge_{|G| \le 2} C \neg \alpha_G.$$

Please try carefully to understand the notation:

α_G the set of muddy children is precisely the set G

$\neg\alpha_G$ the set of muddy children is some other set than G

$\bigwedge_{|G|\leq k} \neg\alpha_G$ the set of muddy children is of size greater than k.

The entailment corresponding to the second round is:

$$\Gamma, C(\bigwedge_{|G|\leq 2} \neg\alpha_G), \alpha_H \vdash \bigwedge_{i\in H} K_i p_i, \qquad \text{where } |H| = 3.$$

The entailment corresponding to the kth round is:

Entailment 2.

$$\Gamma, C(\bigwedge_{|G|\leq k} \neg\alpha_G), \alpha_H \vdash \bigwedge_{i\in H} K_i p_i, \qquad \text{where } |H| = k+1. \qquad (5.4)$$

Please try carefully to understand what this entailment is saying. 'If all the things in Γ are true and if it is common knowledge that the set of muddy children is not of size less than or equal to k and if actually it is of size $k + 1$, then each of those $k + 1$ children can deduce that they are muddy.' Notice how this fits with our intuitive account given earlier in this text.

To prove Entailment 2, take any $i \in H$. It is sufficient to prove that

$$\Gamma, C(\bigwedge_{|G|\leq k} \neg\alpha_G), \alpha_H \vdash K_i p_i.$$

Using $\wedge i$ repeatedly over all values of i, this gives us a proof of Entailment 2. Let G be $H - \{i\}$; the proof that $\Gamma, C(\neg\alpha_G), \alpha_H \vdash K_i p_i$ is given in Figure 5.20. Please follow it carefully and understand how it is just following the steps taken in the informal proof in Section 5.5.1.

The line 14 of the proof in Figure 5.20 applies several instances of $\wedge i$ in sequence and is a legitimate step since the formulas in lines 11-13 had been shown 'for each' element in the respective set.

EXERCISES 5.9
Use the natural deduction rules for propositional logic to justify the proof steps above which are only annotated with 'prop'.

    1. Line 11 in Figure 5.15.

1	α_H	premise
2	$C\neg\alpha_G$	premise as $|G| \leq k$
3	p_j	$\wedge$e 1, for each $j \in G$
4	$\neg p_k$	$\wedge$e 1, for each $k \notin H$
5	$p_j \rightarrow K_i p_j$	in Γ for each $j \in G$
6	$K_i p_j$	$\rightarrow$e 5, 4, for each $j \in G$
7	$\neg p_k \rightarrow K_i \neg p_k$	in Γ for each $k \notin H$
8	$K_i \neg p_k$	$\rightarrow$e 7, 4, for each $k \notin H$
9	$K_i \neg \alpha_G$	CK 2

10	K_i	
11	p_j	K_i e 6 ($j \in G$)
12	$\neg p_k$	K_i e 8 ($k \notin H$)
13	$\neg p_i$	assumption
14	α_G	$\wedge$i 11, 12, 13
15	$\neg \alpha_G$	K_i e 9
16	$\bot$	$\neg$e 14, 15
17	$\neg\neg p_i$	$\neg$i 13–16
18	p_i	$\neg\neg$e 17
19	$K_i p_i$	K_i i 10–18

Fig. 5.20. The proof of Γ, $C(\neg\alpha_G)$, $\alpha_H \vdash K_i p_i$, used to prove 'Entailment 2' for the muddy-children puzzle.

2. Lines 10, 18 and 23 of the proof in Figure 5.16. Of course this requires three separate proofs.
3. Line 14 of the proof in Figure 5.18.
4. Line 10 of the proof for the sequent in (5.3).

EXERCISES 5.10

1. Prove, using the natural deduction rules for KT45^n:

    (a) $K_i(p \wedge q) \leftrightarrow K_i p \wedge K_i q$

    (b) $C(p \wedge q) \leftrightarrow Cp \wedge Cq$

* (c) $K_i Cp \leftrightarrow Cp$
  (d) $C K_i p \leftrightarrow Cp$
* (e) $\neg\phi \rightarrow K_i \neg K_i \phi$.
      Explain what this formula means in terms of knowledge. Do
      you believe it?
  (f) $\neg\phi \rightarrow K_1 K_2 \neg K_2 K_1 \phi$
* (g) $\neg K_1 \neg K_1 \phi \leftrightarrow K_1 \phi$.

2. We will do a natural deduction proof for a simpler version of the
   wise-men problem.

   There are two wise men; as usual, they can see each other's hats
   but not their own. It is common knowledge that there's only one
   white hat available and two red ones. (So at least one of the men is
   wearing a red one.)

   Man 1 informs the second that he doesn't know which hat he is
   wearing. Man 2 says, 'Aha, then I must be wearing a red hat.'.

   (a) Justify man 2's conclusion informally.
   (b) Let p_1, p_2 respectively, mean man 1, 2 respectively, is wearing
       a red hat. (So $\neg p_1$, $\neg p_2$ mean they (respectively) are wearing
       a white one.) Informally justify each of the following premises
       in terms of the description of the problem:

       (i) $K_2 K_1 (p_1 \vee p_2)$
       (ii) $K_2(\neg p_2 \rightarrow K_1 \neg p_2)$
       (iii) $K_2 \neg K_1 p_1$.

   (c) Using natural deduction, prove from these premises that $K_2 p_2$.
   (d) Show that the third premise was essential, by exhibiting a
       model/world which satisfies the first two, but not the conclu-
       sion.
   (e) Now it is easy to answer questions like 'if man 2 were blind
       would he still be able to tell?' and 'if man 1 were blind, would
       man 2 still be able to tell?'.

   ———

5.6 Bibliographic notes

The first systematic approaches to modal logic were made by C. I. Lewis
in the 1950s. The possible-worlds approach, which greatly simplified modal
logic and is now almost synonymous with it, was invented by S. Kripke.
Books devoted to modal logic include [Che80, Gol87, Pop94], where exten-
sive references to the literature may be found. All these books discuss the

soundness and completeness of proof calculi for modal logics. They also investigate which modal logics have the *finite-model property*: if a sequent does not have a proof, there is a finite model which demonstrates that. Not all modal logics enjoy this property, which is important for decidability. Intuitionistic propositional logic has the finite-model property; an animation which generates such finite models (called PORGI) is available from Allen Stoughton's website[1].

The idea of using modal logic to reason about knowledge is due to J. Hintikka. A great deal of work on applying modal logic to multi-agent systems has been done in [FHMV95] and [MvdH95] and other work by those authors. Many examples in this chapter are taken from this literature (some of them are attributed to other people there), though our treatment of them is original.

The natural deduction proof system for modal logic presented in this chapter is based on ideas in [Fit93].

An application of the modal logic KT4 (more precisely, its fragment without negation) as a type system for staged computation in a functional programming language can be found in [DP96].

We should stress that our framework was deliberately 'classical'; the thesis [Sim94] is a good source for discussions of intuitionistic modal logics; it also contains a gentle introduction to basic first-order modal logic.

---

[1] www.cis.ksu.edu/~allen/research.html

6

Binary decision diagrams

6.1 Representing boolean functions

Boolean functions are an important descriptive formalism for many hardware and software systems, such as synchronous and asynchronous circuits, reactive systems and finite-state programs. Representing those systems in a computer in order to reason about them requires an efficient representation for boolean functions. We look at such a representation in this chapter and describe in detail how the systems discussed in Chapter 3 can be verified using the representation.

Definition 6.1 A *boolean variable* x is a variable ranging over the values 0 and 1. We write $x_1, x_2, \ldots$ and $x, y, z, \ldots$ to denote boolean variables. We define the following functions on the set $\{0, 1\}$:

- $\bar{0} \stackrel{\text{def}}{=} 1$ and $\bar{1} \stackrel{\text{def}}{=} 0$;
- $x \cdot y \stackrel{\text{def}}{=} 1$ if x and y have value 1; otherwise $x \cdot y \stackrel{\text{def}}{=} 0$;
- $x + y \stackrel{\text{def}}{=} 0$ if x and y have value 0; otherwise $x + y \stackrel{\text{def}}{=} 1$;
- $x \oplus y \stackrel{\text{def}}{=} 1$ if exactly one of x and y equals 1.

A *boolean function* f of n arguments is a function from $\{0, 1\}^n$ to $\{0, 1\}$. We write $f(x_1, x_2, \ldots, x_n)$, or $f(V)$, to indicate that a syntactic representation of f depends on the boolean variables in V.

Note that $\cdot$, $+$ and $\oplus$ are boolean functions with two arguments, whereas $^-$ is a boolean function that takes one argument. The binary functions $\cdot$, $+$ and $\oplus$ are written in infix notation instead of prefix (i.e. we write $x + y$ instead of $+(x, y)$, etc.).

Example 6.2 In terms of the four functions above, we can define other boolean functions such as

(1). $f(x, y) \stackrel{\text{def}}{=} x \cdot (y + \overline{x})$,

(2). $g(x, y) \stackrel{\text{def}}{=} x \cdot y + (1 \oplus \overline{x})$,

(3). $h(x, y, z) \stackrel{\text{def}}{=} x + y \cdot (x \oplus \overline{y})$,

(4). $k() \stackrel{\text{def}}{=} 1 \oplus (0 \cdot \overline{1})$.

6.1.1 Propositional formulas and truth tables

Truth tables and *propositional formulas* are two different representations of boolean functions. In propositional formulas, $\land$ denotes $\cdot$, $\lor$ denotes $+$, $\neg$ denotes $^-$ and $\top$ and $\bot$ denote 1 and 0, respectively.

Boolean functions are represented by truth tables in the obvious way; for example, the function $f(x, y) \stackrel{\text{def}}{=} \overline{x + y}$ is represented by the truth table on the left:

x	y	$f(x, y)$		p	q	ϕ
1	1	0		T	T	F
0	1	0		F	T	F
1	0	0		T	F	F
0	0	1		F	F	T

On the right, we show the same truth table using the notation of Chapter 1; a formula having this truth table is $\neg(p \lor q)$. In this chapter, we may mix these two notational systems of boolean formulas and formulas of propositional logic whenever it is convenient. You should be able to translate expressions easily from one notation to the other and vice versa.

As representations of boolean functions, propositional formulas and truth tables have different advantages and disadvantages. Truth tables are very space-inefficient: if one wanted to model the functionality of a sequential circuit by a boolean function of 100 variables (a small chip component would easily require this many variables), then the truth table would require 2^{100} (which is more than 10^{30}) lines. Alas, there is not enough storage space (whether paper or particle) in the universe to record the information of 2^{100} different bit vectors of length 100. Once you have computed a truth table, it is easy to see whether the boolean function represented is satisfiable: you just look to see if there is a 1 in the last column of the table. Comparing whether two truth tables represent the same boolean function also seems easy: assuming the two tables are presented with the same order of valuations, we simply check that they are identical. Although these operations seem simple, however, they are computationally intractable because of the fact that the number of lines in the truth table is exponential in the number of variables. Checking satisfiability of a function with n atoms requires of the order of 2^n operations if the function is represented as a truth table. We conclude that checking satisfiability and equivalence is highly inefficient with the truth-table representation.

Representation of boolean functions by propositional formulas is slightly better. Propositional formulas often provide a wonderfully compact and efficient presentation of boolean functions. A formula with 100 variables might only be about 200–300 characters long. However, deciding whether an arbitrary propositional formula is satisfiable is a famous problem in computer science: no efficient algorithms for this task are known, and it is strongly suspected that there aren't any. Similarly, deciding whether two arbitrary propositional formulas f and g denote the same boolean function is suspected to be exponentially expensive.

It is straightforward to see how to perform the boolean operations $\cdot$, $+$, $\oplus$ and $^-$ on these two representations. In the case of truth tables, they involve applying the operation to each line; for example, given truth tables for f and g over the same set of variables (and in the same order), the truth table for $f \oplus g$ is obtained by applying $\oplus$ to the truth value of f and g in each line. If f and g do not have the same set of arguments, it is easy to pad them out by adding further arguments. In the case of representation by propositional formulas, the operations $\cdot$, $\oplus$, etc., are simply syntactic manipulations. For example, given formulas ϕ and ψ representing the functions f and g, the formulas representing $f \cdot g$ and $f \oplus g$ are, respectively, $\phi \wedge \psi$ and $(\phi \wedge \neg\psi) \vee (\neg\phi \wedge \psi)$.

We could also consider representing boolean functions by various sub-classes of propositional formulas, such as conjunctive and disjunctive normal forms. In the case of disjunctive normal form (DNF, in which a formula is a disjunction of conjunctions of literals), the representation is sometimes compact, but in the worst cases it can be very lengthy. Checking satisfiability is a straightforward operation, however, because it is sufficient to find a disjunct which does not have two complementary literals. Unfortunately, there is not a similar way of checking validity. Performing $+$ on two formulas in DNF simply involves inserting $\vee$ between them. Performing $\cdot$ is more complicated; we cannot simply insert $\wedge$ between the two formulas, because the result will not in general be in DNF, so we have to perform lengthy applications of the distributivity rule $\phi \wedge (\psi_1 \vee \psi_2) \equiv (\phi \wedge \psi_1) \vee (\phi \wedge \psi_1)$. Computing the negation of a DNF formula is also expensive. The DNF formula ϕ may be quite short, whereas the length of the disjunctive normal form of $\neg\phi$ can be exponential in the length of ϕ.

The situation for representation in conjunctive normal form is the dual. A summary of these remarks is contained in Figure 6.1 (for now, please ignore the last row).

Representation of boolean functions	compact?	test for satisf'ty	validity	boolean operations ·	+	¯
Prop. formulas	often	hard	hard	easy	easy	easy
Formulas in DNF	sometimes	easy	hard	hard	easy	hard
Formulas in CNF	sometimes	hard	easy	easy	hard	hard
Ordered truth tables	never	hard	hard	hard	hard	hard
Reduced OBDDs	often	easy	easy	medium	medium	easy

Fig. 6.1. Comparing efficiency of five representations of boolean formulas.

EXERCISES 6.1
1. Write down the truth tables for the boolean formulas in Example 6.2. In your table, you may use 0 and 1, or F and T, whatever you prefer. What truth value does the boolean formula of item (4) on page 317 compute?
2. $\oplus$ is the exclusive-or: $x \oplus y \stackrel{def}{=} 1$ if the values of x and y are different; otherwise, $x \oplus y \stackrel{def}{=} 0$. Express this in propositional logic, i.e. find a formula ϕ having the same truth table as $\oplus$.
* 3. Write down a boolean formula $f(x,y)$ in terms of $\cdot$, $+$, $\bar{\ }$, 0 and 1, such that f has the same truth table as $p \to q$.
4. Write down a BNF for the syntax of boolean formulas based on the operations in Definition 6.1.

6.1.2 *Binary decision diagrams*

Binary decision diagrams (BDDs) are another way of representing boolean functions. A certain class of such diagrams will provide the implementational framework for our symbolic model-checking algorithm. Binary decision diagrams were first considered in a simpler form called *binary decision trees*. These are trees whose non-terminal nodes are labelled with boolean variables $x, y, z, \ldots$ and whose terminal nodes are labelled with either 0 or 1. Each non-terminal node has two edges, one dashed line and one solid line. In Figure 6.2 you can see such a binary decision tree with two layers of variables x and y.

Definition 6.3 Let T be a finite binary decision tree. Then T determines a unique boolean function of the variables in non-terminal nodes, in the following way. Given an assignment of 0s and 1s to the boolean variables occurring in T, we start at the root of T and take the dashed line whenever the value of the variable at the current node is 0; otherwise, we travel along the solid line. The function value is the value of the terminal node we reach.

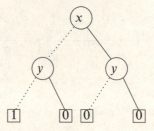

Fig. 6.2. An example of a binary decision tree.

For example, the binary decision tree of Figure 6.2 represents a boolean function $f(x, y)$. To find $f(0, 1)$, start at the root of the tree. Since the value of x is 0 we follow the dashed line out of the node labelled x and arrive at the leftmost node labelled y. Since y's value is 1, we follow the solid line out of that y-node and arrive at the leftmost terminal node labelled 0. Thus, $f(0, 1)$ equals 0. In computing $f(0, 0)$, we similarly travel down the tree, but now following two dashed lines to obtain 1 as a result. You can see that the two other possibilities result in reaching the remaining two terminal nodes labelled 0. Thus, this binary decision tree computes the function $f(x, y) \stackrel{\text{def}}{=} \overline{x + y}$.

EXERCISES 6.2
* 1. Suppose we swap all dashed and solid lines in the binary decision tree of Figure 6.2. Write out the truth table of the resulting binary decision tree and find a formula for it.
* 2. Consider the following truth table:

p	q	r	ϕ
T	T	T	T
T	T	F	F
T	F	T	F
T	F	F	F
F	T	T	T
F	T	F	F
F	F	T	T
F	F	F	F

Write down a binary decision tree which represents the boolean function specified in this truth table.

3. Construct a binary decision tree for the boolean function specified in

Figure 6.2, but now the root should be a y-node and its two successors should be x-nodes.

4. Consider the following boolean function given by its truth table:

x	y	z	$f(x,y,z)$
1	1	1	0
1	1	0	1
1	0	1	0
1	0	0	1
0	1	1	0
0	1	0	0
0	0	1	0
0	0	0	1

(a) Construct a binary decision tree for $f(x,y,z)$ such that the root is an x-node followed by y- and then z-nodes.

(b) Construct another binary decision tree for $f(x,y,z)$, but now let its root be a z-node followed by y- and then x-nodes.

5. Let T be a binary decision tree for a boolean function $f(x_1, x_2, \ldots, x_n)$ of n boolean variables. Suppose that every variable occurs exactly once as one travels down on any path of the tree T. Use mathematical induction to show that T has $2^{n+1} - 1$ nodes.

Binary decision trees are quite close to the representation of boolean functions as truth tables as far as their sizes are concerned. If the root of a binary decision tree is an x-node then it has two subtrees (one for the value of x being 0 and another one for x having value 1). So if f depends on n boolean variables, the corresponding binary decision tree will have at least $2^{n+1} - 1$ nodes (see Exercise 6.2.5). Since f's truth table has 2^n lines, we see that decision trees as such are not a more compact representation of boolean functions. However, binary decision trees often contain some redundancy which we can exploit.

Since 0 and 1 are the only terminal nodes of binary decision trees, we can optimise the representation by having pointers to just one copy of 0 and one copy of 1. For example, the binary decision tree in Figure 6.2 can be optimised in this way and the resulting structure is depicted in Figure 6.3(a). Note that we saved storage space for two redundant terminal 0-nodes, but that we still have as many edges (pointers) as before.

A second optimisation we can do is to remove unnecessary decision points in the tree. In Figure 6.3(a), the right-hand y is unnecessary, because we

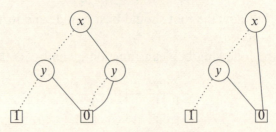

Fig. 6.3. (a) Sharing the terminal nodes of the binary decision tree in Figure 6.2; (b) further optimisation by removing a redundant decision point.

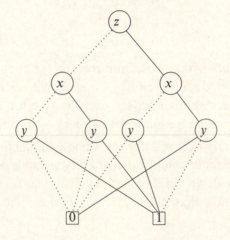

Fig. 6.4. A BDD with duplicated subBDDs.

go to the same place whether it is 0 or 1. Therefore the structure could be further reduced, to the one shown on the right, (b).

All these structures are examples of *binary decision diagrams* (BDDs). They are more general than binary decision trees; the sharing of the leaves means they are not trees. As a third optimisation, we also allow subBDDs to be shared. A subBDD is the part of a BDD occurring below a given node. For example, in the BDD of Figure 6.4, the two inner y-nodes perform the same role, because the subBDDs below them have the same structure. Therefore, one of them could be removed, resulting in the BDD in Figure 6.5(a). Indeed, the left-most y-node could also be merged with the middle one; then the x-node above both of them would become redundant. Removing it would result in the BDD on the right of Figure 6.5, (b).

To summarise, we encountered three different ways of reducing a BDD to a more compact form:

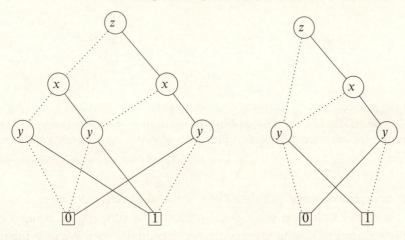

Fig. 6.5. The BDD of Figure 6.4 (a) after removal of one of the duplicate *y*-nodes; (b) after removal of another duplicate *y*-node and then a redundant *x*-decision point.

C1. Removal of duplicate terminals. If a BDD contains more than one terminal 0-node, then we redirect all edges which point to such a 0-node to just one of them. We proceed in the same way with terminal nodes labelled with 1.

C2. Removal of redundant tests. If both outgoing edges of a node *n* point to the same node *m*, then we eliminate that node *n*, sending all its incoming edges to *m*.

C3. Removal of duplicate non-terminals. If two distinct nodes *n* and *m* in the BDD are the roots of structurally identical subBDDs, then we eliminate one of them, say *m*, and redirect all its incoming edges to the other one.

In order to define BDDs precisely, we need a few auxiliary notions.

Definition 6.4 A *directed graph* is a set *G* and a binary relation $\rightarrow$ on *G* (i.e. $\rightarrow \subseteq G \times G$). A *cycle* in a directed graph is a finite path in that graph that begins and ends at the same node, i.e. a path of the form $v_1 \rightarrow v_2 \rightarrow \cdots \rightarrow v_n \rightarrow v_1$. A *directed acyclic graph* (dag) is a directed graph that does not have any cycles. A node of a dag is *initial* if there are no edges pointing to that node. A node is called *terminal* if there are no edges out of that node.

The directed graph in Figure 3.2 has cycles (for example the cycle $s_0 \rightarrow s_1 \rightarrow s_0$) and is not a dag. If we interpret the links in BDDs (whether solid or dashed) as always going in a downwards direction, then the BDDs of this

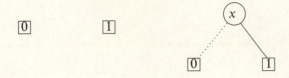

Fig. 6.6. The BDDs (a) B_0, representing the constant 0 boolean function; (b) B_1, representing the constant 1 boolean function; and (c) B_x, representing the boolean variable x.

chapter are also directed graphs. They are also acyclic and have a unique initial node. The optimisations C1–C3 preserve the property of being a dag; and fully reduced BDDs have precisely two terminal nodes. We now formally define BDDs as certain kinds of dags:

Definition 6.5 A *binary decision diagram* (BDD) is a finite dag with a unique initial node, where all terminal nodes are labelled with 0 or 1 and all non-terminal nodes are labelled with a boolean variable. Each non-terminal node has exactly two edges from that node to others: one labelled 0 and one labelled 1 (we represent them as a dashed line and a solid line, respectively).

A BDD is said to be *reduced* if none of the optimisations C1–C3 can be applied (i.e. no more reductions are possible).

All the decision structures we have seen in this chapter (Figures 6.2-6.5) are BDDs, as are the constant functions B_0 and B_1 and the function B_x depicted in Figure 6.6 in that order. If B is a BDD where $V = \{x_1, x_2, \ldots, x_n\}$ is the set of labels of non-terminal nodes, then B determines a boolean function $f(V)$ in the same way as binary decision trees (see Definition 6.3): given an assignment of 0s and 1s to the variables in V, we compute the value of f by starting with the unique initial node. If its variable has value 0, we follow the dashed line; otherwise we take the solid line. We continue for each node until we reach a terminal node. Since the BDD is finite by definition, we eventually reach a terminal node which is labelled with 0 or 1. That label is the result of f for that particular assignment of truth values.

The definition of a BDD does not prohibit that a boolean variable occur more than once on a path in the dag. For example, consider the BDD in Figure 6.7.

Such a representation is wasteful, however. The solid link from the leftmost x to the 0-terminal is never taken, for example, because one can only get to that x-node when x has value 0.

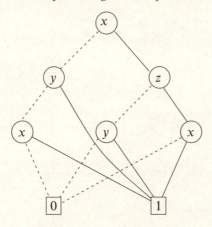

Fig. 6.7. A BDD where some boolean variables occur more than once on an evaluation path.

Thanks to the reductions C1–C3, BDDs can often be quite compact representations of boolean functions. Let us consider how to check satisfiability and perform the boolean operations on functions represented as BDDs. A BDD represents a satisfiable function if a 1-terminal node is reachable from the root along a *consistent path* in a BDD which represents it. A consistent path is one which, for every variable, has only dashed lines or only solid lines leaving nodes labelled by that variable. (In other words, we cannot assign a variable the values 0 and 1 simultaneously.) Checking validity is similar, but we check that no 0-terminal is reachable by a consistent path.

The operations $\cdot$ and $+$ can be performed by 'surgery' on the component BDDs. Given BDDs B_f and B_g representing boolean functions f and g, a BDD representing $f \cdot g$ can be obtained by taking the BDD f and replacing all its 1-terminals by B_g. To see why this is so, consider how to get to a 1-terminal in the resulting BDD. You have to satisfy the requirements for getting to a 1 imposed by both of the BDDs. Similarly, a BDD for $f + g$ can be obtained by replacing all 0 terminals of B_f by B_g. Note that these operations are likely to generate BDDs with multiple occurrences of variables along a path. Later, in Section 6.2, we will see definitions of $+$ and $\cdot$ on BDDs that don't have this undesirable effect.

The complementation operation $^-$ is also possible: a BDD representing $\overline{f}$ can be obtained by replacing all 0-terminals in B_f by 1-terminals and vice versa. Figure 6.8 shows the complement of the BDD in Figure 6.2.

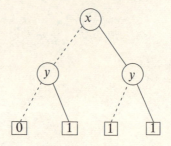

Fig. 6.8. The complement of the BDD in Figure 6.2.

EXERCISES 6.3

* 1. Explain why all reductions C1–C3 on a BDD B result in BDDs which still represent the same function as B.

2. Consider the BDD in Figure 6.7.

   * (a) Specify the truth table for the boolean function $f(x, y, z)$ represented by this BDD.
   (b) Find a BDD for that function which does not have multiple occurrences of variables along any path.

3. Let f be the function represented by the BDD of Figure 6.3(b). Using also the BDDs B_0, B_1 and B_x illustrated in Figure 6.6, find BDDs representing

   (a) $f \cdot x$
   (b) $x + f$
   (c) $\overline{f \cdot 0}$
   (d) $f \cdot 1$.

___

6.1.3 Ordered BDDs

We have seen that the representation of boolean functions by BDDs is often compact, thanks to the sharing of information afforded by the reductions C1–C3. However, BDDs with multiple occurrences of a boolean variable along a path seem rather inefficient. Moreover, there seems no easy way to test for equivalence of BDDs. For example, the BDDs of Figures 6.7 and 6.9 represent the same boolean function (the reader should check this). Neither of them can be optimised further by applying the rules C1–C3. However, testing whether they denote the same boolean function seems to involve as much computational effort as computing the entire truth table for $f(x, y, z)$.

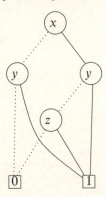

Fig. 6.9. A BDD representing the same function as the BDD of Figure 6.7, but having the variable ordering $[x, y, z]$.

We can improve matters by imposing an ordering on the variables occurring along any path. We then adhere to that same ordering for all the BDDs we manipulate.

Definition 6.6 Let $[x_1, \ldots, x_n]$ be an ordered list of variables without duplications and let B be a BDD all of whose variables occur somewhere in the list. We say that *B has the ordering* $[x_1, \ldots, x_n]$ if all variable labels of B occur in that list and, for every occurrence of x_i followed by x_j along any path in B, we have $i < j$.

An *ordered* BDD (OBDD) is a BDD which has an ordering for some list of variables.

Note that the BDDs of Figures 6.3(a,b) and 6.9 are ordered (with ordering $[x, y, z]$). We don't insist that every variable in the list is used in the paths. Thus, the OBDDs of Figures 6.3 and 6.9 have the ordering $[x, y, z]$ and so does any list having x, y and z in it in that order, such as $[u, x, y, v, z, w]$ and $[x, u, y, z]$. Even the BDDs B_0 and B_1 in Figure 6.6 are OBDDs, a suitable ordering list being the empty list (there are no variables), or indeed *any* list. The BDD B_x of Figure 6.6(c) is also an OBDD, with any list containing x as its ordering.

The BDD of Figure 6.7 is not ordered. To see why this is so, consider the path taken if the values of x and y are 0. We begin with the root, an x-node, and reach a y-node and then an x-node again. Thus, no matter what list arrangement we choose (remembering that no double occurrences are allowed), this path violates the ordering condition. Another example of a BDD that is not ordered can be seen in Figure 6.10. In that case, we cannot

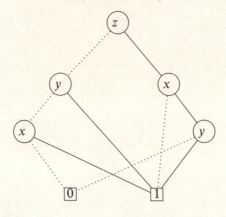

Fig. 6.10. A BDD which does not have an ordering of variables.

find an order since the path for $(x, y, z) \Rightarrow (0, 0, 0)$ — meaning that x, y and z are assigned 0 — shows that y needs to occur before x in such a list, whereas the path for $(x, y, z) \Rightarrow (1, 1, 1)$ demands that x be before y.

It follows from the definition of OBDDs that one cannot have multiple occurrences of any variable along a path.

When operations are performed on two OBDDs, we usually require that they have *compatible variable orderings*. The orderings of B_1 and B_2 are said to be compatible if there are no variables x and y such that x comes before y in the ordering of B_1 and y comes before x in the ordering of B_2. This commitment to an ordering gives us a unique representation of boolean functions as OBDDs.

Theorem 6.7 *The reduced OBDD representing a given function f is unique. That is to say, let B_1 and B_2 be two reduced OBDDs with compatible variable orderings. If B_1 and B_2 represent the same boolean function, then they have identical structure.*

In other words, with OBDDs we cannot get a situation like the one encountered earlier, in which we have two distinct reduced BDDs which represent the same function, provided that the orderings are compatible. It follows that checking equivalence of OBDDs is immediate. Checking whether two OBDDs (having compatible orderings) represent the same function is simply a matter of checking whether they have the same structure[1].

A useful consequence of the theorem above is that, if we apply the reductions C1–C3 to an OBDD until no further reductions are possible, then

---

[1] In an implementation this will amount to checking whether two pointers are equal.

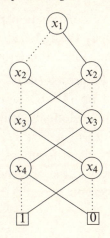

Fig. 6.11. An OBDD for the even parity function for four bits.

we are guaranteed that the result is always the same reduced OBDD. The order in which we applied the reductions does not matter. We therefore say that OBDDs have a *canonical form*, namely their unique reduced OBDD. Most other representations (conjunctive normal forms, etc.) do not have canonical forms.

The algorithms for $\cdot$ and $+$ for BDDs presented in Section 6.1.2 will not work for OBDDs, because they may introduce multiple occurrences of the same variable on a path. We need to develop more sophisticated algorithms for these operations on OBDDs, which exploit the compatible ordering of variables in paths, in the next section.

OBDDs allow compact representations of certain classes of boolean functions which only have exponential representations in other systems, such as truth tables and conjunctive normal forms. As an example consider the *even parity function* $f_{even}(x_1, x_2, \ldots, x_n)$ which is defined to be 1 if there is an even number of variables x_i with value 1; otherwise, it is defined to be 0. Its representation as an OBDD requires only $2n+1$ nodes. Its OBDD for $n = 4$ and the ordering $[x_1, x_2, x_3, x_4]$ can be found in Figure 6.11.

EXERCISES 6.4
1. Figure 6.9 shows a BDD with ordering $[x, y, z]$.

    * (a) Find an equivalent reduced BDD with ordering $[z, y, x]$. (Hint: you already worked out the truth table for this BDD, in Exercise 6.3.2(a). Find first the decision tree with the ordering $[z, y, x]$, and then reduce it using C1–C3.)

(b) Carry out the same construction process for the variable ordering $[y, z, x]$. Does the reduced BDD have more or fewer nodes than the ones for the orderings $[x, y, z]$ and $[z, y, x]$?

2. Consider the BDDs in Figures 6.4-6.10. Determine which of them are OBDDs. If you find an OBDD, you need to specify a list of its boolean variables without double occurrences which demonstrates that ordering.

3. Consider the following boolean formulas. Compute their unique reduced OBDDs with respect to the ordering $[x, y, z]$. It is advisable to first compute a binary decision tree and then to perform the removal of redundancies.

   (a) $f(x, y) \stackrel{\text{def}}{=} x \cdot y$
   * (b) $f(x, y) \stackrel{\text{def}}{=} x + y$
   (c) $f(x, y) \stackrel{\text{def}}{=} x \oplus y$
   * (d) $f(x, y, z) \stackrel{\text{def}}{=} (x \oplus y) \cdot (\overline{x} + z)$.

4. Recall the derived connective $\phi \leftrightarrow \psi$ from Chapter 1 saying that for all valuations ϕ is true if, and only if, ψ is true.

   (a) Define this operator for boolean formulas using the basic operations $\cdot$, $+$, $\oplus$ and $^{-}$ from Definition 6.1.
   (b) Draw a reduced OBDD for the formula $g(x, y) \stackrel{\text{def}}{=} x \leftrightarrow y$ using the ordering $[y, x]$.

5. Consider the even parity function introduced at the end of the last section.

   (a) Define the *odd parity function* $f_{\text{odd}}(x_1, x_2, \ldots, x_n)$.
   (b) Draw an OBDD for the odd parity function for $n = 5$ and the ordering $[x_3, x_5, x_1, x_4, x_2]$. Would the overall structure of this OBDD change if you changed the ordering?
   (c) Show that $f_{\text{even}}(x_1, x_2, \ldots, x_n)$ and $\overline{f_{\text{odd}}(x_1, x_2, \ldots, x_n)}$ denote the same boolean function.

6. Use Theorem 6.7 to show that, if the reductions C1–C3 are applied until no more reduction is possible, the result is independent of the order in which they were applied.

——

The impact of the chosen variable ordering

The size of the OBDD representing the parity functions is independent of the chosen variable ordering. This is because the parity functions are

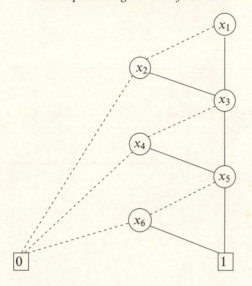

Fig. 6.12. The OBDD for $(x_1 + x_2) \cdot (x_3 + x_4) \cdot (x_5 + x_6)$ with variable ordering $[x_1, x_2, x_3, x_4, x_5, x_6]$.

themselves independent of the order of variables: swapping the values of any two variables does not change the value of the function (such functions are called symmetric).

However, in general the chosen variable ordering makes a significant difference to the size of the OBDD representing a given function. Consider the boolean function $(x_1 + x_2) \cdot (x_3 + x_4) \cdot \cdots \cdot (x_{2n-1} + x_{2n})$; it corresponds to a propositional formula in conjunctive normal form. If we choose the 'natural' ordering $[x_1, x_2, x_3, x_4, \ldots]$, then we can represent this function as an OBDD with $2n + 2$ nodes. Figure 6.12 shows the resulting OBDD for $n = 3$. Unfortunately, if we choose instead the ordering

$$[x_1, x_3, x_5, \ldots, x_{2n-1}, x_2, x_4, x_6, \ldots, x_{2n}]$$

the resulting OBDD requires 2^{n+1} nodes; the OBDD for $n = 3$ can be seen in Figure 6.13.

The sensitivity of the size of an OBDD to the particular variable ordering is a price we pay for all the advantages that OBDDs have over BDDs. Although finding the optimal ordering is itself a computationally expensive problem, there are good heuristics which will usually produce a fairly good ordering. We will say more about that when discussing applications in later sections.

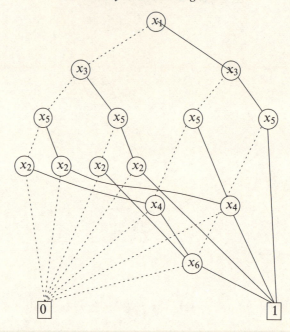

Fig. 6.13. Changing the ordering may have dramatic effects on the size of an OBDD: the OBDD for $(x_1+x_2)\cdot(x_3+x_4)\cdot(x_5+x_6)$ with variable ordering $[x_1, x_3, x_5, x_2, x_4, x_6]$.

The importance of canonical representation

The importance of having a canonical form for OBDDs in conjunction with an efficient test for deciding whether two reduced OBDDs are isomorphic cannot be overestimated. It allows us to perform the following tests:

Absence of redundant variables. If the value of the boolean function $f(x_1, x_2,...,x_n)$ does not depend on the value of x_i, then any reduced OBDD which represents f does not contain any x_i-node.

Test for semantic equivalence. If two functions $f(x_1, x_2,...,x_n)$ and $g(x_1, x_2,...,x_n)$ are represented by OBDDs B_f, respectively B_g, with a compatible ordering of variables, then we can efficiently decide whether f and g are semantically equivalent. We reduce B_f and B_g (if necessary); f and g denote the same boolean functions if, and only if, the reduced OBDDs have identical structure.

Test for validity. We can test a function $f(x_1, x_2,...,x_n)$ for validity (i.e. f always computes 1) in the following way. Compute a reduced OBDD for f. Then f is valid if, and only if, its reduced OBDD is B_1.

Test for implication. We can test whether $f(x_1, x_2,...,x_n)$ implies $g(x_1,$

$x_2, \ldots, x_n$) (i.e. whenever f computes 1, then so does g) by computing the reduced OBDD for $f \cdot \overline{g}$. This is B_0 iff the implication holds.

Test for satisfiability. We can test a function $f(x_1, x_2, \ldots, x_n)$ for satisfiability (f computes 1 for at least one assignment of 0 and 1 values to its variables). The function f is satisfiable iff its reduced OBDD is not B_0.

EXERCISES 6.5

1. Given the boolean formula $f(x_1, x_2, x_3) \stackrel{\text{def}}{=} x_1 \cdot (x_2 + \overline{x_3})$, compute its reduced OBDD for the following orderings:

   (a) $[x_1, x_2, x_3]$
   (b) $[x_3, x_1, x_2]$
   (c) $[x_3, x_2, x_1]$.

2. Compute the reduced OBDD for $f(x, y, z) = x \cdot (z + \overline{z}) + \overline{y} \cdot \overline{x}$ in any ordering you like. Is there a z-node in that reduced OBDD?

3. Consider the boolean formula $f(x, y, z) \stackrel{\text{def}}{=} (\overline{x} + y + \overline{z}) \cdot (x + \overline{y} + z) \cdot (x + y)$. For the variable orderings below, compute the (unique) reduced OBDD B_f of f with respect to that ordering. It is best to write down the binary decision tree for that ordering and then to apply all possible reductions.

   (a) $[x, y, z]$.
   (b) $[y, x, z]$.
   (c) $[z, x, y]$.
   (d) Find an ordering of variables for which the resulting reduced OBDD B_f has a minimal number of edges; i.e. there is no ordering for which the corresponding B_f has fewer edges. (How many possible orderings for x, y and z are there?)

4. Given the truth table

x	y	z	$f(x, y, z)$
1	1	1	0
1	1	0	1
1	0	1	1
1	0	0	0
0	1	1	0
0	1	0	1
0	0	1	0
0	0	0	1

   compute the reduced OBDD with respect to the following ordering of variables:

    (a) $[x, y, z]$

    (b) $[z, y, x]$

    (c) $[y, z, x]$

    (d) $[x, z, y]$.

5. Given the ordering $[p, q, r]$, compute the reduced BDDs for $p \wedge (q \vee r)$
   and $(p \wedge q) \vee (p \wedge r)$ and explain why they are identical.

* 6. Consider the BDD in Figure 6.11.

    (a) Construct its truth table.

    (b) Compute its conjunctive normal form.

    (c) Compare the length of that normal form with the size of the
        BDD. What is your assessment?

6.2 Algorithms for reduced OBDDs

6.2.1 The algorithm reduce

The reductions C1-C3 are at the core of any serious use of OBDDs, for
whenever we construct a BDD we will want to convert it to its reduced
form. In this section, we describe an algorithm reduce which does this
efficiently for ordered BDDs.

  If the ordering of B is $[x_1, x_2, \dots, x_l]$, then B has at most $l + 1$ layers. The
algorithm reduce now traverses B layer by layer in a bottom-up fashion
(beginning with the terminal nodes). In traversing B, it assigns an integer
label $id(n)$ to each node n of B, in such a way that the subOBDDs with root
nodes n and m denote the same boolean function if, and only if, $id(n)$ equals
$id(m)$.

  Since reduce starts with the layer of terminal nodes, it assigns the first
label (say #0) to the first 0-node it encounters. All other terminal 0-nodes
denote the same function as the first 0-node and therefore get the same label
(compare with reduction C1). Similarly, the 1-nodes all get the next label,
say #1.

  Now let us inductively assume that reduce has already assigned integer
labels to all nodes of a layer $> i$ (i.e. all terminal nodes and x_j-nodes with
$j > i$). We describe how nodes of layer i (i.e. x_i-nodes) are being handled.

Definition 6.8 Given a non-terminal node n in a BDD, we define $lo(n)$ to be
the node pointed to via the dashed line from n. Dually, $hi(n)$ is the node
pointed to via the solid line from n.

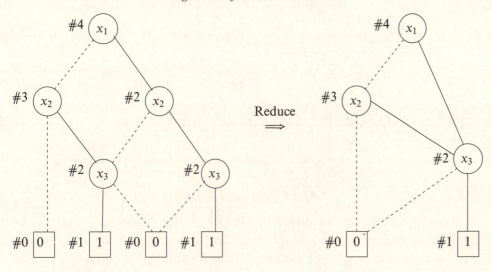

Fig. 6.14. An example execution of the algorithm `reduce`.

Let us describe how the labelling is done. Given an x_i-node n, there are three ways in which it may get its label:

- If the label id(lo(n)) is the same as id(hi(n)), then we set id(n) to be that label. That is because the boolean function represented at n is the same function as the one represented at lo(n) and hi(n). In other words, node n performs a redundant test and can be eliminated by reduction C2.
- If there is another node m such that n and m have the same variable x_i, and id(lo(n)) = id(lo(m)) and id(hi(n)) = id(hi(m)), then we set id(n) to be id(m). This is because the nodes n and m compute the same boolean function (compare with reduction C3).
- Otherwise, we set id(n) to the next unused integer label.

Note that only the last case creates a new label. Consider the OBDD in Figure 6.14(a); each node has an integer label obtained in the manner just described. The algorithm `reduce` then finishes by redirecting edges bottom-up as outlined in C1–C3. The resulting reduced OBDD is in Figure 6.14(b). Since there are efficient bottom-up traversal algorithms for dags, `reduce` is an efficient operation in the number of nodes of an OBDD.

EXERCISES 6.6

1. Perform the execution of `reduce` on the following OBDDs:

    (a) The binary decision *tree* for

(i) $x \oplus y$

(ii) $x \cdot y$

(iii) $x + y$

(iv) $x \leftrightarrow y$.

(b) The OBDD in Figure 6.2.

* (c) The OBDD in Figure 6.4.

———

6.2.2 *The algorithm* apply

Another procedure at the heart of OBDDs is the algorithm apply. It is used to implement operations on boolean functions such as $+$, $\cdot$, $\oplus$ and complementation (via $f \oplus 1$). Given OBDDs B_f and B_g for boolean formulas f and g, the call apply (op, B_f, B_g) computes the reduced OBDD of the boolean formula f op g, where op denotes any function from $\{0,1\} \times \{0,1\}$ to $\{0,1\}$.

The intuition behind the apply algorithm is fairly simple. The algorithm operates recursively on the structure of the two OBDDs:

1. let v be the variable highest in the ordering (=leftmost in the list) which occurs in B_f or B_g.
2. split the problem into two subproblems for v being 0 and v being 1 and solve recursively;
3. at the leaves, apply the boolean operation op directly.

The result will usually have to be reduced to make it into an OBDD. Some reduction can be done 'on the fly' in step 2, by avoiding creating a new node if both branches are equal (in which case return the common result), or if an equivalent node already exists (in which case, use it).

Let us make all this more precise and detailed.

Definition 6.9 Let f be a boolean formula and x a variable.

1. We denote by $f[0/x]$ the boolean formula obtained by replacing all occurrences of x in f by 0. The formula $f[1/x]$ is defined similarly. The expressions $f[0/x]$ and $f[1/x]$ are called *restrictions* of f.
2. We say that two boolean formulas f and g are *semantically equivalent* if they represent the same boolean function (with respect to the boolean variables that they depend upon). In that case, we write $f \equiv g$.

For example, if $f(x, y) \stackrel{\text{def}}{=} x \cdot (y + \overline{x})$, then $f[0/x](x, y)$ equals $0 \cdot (y + \overline{0})$, which is semantically equivalent to 0. Similarly, $f[1/y](x, y)$ is $x \cdot (1 + \overline{x})$, which is semantically equivalent to x.

Restrictions allow us to perform recursion on boolean formulas, by decomposing boolean formulas into simpler ones. For example, if x is a variable in f, then f is equivalent to $\overline{x} \cdot f[0/x] + x \cdot f[1/x]$. To see this, consider the case $x = 0$; the expression computes to $f[0/x]$. When $x = 1$ it yields $f[1/x]$. This observation is known as the *Shannon expansion*, although it can already be found in G. Boole's book '*The Laws of Thought*' from 1854.

Lemma 6.10 (Shannon expansion) *For all boolean formulas f and all boolean variables x (even those not occurring in f) we have*

$$f \equiv \overline{x} \cdot f[0/x] + x \cdot f[1/x]. \tag{6.1}$$

The function `apply` is based on the Shannon expansion for $f \text{ op } g$:

$$f \text{ op } g = \overline{x_i} \cdot (f[0/x_i] \text{ op } g[0/x_i]) + x_i \cdot (f[1/x_i] \text{ op } g[1/x_i]). \tag{6.2}$$

This is used as a control structure of `apply` which proceeds from the roots of B_f and B_g downwards to construct nodes of the OBDD $B_{f \text{ op } g}$. Let r_f be the root node of B_f and r_g the root node of B_g.

1. If both r_f and r_g are terminal nodes with labels l_f and l_g, respectively (recall that terminal labels are either 0 or 1), then we compute the value $l_f \text{ op } l_g$ and let the resulting OBDD be B_0 if that value is 0 and B_1 otherwise.

2. In the remaining cases, at least one of the root nodes is a non-terminal. Suppose that both root nodes are x_i-nodes. Then we create an x_i-node n with a dashed line to apply $(\text{op}, \text{lo}(r_f), \text{lo}(r_g))$ and a solid line to apply $(\text{op}, \text{hi}(r_f), \text{hi}(r_g))$, i.e. we call `apply` recursively on the basis of (6.2).

3. If r_f is an x_i-node, but r_g is a terminal node or an x_j-node with $j > i$, then we know that there is no x_i-node in B_g because the two OBDDs have a compatible ordering of boolean variables. Thus, g is independent of x_i ($g \equiv g[0/x_i] \equiv g[1/x_i]$). Therefore, we create an x_i-node n with a dashed line to apply $(\text{op}, \text{lo}(r_f), r_g)$ and a solid line to apply $(\text{op}, \text{hi}(r_f), r_g)$.

4. The case in which r_g is a non-terminal, but r_f is a terminal or an x_j-node with $j > i$, is handled symmetrically.

The result of this procedure might not be reduced; therefore `apply` finishes by calling the function `reduce` on the OBDD it constructed. An example of

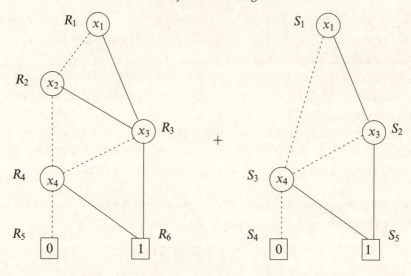

Fig. 6.15. An example of two arguments for a call apply $(+, B_f, B_g)$.

apply (where op is $+$) can be seen in Figures 6.15–6.17. Figure 6.16 shows the recursive descent control structure of apply and Figure 6.17 shows the final result. In this example, the result of apply $(+, B_f, B_g)$ is B_f.

Figure 6.16 shows that numerous calls to apply occur several times with the same arguments. Efficiency could be gained if these were evaluated only the first time and the result remembered for future calls. This programming technique is known as memoisation. As well as being more efficient, it has the advantage that the resulting OBDD requires less reduction. (In this example, using memoisation eliminates the need for the final call to reduce altogether.) Without memoisation, apply is exponential in the size of its arguments, since each non-leaf call generates a further two calls. With memoisation, the number of calls to apply is bounded by $2 \cdot |B_f| \cdot |B_g|$, where $|B|$ is the size of the BDD. This is a worst-time complexity; the actual performance is often much better than this.

EXERCISES 6.7

1. Recall the Shannon expansion in (6.1). Suppose that x does not occur in f at all. Why does the equivalence in (6.1) still hold?

2. Let $f(x, y, z) \stackrel{\text{def}}{=} y + \overline{z} \cdot x + z \cdot \overline{y} + y \cdot x$ be a boolean formula. Compute f's Shannon expansion with respect to

   (a) x
   (b) y
   (c) z.

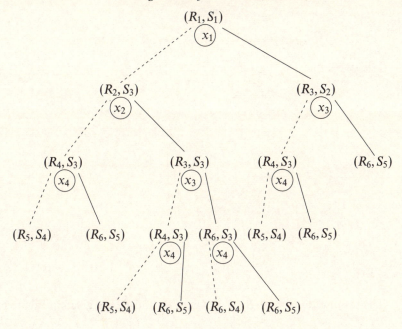

Fig. 6.16. The recursive call structure of `apply` for the example in Figure 6.15 (without memoisation).

3. Show that boolean formulas f and g are semantically equivalent if, and only if, the boolean formula $(\overline{f} + g) \cdot (f + \overline{g})$ computes 1 for all possible assignments of 0s and 1s to their variables.

4. We may use the Shannon expansion to define formally how BDDs determine boolean functions. Let B be a BDD. It is intuitively clear that B determines a *unique* boolean function. Formally, we compute a function f_n inductively (bottom-up) for all nodes n of B:

   - If n is a terminal node labelled 0, then f_n is the constant 0 function.
   - Dually, if n is a terminal 1-node, then f_n is the constant 1 function.
   - If n is a non-terminal node labelled x, then we already have defined the boolean functions $f_{lo(n)}$ and $f_{hi(n)}$ and set f_n to be $\overline{x} \cdot f_{lo(n)} + x \cdot f_{hi(n)}$.

   If i is the initial node of B, then f_i is the boolean function represented by B. Observe that we could apply this definition as a *symbolic evaluation* of B resulting in a boolean formula. For example, the BDD of Figure 6.3 renders $\overline{x} \cdot (\overline{y} \cdot 1 + y \cdot 0) + x \cdot 0$. Compute the boolean formulas obtained in this way for the following BDDs:

   (a) the BDD in Figure 6.5(b)

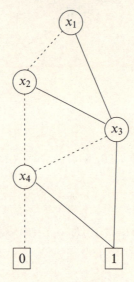

Fig. 6.17. The result of apply $(+, B_f, B_g)$ (where B_f and B_g are given in Figure 6.15).

    (b) the BDDs in Figure 6.6

    (c) the BDD in Figure 6.11.

* 5. Consider a ternary (= takes three arguments) boolean connective $f \rightarrow (g, h)$ which is equivalent to g when f is true; otherwise, it is equivalent to h.

    (a) Define this connective using any of the operators $+$, $\cdot$, $\oplus$ and $\bar{\ }$.

    (b) Recall Exercise 6.7.4. Use the ternary operator above to write f_n as an expression of $f_{\text{lo}(n)}$, $f_{\text{hi}(n)}$ and its label x.

    (c) Use mathematical induction (on what?) to prove that, if the root of f_n is an x-node, then f_n is independent of any y which comes before x in an assumed variable ordering.

6. Explain why apply (op, B_f, B_g) (where B_f and B_g have compatible ordering) produces an OBDD with an ordering compatible with that of B_f and B_g.

7. Explain why the four cases of the control structure for apply are exhaustive, i.e. there are no other possible cases in its execution.

8. Consider the reduced OBDDs B_f and B_g in Figure 6.18. Recall that, in order to compute the reduced OBDD for f op g, you need to

    ● construct the tree showing the recursive descent of apply (op, B_f, B_g) as done in Figure 6.17;

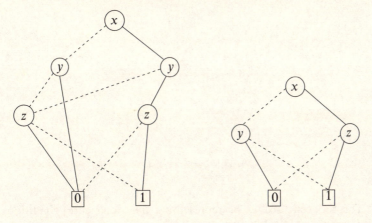

Fig. 6.18. The reduced OBDDs B_f and B_g (see exercises)

- use that tree to simulate apply (op, B_f, B_g);
- reduce, if necessary, the resulting OBDD.

Perform these steps on the OBDDs of Figure 6.18 for the operation 'op' being

    (a) +

    (b) ⊕

    (c) ·

9. Let B_f be the OBDD in Figure 6.11. Compute apply $(⊕, B_f, B_1)$ and reduce the resulting OBDD. If you did everything correctly, then this OBDD should be isomorphic to the one obtained from swapping 0- and 1-nodes in Figure 6.11.

* 10. Consider the OBDD B_c in Figure 6.19 which represents the 'don't care' conditions for comparing the boolean functions f and g represented in Figure 6.18. This means that we want to compare whether f and g are equal for all values of variables except those for which c is true (i.e. we 'don't care' when c is true).

    (a) Show that the boolean formula $(\overline{f \oplus g}) + c$ is valid (always computes 1) if, and only if, f and g are equivalent on all values for which c evaluates to 0.

    (b) Proceed in three steps as on page 340 to compute the reduced OBDD for $(\overline{f \oplus g}) + c$ from the OBDDs for f, g and c. Which call to apply needs to be first?

11. We say that $v \in \{0, 1\}$ is a (left)-controlling value for the operation

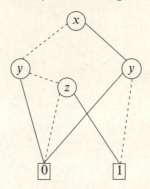

Fig. 6.19. The reduced OBDD B_c representing the 'don't care' conditions for the equivalence test of the OBDDs in Figure 6.18.

op, if either $v \text{ op } x = 1$ or $v \text{ op } x = 0$ for all values of x. We say that v is a controlling value if it is a left- and right-controlling value.

(a) Define the notion of a right-controlling value.

(b) Give examples of operations with controlling values.

(c) Describe informally how apply can be optimised when op has a controlling value.

(d) Could one still do some optimisation if op had only a left- or right-controlling value?

12. We showed that the worst-time complexity of apply is $O(|B_f| \cdot |B_g|)$. Show that this upper bound is *hard*, i.e. it cannot be improved:

(a) Consider the functions $f(x_1, x_2, \ldots, x_{2n+2m}) \stackrel{\text{def}}{=} x_1 \cdot x_{n+m+1} + \cdots + x_n \cdot x_{2n+m}$ and $g(x_1, x_2, \ldots, x_{2n+2m}) \stackrel{\text{def}}{=} x_{n+1} \cdot x_{2n+m+1} + \cdots + x_{n+m} \cdot x_{2n+2m}$ which are in *sum-of-product form*. Compute the sum-of-product form of $f + g$.

(b) Choose the ordering $[x_1, x_2, \ldots, x_{2n+2m}]$ and argue that the OBDDs B_f and B_g have 2^{n+1} and 2^{m+1} edges, respectively.

(c) Use the result from part (a) to conclude that B_{f+g} has 2^{n+m+1} edges, i.e. $0.5 \cdot |B_f| \cdot |B_g|$.

___

6.2.3 *The algorithm* restrict

Given an OBDD B_f representing a boolean formula f, we need an algorithm restrict such that the call $\text{restrict}(0, x, B_f)$ computes the reduced OBDD representing $f[0/x]$ using the same variable ordering as B_f. The algorithm for restrict(0, x, B_f) works as follows. For each node n labelled with x, incoming edges are redirected to lo(n) and n is removed. Then we call reduce on the resulting OBDD. The call restrict (1, x, B_f) proceeds similarly, only we now redirect incoming edges to hi(n).

EXERCISES 6.8

1. Let f be the reduced OBDD represented in Figure 6.5(b). Compute the reduced OBDD for the restrictions:

    (a) $f[0/x]$

 * (b) $f[1/x]$

    (c) $f[1/y]$

 * (d) $f[0/z]$.

* 2. Suppose that we intend to modify the algorithm restrict so that it is capable of computing reduced OBDDs for a general composition $f[g/x]$.

    (a) Generalise Equation (6.1) to reflect the intuitive meaning of the operation $[g/x]$.

    (b) What fact about OBDDs causes problems for computing this composition *directly*?

    (c) How can we compute this composition given the algorithms discussed so far?

3. We define *read*-1-BDDs as BDDs B where each boolean variable occurs at most once on any evaluation path of B. In particular, read-1-BDDs need not possess an ordering on their boolean variables. Clearly, every OBDD is a read-1-BDD; but not every read-1-BDD is an OBDD (see Figure 6.10). In Figure 6.20 we see a BDD which is not a read-1-BDD; the path for $(x, y, z) \Rightarrow (1, 0, 1)$ 'reads' the value of x twice.

    Critically assess the implementation of boolean formulas via OBDDs to see which implementation details could be carried out for read-1-BDDs as well. Which implementation aspects would be problematic?

4. (For those who have had a course on finite automata.) Every boolean function f in n arguments can be viewed as a subset L_f of $\{0, 1\}^n$; defined to be the set of all those bit vectors $(v_1, v_2, \ldots, v_n)$ for which f computes 1. Since this is a finite set, L_f is a regular language and has therefore a deterministic finite automaton with a minimal number of states which accepts L_f. Can you match some of the OBDD operations with those known for finite automata? How close is the correspondence? (You may have to consider non-reduced OBDDs.)

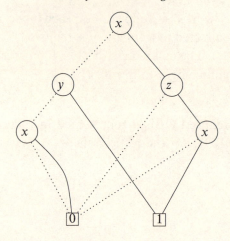

Fig. 6.20. An example of a BDD which is not a read-1-BDD.

5.   (a) Show that every boolean function in n arguments can be represented as a boolean formula of the grammar

$$f ::= 0 \mid x \mid \bar{f} \mid f_1 + f_2.$$

(b) Why does this also imply that every such function can be represented by a reduced OBDD in any variable ordering?

6. Use mathematical induction on n to prove that there are exactly $2^{(2^n)}$ many different boolean functions in n arguments.

———

6.2.4 *The algorithm* exists

A boolean function can be thought of as putting a constraint on the values of its argument variables. For example, the function $x + (\bar{y} \cdot z)$ evaluates to 1 only if x is 1; or y is 0 and z is 1 — this is a constraint on x, y, and z.

It is useful to be able to express the relaxation of the constraint on a subset of the variables concerned. To allow this, we write $\exists x. f$ for the boolean function f with the constraint on x relaxed. Formally, $\exists x. f$ is defined as $f[0/x] + f[1/x]$; that is, $\exists x. f$ is true if f could be made true by putting x to 0 or to 1.

Given that

$$\exists x. f \overset{\text{def}}{=} f[0/x] + f[1/x], \tag{6.3}$$

the exists algorithm can be implemented in terms of the algorithms apply

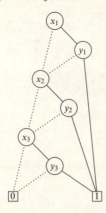

Fig. 6.21. A BDD B_f to illustrate the exists algorithm.

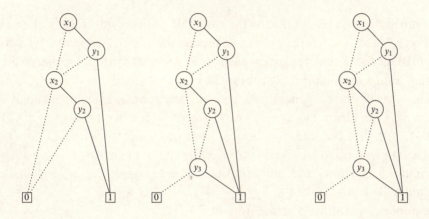

Fig. 6.22. restrict$(0, x_3, B_f)$ and restrict$(1, x_3, B_f)$ and the result of applying $+$ to them.

and restrict as apply$(+, \text{restrict}\,(0, x, B_f), \text{restrict}\,(1, x, B_f))$. Consider, for example, the OBDD B_f for the function $f \stackrel{\text{def}}{=} x_1 \cdot y_1 + x_2 \cdot y_2 + x_3 \cdot y_3$, shown in Figure 6.21. Figure 6.22 shows restrict$(0, x_3, B_f)$ and restrict$(1, x_3, B_f)$ and the result of applying $+$ to them. (In this case the apply function happens to return its second argument.)

We can improve the efficiency of this algorithm. Consider what happens during the apply stage of apply$(+, \text{restrict}\,(0, x, B_f), \text{restrict}\,(1, x, B_f))$. In that case, the apply algorithm works on two BDDs which are identical all the way down to the level of the x-nodes; therefore the returned BDD also has that structure down to the x-nodes. At the x-nodes, the two argument BDDs differ, so the apply algorithm will compute the apply of $+$ to these

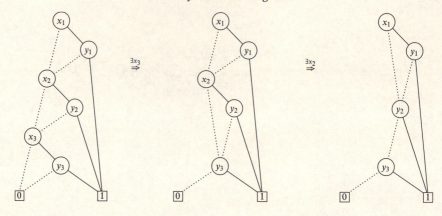

Fig. 6.23. OBDDs for f, $\exists x_3.f$ and $\exists x_2.\exists x_3.f$.

two subBDDs and return that as the subBDD of the result. This is illustrated in Figure 6.22. Therefore, we can compute the OBDD for $\exists x.f$ by taking the OBDD for f and replacing each node labelled with x by the result of calling apply on $+$ and its two branches.

This can easily be generalised to a sequence of exists operations. We write $\exists \hat{x}.f$ to mean $\exists x_1.\exists x_2.\ldots.\exists x_n.f$, where $\hat{x}$ denotes $(x_1, x_2, \ldots, x_n)$. The OBDD for this boolean function is obtained from the OBDD for f by replacing *every* node labelled with an x_i by the $+$ of its two branches.

Figure 6.23 shows the computation of $\exists x_3.f$ and $\exists x_2.\exists x_3.f$ (which is semantically equivalent to $x_1 \cdot y_1 + y_2 + y_3$) in this way.

The boolean quantifier $\forall$ is the dual of $\exists$:

$$\forall x.f \overset{\text{def}}{=} f[0/x] \cdot f[1/x],$$

asserting that f could be made false by putting x to 0 or to 1.

EXERCISES 6.9

1. Use the exists algorithm to compute the OBDDs for

    (a) $\exists x_3.f$, given the OBDD for f in Figure 6.11.

    (b) $\forall y.g$, given the OBDD for g in Figure 6.9.

    (c) $\exists x_2.\exists x_3.x_1 \cdot y_1 + x_2 \cdot y_2 + x_3 \cdot y_3$.

2. Let f be a boolean function depending on n variables.

    (a) Show:

        (i) The formula $\exists x.f$ depends on all those variables that f depends upon, except x.

Boolean formula f	Representing OBDD B_f
0	B_0 (Fig. 6.6(a))
1	B_1 (Fig. 6.6(b))
x	B_x (Fig. 6.6(c))
$\overline{f}$	swap the 0- and 1-nodes in B_f
$f + g$	apply $(+, B_f, B_g)$
$f \cdot g$	apply $(\cdot, B_f, B_g)$
$f \oplus g$	apply $(\oplus, B_f, B_g)$
$f[1/x]$	restrict $(1, x, B_f)$
$f[0/x]$	restrict $(0, x, B_f)$
$\exists x.f$	apply $(+, B_{f[0/x]}, B_{f[1/x]})$
$\forall x.f$	apply $(\cdot, B_{f[0/x]}, B_{f[1/x]})$

Fig. 6.24. Translating boolean formulas f to OBDDs B_f, given a fixed, global ordering on boolean variables.

(ii) If f computes to 1 with respect to a valuation ρ, then $\exists x.f$ computes 1 with respect to the same valuation.

(iii) If $\exists x.f$ computes to 1 with respect to a valuation ρ, then there is a valuation ρ' for f which agrees with ρ for all variables other than x such that f computes to 1 under ρ'.

(b) Can the statements above be shown for the function value 0?

3. Let ϕ be a boolean formula.

* (a) Show that ϕ is satisfiable if, and only if, $\exists x.\phi$ is satisfiable.

(b) Show that ϕ is valid if, and only if, $\forall x.\phi$ is valid.

(c) Generalise the two facts above to nested quantifications $\exists \hat{x}$ and $\forall \hat{x}$. (Use induction on the number of quantified variables.)

4. Show that $\forall \hat{x}.f$ and $\overline{\exists \hat{x}.\overline{f}}$ are semantically equivalent. Use induction on the number of arguments in the vector $\hat{x}$.

The translation of boolean formulas into OBDDs using the algorithms of this section is summarised in Figure 6.24.

Algorithm	Input OBDD(s)	Output OBDD	Time-complexity
`reduce`	B	reduced B	$O(|B| \cdot \log|B|)$
`apply`	B_f, B_g (reduced)	$B_{f \text{ op } g}$ (reduced)	$O(|B_f| \cdot |B_g|)$
`restrict`	B_f (reduced)	$B_{f[0/x]}$ or $B_{f[1/x]}$ (reduced)	$O(|B_f| \cdot \log|B_f|)$
$\exists$	B_f (reduced)	$B_{\exists x_1 . \exists x_2 \dots \exists x_n . f}$ (reduced)	NP-complete

Fig. 6.25. Upper bounds in terms of the input OBDD(s) for the worst-case running times of our algorithms needed in our implementation of boolean formulas.

6.2.5 *Assessment of OBDDs*

Time complexities for computing OBDDs

We can measure the complexity of the algorithms of the preceding section by giving upper bounds for the running time in terms of the sizes of the input OBDDs. The table in Figure 6.25 summarises these upper bounds (some of those upper bounds may require more sophisticated versions of the algorithms than the versions presented in this chapter). All the operations except nested boolean quantification are practically efficient in the size of the participating OBDDs. Thus, modelling very large systems with this approach will work if the OBDDs which represent the systems don't grow too large too fast. If we can somehow control the size of OBDDs, e.g. by using good heuristics for the choice of variable ordering, then these operations are computationally feasible. It has already been shown that OBDDs modelling certain classes of systems and networks don't grow excessively.

The expensive computational operations are the nested boolean quantifications $\exists z_1 . \dots . \exists z_n . f$ and $\forall z_1 . \dots . \forall z_n . f$. By Exercise 6.10.1, the computation of the OBDD for $\exists z_1 . \dots . \exists z_n . f$, given the OBDD for f, is an NP-complete problem; thus, it is unlikely that there exists an algorithm with a feasible worst-time complexity. This is not to say that boolean functions modelling practical systems may not have efficient nested boolean quantifications. The performance of our algorithms can be improved by using further optimisation techniques, such as parallelisation.

Note that the operations `apply`, `restrict`, etc. are only efficient in the size of the input OBDDs. So if a function f does not have a compact representation as an OBDD, then computing with its OBDD will not be efficient. There are such nasty functions; indeed, one of them is *integer multiplication*. Let $b_{n-1}b_{n-2}\dots b_0$ and $a_{n-1}a_{n-2}\dots a_0$ be two n-bit integers, where b_{n-1} and a_{n-1} are the most significant bits and b_0 and a_0 are the least significant bits. The multiplication of these two integers results in a $2n$-bit integer. Thus, we may think of multiplication as $2n$ many boolean functions

f_i in $2n$ variables (n bits for input b and n bits for input a), where f_i denotes the ith output bit of the multiplication. The following negative result, due to R. E. Bryant, shows that OBDDs cannot be used for implementing integer multiplication.

Theorem 6.11 *Any OBDD representation of f_{n-1} has at least a number of vertices proportional to 1.09^n, i.e. its size is exponential in n.*

EXERCISES 6.10
(For those who know about complexity classes.)

1. Show that 3SAT can be reduced to nested existential boolean quantification. Given an instance of 3SAT, we may think of it as a boolean formula f in product-of-sums form $g_1 \cdot g_2 \cdot \cdots \cdot g_n$, where each g_i is of the form $(l_1 + l_2 + l_3)$ with each l_j being a boolean variable or its complementation. For example, f could be $(x + \bar{y} + z) \cdot (x_5 + x + \bar{x}_7) \cdot (\bar{x}_2 + z + x) \cdot (x_4 + \bar{x}_2 + \bar{x}_4)$.

    (a) Show that you can represent each function g_i with an OBDD of no more than three non-terminals, *independently of the chosen ordering*.

    (b) Introduce n new boolean variables $z_1, z_2, \ldots, z_n$. We write $\sum_{1 \le i \le n} f_i$ for the expression $f_1 + f_2 + \cdots + f_n$ and $\prod_{1 \le i \le n} f_i$ for $f_1 \cdot f_2 \cdot \cdots \cdot f_n$. Consider the boolean formula h, defined as

    $$\sum_{1 \le i \le n} \left(\bar{g}_i \cdot z_i \cdot \prod_{1 \le j < i} \bar{z}_j \right). \tag{6.4}$$

    Choose any ordering of variables whose list begins as in $[z_1, z_2, \ldots, z_n, \ldots]$. Draw the OBDD for h (draw only the root nodes for $\bar{g}_i$).

    (c) Argue that the OBDD above has at most $4n$ non-terminal nodes.

    (d) Show that f is satisfiable if, and only if, the OBDD for $\exists z_1. \exists z_2. \ldots. \exists z_n.h$ is not equal to B_1.

    (e) Explain why the last item shows a reduction of 3SAT to nested existential quantification.

2. Show that the problem of finding an optimal ordering for representing boolean functions as OBDDs is in coNP.

3. Recall that $\exists x.f$ is defined as $f[1/x] + f[0/x]$. Since we have efficient

algorithms for restriction and $+$, we obtain hereby an efficient algorithm for $\exists z_1 \ldots \exists z_n.f$. Thus, P equals NP! What is wrong with this argument?

——

Extensions and variations of OBDDs

There are many variations and extensions to the OBDD data structure. Many of them can implement certain operations more efficiently than their OBDD counterparts, but it seems that none of them perform as well as OBDDs overall. In particular, one feature which many of the variations lack is the canonical form; therefore they lack an efficient algorithm for deciding when two objects denote the same boolean function.

One kind of variation allows non-terminal nodes to be labelled with binary operators as well as boolean variables. *Parity OBDDs* are like OBDDs in that there is an ordering on variables and every variable may occur at most once on a path; but some non-terminal nodes may be labelled with $\oplus$, the exclusive-or operation. The meaning is that the function represented by that node is the exclusive-or of the boolean functions determined by its children. Parity OBDDs have similar algorithms for `apply`, `restrict`, etc. with the same performance, but they do not have a canonical form. Checking for equivalence cannot be done in constant time. There is, however, a cubic algorithm for determining equivalence; and there are also efficient probabilistic tests. Another variation of OBDDs allows complementation nodes, with the obvious meaning. Again, the main disadvantage is the lack of canonical form.

One can also allow non-terminal nodes to be unlabelled and to branch to more than two children. This can then be understood either as non-deterministic branching, or as probabilistic branching: throw a pair of dice to determine where to continue the path. Such methods may compute wrong results; one then aims at repeating the test to keep the (probabilistic) error as small as desired. This method of repeating probabilistic tests is called *probabilistic amplification*. Unfortunately, the satisfiability problem for probabilistic branching OBDDs is NP-complete. On a good note, probabilistic branching OBDDs can *verify* integer multiplication.

The development of extensions or variations of OBDDS which are customised to certain classes of boolean functions is an important area of ongoing research.

6.3 Symbolic model checking

The use of BDDs in model checking resulted in a significant breakthrough in verification in the early 1990s, because they have allowed systems with much larger state spaces to be verified. In this section, we describe in detail how the model-checking algorithm presented in Chapter 3 can be implemented using OBDDs as the basic data structure.

The pseudo-code presented in Section 3.5.2 takes as input a CTL formula ϕ and returns the set of states of the given model which satisfy ϕ. Inspection of the code shows that the algorithm consists of manipulating intermediate sets of states. We show in this section how the model and the intermediate sets of states can be stored as OBDDs; and how the operations required in that pseudo-code can be implemented in terms of the operations on OBDDs which we have seen in this chapter.

We start by showing how sets of states are represented with OBDDs, together with some of the operations required. Then, we extend that to the representation of the transition system; and finally, we show how the remainder of the required operations is implemented.

Model checking using OBDDs is called *symbolic model checking*. The term emphasises that individual states are not represented; rather, sets of states are represented symbolically, namely, those which satisfy the formula being checked.

6.3.1 Representing subsets of the set of states

Let S be a finite set (we forget for the moment that it is a set *of states*). The task is to represent the various subsets of S as OBDDs. Since OBDDs encode boolean functions, we need somehow to code the elements of S as boolean values. The way to do this in general is to assign to each element $s \in S$ a unique vector of boolean values $(v_1, v_2, \ldots, v_n)$, each $v_i \in \{0, 1\}$. Then, we represent a subset T by the boolean function f_T which maps $(v_1, v_2, \ldots, v_n)$ onto 1 if $s \in T$ and maps it onto 0 otherwise.

There are 2^n boolean vectors $(v_1, v_2, \ldots, v_n)$ of length n. Therefore, n should be chosen such that $2^{n-1} < |S| \leq 2^n$, where $|S|$ is the number of elements in S. If $|S|$ is not an exact power of 2, there will be some vectors which do not correspond to any element of S; they are just ignored. The function $f_T : \{0, 1\}^n \to \{0, 1\}$ which tells us, for each s, represented by $(v_1, v_2, \ldots, v_n)$, whether it is in the set T or not, is called the *characteristic function* of T.

In the case that S is the set of states of a CTL model $\mathcal{M} = (S, \to, L)$ (see Definition 3.4), there is a natural way of choosing the representation of S

as boolean vectors. The labelling function $L : S \to \mathcal{P}(\text{Atoms})$ gives us the encoding. We assume a fixed ordering on the set Atoms, say $x_1, x_2, \ldots, x_n$, and then represent $s \in S$ by the vector $(v_1, v_2, \ldots, v_n)$, where, for each i, v_i equals 1 if $x_i \in L(s)$ and v_i is 0 otherwise. In order to guarantee that each s has a unique representation as a boolean vector, we require that, for all $s_1, s_2 \in S$, $L(s_1) = L(s_2)$ implies $s_1 = s_2$. If this is not the case, perhaps because $2^{|\text{Atoms}|} < |S|$, we can add extra atomic propositions in order to make enough distinctions (*Cf.* introduction of the turn variable for mutual exclusion in Section 3.6.3.)

From now on, we refer to a state $s \in S$ by its representing boolean vector $(v_1, v_2, \ldots, v_n)$, where v_i is 1 if $x_i \in L(s)$ and 0 otherwise. As an OBDD, this state is represented by the OBDD of the boolean function

$$l_1 \cdot l_2 \cdot \cdots \cdot l_n,$$

where l_i is x_i if $x_i \in L(s)$ and $\overline{x_i}$ otherwise. The set of states $\{s_1, s_2, \ldots, s_m\}$ is represented by the OBDD of the boolean function

$$(l_{11} \cdot l_{12} \cdot \cdots \cdot l_{1n}) + (l_{21} \cdot l_{22} \cdot \cdots \cdot l_{2n}) + \cdots + (l_{m1} \cdot l_{m2} \cdot \cdots \cdot l_{mn}),$$

where $l_{i1} \cdot l_{i2} \cdot \cdots \cdot l_{in}$ represents state s_i.

The key point which makes this representation interesting is that the OBDD representing a set of states may be quite small.

Example 6.12 Consider the CTL model in Figure 6.26, given by:

$$
\begin{aligned}
S &\stackrel{\text{def}}{=} \{s_0, s_1, s_2\} \\
\to &\stackrel{\text{def}}{=} \{(s_0, s_1), (s_1, s_2), (s_2, s_0), (s_2, s_2)\} \\
L(s_0) &\stackrel{\text{def}}{=} \{x_1\} \\
L(s_1) &\stackrel{\text{def}}{=} \{x_2\} \\
L(s_2) &\stackrel{\text{def}}{=} \emptyset.
\end{aligned}
$$

Note that it has the property that, for all states s_1 and s_2, $L(s_1) = L(s_2)$ implies $s_1 = s_2$, i.e. a state is determined entirely by the atomic formulas true in it. Sets of states may be represented by boolean values and by boolean formulas with the ordering $[x_1, x_2]$, as shown in Figure 6.27.

Notice that the vector $(1, 1)$ and the corresponding function $x_1 \cdot x_2$ are unused. Therefore, we are free to include it in the representation of a subset of S or not; so we may choose to include it or not in order to optimise the size of the OBDD. For example, the subset $\{s_0, s_1\}$ is better represented by the boolean function $x_1 + x_2$, since its OBDD is smaller than that for $x_1 \cdot \overline{x_2} + \overline{x_1} \cdot x_2$ (Figure 6.28).

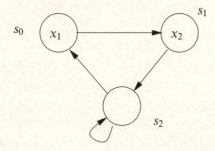

Fig. 6.26. A simple CTL model (Example 6.12).

set of states	representation by boolean values	representation by boolean function
$\emptyset$		0
$\{s_0\}$	$(1,0)$	$x_1 \cdot \overline{x_2}$
$\{s_1\}$	$(0,1)$	$\overline{x_1} \cdot x_2$
$\{s_2\}$	$(0,0)$	$\overline{x_1} \cdot \overline{x_2}$
$\{s_0, s_1\}$	$(1,0), (0,1)$	$x_1 \cdot \overline{x_2} + \overline{x_1} \cdot x_2$
$\{s_0, s_2\}$	$(1,0), (0,0)$	$x_1 \cdot \overline{x_2} + \overline{x_1} \cdot \overline{x_2}$
$\{s_1, s_2\}$	$(0,1), (0,0)$	$\overline{x_1} \cdot x_2$
S	$(1,0), (0,1), (0,0)$	$x_1 \cdot \overline{x_2} + \overline{x_1} \cdot x_2 + \overline{x_1} \cdot \overline{x_2}$

Fig. 6.27. Representation of subsets of states of the model of Figure 6.26.

In order to justify the claim that the representation of subsets of S as OBDDs will be suitable for the algorithm presented in Section 3.5.2, we need to look at how the operations on subsets which are used in that algorithm can be implemented in terms of the operations we have defined on OBDDs. The operations in that algorithm are:

- Intersection, union and complementation of subsets. It is clear that these are represented by the boolean functions $\cdot$, $+$ and $^-$ respectively. The implementation via OBDDs of $\cdot$ and $+$ uses the `apply` algorithm (Section 6.2.2).
- The functions

$$\mathrm{pre}_\exists(X) = \{s \in S \mid \text{exists } s', (s \to s' \text{ and } s' \in X)\}$$
$$\mathrm{pre}_\forall(X) = \{s \mid \text{for all } s', (s \to s' \text{ implies } s' \in X)\}.$$

The function $\mathrm{pre}_\exists$ (instrumental in $\mathrm{SAT}_{\mathrm{EX}}$ and $\mathrm{SAT}_{\mathrm{EU}}$) takes a subset X of states and returns the set of states which can make a transition into X. The function $\mathrm{pre}_\forall$, used in $\mathrm{SAT}_{\mathrm{AF}}$, takes a set X and returns the set of states which can make a transition *only* into X. In order to see how

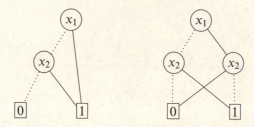

Fig. 6.28. Two OBDDs for the set $\{s_0, s_1\}$ (Example 6.12).

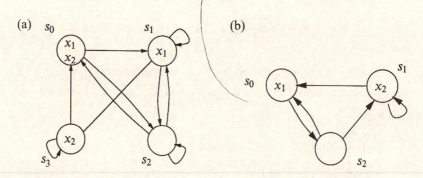

Fig. 6.29. (a) A CTL model with four states. (b) A CTL model with three states.

these are implemented in terms of OBDDs, we need first to look at how the transition relation itself is represented.

EXERCISES 6.11

* 1. Consider the CTL model in Figure 6.29(a). Using the ordering $[x_1, x_2]$, draw the OBDD for the subsets $\{s_0, s_1\}$ and $\{s_0, s_2\}$.
2. Consider the CTL model in Figure 6.29(b). Because the number of states is not an exact power of 2, there are more than one OBDDs representing any given set of states. Using again the ordering $[x_1, x_2]$, draw all possible OBDDs for the subset
    (a) $\{s_0, s_1\}$
    (b) $\{s_0, s_2\}$.

_____

6.3.2 Representing the transition relation

The transition relation $\rightarrow$ of a model $\mathcal{M} = (S, \rightarrow, L)$ is a subset of $S \times S$. We have already seen that subsets of a given finite set may be represented as OBDDs by considering the characteristic function of a binary encoding.

Just like in the case of subsets of S, the binary encoding is naturally given by the labelling function L. Since $\rightarrow$ is a subset of $S \times S$, we need two copies of the boolean vectors. Thus, the link $s \rightarrow s'$ is represented by the pair of boolean vectors $((v_1, v_2, \ldots, v_n), (v'_1, v'_2, \ldots, v'_n))$, where v_i is 1 if $p_i \in L(s)$ and 0 otherwise; and similarly, v'_i is 1 if $p_i \in L(s')$ and 0 otherwise. As an OBDD, the link is represented by the OBDD for the boolean function

$$(l_1 \cdot l_2 \cdots \cdots l_n) \cdot (l'_1 \cdot l'_2 \cdots \cdots l'_n)$$

and a set of links (for example, the entire relation $\rightarrow$) is the OBDD for the $+$ of such formulas.

Example 6.13 To compute the OBDD for the transition relation of Figure 6.26, we first show it as a truth table (Figure 6.30(a)). Each 1 in the final column corresponds to a link in the transition relation and each 0 corresponds to the absence of a link. The boolean function is obtained by taking the disjunction of the rows having 1 in the last column and is

$$f^\rightarrow \overset{\text{def}}{=} \overline{x}_1 \cdot \overline{x}_2 \cdot \overline{x}'_1 \cdot \overline{x}'_2 + \overline{x}_1 \cdot \overline{x}_2 \cdot x'_1 \cdot \overline{x}'_2 + x_1 \cdot \overline{x}_2 \cdot \overline{x}'_1 \cdot x'_2 + \overline{x}_1 \cdot x_2 \cdot \overline{x}'_1 \cdot \overline{x}'_2.$$
$$(6.5)$$

The rows marked $-$ in the final columns of Figure 6.30 are the 'don't care' links, that is, those which refer to the state $(1, 1)$ which is an artifact of the binary representation and which we ignore. We can include or exclude these links as we wish; therefore we might as well include those which help make the final OBDD more compact. It turns out that it is usually more efficient to interleave unprimed and primed variables in the OBDD variable ordering for $\rightarrow$. We therefore use $[x_1, x'_1, x_2, x'_2]$ rather than $[x_1, x_2, x'_1, x'_2]$. Figure 6.30(b) shows the truth table redrawn with the interleaved ordering of the columns and the rows *reordered lexicographically*. In considering which of the 'don't care' rows to include, we group them with their neighbours in order to form blocks of 0s and 1s. For example, we treat the first and second $-$ in the second block as a 1 and a 0, respectively, since then the resulting block $1, 1, 0, 0$ can be computed in the OBDD without reference to the variable x'_2. If the last three $-$s are treated as 0, then the value for that block is independent of x_2 and x'_2. The resulting OBDD is shown in Figure 6.31.

6.3.3 Implementing the functions $\text{pre}_\exists$ and $\text{pre}_\forall$

It remains to show how an OBDD for $\text{pre}_\exists(X)$ and $\text{pre}_\forall(X)$ can be computed, given OBDDs B_X for X and $B_\rightarrow$ for the transition relation $\rightarrow$. First we observe that $\text{pre}_\forall$ can be expressed in terms of complementation and $\text{pre}_\exists$,

Binary decision diagrams

356

x_1	x_2	x_1'	x_2'	$\rightarrow$
0	0	0	0	1
0	0	0	1	0
0	0	1	0	1
0	0	1	1	—
0	1	0	0	1
0	1	0	1	0
0	1	1	0	0
0	1	1	1	—
1	0	0	0	0
1	0	0	1	1
1	0	1	0	0
1	0	1	1	—
1	1	0	0	—
1	1	0	1	—
1	1	1	0	—
1	1	1	1	—

x_1	x_1'	x_2	x_2'	$\rightarrow$
0	0	0	0	1
0	0	0	1	0
0	0	1	0	1
0	0	1	1	0
0	1	0	0	1
0	1	0	1	—
0	1	1	0	0
0	1	1	1	—
1	0	0	0	0
1	0	0	1	1
1	0	1	0	—
1	0	1	1	—
1	1	0	0	0
1	1	0	1	—
1	1	1	0	—
1	1	1	1	—

Fig. 6.30. The truth table for the transition relation of Figure 6.26 (see Example 6.13). The left version shows the ordering of variables $[x_1, x_2, x_1', x_2']$, while the right one orders the variables $[x_1, x_1', x_2, x_2']$ (the rows are ordered lexicographically).

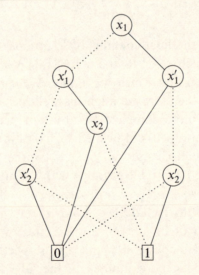

Fig. 6.31. An OBDD for the transition relation of Example 6.13.

as follows:

$$\text{pre}_\forall(X) = S - \text{pre}_\exists(S - X),$$

where we write $S - Y$ for the set of all $s \in S$ which are not in Y. Therefore, we need only explain how to compute the OBDD for $\text{pre}_\exists(X)$ in terms of

B_X and $B_\to$. Recall that

$$\text{pre}_\exists(X) = \{s \mid \text{exists } s', (s \to s' \text{ and } s' \in X)\};$$

this suggests that one should proceed as follows:

1. Rename the variables in B_X to their primed versions; call the resulting OBDD $B_{X'}$.
2. Compute the OBDD for `exists(`$\hat{x}'$`, apply(`$\cdot, B_\to, B_{X'}$`))` using the `apply` and `exists` algorithms (Sections 6.2.2 and 6.2.4).

EXERCISES 6.12
1. Consider the CTL model in Figure 6.29(a).

   (a) Work out the truth table for the transition relation, ordering the columns $[x_1, x_1', x_2, x_2']$. There should be as many 1s in the final column as there are arrows in the transition relation. There is no freedom in the representation in this case, since the number of states is an exact power of 2.
   (b) Draw the OBDD for this transition relation, using the variable ordering $[x_1, x_1', x_2, x_2']$.

2. Apply the algorithm of Section 3.5.2, but now interpreted over OBDDs in the ordering $[x_1, x_2]$, to compute the set of states of the CTL model in Figure 6.29(b) which satisfy

   (a) $AG (x_1 \lor \neg x_2)$;
   (b) $E[x_2 \text{ U } x_1]$.

   Show the OBDDs which are computed along the way.
3. Explain why `exists(`$\hat{x}'$`, apply(`$\cdot, B_\to, B_{X'}$`))` faithfully implements the meaning of $\text{pre}_\exists(X)$.

6.3.4 Synthesising OBDDs

The method used in Example 6.13 for producing an OBDD for the transition relation was to compute first the truth table and then an OBDD which might not be in its fully reduced form; hence the need for a final call to the `reduce` function. However, this procedure would be unacceptable if applied to realistically sized systems with a large number of variables, for the truth table's size is exponential in the number of boolean variables. The key idea and attraction of applying OBDDs to finite systems is therefore to take a system description in a language such as SMV and to synthesise the

OBDD directly, without having to go via intermediate representations (such as binary decision *trees* or truth tables) which are exponential in size.

SMV allows us to define the next value of a variable in terms of the current values of variables (see the examples of code in Section 3.6, page 181)[1]. This can be compiled into a set of boolean functions f_i, one for each variable x_i, which define the next value of x_i in terms of the current values of all the variables. In order to cope with non-deterministic assignment (such as the assignment to status in the example on page 182), we extend the set of variables by adding unconstrained variables which model the input. Each x_i' is a deterministic function of this enlarged set of variables; thus,

$$x_i' \leftrightarrow f_i,$$

where $f \leftrightarrow g = 1$ if, and only if, f and g compute the same values, i.e. it is a shorthand for $\overline{f} \oplus g$.

The boolean function representing the transition relation is therefore of the form

$$\prod_{1 \leq i \leq n} x_i' \leftrightarrow f_i, \tag{6.6}$$

where $\prod_{1 \leq i \leq n} g_i$ is a shorthand for $g_1 \cdot g_2 \cdot \ldots \cdot g_n$. Note that the $\prod$ ranges only over the non-input variables. So, if u is an input variable, the boolean function does not contain any $u' \leftrightarrow f_u$.

Figure 6.24 showed how the reduced OBDD could be computed from the parse tree of such a boolean function. Thus, it is possible to compile SMV programs into OBDDs such that their specifications can be executed according to the pseudo-code of the function SAT, now interpreted over OBDDs. In Section 3.7, we will see that this OBDD implementation can be extended to simple fairness constraints.

Modelling sequential circuits

As a further application of OBDDs to verification, we show how OBDDs representing circuits may be synthesised.

Synchronous circuits. Suppose that we have a design of a sequential circuit such as the one in Figure 6.32. This is a synchronous circuit (meaning that all the state variables are updated synchronously in parallel) whose functionality can be described by saying what the values of the registers x_1 and x_2 in the

---

[1] SMV also allows next values to be defined in terms of next values, i.e. the keyword next to appear in expressions on the right-hand side of :=. This is useful for describing synchronisations, for example, but we ignore that feature here.

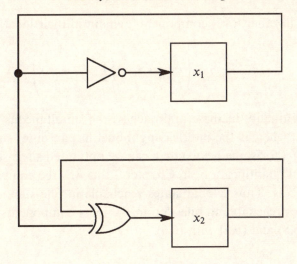

Fig. 6.32. A simple synchronous circuit with two registers.

next state of the circuit are. The function $f^{\rightarrow}$ coding the possible next states of the circuits is

$$(x_1' \leftrightarrow \overline{x}_1) \cdot (x_2' \leftrightarrow x_1 \oplus x_2). \qquad (6.7)$$

This may now be translated into an OBDD by the methods summarised in Figure 6.24.

Asynchronous circuits. The symbolic encoding of synchronous circuits is in its logical structure very similar to the encoding of $f^{\rightarrow}$ for CTL models; compare the codings in (6.7) and (6.6). In asynchronous circuits, or processes in SMV, the logical structure of $f^{\rightarrow}$ changes. As before, we can construct functions f_i which code the possible next state in the *local component*, or the SMV process, i. For asynchronous systems, there are two principal ways of composing these functions into global system behaviour:

• In a *simultaneous model*, a global transition is one in which any number of components may make their local transition. This is modelled as

$$f^{\rightarrow} \stackrel{\text{def}}{=} \prod_{i=1}^{n} \left((x_i' \leftrightarrow f_i) + (x_i' \leftrightarrow x_i) \right). \qquad (6.8)$$

• In an *interleaving model*, exactly one local component makes a local transition; all other local components remain in their local state:

$$f^{\rightarrow} \overset{\text{def}}{\equiv} \sum_{i=1}^{n}\left((x_i' \leftrightarrow f_i) \cdot \prod_{j \neq i}(x_j' \leftrightarrow x_j) \right). \tag{6.9}$$

Observe the duality in these approaches: the simultaneous model has an outer product, whereas the interleaving model has an outer sum. The latter, if used in $\exists \hat{x}'.f$ ('for some next state'), can be optimised since sums distribute over existential quantification; in Chapter 2 this was the equivalence $\exists x.(\phi \lor \psi) \equiv \exists x.\phi \lor \exists x.\psi$. Thus, global states reachable in one step are the 'union' of all the states reachable in one step in the local components; compare the formulas in (6.8) and (6.9) with (6.6).

EXERCISES 6.13

1. (a) Simulate the evolution of the circuit in Figure 6.32 with initial state 01. What do you think that it computes?

    (b) Write down the explicit CTL model $(S, \rightarrow, L)$ for this circuit.

2. Consider the sequential synchronous circuit in Figure 6.33.

    (a) Construct the functions f_i for $i = 1, 2, 3$.

    (b) Code the function $f^{\rightarrow}$.

    (c) Recall from Chapter 2 that $(\exists x.\phi) \land \psi$ is semantically equivalent to $\exists x.(\phi \land \psi)$ if x is not free in ψ.

    (i) Why is this also true in our setting of boolean formulas?

    (ii) Apply this law to push the $\exists$ quantifications in $f^{\rightarrow}$ as far inwards as possible. This is an often useful optimisation in checking synchronous circuits.

3. Consider the boolean formula for the 2-bit comparator:

$$f(x_1, x_2, y_1, y_2) \overset{\text{def}}{=} (x_1 \leftrightarrow y_1) \cdot (x_2 \leftrightarrow y_2).$$

    (a) Draw its OBDD for the ordering $[x_1, y_1, x_2, y_2]$.

    (b) Draw its OBDD for the ordering $[x_1, x_2, y_1, y_2]$ and compare that with the one above.

4. (a) Can you use Equation (6.6) to code the transition relation $\rightarrow$ of the model in Figure 6.26?

    (b) Can you do it with Equation (6.9)?

    (c) With Equation (6.8)?

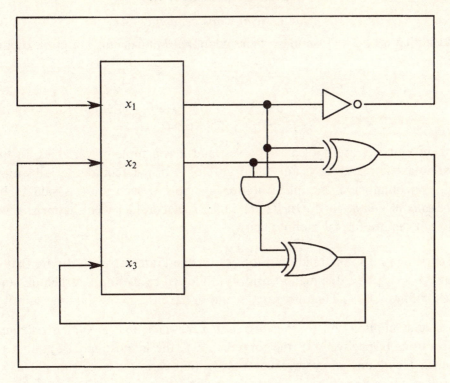

Fig. 6.33. A synchronous circuit for a modulo 8 counter.

6.4 A relational mu-calculus

We saw in Section 3.9 that evaluating the set of states satisfying a CTL formula in a model may involve the computation of a fixed point of an operator. For example, $[\![\text{EF}\,\phi]\!]$ is the least fixed point of the operator $F : \mathcal{P}(S) \to \mathcal{P}(S)$ given by

$$F(X) = [\![\phi]\!] \cup \text{pre}_\exists(X).$$

In this section, we introduce a syntax for referring to fixed points in the context of boolean formulas. Fixed-point invariants frequently occur in all sorts of applications (for example, the common-knowledge operator C_G in Chapter 5), so it makes sense to have an intermediate language for expressing such invariants syntactically. This language also provides a formalism for describing interactions and dependences of such invariants. We will see shortly that symbolic model checking in the presence of simple fairness constraints exhibits such more complex relationships between invariants.

6.4.1 Syntax and semantics

Definition 6.14 The formulas of the relational mu-calculus are given by the grammar

$$v \quad ::= \quad x \mid Z$$
$$f \quad ::= \quad 0 \mid 1 \mid v \mid \overline{f} \mid f_1 + f_2 \mid f_1 \cdot f_2 \mid f_1 \oplus f_2 \mid \qquad (6.10)$$
$$\exists x.f \mid \forall x.f \mid \mu Z.f \mid \nu Z.f \mid f[\hat{x} := \hat{x}'],$$

where x and Z are boolean variables, and $\hat{x}$ is a tuple of variables. In the formulas $\mu Z.f$ and $\nu Z.f$, any occurrence of Z in f is required to fall within an even number of complementation symbols $^-$; such an f is said to be *formally monotone* in Z. (In Exercise 6.15.7 we consider what happens if we do not require formal monotonicity.)

Convention 6.15 The binding priorities for the grammar in (6.10) are that $^-$, and $[\hat{x} := \hat{x}']$ have the highest priority; followed by $\exists x$ and $\forall y$; then μZ and νZ; followed by $\cdot$. The operators $+$ and $\oplus$ have the lowest binding priority.

The symbols μ and ν are called *least fixed-point* and *greatest fixed-point* operators, respectively. In the formula $\mu Z.f$, the interesting case is that in which f contains an occurrence of Z. In that case, f can be thought of as a function, taking Z to f. The formula $\mu Z.f$ is intended to mean the least fixed point of that function. Similarly, $\nu Z.f$ is the greatest fixed point of the function. We will see how this is done in the semantics.

The formula $f[\hat{x} := \hat{x}']$ expresses an explicit substitution which forces f to be evaluated using the values of x_i' rather than x_i. (Recall that the primed variables refer to the next state.) Thus, this syntactic form is not a meta-operation denoting a substitution, but an explicit syntactic form in its own right. The substitution will be made on the semantic side, not the syntactic side. This difference will become clear when we present the semantics of $\models$.

A valuation ρ for f is an assignment of values 0 or 1 to all variables v. We define a *satisfaction relation* $\rho \models f$ inductively over the structure of such formulas f, given a valuation ρ.

Definition 6.16 Let ρ be a valuation and v a variable. We write $\rho(v)$ for the value of v assigned by ρ. We define $\rho[v \mapsto 0]$ to be the *updated valuation* which assigns 0 to v and $\rho(w)$ to all other variables w. Dually, $\rho[v \mapsto 1]$ assigns 1 to v and $\rho(w)$ to all other variables w.

For example, if ρ is the valuation represented by $(x, y, Z) \Rightarrow (1, 0, 1)$ — meaning that $\rho(x) = 1$, $\rho(y) = 0$, $\rho(Z) = 1$ and $\rho(v) = 0$ for all other variables v — then $\rho[x \mapsto 0]$ is represented by $(x, y, Z) \Rightarrow (0, 0, 1)$, whereas

$\rho[Z \mapsto 0]$ is $(x, y, Z) \Rightarrow (1, 0, 0)$. The assumption that valuations assign values to all variables is rather mathematical, but avoids some complications which have to be addressed in implementations (see Exercise 6.14.3).

Updated valuations allow us to define the satisfaction relation for all formulas without fixed points:

Definition 6.17 We define a satisfaction relation $\rho \vDash f$ for formulas f without fixed-point subformulas with respect to a valuation ρ by structural induction:

- $\rho \nvDash 0$
- $\rho \vDash 1$
- $\rho \vDash v$ iff $\rho(v)$ equals 1
- $\rho \vDash \overline{f}$ iff $\rho \nvDash f$
- $\rho \vDash f + g$ iff $\rho \vDash f$ or $\rho \vDash g$
- $\rho \vDash f \cdot g$ iff $\rho \vDash f$ and $\rho \vDash g$
- $\rho \vDash f \oplus g$ iff $\rho \vDash (f \cdot \overline{g} + \overline{f} \cdot g)$
- $\rho \vDash \exists x.f$ iff $\rho[x \mapsto 0] \vDash f$ or $\rho[x \mapsto 1] \vDash f$
- $\rho \vDash \forall x.f$ iff $\rho[x \mapsto 0] \vDash f$ and $\rho[x \mapsto 1] \vDash f$
- $\rho \vDash f[\hat{x} := \hat{x}']$ iff $\rho[\hat{x} := \hat{x}'] \vDash f$,

where $\rho[\hat{x} := \hat{x}']$ is the valuation which assigns the same values as ρ, but for each x_i it assigns $\rho(x_i')$.

The semantics of boolean quantification closely resembles the one for the quantifiers of predicate logic. The crucial difference, however, is that boolean formulas are only interpreted over the fixed universe of values $\{0, 1\}$, whereas predicate formulas may take on values in all sorts of finite and infinite models.

To see the definition of $\vDash$ at work, let ρ be such that $\rho(x_1')$ equals 0 and $\rho(x_2')$ is 1. We evaluate $\rho \vDash (x_1 + \overline{x}_2)[\hat{x} := \hat{x}']$ which holds iff $\rho[\hat{x} := \hat{x}'] \vDash (x_1 + \overline{x}_2)$. Thus, we need $\rho[\hat{x} := \hat{x}'] \vDash x_1$ or $\rho[\hat{x} := \hat{x}'] \vDash \overline{x}_2$ to be the case. Now, $\rho[\hat{x} := \hat{x}'] \vDash x_1$ cannot be, for this would mean that $\rho(x_1')$ equals 1. Since $\rho[\hat{x} := \hat{x}'] \vDash \overline{x}_2$ would imply that $\rho[\hat{x} := \hat{x}'] \nvDash x_2$, we infer that $\rho[\hat{x} := \hat{x}'] \nvDash \overline{x}_2$ because $\rho(x_2')$ equals 1. In summary, we demonstrated that $\rho \nvDash (x_1 + \overline{x}_2)[\hat{x} := \hat{x}']$.

We now extend the definition of $\vDash$ to the fixed-point operators μ and ν. Their semantics will have to reflect their meaning as least, respectively, greatest, fixed-point operators. We define the semantics of $\mu Z.f$ via its syntactic approximants which unfold the meaning of $\mu Z.f$:

$$\mu_0 Z.f \overset{\text{def}}{=} 0$$
$$\mu_{m+1} Z.f \overset{\text{def}}{=} f[\mu_m Z.f/Z] \qquad (m \ge 0). \tag{6.11}$$

The unfolding is achieved by a meta-operation $[g/Z]$ which, when applied to a formula f, replaces all free occurrences of Z in f with g. Thus, we view μZ as a binding construct similar to the quantifiers $\forall x$ and $\exists x$, and $[g/Z]$ is similar to the substitution $[t/x]$ in predicate logic. For example, $(x_1 + \exists x_2.(Z \cdot x_2))[\overline{x}_1/Z]$ is the formula $x_1 + \exists x_2.(\overline{x}_1 \cdot x_2)$, whereas $((\mu Z.x_1 + Z) \cdot (x_1 + \exists x_2.(Z \cdot x_2)))[\overline{x}_1/Z]$ equals $(\mu Z.x_1 + Z) \cdot (x_1 + \exists x_2.(\overline{x}_1 \cdot x_2))$. See exercise 3 on page 365 for a formal account of this meta-operation.

With these approximants we can define:

$$\rho \vDash \mu Z.f \text{ iff } (\rho \vDash \mu_m Z.f \text{ for some } m \ge 0). \tag{6.12}$$

Thus, to determine whether $\mu Z.f$ is true with respect to a valuation ρ, we have to find some $m \ge 0$ such that $\rho \vDash \mu_m Z.f$ holds. A sensible strategy is to try to prove this for the smallest such m possible, if indeed such an m can be found. For example, in attempting to show $\rho \vDash \mu Z.Z$, we try $\rho \vDash \mu_0 Z.Z$, which fails since the latter formula is just 0. Now, $\mu_1 Z.Z$ is defined to be $Z[\mu_0 Z.Z/Z]$ which is just $\mu_0 Z.Z$ again. We can now use mathematical induction on $m \ge 0$ to show that $\mu_m Z.Z$ equals $\mu_0 Z.Z$ for all $m \ge 0$. By (6.12), this implies $\rho \nvDash \mu Z.Z$.

The semantics for $\nu Z.f$ is similar. First, let us define a family of approximants $\nu_0 Z.f$, $\nu_1 Z.f$, ... by

$$\nu_0 Z.f \overset{\text{def}}{=} 1$$
$$\nu_{m+1} Z.f \overset{\text{def}}{=} f[\nu_m Z.f/Z] \qquad (m \ge 0). \tag{6.13}$$

Note that this definition only differs from the one for $\mu_m Z.f$ in that the first approximant is defined to be 1 instead of 0.

Recall how the greatest fixed point for $EG\,\phi$ requires that ϕ holds on all states of some path. Such invariant behaviour cannot be expressed with a condition such as in (6.12), but is adequately defined by demanding that

$$\rho \vDash \nu Z.f \text{ iff } (\rho \vDash \nu_m Z.f \text{ for all } m \ge 0). \tag{6.14}$$

A dual reasoning to the above shows that $\rho \vDash \nu Z.Z$ holds, regardless of the nature of ρ.

One informal way of understanding the definitions in (6.12) and (6.14) is that $\rho \vDash \mu Z.f$ is false until, and if, it is proven to hold; whereas $\rho \vDash \nu Z.f$ is true until, and if, it is proven to be false. The temporal aspect is encoded by the unfolding of the recursion in (6.11), or in (6.13).

To prove that this recursive way of specifying $\rho \vDash f$ actually is well defined, one has to consider more general forms of induction which keep track not only of the height of f's parse tree, but also of the number of syntactic approximants $\mu_m Z.g$ and $\nu_n Z.h$, as well as their 'degree' (in this case, m and n). This can be done, though we won't discuss the details here.

EXERCISES 6.14

1. Let ρ be the valuation for which $(x, y, z) \Rightarrow (0, 1, 1)$. Compute whether $\rho \vDash f$ holds for the following boolean formulas:

   (a) $x \cdot (y + \overline{z} \cdot (y \oplus x))$
   (b) $\exists x.(y \cdot (x + z + \overline{y}) + x \cdot \overline{y})$
   (c) $\forall x.(y \cdot (x + z + \overline{y}) + x \cdot \overline{y})$
   (d) $\exists z.(x \cdot \overline{z} + \forall x.((y + (x + \overline{x}) \cdot z)))$
   * (e) $\forall x.(y + \overline{z})$.

* 2. Use (6.14) and the definition of the satisfaction relation for formulas of the relational mu-calculus to prove $\rho \vDash \nu Z.Z$ for all valuations ρ. In this case, f equals Z and you need to show (6.14) by mathematical induction on $m \geq 0$.

3. An implementation which decides $\vDash$ and $\nvDash$ for the relational mu-calculus obviously cannot represent valuations which assign semantic values 0 or 1 to all, i.e. infinitely many variables. Thus, it makes sense to consider $\vDash$ as a relation between pairs (ρ, f), where ρ only assigns semantic values to all *free* variables of f.

   (a) Assume that νZ and μZ, $\exists x$, $\forall x$, and $[\hat{x} := \hat{x}']$ are binding constructs similar to the quantifiers in predicate logic. Define formally the set of free variables for a formula f of the relational mu-calculus. (Hint: You should define this by structural induction on f. Also, which variables get bound in $f[\hat{x} := \hat{x}']$?)

   (b) Recall the notion of t being free for x in ϕ which we discussed in Section 2.2.3. Define what 'g is free for Z in f' should mean and find an example, where g is not free for Z in f.

   (c) Explain informally why we can decide whether $\rho \vDash f$ holds, provided that ρ assigns values 0 or 1 to all free variables of f. Explain why this answer will be independent of what ρ does to variables which are bound in f. Why is this relevant for an implementation framework?

4. Let ρ be the valuation for which $(x, x', y, y') \Rightarrow (0, 1, 1, 1)$. Determine whether $\rho \vDash f$ holds for the following formulas f (recall that we write

$f \leftrightarrow g$ as an abbreviation for $\bar{f} \oplus g$, meaning that f computes 1 iff g computes 1):

(a) $\exists x.(x' \leftrightarrow (\bar{y} + y' \cdot x))$

(b) $\forall x.(x' \leftrightarrow (\bar{y} + y' \cdot x))$

(c) $\exists x'.(x' \leftrightarrow (\bar{y} + y' \cdot x))$

(d) $\forall x'.(x' \leftrightarrow (\bar{y} + y' \cdot x))$.

5. Let ρ be a valuation with $\rho(x_1') = 1$ and $\rho(x_2') = 0$. Determine whether $\rho \vDash f$ holds for the following:

(a) $\bar{x}_1[\hat{x} := \hat{x}']$

(b) $(x_1 + \bar{x}_2)[\hat{x} := \hat{x}']$

(c) $(\bar{x}_1 \cdot \bar{x}_2)[\hat{x} := \hat{x}']$.

6. Evaluate $\rho \vDash (\exists x_1.(x_1 + \bar{x}_2))[\hat{x} := \hat{x}']$ and explain how the valuation ρ changes in that process. In particular, $[\hat{x} := \hat{x}']$ replaces x_i by x_i', but why does this not interfere with the binding quantifier $\exists x_1$?

7. (a) How would you define the notion of semantic entailment for the relational mu-calculus?

   (b) Define formally when two formulas of the relational mu-calculus are semantically equivalent.

6.4.2 Coding CTL models and specifications

Given a CTL model $\mathcal{M} = (S, \rightarrow, L)$, the μ and ν operators permit us to translate any CTL formula ϕ into a formula, f^ϕ, of the relational mu-calculus such that f^ϕ represents the set of states $s \in S$ with $s \vDash \phi$. Since we already saw how to represent subsets of states as such formulas, we can then capture the model-checking problem

$$\mathcal{M}, I \overset{?}{\vDash} \phi \qquad (6.15)$$

of whether all *initial* states $s \in I$ satisfy ϕ, in purely symbolic form: we answer in the affirmative if $f^I \cdot \overline{f^\phi}$ is unsatisfiable, where f^I is the characteristic function of $I \subseteq S$. Otherwise, the logical structure of $f^I \cdot \overline{f^\phi}$ may be exploited to extract debugging information for correcting the model $\mathcal{M}$ in order to make (6.15) true.

Recall how we can represent the transition relation $\rightarrow$ as a boolean formula $f^\rightarrow$ (see Section 6.3.2). As before, we assume that states are coded as bit vectors $(v_1, v_2, \ldots, v_n)$ and so the free boolean variables of all functions

f^ϕ are subsumed by the vector $\hat{x}$. The coding of the CTL formula ϕ as a function f^ϕ in the relational mu-calculus is now given inductively as follows:

$$f^x \overset{\text{def}}{=} x \quad \text{for variables } x$$
$$f^\perp \overset{\text{def}}{=} 0$$
$$f^{\neg\phi} \overset{\text{def}}{=} \overline{f^\phi}$$
$$f^{\phi\wedge\psi} \overset{\text{def}}{=} f^\phi \cdot f^\psi$$
$$f^{\text{EX}\,\phi} \overset{\text{def}}{=} \exists\hat{x}'.(f^\rightarrow \cdot f^\phi[\hat{x} := \hat{x}']).$$

The clause for EX deserves explanation. The variables x_i refer to the current state, whereas x_i' refer to the next state. The semantics of CTL says that $s \vDash \text{EX}\,\phi$ if, and only if, there is some s' with $s \to s'$ and $s' \vDash \phi$. The boolean formula encodes this definition, computing 1 precisely when this is the case. If $\hat{x}$ models the current state s, then $\hat{x}'$ models a possible successor state if $f^\rightarrow$, a function in $(\hat{x}, \hat{x}')$, holds. We use the nested boolean quantifier $\exists\hat{x}'$ in order to say 'there is *some* successor state'. Observe also the desired effect of $[\hat{x} := \hat{x}']$ performed on f^ϕ, thereby 'forcing' ϕ to be true at some next state[1].

The clause for EF is more complicated and involves the μ operator. Recall the equivalence

$$\text{EF}\,\phi \equiv \phi \vee \text{EX}\,\text{EF}\,\phi. \tag{6.16}$$

Therefore, $f^{\text{EF}\,\phi}$ has to be equivalent to $f^\phi + f^{\text{EX}\,\text{EF}\,\phi}$ which in turn is equivalent to $f^\phi + \exists\hat{x}'.(f^\rightarrow \cdot f^{\text{EF}\,\phi}[\hat{x} := \hat{x}'])$. Now, since EF involves computing the *least* fixed point of the operator derived from the Equivalence (6.16), we obtain

$$f^{\text{EF}\,\phi} \overset{\text{def}}{=} \mu Z.(f^\phi + \exists\hat{x}'.(f^\rightarrow \cdot Z[\hat{x} := \hat{x}'])). \tag{6.17}$$

Note that the substitution $Z[\hat{x} := \hat{x}']$ means that the boolean function Z should be made to depend on the x_i' variables, rather than the x_i variables. This is because the evaluation of $\rho \vDash Z[\hat{x} := \hat{x}']$ results in $\rho[\hat{x} := \hat{x}'] \vDash Z$, where the latter valuation satisfies $\rho[\hat{x} := \hat{x}'](x_i) = \rho(x_i')$. Then, we use the modified valuation $\rho[\hat{x} := \hat{x}']$ to evaluate Z.

---

[1] Exercise 6 on page 366 should give you a feel for how the semantics of $f[\hat{x} := \hat{x}']$ does not interfere with potential $\exists\hat{x}'$ or $\forall\hat{x}'$ quantifiers within f. For example, to evaluate $\rho \vDash (\exists\hat{x}'.f)[\hat{x} := \hat{x}']$, we evaluate $\rho[\hat{x} := \hat{x}'] \vDash \exists\hat{x}'.f$, which is true if we can find some values $(v_1, v_2, \ldots, v_n) \in \{0,1\}^n$ such that $\rho[\hat{x} := \hat{x}'][x_1' \mapsto v_1][x_2' \mapsto v_2]\ldots[x_n' \mapsto v_n] \vDash f$ is true. Observe that the resulting environment binds all x_i' to v_i, but for all other values it binds them according to $\rho[\hat{x} := \hat{x}']$; since the latter binds x_i to $\rho(x_i')$ which is the 'old' value of x_i', this is exactly what we desire in order to prevent a clash of variable names with the intended semantics.

Recall that an OBDD implementation synthesises formulas in a bottom-up fashion, so a reduced OBDD for $\exists\hat{x}'.f$ will not contain any x_i' nodes as its function does not depend on those variables. Thus, OBDDs also avoid such name clash problems.

Since EF ϕ is equivalent to E[T U ϕ], we can generalise our coding of EF ϕ accordingly:

$$f^{E[\phi U \psi]} \stackrel{\text{def}}{=} \mu Z.\,(f^\psi + f^\phi \cdot \exists \hat{x}'.\,(f^\rightarrow \cdot Z[\hat{x} := \hat{x}'])). \tag{6.18}$$

The coding of AF is similar to the one for EF in (6.17), except that 'for some' (boolean quantification $\exists \hat{x}'$) gets replaced by 'for all' (boolean quantification $\forall \hat{x}'$):

$$f^{AF\,\phi} \stackrel{\text{def}}{=} \mu Z.\,(f^\phi + \forall \hat{x}'.\,(f^\rightarrow \cdot Z[\hat{x} := \hat{x}'])). \tag{6.19}$$

Notice how the semantics of $\mu Z.f$ in (6.12) reflects the intended meaning of the AF connective. The mth approximant of $f^{AF\,\phi}$, which we write as $f_m^{AF\,\phi}$, represents those states where all paths reach a ϕ-state within m steps.

This leaves us with coding EG, for then we have provided such a coding for an adequate fragment of CTL (recall Theorem 3.8). Because EG involves computing greatest fixed points, we make use of the ν operator:

$$f^{EG\,\phi} \stackrel{\text{def}}{=} \nu Z.\,(f^\phi \cdot \exists \hat{x}'.\,(f^\rightarrow \cdot Z[\hat{x} := \hat{x}'])). \tag{6.20}$$

Observe that this does follow the logical structure of the semantics of EG: we need to show ϕ in the present state and then we have to find some successor state satisfying EG ϕ. The crucial point is that this obligation never ceases; this is exactly what we ensured in (6.14).

Let us see these codings in action on the model of Figure 6.26. We want to perform a symbolic model check of the formula EX $(x_1 \vee \neg x_2)$. You should verify, using e.g. the labelling algorithm from Chapter 3, that $[\![EX\,(x_1 \vee \neg x_2)]\!] = \{s_1, s_2\}$. Our claim is that the resulting formula $f^{EX\,(x_1 \vee \neg x_2)}$ computes the same set symbolically. First, we compute the formula $f^\rightarrow$ which represents the transition relation $\rightarrow$:

$$f^\rightarrow = (x_1' \leftrightarrow \overline{x}_1 \cdot \overline{x}_2 \cdot u) \cdot (x_2' \leftrightarrow x_1),$$

where u is an input variable used to model the non-determinism (compare the form (6.6) for the transition relation in Section 6.3.4). Thus, we obtain

$$
\begin{aligned}
f^{EX\,(x_1 \vee \neg x_2)} &= \exists x_1'.\exists x_2'.(f^\rightarrow \cdot f^{x_1 \vee \neg x_2}[\hat{x} := \hat{x}']) \\
&= \exists x_1'.\exists x_2'.((x_1' \leftrightarrow \overline{x}_1 \cdot \overline{x}_2 \cdot u) \cdot (x_2' \leftrightarrow x_1) \cdot (x_1' + \overline{x}_2')).
\end{aligned}
$$

To see whether s_0 satisfies EX $(x_1 \vee \neg x_2)$, we evaluate $\rho_0 \vDash f^{EX\,(x_1 \vee \neg x_2)}$, where $\rho_0(x_1) = 1$ and $\rho_0(x_2) = 0$ (the value of $\rho_0(u)$ does not matter). We find that this does not hold, whence $s_0 \nvDash EX\,(x_1 \vee \neg x_2)$. Likewise, we verify $s_1 \vDash EX\,(x_1 \vee \neg x_2)$ by showing $\rho_1 \vDash f^{EX\,(x_1 \vee \neg x_2)}$; and $s_2 \vDash EX\,(x_1 \vee \neg x_2)$ by showing $\rho_2 \vDash f^{EX\,(x_1 \vee \neg x_2)}$, where ρ_i is the valuation representing state s_i.

As a second example, we compute $f^{\text{AF}(\neg x_1 \wedge \neg x_2)}$ for the model in Figure 6.26. First, note that all three[1] states satisfy $\text{AF}(\neg x_1 \wedge \neg x_2)$, if we apply the labelling algorithm to the explicit model. Let us verify that the symbolic encoding matches this result. By (6.19), we have that $f^{\text{AF}(\neg x_1 \wedge \neg x_2)}$ equals

$$\mu Z. \left((\overline{x}_1 \cdot \overline{x}_2) + \forall x_1'.\forall x_2'.(x_1' \leftrightarrow \overline{x}_1 \cdot \overline{x}_2 \cdot u) \cdot (x_2' \leftrightarrow x_1) \cdot Z[\hat{x} := \hat{x}'] \right). \quad (6.21)$$

By (6.12), we have $\rho \vDash f^{\text{AF}(\neg x_1 \wedge \neg x_2)}$ iff $\rho \vDash f_m^{\text{AF}(\neg x_1 \wedge \neg x_2)}$ for some $m \geq 0$. Clearly, we have $\rho \nvDash f_0^{\text{AF}(\neg x_1 \wedge \neg x_2)}$. Now, $f_1^{\text{AF}(\neg x_1 \wedge \neg x_2)}$ equals

$$((\overline{x}_1 \cdot \overline{x}_2) + \forall x_1'.\forall x_2'.(x_1' \leftrightarrow \overline{x}_1 \cdot \overline{x}_2 \cdot u) \cdot (x_2' \leftrightarrow x_1) \cdot Z[\hat{x} := \hat{x}'])[0/Z].$$

Since $[0/Z]$ is a meta-operation, the latter formula is just

$$(\overline{x}_1 \cdot \overline{x}_2) + \forall x_1'.\forall x_2'.(x_1' \leftrightarrow \overline{x}_1 \cdot \overline{x}_2 \cdot u) \cdot (x_2' \leftrightarrow x_1) \cdot 0[\hat{x} := \hat{x}'].$$

Thus, we need to evaluate the disjunction $(\overline{x}_1 \cdot \overline{x}_2) + \forall x_1'.\forall x_2'.(x_1' \leftrightarrow \overline{x}_1 \cdot \overline{x}_2 \cdot u) \cdot (x_2' \leftrightarrow x_1) \cdot 0[\hat{x} := \hat{x}']$ at ρ. In particular, if $\rho(x_1) = 0$ and $\rho(x_2) = 0$, then $\rho \vDash \overline{x}_1 \cdot \overline{x}_2$ and so $\rho \vDash (\overline{x}_1 \cdot \overline{x}_2) + \forall x_1'.\forall x_2'.(x_1' \leftrightarrow \overline{x}_1 \cdot \overline{x}_2 \cdot u) \cdot (x_2' \leftrightarrow x_1) \cdot 0[\hat{x} := \hat{x}']$. Thus, $s_2 \vDash \text{AF}(\neg x_1 \wedge \neg x_2)$ holds.

Similar reasoning establishes that the formula in (6.21) renders a correct coding for the remaining two states as well, which you are invited to verify as an exercise.

EXERCISES 6.15

1. Using the model of Figure 6.26, determine whether $\rho \vDash f^{\text{EX}(x_1 \vee \neg x_2)}$ holds, where ρ is

    (a) $(x_1, x_2) \Rightarrow (1, 0)$
    (b) $(x_1, x_2) \Rightarrow (0, 1)$
    (c) $(x_1, x_2) \Rightarrow (0, 0)$.

2. Let S be $\{s_0, s_1\}$, with $s_0 \to s_0$, $s_0 \to s_1$ and $s_1 \to s_0$ as possible transitions and $L(s_0) = \{x_1\}$ and $L(s_1) = \emptyset$. Compute the boolean function $f^{\text{EX}(\text{EX} \neg x_1)}$.

3. Equations (6.17), (6.19) and (6.20) define $f^{\text{EF}\phi}$, $f^{\text{AF}\phi}$ and $f^{\text{EG}\phi}$. Write down a similar equation to define $f^{\text{AG}\phi}$.

4. Define a direct coding $f^{\text{AU}\phi}$ by modifying (6.18) appropriately.

5. Mimic the example checks on page 368 for the connective AU: consider the model of Figure 6.26. Note that $\llbracket \text{E}[(x_1 \vee x_2) \, \text{U} \, (\neg x_1 \wedge \neg x_2)] \rrbracket$ equals $\{s_0, s_1, s_2\}$, the entire state set. Thus, if your coding is correct then the boolean formula $f^{\text{E}[x_1 \vee x_2 \text{U} \neg x_1 \wedge \neg x_2]}$ should compute 1 for all bit vectors different from $(1, 1)$.

---

[1] Since we have added the variable u, there are actually six states; they all satisfy the formula.

(a) Verify that your coding is indeed correct.

(b) Find a boolean formula without fixed points which is semantically equivalent to $f^{\text{E}[(x_1 \lor x_2) \text{U}(\neg x_1 \land \neg x_2)]}$.

6.   (a) Use (6.20) to compute $f^{\text{EG} \neg x_1}$ for the model in Figure 6.26.

(b) Show that $f^{\text{EG} \neg x_1}$ faithfully models the set of all states which satisfy EG $\neg x_1$.

7. In the grammar (6.10) for the relational mu-calculus, it was stated that, in the formulas $\mu Z.f$ and $\nu Z.f$, any occurrence of Z in f is required to fall within an even number of complementation symbols $^{-}$. In this exercise, we investigate what happens if we drop this requirement.

(a) Consider the expression $\mu Z.\overline{Z}$. We already saw that our relation ρ is total in the sense that either $\rho \vDash f$ or $\rho \nvDash f$ holds for all choices of valuations ρ and relational mu-calculus formulas f. But formulas like $\mu Z.\overline{Z}$ are not formally monotone. For let ρ be any valuation. Use mutual mathematical induction to show that

(i) $\rho \nvDash \mu_m Z.\overline{Z}$ for all even numbers $m \geq 0$

(ii) $\rho \vDash \mu_m Z.\overline{Z}$ for all odd numbers $m \geq 1$

Infer from these two items that $\rho \vDash \mu Z.\overline{Z}$ holds according to (6.12).

(b) Consider *any* environment ρ. Use mathematical induction on m (and maybe an analysis on ρ) to show:

If $\rho \vDash \mu_m Z.(x_1 + x_2 \cdot \overline{\overline{Z}})$ for some $m \geq 0$, then $\rho \vDash \mu_k Z.(x_1 + x_2 \cdot \overline{\overline{Z}})$ for all $k \geq m$.

(c) In general, if f is formally monotone in Z then $\rho \vDash \mu_m Z.f$ implies $\rho \vDash \mu_{m+1} Z.f$. State a similar property for the greatest fixed-point operator ν.

8. Given the CTL model in Figure 6.32:

* (a) code the function $f^{\text{EX}(x_1 \land \neg x_2)}$

(b) code the function $f^{\text{AG}(\text{AF} \neg x_1 \land \neg x_2)}$

* (c) find a boolean formula *without any fixed points* which is semantically equivalent to $f^{\text{AG}(\text{AF} \neg x_1 \land \neg x_2)}$.

9. Consider the sequential synchronous circuit in Figure 6.33. Evaluate $\rho \vDash f^{\text{EX} x_2}$, where ρ equals

(a) $(x_1, x_2, x_3) \Rightarrow (1, 0, 1)$

(b) $(x_1, x_2, x_3) \Rightarrow (0, 1, 0)$.

10. Prove

    Theorem 6.18 *Given a coding for a finite CTL model, let ϕ be a CTL formula. Then $[\![\phi]\!]$ corresponds to the set of valuations ρ such that $\rho \vDash f^{\phi}$.*

    by structural induction on ϕ. You may first want to show that the evaluation of $\rho \vDash f^{\phi}$ depends only on the values $\rho(x_i)$, i.e. it does not matter what ρ assigns to x_i' or Z.

11. Argue that Theorem 6.18 above remains valid for arbitrary CTL formulas as long as we translate formulas ϕ which are not in the adequate fragment into semantically equivalent formulas ψ in that fragment and define f^{ϕ} to be f^{ψ}.

12. Derive the formula $f^{\mathrm{AF}(\neg x_1 \wedge x_2)}$ for the model in Figure 6.29(b) and evaluate it for the valuation corresponding to state s_2 to determine whether $s_2 \vDash \mathrm{AF}(\neg x_1 \wedge x_2)$ holds.

13. Repeat the last exercise with $f^{\mathrm{E}[x_1 \vee \neg x_2 \mathrm{U} x_1]}$.

14. Recall the way the labelling algorithms 1 and 2 operate in Chapter 3. Does our symbolic coding mimic either or both of them, or neither?

――――

Symbolic model checking with fairness

In Chapter 3, we sketched how SMV could use fairness assumptions which were not expressible entirely within CTL and its semantics. The addition of fairness could be achieved by restricting the ordinary CTL semantics to fair computation paths, or fair states. Formally, we were given a set $C = \{\psi_1, \psi_2, \dots, \psi_k\}$ of CTL formulas, called the *fairness constraints*, and we wanted to check whether $s \vDash \phi$ holds for a CTL formula ϕ and all initial states s, with the additional fairness constraints in C. Since $\bot, \neg, \wedge, \mathrm{EX}$, EU and EG form an adequate set of connectives for CTL, we may restrict this discussion to only these operators. Clearly, the propositional connectives won't change their meaning with the addition of fairness constraints. Therefore, it suffices to provide symbolic codings for the fair connectives $\mathrm{E}_C\mathrm{X}$, $\mathrm{E}_C\mathrm{U}$ and $\mathrm{E}_C\mathrm{G}$ from Chapter 3. The key is to represent the set of fair states symbolically as a boolean formula fair defined as

$$\text{fair} \stackrel{\text{def}}{=} f^{\mathrm{E}_C\mathrm{G}\top} \tag{6.22}$$

which uses the (yet to be defined) function $f^{\mathrm{E}_C\mathrm{G}\phi}$ with $\top$ as an instance. Assuming that the coding of $f^{\mathrm{E}_C\mathrm{G}\phi}$ is correct, we see that fair computes 1 in a state s if, and only if, there is a fair path with respect to C that begins in s. We say that such an s is a *fair state*.

As for E_CX, note that $s \vDash E_CX\phi$ if, and only if, there is some next state s' with $s \rightarrow s'$ and $s' \vDash \phi$ such that s' is a fair state. This immediately renders

$$f^{E_CX\phi} \stackrel{\text{def}}{=} \exists \hat{x}'.(f^{\rightarrow} \cdot (f^{\phi} \cdot \text{fair})[\hat{x} := \hat{x}']). \tag{6.23}$$

Similarly, we obtain

$$f^{E_C[\phi_1 U\phi_2]} \stackrel{\text{def}}{=} \mu Z.(f^{\psi} \cdot \text{fair} + f^{\phi} \cdot \exists \hat{x}'.(f^{\rightarrow} \cdot Z[\hat{x} := \hat{x}'])). \tag{6.24}$$

This leaves us with the task of coding $f^{E_CG\phi}$. It is this last connective which reveals the complexity of fairness checks at work. Because the coding of $f^{E_CG\phi}$ is rather complex, we proceed in steps. It is convenient to have the EX and EU functionality also at the level of boolean formulas directly. For example, if f is a boolean function in $\hat{x}$, then $\text{checkEX}(f)$ codes the boolean formula which computes 1 for those vectors $\hat{x}$ which have a next state $\hat{x}'$ for which f computes 1:

$$\text{checkEX}(f) \stackrel{\text{def}}{=} \exists \hat{x}'.(f^{\rightarrow} \cdot f[\hat{x} := \hat{x}']). \tag{6.25}$$

Thus, $f^{E_CX\phi}$ equals $\text{checkEX}(f^{\phi} \cdot \text{fair})$. We proceed in the same way for functions f and g in n arguments $\hat{x}$ to obtain $\text{checkEU}(f, g)$ which computes 1 at $\hat{x}$ if there is a path that realises the f U g pattern:

$$\text{checkEU}(f, g) \stackrel{\text{def}}{=} \mu Y.g + (f \cdot \text{checkEX}(Y)). \tag{6.26}$$

With this in place, we can code $f^{E_CG\phi}$ quite easily:

$$f^{E_CG\phi} \stackrel{\text{def}}{=} \nu Z.f^{\phi} \cdot \prod_{i=1}^{k} \text{checkEX}(\text{checkEU}(f^{\phi}, Z \cdot f^{\psi_i})). \tag{6.27}$$

Note that this coding has a least fixed point (checkEU) in the body of a greatest fixed point. This is computationally rather involved since the call of checkEU contains Z, the recursion variable of the outer greatest fixed point, as a free variable; thus these recursions are nested and inter-dependent. Observe how this coding operates: to have a fair path from $\hat{x}$ on which ϕ holds globally, we need ϕ to hold at $\hat{x}$; and for all fairness constraints ψ_i there has to be a next state $\hat{x}'$, where the whole property is true again (enforced by the free Z) and each fairness constraint is realised eventually on that path. The recursion in Z constantly reiterates this reasoning, so if this function computes 1, then there is a path on which ϕ holds globally and where each ψ_i is true infinitely often.

EXERCISES 6.16

1. Consider the equations in (6.22) and (6.27). The former defines fair in terms of f^{EcGT}, whereas the latter defines $f^{\text{EcG}\phi}$ for general ϕ. Why is this unproblematic, i.e. non-circular?

2. Given a fixed CTL model $\mathcal{M} = (S, \rightarrow, L)$, we saw how to code formulas f^{ϕ} representing the set of states $s \in S$ with $s \vDash \phi$, ϕ being a CTL formula of an adequate fragment.

    (a) Assume the coding without consideration of simple fairness constraints. Use structural induction on the CTL formula ϕ to show that

        (i) the free variables of f^{ϕ} are among $\hat{x}$, where the latter is the vector of boolean variables which code states $s \in S$;
        (ii) all fixed-point subformulas of f^{ϕ} are formally monotone.

    (b) Show these two assertions if f^{ϕ} also encodes simple fairness constraints.

3. Consider the pseudo-code for the function SAT in Section 3.5.2. We now want to modify it so that the resulting output is not a set, or an OBDD, but a formula of the relational mu-calculus; thus, we complete the table in Figure 6.24 on page 347 to give formulas of the relational mu-calculus. For example, the output for $\top$ would be 1 and the output for EU ψ would be a recursive call to SAT informed by (6.18). Do you have a need for a separate function which handles least or greatest fixed points?

4. (a) Write pseudo-code for a function $\text{SAT}_{\text{rel\_mu}}$ which takes as input a formula of the relational mu-calculus, f, and synthesises an OBDD B_f, representing f. Assume that there are no fixed-point subexpressions of f such that their recursive body contains a recursion variable of an outwards fixed point. Thus, the formula in (6.27) is not allowed. The fixed-point operators μ and ν require separate subfunctions which iterate the fixed-point meaning informed by (6.12), respectively (6.14). Some of your clauses may need further comment. E.g. how do you handle the constructor $[\hat{x} := \hat{x}']$?

    (b) Explain what goes wrong if the input to your code is the formula in (6.27).

5. If f is a formula with a vector of n free boolean variables $\hat{x}$, then the iteration of $\mu Z.f$, whether as OBDD implementation, or as in (6.12), may require up to 2^n recursive unfoldings to compute its meaning.

Clearly, this is unacceptable. Given the symbolic encoding of a CTL model $\mathcal{M} = (S, \rightarrow, L)$ and a set $I \subseteq S$ of initial states, we seek a formula that represents all states which are reachable from I on some finite computation path in $\mathcal{M}$. Using the extended Until operator in (6.26), we may express this as $\text{checkEU}(f^I, \top)$, where f^I is the characteristic function of I. We can 'speed up' this iterative process with a technique called 'iterative squaring':

$$\mu Y.(f^{\rightarrow} \cdot \exists \hat{w}.(Y[\hat{x} := \hat{x}'][\hat{w} := \hat{w}'] \cdot Y[\hat{x} := \hat{x}'][\hat{w} := \hat{w}'])). \quad (6.28)$$

Note that this formula depends on the same boolean variables as $f^{\rightarrow}$, i.e. the pair $(\hat{x}, \hat{x}')$. Explain *informally*:

If we apply (6.12) m times to the formula in (6.28), then this has the same semantic 'effect' as applying this rule 2^m times to $\text{checkEU}(f^I, \top)$.

Thus, one may *first* compute the set of states reachable from any initial state and then restrict model checking to those states. Note that this reduction does not alter the semantics of $s \vDash \phi$ for initial states s, so it is a sound technique; it sometimes improves, other times worsens, the performance of symbolic model checks.

6.5 Bibliographic notes

Ordered binary decision diagrams are due to R. E. Bryant [Bry86]. Binary decision diagrams were introduced by C. Y. Lee [Lee59] and S. B. Akers [Ake78]. For a nice survey of these ideas see [Bry92]. For the limitations of OBDDs as models for integer multiplication as well as interesting connections to VLSI design see [Bry91]. A general introduction to the topic of computational complexity and its tight connections to logic can be found in [Pap94]. The modal mu-calculus was invented by D. Kozen [Koz83]; for more on that logic and its application to specifications and verification see [Bra91].

The use of BDDs in model checking was proposed by the team of authors J. R. Burch, E. M. Clarke, K. L. McMillan, D. L. Dill and J. Hwang [BCM$^+$90, CGL93, McM93].

Bibliography

[Ake78] S. B. Akers. Binary decision diagrams. *IEEE Transactions on Computers*, C-27(6):509–516, 1978.

[AO91] K. R. Apt and E.-R. Olderog. *Verification of Sequential and Concurrent Programs*. Springer-Verlag, 1991.

[Bac86] R. C. Backhouse. *Program Construction and Verification*. Prentice Hall, 1986.

[BCM+90] J. R. Burch, J. M. Clarke, K. L. McMillan, D. L. Dill, and J. Hwang. Symbolic model checking: 10^{20} states and beyond. In *IEEE Symposium on Logic in Computer Science*. IEEE Computer Society Press, 1990.

[BEKV94] K. Broda, S. Eisenbach, H. Khoshnevisan, and S. Vickers. *Reasoned Programming*. Prentice Hall, 1994.

[BJ80] G. Boolos and R. Jeffrey. *Computability and Logic*. Cambridge University Press, 2nd edition, 1980.

[Boo54] George Boole. *An Investigation of the Laws of Thought*. Dover, New York, 1854.

[Bra91] J. C. Bradfield. *Verifying Temporal Properties of Systems*. Birkhäuser, Boston, 1991.

[Bry86] R. E. Bryant. Graph-based algorithms for boolean function manipulation. *IEEE Transactions on Compilers*, C-35(8), 1986.

[Bry91] R. E. Bryant. On the Complexity of VLSI Implementations and Graph Representations of Boolean Functions with Applications to Integer Multiplication. *IEEE Transactions on Computers*, 40(2):205–213, February 1991.

[Bry92] R. E. Bryant. Symbolic Boolean Manipulation with Ordered Binary-decision Diagrams. *ACM Computing Surveys*, 24(3):293–318, September 1992.

[CE81] E. M. Clarke and E. A. Emerson. Synthesis of synchronization skeletons for branching time temporal logic. In D. Kozen, editor, *Logic of Programs Workshop*, number 131 in LNCS. Springer Verlag, 1981.

[CGL93] E. Clarke, O. Grumberg, and D. Long. Verification tools for finite-state concurrent systems. In *A Decade of Concurrency*, number 803 in Lecture Notes in Computer Science, pages 124–175. Springer Verlag, 1993.

[CGL94] E. M. Clarke, O. Grumberg, and D. E. Long. Model checking and Abstraction. *ACM Transactions on Programming Languages and Systems*, 16(5):1512–1542, September 1994.

[Che80] B. F. Chellas. *Modal Logic – an Introduction*. Cambridge University Press, 1980.

[Dam96] D. R. Dams. *Abstract Interpretation and Partition Refinement for Model Checking*. PhD thesis, Institute for Programming Research and Algorithmics. Eindhoven University of Technology, July 1996.

[Dij76] E. W. Dijkstra. *A Discipline of Programming*. Prentice Hall, 1976.

[DP96] R. Davies and F. Pfenning. A Modal Analysis of Staged Computation. In *23rd Annual ACM Symposium on Principles of Programming Languages*. ACM Press, January 1996.

[EN94] R. Elmasri and S. B. Navathe. *Fundamentals of Database Systems*. Benjamin/Cummings, 1994.

[FHMV95] Ronald Fagin, Joseph Y. Halpern, Yoram Moses, and Moshe Y. Vardi. *Reasoning about Knowledge*. MIT Press, Cambridge, 1995.

[Fit93] M. Fitting. Basic modal logic. In D. Gabbay, C. Hogger, and J. Robinson, editors, *Handbook of Logic in Artificial Intelligence and Logic Programming*, volume 1. Oxford University Press, 1993.

[Fit96] M. Fitting. *First-Order Logic and Automated Theorem Proving*. Springer, 2nd edition, 1996.

[Fra92] N. Francez. *Program Verification*. Addison-Wesley, 1992.

[Fre03] G. Frege. *Grundgesetze der Arithmetik, begriffsschriftlich abgeleitet*. 1903. Volumes I and II (Jena).

[Gal87] J. H. Gallier. *Logic for Computer Science*. John Wiley, 1987.

[Gen69] G. Gentzen. Investigations into logical deduction. In M. E. Szabo, editor, *The Collected Papers of Gerhard Gentzen*, chapter 3, pages 68–129. North-Holland Publishing Company, 1969.

[Gol87] R. Goldblatt. *Logics of Time and Computation*. CSLI Lecture Notes, 1987.

[Gri82] D. Gries. A note on a standard strategy for developing loop invariants and loops. *Science of Computer Programming*, 2:207–214, 1982.

[Ham78] A. G. Hamilton. *Logic for Mathematicians*. Cambridge University Press, 1978.

[Hoa69] C. A. R. Hoare. An axiomatic basis for computer programming. *Communications of the ACM*, 12:576–580, 1969.

[Hod77] W. Hodges. *Logic*. Penguin Books, 1977.

[Hod83] W. Hodges. Elementary predicate logic. In D. Gabbay and F. Guenthner, editors, *Handbook of Philosophical Logic*, volume 1. Dordrecht: D. Reidel, 1983.

[Hol90] G. Holzmann. *Design and Validation of Computer Protocols*. Prentice Hall, 1990.

[Koz83] D. Kozen. Results on the propositional mu-calculus. *Theoretical Computer Science*, 27:333–354, 1983.

[Lee59] C. Y. Lee. Representation of switching circuits by binary-decision programs. *Bell System Technical Journal*, 38:985–999, 1959.

[Lon83] D. E. Long. *Model Checking, Abstraction, and Compositional Verification*. PhD thesis, School of Computer Science, Carnegie Mellon University, July 1983.

[McM93] K. L. McMillan. *Symbolic Model Checking*. Kluwer Academic Publishers, 1993.

[MP91] Z. Manna and A. Pnueli. *The Temporal Logic of Reactive and Concurrent Systems: Specification*. Springer-Verlag, 1991.

[MP95] Z. Manna and A. Pnueli. *Temporal Verification of Reactive Systems: Safety*.

Springer-Verlag, 1995.

[MvdH95] J.-J. Ch. Meyer and W. van der Hoek. *Epistemic Logic for AI and Computer Science*, volume 41 of *Cambridge Tracts in Theoretical Computer Science*. Cambridge University Press, 1995.

[Pap94] C. H. Papadimitriou. *Computational Complexity*. Addison Wesley, 1994.

[Pau91] L.C. Paulson. *ML for the Working Programmer*. Cambridge University Press, 1991.

[Pnu81] A. Pnueli. A temporal logic of programs. *Theoretical Computer Science*, 13:45–60, 1981.

[Pop94] S. Popkorn. *First Steps in Modal Logic*. Cambridge University Press, 1994.

[Pra65] D. Prawitz. *Natural Deduction: A Proof-Theoretical Study*. Almqvist & Wiksell, 1965.

[QS81] J. P. Quielle and J. Sifakis. Specification and verification of concurrent systems in CESAR. In *Proceedings of the Fifth International Symposium on Programming*, 1981.

[Ros97] A. W. Roscoe. *The Theory and Practice of Concurrency*. Prentice Hall, 1997.

[SA91] V. Sperschneider and G. Antoniou. *Logic, A Foundation for Computer Science*. Addison Wesley, 1991.

[Sch92] U. Schoening. *Logik für Informatiker*. B. I. Wissenschaftsverlag, 1992.

[Sch94] D. A. Schmidt. *The Structure of Typed Programming Languages*. Foundations of Computing. The MIT Press, 1994.

[Sim94] A. K. Simpson. *The Proof Theory and Semantics of Intuitionistic Modal Logic*. PhD thesis, The University of Edinburgh, Department of Computer Science, 1994.

[Tay98] R. G. Taylor. *Models of Computation and Formal Languages*. Oxford University Press, 1998.

[Ten91] R. D. Tennent. *Semantics of Programming Languages*. Prentice Hall, 1991.

[Tur91] R. Turner. *Constructive Foundations for Functional Languages*. McGraw Hill, 1991.

[vD89] D. van Dalen. *Logic and Structure*. Universitext. Springer-Verlag, 3rd edition, 1989.

[Wei98] M. A. Weiss. *Data Structures and Problem Solving Using Java*. Addison-Wesley, 1998.

Index